**Business Calculations
for Bankers**

Banking Certificate Series

Business Calculations for Bankers

Helen V Coult, BSc, ACIB, DipFS

Series Editor: David Palfreman BA

The Chartered Institute of Bankers

Recommended reading for
the Banking Certificate

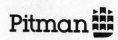

PITMAN PUBLISHING
128 Long Acre, London WC2E 9AN

A Division of Longman Group UK Limited

© Helen Coult, 1990

First published in Great Britain 1990

British Library Cataloguing in Publication Data

Coult, Helen V.
    Business calculations for bankers
    1. Accounting
    I. Title
    657.833

    ISBN 0–273–02884–7

Printed and bound in Great Britain

Contents

Introduction

Are you wondering why Business Calculations appears on the Banking Certificate Syllabus? Surely all young bankers can add up, you may say. Well, I certainly hope that is the case, but Business Calculations is not just 'sums'.

BASIC SKILLS

Each of us has experienced a different level of mathematics teaching at school. Some may have enjoyed the subject, but many will have had problems with some aspects. The first aim of the course is therefore to bring all students up to speed on fairly basic mathematical skills — filling in any gaps in their knowledge. If you feel you are completely comfortable working with numbers, just dip into the first few chapters to make sure. If you have any doubts, then work through the appropriate sections.

Numbers are only meaningful in banking if you know how to apply them, so most of the rest of the chapters deal with the use of numbers in real business situations.

SIMPLE AND COMPOUND INTEREST

The calculation of interest is a vital part of any bank's daily operations — both interest on loans and interest on deposits. Although such calculations are usually performed by computers these days, it is important that you understand how they are performed so that you can explain them to your customers. If a customer asks you roughly how much interest they will have to pay on a loan of £1850 over two years at $14\frac{1}{2}\%$, they will not be impressed if you tell them you have no idea. Having studied this book you should have no difficulty in answering that question.

APR

Similarly, it is important for all bankers to understand the meaning of APR (Annual Percentage Rate) so that you can help your customers choose the best loan product for their needs.

INTRODUCTION TO COMPUTERS

Computers are taken for granted in banks nowadays but are you a slave to the computer, or do you know enough about it to make the computer work for you? This book will not turn you into a programmer, but it will help you understand some of the jargon which often hides the usefulness of a computer to the business it serves.

INTRODUCTION TO STATISTICS

Information, whether derived from a computer or elsewhere, is only of value if it is displayed in a way which is clear, unambiguous and easy to assimilate. A basic understanding of statistics and the use of graphs and diagrams will enable you to communicate information (whether to your manager, your colleagues or your customers) in a straightforward manner.

BASIC ACCOUNTING

You will certainly have studied arithmetic in school; you will probably have learnt to draw graphs and you may well have studied or used a computer; however, the subject within Business Calculations which is most likely to be completely new to you is Accountancy. I am well aware that this can be a difficult area for a banking student to grasp, so this book goes out of its way to explain clearly and simply the underlying principles of accounts and double-entry bookkeeping. Inevitably, in introducing such a wide topic, I have had to go into more depth than strictly necessary in some parts in order to explain the various ideas which underpin the whole subject. Don't let this put you off. Remember that the questions in the examination will be quite straightforward, so long as you have understood the basics.

THE EXAMINATION

Which brings us to the examination itself. When I set the papers, I will not be trying to trick you or catch you out, but I will be testing your **understanding** of the various parts of the syllabus, not just your ability to learn parrot-fashion.

The first section of the paper is a compulsory question with ten short parts, each worth four marks. Some parts will ask you to state a formula and explain what it means, or to carry out a simple calculation. Some will ask you to give a brief definition of one of the concepts found in the major syllabus areas and some will ask you to solve an equation and so on.

In the second section you have a choice of three questions out of four. These will often apply the basic knowledge you have acquired in your studies to real-life banking or business situations. This is where the **understanding** of concepts is so important, as you must be able to deal with problems which may be a little different or expressed in a different way from the examples in your text books.

Clearly, in a question worth 20 marks I will be expecting you to demonstrate a much deeper knowledge of each topic than that required for the four mark parts of question one. I may set questions which cover more than one area of the syllabus.

STUDY AND REVISION

Many people find studying much harder once they have left school. Without the discipline of a day divided up into lessons and planned out for you, it is easy to let the competing attractions of sports, friends and social life monopolise your free time and feel that 'I don't have time to study'. This is particularly true if you are studying at home rather than at day release or evening classes.

No-one can make you study, but remember that it is **your** career which will suffer in the long term. It may sound trite, but it is nonetheless true, that if you give up some time to study now, you will reap the rewards for the rest of your banking career. The Chartered Institute of Bankers is dedicated to the idea of professional qualifications for all those who work in banking, and seek promotion to management levels.

If you are at college, your tutors will guide you through the syllabus. If you are studying at home I suggest you work steadily through this book, making notes of the important concepts, formulae etc. as you go.

When it comes to revision, get as much practice as you can in answering questions from previous papers (which are published by the Chartered Institute of Bankers with examiners' reports and model answers, after every session). Make use of other text books and question/answer books too to give a different slant on topics you may have found tricky. Talk to your manager or supervisor if you want to know more about the way banks operate. Take every opportunity to practice what you are learning in your every day work – that is the reason for studying: to make you better at your job.

Finally, when you sit the examination, well prepared and confident, I hope I will be able to mark your paper and say 'Credit Pass – fully competent'.

Good luck!
HVC 1990

ACKNOWLEDGEMENTS

In writing this book I have received much help and encouragement from a number of people, both at the Chartered Institute of Bankers and from my colleagues at the Midland Bank. I should like to express my appreciation of their assistance and forbearance in checking and verifying procedures, etc.

I should also like to thank Dr P G Whitehead and Geoffrey Whitehead for permission to use certain material and artwork from their book, *Statistics for Business*. Finally, may I thank my secretary, Nina Clark, for her considerable efforts in typing and supervising the manuscript.

1 Business calculations and the banker

OBJECTIVES

After studying this chapter you should:
1 Understand why basic arithmetical skills are essential to successful banking;
2 Understand the general subject area covered in this book;
3 Appreciate how important the use of a calculator is in the course and at all levels in banking;
4 Know how to tackle the course and how important regular study is at each stage.

1 THE IMPORTANCE OF BUSINESS CALCULATIONS

Business calculations are essential to bankers, and everyone else in business. Although most of the hard labour of calculations has been removed now that the electronic calculator and the computer can process data (numbers, facts) at electronic speeds, it is still essential to know enough mathematics to appreciate whether an answer is likely to be correct or hopelessly wrong. Even the smallest mis-key can lead to a ridiculous answer, and the person who does not appreciate that the answer is ridiculous and accepts it because the machine gave it, can cost his/her bank a lot of money. Perhaps worse, the error may mean we charge a customer unfairly and do customer relations a great deal of harm. This sort of basic understanding of what an answer should be cannot be acquired in a day, or even a month. You have to keep plodding away at the various aspects of business calculations before you develop that feeling – a sort of sixth sense – which tells you that the answer the calculator has just provided cannot possibly be right.

Fortunately, most young bankers already have a reasonable background in mathematics, though some critics say that the business aspects of mathematics are not always taught well in the last two years of schooling, the students having moved on – quite rightly – to other things. If you feel that your grasp of mathematics is at all rusty then you will be able to polish it up in the early chapters of this book.

1.1 Annual Percentage Rates

Banking is chiefly concerned with money; with funds deposited by customers for safe keeping and with loans made to those in need of funds, who are prepared to buy the use of the bank's money by paying a fair price for it. This price is called 'interest'. Interest rates vary considerably. In the days of 'cheap money' from 1745–1946 almost anyone could borrow money at $2\frac{1}{2}\%$ per annum (a year) interest – today many people using store credit cards pay as much as 35% per annum interest. You will see the APR (annual percentage rate) displayed on all sorts of documents. These rates are controlled by the Office of Fair Trading under the Consumer Credit Act, 1974. Banks are very much concerned with APR rates, and they form an important section of your syllabus, and of this book. Not only must the true APR rate be shown on every loan calculation, but every credit card that is issued must be accompanied by a credit agreement stating what the APR rate is at the time of issue. This enables the customer to compare one lender's rates with another, on an equal basis. It is very important to understand APR rates and how they are calculated, though in everyday practice we refer to tables provided by the bank for easy reference.

1.2 The accounts of customers

Accounting is a special class of business calculations – indeed the very first accountancy textbook published in 1494 by a banker from Lombardy in Northern Italy was simply called *summa* (Latin – sums of money). All the time, as bankers, we are dealing with customers' accounts. They have current accounts, deposit accounts, high interest cheque accounts, investment accounts, etc. Even more important, when asking for a loan they present their own financial accounts, usually running back over several years. You must be able to understand these accounts; to sort the sheep from the goats as far as reliability is concerned. You must be able to read their Balance Sheets so that you know what assets they have and what liabilities they already owe to other banks, or in the case of companies to debenture holders (people who have loaned them money against a security called a debenture which gives a prior right to repayment). This is another part of your syllabus – very simple as far as Business Calculations goes but with a great many ideas which may be new to you if you have never studied accounts before.

1.3 Computerisation

Today the banking system is increasingly computerised. Of course, most of the programming for this aspect of banking is done by specialist computer centres and unless you work in one of those departments you will not need to be trained as a computer programmer. Nevertheless, many of you will be operating computer equipment in your branches: terminals connected to the computer centre; micro-computers used to monitor branch performance, to help in Balance Sheet analysis and so on; or counter terminals used by cashiers. We all need to have a nodding acquaintance with computerisation and understand the 'jargon'. 'Jargon' is a much abused word, because everyone feels that the computer specialists are trying to 'blind us with science' with their latest 'buzz' words. Really this is not so. Every subject has its

specialist vocabulary, and if we want to understand the subject we have to learn the 'jargon' that has been developed to make sense of the new processes and procedures. Don't be put off by a new word. Ask what it means, and add it to your vocabulary. The chapters about computers in this book are relatively simple, and our syllabus clearly states that it is not the intention that students should become computer experts.

1.4 Statistics

Statistics are numerical facts, systematically collected and presented. As bankers we meet statistics in every aspects of our work. Customers present figures for output, turnover, gross profit and net profit, costings, break-even analyses, charts and tables. We need some understanding of statistics to follow all this information, and make judgments about loans and overdrafts based upon our understanding. We also need statistics to discover the bank's own results, and make business decisions which will improve our efficiency. Such statistics and ratios as:

(a)   How many current accounts has Branch A?
(b)   What is the average balance outstanding?
(c)   What percentage of current account holders have a credit card?
(d)   What is the average activity per day at each cashier's window?
(e)   What is the activity at each ATM (Automated Teller Machine)?

Such statistical controls alert management to changes in the prosperity of particular areas, and the possibilities of marketing new products (such as pension funds, units trusts, insurance policies, etc.). They help manpower planning, in training staff to use new skills and in investment decisions about new methods of work.

The sections of statistical work in this course are relatively simple, but they are an important aspect of banking and have implications for studies at higher levels.

2   THE USE OF CALCULATORS

Banking examinations reflect real life in that they recognise that almost everyone in every situation uses an electronic calculator today. The saving in time, for example when doing a long division sum, is so great that no-one would consider a rule saying that all workings have to be set down manually. However, some parts of the examination may ask you to show your workings for two reasons: firstly to make sure you understand the underlying principle of the calculation, and are not just relying on the calculator to think for you; secondly so that if you *do* make a mistake in your calculation somewhere the examiner may be able to give you *some* marks for method, even if the final answer is not correct. Therefore it is permitted to take into the examination room a non-programmable pocket calculator, and although it is not essential, you will find it very helpful to have such a calculator and use it throughout the course. Calculators which are noisy (like most printing calculators) are not allowed, for the rules say that the calculator must be one which will not distract other candidates. A suitable calculator is illustrated in Fig. 1.1 and you should obtain one as soon as possible. Assistants in many shops know very little about the calculators they are selling, and you may find it difficult to get advice. So long as the calculator you buy

Fig. 1.1   The Sharp Elsi Mate EL-351A calculator

has all the keys shown in the illustration (see Fig. 1.1) you will be all right, but please note that some designs combine keys, for instance the RM key (recall memory) and the CM key (clear memory) may be combined into an RCM key. This recalls the memory at one touch and clears the memory if you touch the same key a second time. Similarly the CE key (clear last entry) and the C key (clear the whole calculator) may be combined into a CEC (clear last entry and all clear) key. The first touch clears the last entry for rekeying, but a second touch clears the whole calculator and you must start from the beginning again. On some models they are labelled C (clear entry) and AC (all clear) just to confuse the issue. Don't be seduced by the sales assistant into paying a great deal for a complicated 'scientific' calculator unless you need one for other purposes. It will not be any quicker, or more reliable, and the extra buttons may just lead to confusion and errors.

Whichever calculator you buy you will need to get used to its special method of working so that you are thoroughly familiar with it before you get into the examination room. It is a bad mistake to buy a new calculator just before the examination unless it is exactly the same type as you have been using already. Buy a new one of the same type and you are prepared for any breakdown. The calculator shown in Fig. 1.1 happens to be solar powered. The advantage is that the battery cannot run out, and so long as there is at least the same amount of light as you would get from a 60 watt bulb you will find the solar power is satisfactory. If you do buy a battery model be sure you have a new battery in the calculator, or a back-up calculator, before you enter the examination room.

Throughout this book where a new type of calculation is shown the instructions for doing the calculation manually are given, and then a section headed 'Using the

calculator' shows you how to do the same type of calculation on the calculator. In every case the calculator referred to is the one shown in Fig. 1.1 but if you have a different calculator and the method specified does not work for some reason you will have to refer to the instruction booklet supplied with the calculator you are using.

3 NOTE-TAKING AND MATERIALS

When using this book it is essential to do as much practice as you feel you need to develop absolute facility with all the different types of calculation covered. Whether you are studying at college, by correspondence, or by self-study, your own drive is essential to get the extra work done that you need. Disregard what other people do; only *you* know whether you are completely confident about a topic. Do enough practice until you are sure you have mastered it.

On the other hand, there are in every syllabus some pieces you will find difficult. Don't get downhearted and think the subject is beyond you – it isn't. Leave the chapter for one month, and then have another go. What seems difficult at the first attempt seems a lot easier a month later and child's play three months later. Keep coming back – getting some help with the topic if you can.

As far as materials go I would suggest that you need these things:

(a) a lever arch file
(b) some brown paper – old large envelopes are fine
(c) a two hole punch. You can buy quite good ones for about 50 pence
(d) your calculator
(e) plenty of paper – preferably A4 size – and if you can buy it already punched that is an advantage.

3.1 A lever arch file

This is much better than a ring binder. If you drop it it won't burst open, and you can open it easily at any point you wish to add extra material. For example you may see

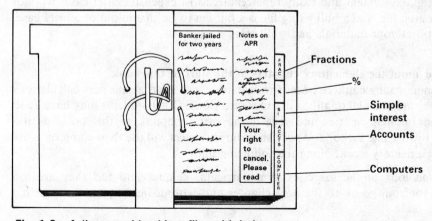

Fig. 1.2 A 'lever-arch' subject file, with index

newspaper stories or financial articles of interest to you – perhaps they have a good statistical diagram or graph that is interesting. Cut these out and add them to your file. It makes revision more varied and builds your background on banking. Figure 1.2 illustrates the system.

3.2   The brown paper

Use these sheets to make index pages which enable you to have a separate section of your file for each chapter in the book. The first section should be labelled SYLLABUS and should contain a photocopy of the syllabus, taken from your CIB brochure. As you learn each part give it a tick and you will soon feel you are making progress. The following index pages should show the chapters in the book, and the subject of each chapter, i.e. 2: Basic numerical skills. Put any notes you make on a chapter in the appropriate section and when you've done a set of exercises file them in the correct place. A quick glance through later will recall the whole subject to you – or it may remind you that this is a subject you are still not happy with, and a bit more work is required.

3.3   The two hole punch

Obviously this enables you to file everything in the lever arch file easily and quickly. Some people fret about getting the holes exactly in the centre of the paper so it looks neat in the binder. Don't worry about such trifles. If you are collecting documents, forms, newspaper articles, etc, it is bound to look a bit of a jumble. What you want is an interesting collection about the whole subject area – with evidence of a lot of hard work – the exercises you have done.

   One final thing. The disadvantage about a lever arch file is that it is rather bulky. If you are attending courses you can probably make one lever arch file do for all subjects until you get half way through the course, when you should unload the early material into another file which can be left at home. The file with your current material and your text books is most easily carried in a plastic carrier bag. It may not look very beautiful, but it is cheap, convenient and easily replaceable. Most expensive brief cases will not hold a lever arch file, and a bulky ring file is a burden to get in and out of a brief case.

   Now – collect your materials and we'll start work.

Special note about the elementary chapters at the start of this book
There are some young bankers who are not particularly good at business calculations although they may be well qualified in other directions. Other students may have good qualifications in mathematics and regard the early chapters of this book as too elementary by far. The author and publishers hope readers will use their common sense about this elementary work, along the following lines:

   (a)   If you look at the exercises in a particular chapter and feel they are too elementary for you, go on to the next chapter until you do find the correct starting point.
   (b)   If you feel at all rusty on the topic under discussion refresh your memory by

doing the exercises. They are not too numerous, the answers are conveniently placed, and you are free to move on as soon as you feel you have revised the topic sufficiently.

(c)   If you are really weak at Business Calculations do the whole set of exercises on each topic and make sure you understand the principles outlined in each chapter. There is plenty of time to do the whole book in one year if you plod steadily through it.

2 Basic numerical skills – number and money

OBJECTIVES

At the end of this chapter you should:
1 Understand both our number system and our money system as decimal systems;
2 Appreciate the meaning of place value;
3 Be able to deal with the four rules (addition, subtraction, multiplication and division) of number – both manually and using an electronic calculator;
4 Be able to deal with the four rules of money – both manually and using an electronic calculator.

1 THE NUMBER SYSTEM AS A DECIMAL SYSTEM

We all know the term 'decimal system' because at school we learn quite a lot about decimal fractions, such as 0.5, 0.25, 0.125 etc. What we sometimes don't realise is that the number system used for whole numbers is also a decimal system. The term 'decimal system' simply means a system based upon 10, from the Latin for 10, which is *decem*. In our number system 10 units makes one ten, and 10 tens make one hundred and 10 hundreds make one thousand. Thus if 8 units are added to 6 units making 14 units in all the 14 means one ten and four units. This is written down:

$$8 + 6 = 14$$

With the decimal number system very large numbers can be written down – for example, there are 365 days in the year and 366 days in a leap year. Similarly there are 100 years in a century and 1000 years in a millenium. There are 63,360 inches in the imperial mile, and the National Blue Book on Income and Expenditure tells us the gross national income of the UK is something in excess of £400,000,000,000; four hundred thousand million pounds. In the ancient Maya numerical system, which was not a decimal system, the symbol for one million was a drawing of a man with his hands held up to heaven in amazement. Just how they would have set down £400,000,000,000 it is difficult to imagine.

Place value The real secret of the decimal system is the idea of place value. There are only nine numbers plus the zero sign 0. With these ten symbols we can represent any number, for the place where the number is written tells us how big the number is. The first three places in any number are hundreds, tens and units:

> HTU
> 1 6 7   This number is one hundred and sixty seven.

We then move into a larger group of numbers, the thousands, which again have hundreds, tens and units.

> HTU HTU
> 2 6 3 , 1 6 7

This number is two hundred and sixty three thousand one hundred and sixty seven. Notice that when we reach the comma we say 'thousand', to acknowledge that we have left the thousands behind, and are about to give the smaller numbers now.

We then move into the millions, which are thousands of thousands

> HTU HTU HTU
> 2 1 4 , 2 6 3 , 1 6 7

Two hundred and fourteen million, two hundred and sixty three thousand, one hundred and sixty seven.

Place values above millions move on to the billions. One billion is a thousand million, though if you look in a dictionary you will see it says a million million. This is an early English meaning, which is not very sensible, because we must have a name for thousands of millions, and the UK for all practical purposes has adopted the American definition of one billion as a thousand million. The term is commonly used to describe a very rich person – a billionaire (someone who has a thousand million pounds), and it is also used in the National Income Statistics and by the Chancellor of the Exchequer, on Budget Day.

Notice that the figures for convenience are grouped in threes. Commas are used between the groups, except when using scientific measurements like grams, metres, etc. where by international agreement commas are not used, and a 'thin space' is used instead. As this is a banking textbook, with some statistical work closely related to banking we will include the commas every third place, to show thousands, millions, etc.

It is very important to be able to read numbers correctly, and to be able to write them down when you are given them – for example by a customer over the telephone. There can't be many banking students who are weak at reading numbers, but if you are not very good on this point consider the numbers below. Basically, the reading of numbers depends on understanding place value.

41	Forty-one (tens and units)
68	Sixty-eight (tens and units)
341	Three hundred and forty-one (HTU)
768	Seven hundred and sixty-eight (HTU)
9,341	Nine thousand three hundred and forty one
9,001	Nine thousand and one (where we have some noughts we say 'and')
9,017	Nine thousand and seventeen
209,016	Two hundred and nine thousand and sixteen
1,245,007	One million two hundred and forty five thousand, and seven

Note that each time we get to a comma we should say the figure represented by that place value – for example in 9,341 we said the nine, then the word thousand (because the comma separates the thousands from the hundreds, tens and units). In 1,245,007 we say 'one', then the word 'million' (because this comma separates the millions from the thousands) then 'two hundred and forty five', then the word 'thousands', and finally 'and seven'.

If you are at all weak at reading numbers try Exercises 2.1 and 2.2 now.

1.1   A note about answers

In this book, to save you the tedious business of always looking at the back of the book to see if you have the correct answer, the answers to each set of questions are given at the end of each chapter. Keep a piece of thin card handy to mark the answer section while you try the questions, and check on each one as you do it. The answers have been very carefully checked, so if your answer does not agree with the book's answer it is probable you have an error. However, every new book may have an odd slip in it, so the author does apologise for possible genuine errors. You may take it there will not be many of them.

■ EXERCISE 2.1
Write down the following numbers in figures.

  (a) Forty nine.
  (b) One thousand seven hundred and fifty-seven.
  (c) Eleven thousand and twenty-three.
  (d) One million one hundred and eighty four thousand and ten.
  (e) Seventeen million five hundred thousand and twenty three.
  (f) Nine thousand two hundred and eighty-four.
  (g) One hundred and seven thousand, two hundred and forty five.
  (h) Nine million two hundred and six thousand one hundred and twenty.
  (i) Seventeen billion, two hundred and two million, and nineteen.
  (j) Four hundred billion.

■ EXERCISE 2.2
Read off these numbers without looking at the answers. Then read them off again, checking with the answers on page 18 that you got them right.

  (a) 41   **(b)** 384   **(c)** 2,901   **(d)** 175,021   **(e)** 800,027,109

2   THE FOUR RULES OF NUMBER AND MONEY

The four basic rules of number and money are addition, subtraction, multiplication and division. Once again we can perhaps assume that every student of banking is able to perform these elementary calculations, but, just in case, we have a short revision section which enables you to check that you are not rusty on these basic skills. The simplest thing is to turn straight to the exercises in each section and try some of them manually and some more using an electronic calculator. If you get even one sum wrong it looks as if you are a bit weak, so do the whole set. More importantly, watch your every-day calculations at the bank and be careful not to make any slips.

3 ADDITION OF NUMBER (the plus sign +)

The addition of numbers is called totting. We can add numbers across the page horizontally, which is called cross-totting.

$5 + 6 + 7 + 3 = 21$ (Say $5 + 6 = 11$; plus $7 = 18$; plus $3 = 21$)

$13 + 8 + 29 + 14 = 64$ (Do the units first: $3 + 8 = 11$; plus $9 = 20$; plus $4 = 24$. Write down the 4 and carry the 2 tens. Now add the tens $2 + 1 = 3$; $+2 = 5 + 1 = 6$)

Alternatively we can add numbers vertically, which is called long totting.

3,725
4,916
204
17,302
26,147
12 1

Add the units column first which comes to 17. Put 7 in the units column of the answer and carry the one ten. Add this in with the tens column which comes to 4 tens. Put this in the answer and add the hundreds. Carrying figures can be put in at the very bottom of the sum under the answer, or squeezed in at the bottom of the column above the line. In a printed book like this, it is clearer if we show them under the answer.

Using the calculator

CALCULATION: As above

SEQUENCE Ⓒ 3,725 ⊞ 4,916 ⊞ 204 ⊞ 17,302 ⊟

DISPLAY 0 3,725 3,725 4,916 8,641 204 8,845 17,302 26,147

ANSWER 26,147

With some tots it is helpful to use sub-totals, which reduce the chances of errors, and make checking easier. For example; using a sub total at every fifth line, we have:

175	
264	
392	
721	
164	1,716
429	
656	
727	
491	
634	2,937
437	
621	
736	
429	
715	2,938
	7,591

Note
When using the calculator with sub-totals use the memory to keep the sub-totals. When the first sub-total is found touch the M + key to add it to the memory. When the second sub-total is found add that to the memory to. When the third sub-total is found add that to the memory and touch the RM (recall memory) key. The answer will then appear.

■ **EXERCISE 2.3**
Copy and complete, or use the calculator and write down the answer only.

(a) 27 + 16 + 54 =   (b) 15 + 21 + 77 =
(c) 13 + 27 + 49 =   (d) 33 + 85 + 79 =
(e) 136 + 245 + 721 =   (f) 149 + 238 + 725 =
(g) 429 + 436 + 825 =   (h) 451 + 636 + 924 =
(i) 12,246 + 17,345 + 14,921 =   (j) 27,248 + 19,306 + 7,215 =

■ **EXERCISE 2.4**
Copy and complete, or use the calculator and write down the answer only.

(a)	7,265	(b)	5,816	(c)	17,295
	381		1,495		14,316
	+ 4,295		+ 787		+ 16,295

(d)	19,264	(e)	27,495	(f)	19,206
	13,712		13,621		15,319
	16,218		8,724		17,425
	+ 14,725		+ 15,388		+ 24,614

■ **EXERCISE 2.5**
Copy and complete, or use the calculator and write down the answer only.

(a)	125	(b)	436	(c)	1,492
	363		972		3,361
	872		365		4,705
	581		749		6,006
	677		221		5,159
	249		607		4,724
	463		133		860
	772		718		7,384
	163		309		2,925
	941		446		6,616
	542		650		498
	676		272		9,726
	118		963		1,310
	829		509		7,495
	475		672		2,066

4 SUBTRACTION OF NUMBER

Numbers can be subtracted horizontally or vertically. For example

$127 - 15 = 112$ (do the units first: 5 from 7 leaves 2 and the tens, etc)
$436 - 129 = 307$ (9 from 6 you cannot, take a 10, 9 from 10 is 1 and 6 = 7 etc)

or

$$\begin{array}{r} 7,361 \\ -\ 2,565 \\ \hline 4,796 \\ \hline \end{array}$$

(To check your answer add the answer you found to the number you took away. $4,796 + 2,565 = 7,361$ This gives you the number you started with.)

Using the calculator

CALCULATION: As above

SEQUENCE   Ⓒ   7,361   ⊟   2,565   ⊟

DISPLAY   0   7,361   7,361   2,565   4,796

ANSWER   4,796

■ EXERCISE 2.6

Copy and complete, or use the calculator and write down the answer only.

(a) $149 - 86 =$ (b) $372 - 194 =$
(c) $486 - 327 =$ (d) $519 - 394 =$

(e) $\begin{array}{r} 1,736 \\ -\ \ \ 859 \\ \hline \\ \hline \end{array}$ (f) $\begin{array}{r} 5,964 \\ -\ 3,827 \\ \hline \\ \hline \end{array}$ (g) $\begin{array}{r} 7,236 \\ -\ 4,216 \\ \hline \\ \hline \end{array}$

(h) $\begin{array}{r} 27,324 \\ -\ 14,917 \\ \hline \\ \hline \end{array}$ (i) $\begin{array}{r} 36,295 \\ -\ 17,488 \\ \hline \\ \hline \end{array}$ (j) $\begin{array}{r} 317,864 \\ -\ 75,694 \\ \hline \\ \hline \end{array}$

5 MULTIPLICATION OF NUMBER

Multiplication is a simplified form of addition. If we have a number (say 7,216) seven times we could set it down seven times and add up the seven numbers to get a grand total. More easily, provided we know our seven times table, we can set the calculation down as follows:

$$\begin{array}{r} 7,216 \\ \times\ 7 \\ \hline 50,512 \\ \hline \end{array}$$ (say $7 \times 6 = 42$, put down the 2 units and carry the 4 tens into the tens column, etc)

1 14

With bigger numbers we have place value coming into the picture as well

7,216	Multiplying by 7 is the same as in the previous example
× 37	Multiplying by 30 means we must move the answer one place value to the left
50,512	by putting a 0 in the units column, and multiply by 3.
216,480	
266,992	

More simply, today, we can use the calculator.

Using the calculator

CALCULATION: As above

SEQUENCE   ◻   7,216   ☒   37   ◻

DISPLAY   0   7,216   7,216   37   266,992

ANSWER   266,992

■ EXERCISE 2.7
Set down these calculations and complete them, or use the calculator and just record the answers.

(a) 127×7 (b) 136×15 (c) 295×18
(d) $1,275 \times 30$ (e) $1,386 \times 65$ (f) $2,742 \times 48$
(g) $17,259 \times 68$ (h) $23,265 \times 42$ (i) $47,560 \times 28$
(j) $1,864 \times 275$

6   DIVISION OF NUMBER

Division is a simplified form of subtraction. If we want to share 240 items between five people we could take five away from the 240 to give them one each, and then take another five away to give them another one each etc. More simply if we know our tables we can set the sum down and divide it.

4	
5⌐240	5 into 24 goes 4 ($4 \times 5 = 20$) and 4 over
48	Take the 4 tens left over into the units row
	5 into 40 units goes 8 units

More simply, today, we can use the calculator.

Using the calculator

CALCULATION: As above

SEQUENCE   ◻   240   ⊞   5   ◻

DISPLAY   0   240   240   5   48

ANSWER   48

But note - not all numbers will divide exactly

CALCULATION: 1276 ÷ 5

SEQUENCE   ⓒ 1,276   ⊞   5   ⊟

DISPLAY   0   1,276 1,276   5   255.2

ANSWER   255.2

The calculator always works out the answer fully, giving the fractional part of the answer as a decimal fraction. In this case it is .2. We have to get used to these decimal fractions for the calculator cannot give an answer in a common (vulgar) fraction. The answer is $255\frac{1}{5}$ as a vulgar fraction.

■ EXERCISE 2.8

Set down the calculations and complete them, or use a calculator and just record the answers.

(a) 425 ÷ 5   (b) 798 ÷ 6   (c) 1,428 ÷ 12
(d) 2,350 ÷ 7   (e) 4,612 ÷ 15   (f) 72,000 ÷ 16
(g) 48,540 ÷ 32   (h) 72,646 ÷ 18   (i) 11,846 ÷ 19
(j) 712,645 ÷ 15

■ EXERCISE 2.9

(a) 7,250 ÷ 25   (b) 12,000 ÷ 42   (c) 38,000 ÷ 35
(d) 46,500 ÷ 76   (e) 92,500 ÷ 84   (f) 112,000 ÷ 62
(g) 74,625 ÷ 95   (h) 95,825 ÷ 74   (i) 71,645 ÷ 66
(j) 80,450 ÷ 17

6.1 Changing the decimal fraction to a vulgar fraction

The answers to many of these division sums come out to answers with a long decimal fraction (as long as the display panel on the calculator). We could simplify these answers by giving them correct to one or two decimal places. This is explained in Section 7.1 below. Alternatively, if you want to find out what that decimal fraction is as a vulgar fraction (see Chapter 3), you can find it by the following method:

Record the answer shown on the calculator on a piece of paper. Using Exercise 2.9(b) as an example

Answer = 285.71428   Now, using the calculator, proceed as follows.
Multiply the whole numbers 285 by the original divisor 42 = 11,970. The original amount to be divided was 12,000. Since the whole numbers came to 11,970 there was a remainder of 30.
As a vulgar fraction $30 \div 42 = \frac{30}{42} = \frac{5}{7}$ (cancelling by 6).

The answer was therefore $285\frac{5}{7}$.
Check the $\frac{5}{7}$ on your calculator. It is 0.7142857, the same as in the answer to 2.9(b) but with more figures (because there were no whole numbers to use up the display).

7 THE MONEY SYSTEM IN THE UK

The UK money system is a decimal system based on pounds sterling, with the £1 divided up into 100 pence. There are 1p, 2p, 5p, 10p, 20p, (a few 25p) 50p, £1 and £2 coins. There are £5, £10, £20 and £50 notes in common circulation and other values are issued for special purposes. Neither the coins nor the notes have intrinsic value (the metal or paper are not worth as much as the face value). Their value arises because they are designated 'legal tender'. This means that Parliament has decreed they may be tendered (offered) in settlement of debts and the creditor must accept them as valid payments. Because it would be unfair to burden a creditor with huge loads of coinage, coins are only legal tender up to the stated limits. Bronze coins (1p and 2p) are legal tender up to 20 pence. Of the cupro-nickel coins, 5p and 10p coins are legal tender up to £5 and 20p and 50p coins up to £10. For the present time £1 coins are legal tender to any amount, and so are notes. Parliament's rules only apply in the UK, so that at times of financial crisis UK notes are sometimes refused by hoteliers abroad, because they are not sure of their value. Not being legal tender abroad no-one is obliged to accept them, and, if the value of the pound is falling, they may refuse them.

7.1 Correcting-up, or rounding, with the decimal system

In any decimal system, whether it is number or money, we can correct-up, or round the figures to any decimal place we like. We only need to calculate to one more decimal place than the answer requires (although a calculator will work the answer out until the whole display is filled). For example, suppose we are asked to calculate to the nearest whole number then we need only work to one decimal place. Suppose we had the following answers:

- (a)   127.2
- (b)   127.5
- (c)   127.7
- (d)   127.9
- (e)   127.1

We want the answer correct to the nearest whole number. The rules are:

1   If the tenths figure (the first decimal place) is less than half (5 tenths is half) disregard it. Therefore (a) and (e) above would have the answer 127 to the nearest whole number.
2   If the tenths figure is more than half (i.e. 6, 7, 8 or 9) count the extra bit as a whole one, so (c) and (d) above would be 128 to the nearest whole number.
3   If the tenths figure is 5, which is exactly half way, we look to see if the calculation goes any further – for example for 127.53 the extra few hundreths make the fraction more than half and we round up to the next figure, giving 128 correct to the nearest whole number.

If the calculation goes no further, the usual rule in every day banking is to round up, so (b) above would be rounded up to 128. In statistics there is a special rule to avoid bias in a long series of numbers, which is to round to the nearest even number. So 127.5 would be rounded up to 128, whereas 126.5 would be rounded down to 126 because that is the nearest even number.

For the purposes of this course in Business Calculations for banking we will use the common rule that a number ending in a 5 is rounded up.

7.2 Writing money

When writing money it is important to do it correctly. The rules are:

(a) We can write with a £ sign, in which case we do not need any other symbols. So £195.16 is correct and so is £0.55, but £195.16p is incorrect − we don't need the pence symbol.

(b) Amounts less than £1 can be written with a £ sign as shown above (£0.55) or without a £ sign, but with a symbol p for pence. The p does not have an abbreviation point; it is a symbol. Thus 55p is correct but 55p. is incorrect (except at the end of a sentence).

■ **EXERCISE 2.10**

1 Expenditures at three branches in an area are as follows for the months of July. Using long-totting and cross-totting find

(a) the total costs for each branch
(b) the total costs under each expense heading
(c) the grand total for the sub-area.

	Branch A £	Branch B £	Branch C £	Total £
Capital items	17,214.40	32,815.50	40,250.65	?
Consumables	3,421.63	3,725.64	5,185.48	?
Salaries	48,605.10	37,591.50	59,820.64	?
Overhead expenses	11,784.60	9,695.80	17,346.52	?
				?

2 Loan details for the three branches were as follows during July. Find the outstanding loans at 31 July for **(a)** each branch and **(b)** the area, by completing the missing totals below.

	Branch A £	Branch B £	Branch C £	Total £
Loans outstanding 1 July	153,812.50	138,274.20	280,434.62	?
New loans in July	47,386.75	42,516.60	86,925.50	?
Interest added	+ 3,018.60	+ 2,816.24	+ 5,162.50	+ ?
	?	?	?	?
Repayments in July	− 18,286.20	− 15,525.60	− 22,920.40	− ?
Totals	?	?	?	?

3 An area head office buys the following items for branches in its area. What is the total cost?

(a) 14 pedestal desks at £459.50 each.
(b) 8 swivel chairs at £97.75 each.

(c)   16 computer workstations at £525.00 each.

(d)   4 safes at £483.33 each.

(e)   18 coffee centres at £121.17 each.

4   The Head Office of a brank is seeking to evaluate the capital costs of employing staff at branches. It is decided to find the average capital cost per employee at each of ten branches chosen on a random basis. The figures are as shown below. Calculate the average cost for each branch. (Answers to the nearest whole pound.)

Branch	Capital cost for year just ended (£)	Number of Employees
A	84,286.50	12
B	62,160.60	7
C	185,942.30	29
D	226,485.60	36
E	90,246.36	14
F	121,248.60	15
G	184,246.40	25
H	275,732.75	48
I	654,060.55	116
J	348,228.00	72

■ ANSWERS

Exercise 2.1   **(a)** 49   **(b)** 1,757   **(c)** 11,023   **(d)** 1,184,010   **(e)** 17,500,023
(f) 9,284   **(g)** 107,245   **(h)** 9,206,120   **(i)** 17,202,000,019   **(j)** 400,000,000,000

Exercise 2.2   **(a)** Forty-one   **(b)** Three hundred and eighty four   **(c)** Two thousand nine hundred and one   **(d)** One hundred and seventy five thousand, and twenty one **(e)** Eight hundred million, twenty seven thousand, one hundred and nine

Exercise 2.3   **(a)** 97   **(b)** 113   **(c)** 89   **(d)** 197   **(e)** 1,102   **(f)** 1,112
(g) 1,690   **(h)** 2,011   **(i)** 44,512   **(j)** 53,769

Exercise 2.4   **(a)** 11,941   **(b)** 8,098   **(c)** 47,906   **(d)** 63,919   **(e)** 65,228
(f) 76,564

Exercise 2.5   **(a)** 7,846   **(b)** 8,022   **(c)** 64,327

Exercise 2.6   **(a)** 63   **(b)** 178   **(c)** 159   **(d)** 125   **(e)** 877   **(f)** 2,137
(g) 3,020   **(h)** 12,407   **(i)** 18,807   **(j)** 242,170

Exercise 2.7   **(a)** 889   **(b)** 2,040   **(c)** 5,310   **(d)** 38,250   **(e)** 90,090
(f) 131,616   **(g)** 1,173,612   **(h)** 977,130   **(i)** 1,331,680   **(j)** 512,600

Exercise 2.8 (a) 85 (b) 133 (c) 119 (d) 335.71428 (e) 307.46666
(f) 4,500 (g) 1,516.875 (h) 4,035.8888 (i) 623.47368 (j) 47,509.666

Exercise 2.9 (a) 290 (b) 285.71428 (c) 1085.7142 (d) 611.8421
(e) 1,101.1904 (f) 1,806.4516 (g) 785.52631 (h) 1294.9324 (i) 1,085.5303
(j) 4732.3529

Exercise 2.10
1 A = £81,025.73 B = £83,828.44 C = £122,603.29 Capital items £90,280.55
Consumables £12,332.75 Salaries £146,017.24 Overheads £38,826.92 Grand total
£287,457.46.
2 Loans at start £572,521.32 New loans £176,828.85 Interest £10,997.34 Grand
total £760,347.51 less total repayments £56,732.20 Final outstandings £703,615.31
of which Branch A £185,931.65 B £168,081.44 C £349,602.22.
3 Total cost = £19,729.38
4 A = £7,024 B = £8,880 C = £6,412 D = £6,291 E = £6,446 F = £8,083
G = £7,370 H = £5,744 I = £5,638 J = £4,837.

3 Fractions

OBJECTIVES

At the end of this chapter you should:
1. Have revised the vocabulary used in discussing vulgar fractions, or common fractions;
2. Be able to add, subtract, multiply and divide numbers including fractions;
3. Understand the meaning of brackets when used in fractions calculations;
4. Be able to solve quite difficult fractions sums.

---

1 THE VOCABULARY OF FRACTIONS

A fraction is a quantity which is less than one whole unit. The commonest fractions in day to day use are $\frac{1}{2}$, $\frac{1}{3}$, $\frac{1}{4}$, $\frac{1}{5}$ etc. When written in this way the top figure is called the **numerator**, which means **the number of parts we have**. The bottom number is called the **denominator**, which means **the name of the part** under consideration. So with $\frac{1}{5}$, $\frac{2}{5}$, $\frac{3}{5}$, and $\frac{4}{5}$ the name of the part in each case is 'fifths' but the top number tells us we have one fifth, two fifths, three fifths etc. When we get to $\frac{5}{5}$ that is a whole unit and is said to **cancel down**

$$\frac{\overset{1}{\cancel{5}}}{\underset{1}{\cancel{5}}} = 1 \text{ (five fifths makes one whole unit)}$$

Cancelling is dividing the numerator of a fraction and the denominator of a fraction by the same number. Thus $\frac{10}{15}$ cancels down to $\frac{2}{3}$, because both the numerator and the denominator divide by 5. The fraction is said to be '*in its lowest terms*' when it will not cancel any more. So $\frac{2}{3}$ is in its lowest terms.

A number made up of whole numbers and fractions is called a **mixed number**. So $1\frac{4}{5}$ is a mixed number. In some fractions calculations we cannot deal with mixed numbers and have to turn the mixed number into a 'top-heavy' fraction, showing that the fraction is larger than a whole number. For example $1\frac{4}{5} = \frac{9}{5}$ (five fifths in the whole unit and four more fifths). The correct mathematical term for a top-heavy fraction is an **improper fraction**.

We shall meet further pieces of fractions vocabulary later in the chapter.

■ **EXERCISE 3.1**

Change these mixed numbers to improper fractions.

(a) $1\frac{1}{2}$ (b) $2\frac{3}{4}$ (c) $3\frac{4}{5}$ (d) $5\frac{1}{2}$ (e) $6\frac{1}{3}$

(f) $7\frac{3}{4}$ (g) $5\frac{2}{3}$ (h) $2\frac{7}{10}$ (i) $3\frac{1}{6}$ (j) $12\frac{1}{2}$

■ **EXERCISE 3.2**

Change these improper fractions to mixed numbers.

(a) $\frac{3}{2}$ (b) $\frac{4}{3}$ (c) $\frac{7}{6}$ (d) $\frac{5}{3}$ (e) $\frac{19}{6}$

(f) $\frac{16}{7}$ (g) $\frac{16}{5}$ (h) $\frac{23}{9}$ (i) $\frac{29}{12}$ (j) $\frac{17}{10}$

■ **EXERCISE 3.3**

Cancel these fractions to their lowest terms.

(a) $\frac{2}{4}$ (b) $\frac{2}{6}$ (c) $\frac{4}{6}$ (d) $\frac{15}{20}$ (e) $\frac{25}{30}$

(f) $\frac{66}{72}$ (g) $\frac{45}{60}$ (h) $\frac{24}{48}$ (i) $\frac{75}{100}$ (j) $\frac{17}{34}$

2 ADDITION AND SUBTRACTION OF FRACTIONS

We can add fractions and subtract fractions if they have the same denominator. We simply add the numerators, or subtract the numerators as required:

$$\frac{2}{5} + \frac{2}{5} = \frac{4}{5}$$
$$\frac{4}{7} - \frac{2}{7} = \frac{2}{7}$$

Sometimes the numerator becomes larger than the denominator and we can give the final answer as a mixed number

$$\frac{4}{9} + \frac{5}{9} + \frac{7}{9} = \frac{16}{9} = 1\frac{7}{9}$$

If the fractions to be added have different denominators we cannot proceed with the calculation, until we have changed them to a **common denominator**. For example

$$\frac{1}{2} + \frac{2}{3}$$

To find the common denominator look at the larger denominator 3. The common denominator will be a multiple of 3, i.e. 6, 9, 12, 15 etc. Since the best common denominator is the **lowest common denominator** we ask ourselves 'Will two go into 6?' The answer is yes – it goes 3 times. Then 6 is the lowest common denominator, because it is the **lowest common multiple** of 2 and 3. We now change $\frac{1}{2}$ into $\frac{3}{6}$ and $\frac{2}{3}$ into $\frac{4}{6}$.

$$\frac{1}{2} + \frac{2}{3} = \frac{3+4}{6} = \frac{7}{6} = 1\frac{1}{6}$$

In addition of fractions, where mixed numbers are concerned add the whole units first, and then find the common denominator and add the fractions. For example:

$$1\frac{1}{2} + 2\frac{3}{4} + 3\frac{7}{8} = 6\frac{4+6+7}{8} = 6\frac{17}{8} = 8\frac{1}{8}$$

(The $\frac{17}{8}$ becomes $2\frac{1}{8}$ (because $\frac{8}{8} = 1$ unit) making $8\frac{1}{8}$ in all).

■ **EXERCISE 3.4**

Add up the following:

(a) $\frac{3}{4} + \frac{5}{8}$ (b) $\frac{3}{7} + \frac{2}{3}$

(c) $\frac{5}{8} + \frac{3}{4} + \frac{7}{12}$ (d) $1\frac{1}{4} + 2\frac{1}{2} + 3\frac{7}{8}$

(e) $2\frac{7}{12} + 3\frac{3}{4} + 2\frac{1}{5}$ (f) $4\frac{3}{5} + 2\frac{7}{10} + 1\frac{1}{20}$

(g) $3\frac{1}{8} + 2\frac{11}{24} + 1\frac{1}{2}$ (h) $2\frac{5}{8} + 2\frac{3}{4} + 7\frac{11}{16}$

(i) $4\frac{1}{2} + 2\frac{2}{3} + 1\frac{3}{14}$ (j) $5\frac{7}{10} + 3\frac{2}{5} + 1\frac{3}{4}$

In subtracting mixed numbers, subtract the whole numbers first and then find the common denominator and subtract the fractions. For example:

$$4\frac{3}{4} - 2\frac{2}{3} = 2\frac{9-8}{12} = 2\frac{1}{12}$$

Sometimes the fraction to be subtracted is bigger than the other fraction. For example:

$$17\frac{1}{3} - 3\frac{3}{4} = 14\frac{4-9}{12}$$

Clearly, as we cannot take 9 from 4 we must use one of the whole units. One unit is twelve twelfths so we have:

$$14\frac{4-9}{12} = 13\frac{16-9}{12} \quad \text{(the unit has turned into } \tfrac{12}{12} \text{ making } \tfrac{16}{12} \text{ in all)}$$

$$= 13\frac{7}{12}$$

■ **EXERCISE 3.5**

Subtract the following:

(a) $\frac{5}{8} - \frac{1}{4}$ (b) $\frac{7}{10} - \frac{3}{5}$

(c) $3\frac{1}{2} - 1\frac{3}{10}$ (d) $4\frac{2}{3} - 2\frac{3}{4}$

(e) $5\frac{1}{3} - 2\frac{11}{12}$ (f) $7\frac{3}{8} - 4\frac{15}{32}$

(g) $9\frac{3}{7} - 4\frac{1}{2}$ (h) $5\frac{2}{3} - 2\frac{11}{12}$

(i) $9\frac{3}{5} - 3\frac{17}{20}$ (j) $14\frac{1}{5} - 7\frac{3}{8}$

3 MULTIPLICATION OF FRACTIONS

To multiply fractions the rules are:

(a) Cancel if you can.
(b) Multiply the numerators and multiply the denominators.

For example:

$$\frac{1}{\cancel{2}} \times \frac{\cancel{2}^{\,1}}{3} = \frac{1}{3} \text{ (cancelling by 2)}$$

and

$$\frac{\cancel{3}^{\,1}}{5} \times \frac{7}{\cancel{15}_{\,5}} = \frac{7}{25} \text{ (cancelling by 3)}$$

If mixed numbers enter into the multiplication we cannot multiply until we have turned the mixed number into an improper fraction

$$1\frac{1}{2} \times 2\frac{1}{3} = \frac{\overset{1}{\cancel{3}}}{2} \times \frac{7}{\underset{1}{\cancel{3}}} \quad \text{(cancelling by 3)}$$

$$= \frac{7}{2} = 3\frac{1}{2}$$

Note that if the result is an improper fraction we turn it back into a mixed number for the final answer.

■ EXERCISE 3.6

Solve these multiplication of fractions sums.

(a) $\frac{2}{3} \times \frac{3}{4}$ (b) $\frac{3}{8} \times \frac{7}{9}$

(c) $\frac{4}{5} \times \frac{3}{8}$ (d) $\frac{7}{12} \times \frac{5}{14}$

(e) $1\frac{1}{2} \times 1\frac{2}{3}$ (f) $1\frac{3}{4} \times 2\frac{3}{7}$

(g) $3\frac{1}{8} \times 2\frac{1}{5} \times 1\frac{1}{11}$ (h) $1\frac{1}{3} \times \frac{7}{16} \times 1\frac{1}{21}$

(i) $4\frac{1}{2} \times 2\frac{1}{3} \times 3\frac{3}{7}$ (j) $2\frac{1}{7} \times 1\frac{1}{8} \times 3\frac{1}{5}$

4 DIVISION OF FRACTIONS

To divide fractions the rules are:

   (a)   Turn the divisor upside down and multiply, which, as before, means

   (b)   Cancel if you can

   (c)   Multiply the numerators and multiply the denominators.

For example:

$$\frac{1}{2} \div \frac{1}{4} = \frac{1}{\underset{1}{\cancel{2}}} \times \frac{\overset{2}{\cancel{4}}}{1} \quad \text{(turning the divisor upside down and then cancelling by 2)}$$

This is a sensible way to arrive at the answer, because if we ask ourselves $\frac{1}{2} \div \frac{1}{4}$ (How many times does $\frac{1}{4}$ go into $\frac{1}{2}$?) the answer is clearly 2. Again:

$$\frac{3}{8} \div \frac{3}{24} = \frac{\overset{1}{\cancel{3}}}{\underset{1}{\cancel{8}}} \times \frac{\overset{3}{\cancel{24}}}{\underset{1}{\cancel{3}}} = 3.$$

If the calculation includes mixed numbers we must turn them into improper fractions before we turn the divisor upside down and multiply.

For example:

$$2\frac{1}{4} \div 1\frac{1}{2} = \frac{9}{4} \div \frac{3}{2} = \frac{\overset{3}{\cancel{9}}}{\underset{2}{\cancel{4}}} \times \frac{\overset{1}{\cancel{2}}}{\underset{1}{\cancel{3}}} = \frac{3}{2} = 1\frac{1}{2}$$

At the end we must turn the improper fraction $(\frac{3}{2})$ back into a mixed number $(1\frac{1}{2})$.

■ EXERCISE 3.7

Solve these division of fractions sums.

(a) $\frac{5}{8} \div \frac{3}{4}$ (b) $\frac{7}{12} \div \frac{2}{3}$

(c) $\frac{4}{9} \div \frac{5}{6}$ (d) $\frac{3}{4} \div \frac{4}{5}$

(e) $1\frac{1}{2} \div 2\frac{1}{4}$ (f) $3\frac{1}{8} \div 1\frac{1}{4}$

(g) $4\frac{1}{2} \div 3\frac{3}{5}$ **(h)** $7\frac{1}{2} \div 1\frac{2}{3}$

(i) $3\frac{3}{10} \div 1\frac{3}{8}$ **(j)** $10\frac{2}{3} \div 2\frac{2}{9}$

5   PRACTICAL BANKING PROBLEMS INVOLVING FRACTIONS

In some banking departments simple problems arise which involve fractions.

Example

An inheritance of £24,720 (all taxes and charges having been deducted) is to be shared so that $\frac{2}{5}$ goes to the older son, Tom, and $\frac{1}{3}$ to the younger son Peter. What fraction is left for the daughter, Sue, and how much will each get.

Calculations

The boys take $\frac{2}{5} + \frac{1}{3} = \frac{6+5}{15} = \frac{11}{15}$

Therefore the fraction left for the daughter must be $\frac{4}{15}$.

Therefore they will receive as follows:

Tom: $£\overset{4\,944}{\cancel{24{,}720}} \times \frac{2}{\cancel{5}_1} = £9{,}888$

Peter: $£\overset{8\,240}{\cancel{24{,}720}} \times \frac{1}{\cancel{3}_1} = £8{,}240$

Sue: $£\overset{\overset{1\,648}{4\,944}}{\cancel{24{,}720}} \times \frac{4}{\cancel{\cancel{15}}_1} = £6{,}592$

(Check: £9,888 + £8,240 + £6,592 = £24,720)

■ EXERCISE 3.8

Solve each of these simple problems.

1 An investment manager is instructed to invest £173,250 for a ward of court in such a way that $\frac{2}{5}$ are in gilt-edged securities, $\frac{1}{4}$ in equities (ordinary shares) and the balance in a high interest investment account.

  (a) What fraction is put in the high interest account?

  (b) What are the three sums of money available for each investment? (Answers correct to the nearest £1.)

2 A bank's total earnings of £5,840 million are used as follows:

  (i) $\frac{1}{2}$ to cover interest to depositors

  (ii) $\frac{1}{16}$ to cover doubtful debts

  (iii) $\frac{1}{4}$ to cover operating expenses

(iv) $\frac{1}{12}$ to pay dividends to shareholders

(v) the balance is put to reserves.

(a) What fraction goes to reserves?

(b) What is the amount used under each of the headings (i)–(v) above. (Answers correct to the nearest £million.)

3 The assets of a partnership business are split in the following ways:

(i) $\frac{3}{8}$ in the form of fixed assets

(ii) $\frac{1}{4}$ in the form of stock

(iii) $\frac{1}{5}$ in the form of debtors

(iv) the balance is in cash at the bank.

The total of the assets is £136,240.

(a) What is the fraction of assets in cash at the bank?

(b) What is the value of each of the assets (i)–(iv) above?

6   MORE DIFFICULT FRACTION SUMS

In many calculations which involve fractions we do meet problems which involve all the processes – addition, subtraction, multiplication and division. In these situations we can get different answers according to which part we do first. For example:

Method 1 $\frac{1}{2} + \frac{1}{2} \times 2$

Doing the addition first we get:

$= 1 \times 2$
$= \underline{\underline{2}}$

Method 2 $\frac{1}{2} + \frac{1}{2} \times 2$

Doing the multiplication first we get

$\frac{1}{2} + \frac{1}{2} \times 2$
$= \frac{1}{2} + 1$
$= \underline{\underline{1\frac{1}{2}}}$

Clearly we must have a rule to tell us which part to do first.

The rule, attributed to the late Mr E J Hopkins is called the 'BODMAS' rule

Brackets first

Of next (of is like a bracket containing a multiplication sign) – for example in finding $1\frac{1}{4} \div \frac{3}{8}$ of 24 we calculate $\frac{3}{8}$ of 24 before we do the division

Division next

Multiplication before addition and subtraction

Addition next and

Subtraction last of all

So in the example used above, the correct method is Method 2, but if we want to do the addition part first we must give it priority by putting it in brackets, because brackets are done first. It would then become $(\frac{1}{2} + \frac{1}{2}) \times 2 = 1 \times 2 = \underline{\underline{2}}$

Example 1

$$1\frac{1}{2} \times 1\frac{2}{3} + 2\frac{1}{4} \quad \text{(do the multiplication before the addition)}$$

$$= \overset{1}{\cancel{\frac{3}{2}}} \times \frac{5}{\cancel{3}_1} + 2\frac{1}{4}$$

$$= \frac{5}{2} + 2\frac{1}{4}$$

$$= 2\frac{1}{2} + 2\frac{1}{4}$$

$$= \underline{\underline{4\frac{3}{4}}}$$

Example 2

$$1\frac{3}{8} \div (\frac{2}{3} + \frac{5}{8}) \qquad \text{(brackets first)}$$

$$= 1\frac{3}{8} \div (\frac{16+15}{24})$$

$$= 1\frac{3}{8} \div (\frac{31}{24})$$

$$= 1\frac{3}{8} \div 1\frac{7}{24}$$

$$= \frac{11}{\cancel{8}_1} \times \frac{\overset{3}{\cancel{24}}}{31} \qquad \text{(cancelling by 8)}$$

$$= \frac{33}{31}$$

$$= \underline{\underline{1\frac{2}{31}}}$$

Note

It is bad practice to break a complex calculation up into little bits and work them out separately. There is a danger of forgetting to put them back together again. When doing the first part of the calculation (the part in brackets) ignore the other part, but set it down each time untouched while you are working on the part in brackets. Then when the brackets part is solved all is ready to proceed with the rest of the calculation.

■ EXERCISE 3.9
Solve these complex fractions sums.

(a) $\frac{1}{2} + \frac{2}{3} \times \frac{9}{10}$

(b) $1\frac{1}{4} - \frac{3}{8} \times \frac{5}{6}$

(c) $2\frac{1}{2} - \frac{3}{5} \div \frac{1}{2}$

(d) $\frac{3}{4} \times \frac{2}{3} - \frac{2}{5} \div 2\frac{2}{3}$

(e) $1\frac{1}{2} \div (\frac{5}{6} + \frac{3}{5})$

(f) $(\frac{2}{3} + \frac{3}{8}) \div 1\frac{5}{6}$

(g) $(4\frac{1}{2} + 2\frac{2}{3}) \div 1\frac{3}{8}$

(h) $(7\frac{1}{2} + 5\frac{1}{3}) \div (\frac{3}{8} \times 1\frac{1}{3})$

(i) $(3\frac{3}{4} - 2\frac{2}{3}) \div (3\frac{1}{8} + 2\frac{5}{6})$

(j) $(17\frac{1}{2} - 4\frac{1}{5}) \div (4\frac{1}{4} + 2\frac{2}{5})$

■ ANSWERS

Exercise 3.1 (a) $\frac{3}{2}$ (b) $\frac{11}{4}$ (c) $\frac{19}{5}$ (d) $\frac{11}{2}$ (e) $\frac{19}{3}$ (f) $\frac{31}{4}$ (g) $\frac{17}{3}$ (h) $\frac{27}{10}$ (i) $\frac{19}{6}$ (j) $\frac{25}{2}$

Exercise 3.2 (a) $1\frac{1}{2}$ (b) $1\frac{1}{3}$ (c) $1\frac{1}{6}$ (d) $1\frac{2}{3}$ (e) $3\frac{1}{6}$ (f) $2\frac{2}{7}$ (g) $3\frac{1}{5}$ (h) $2\frac{5}{9}$ (i) $2\frac{5}{12}$ (j) $1\frac{7}{10}$

Exercise 3.3 (a) $\frac{1}{2}$ (b) $\frac{1}{3}$ (c) $\frac{2}{3}$ (d) $\frac{3}{4}$ (e) $\frac{5}{6}$ (f) $\frac{11}{12}$ (g) $\frac{3}{4}$ (h) $\frac{1}{2}$ (i) $\frac{3}{4}$ (j) $\frac{1}{2}$

Exercise 3.4 (a) $1\frac{3}{8}$ (b) $1\frac{2}{21}$ (c) $1\frac{23}{24}$ (d) $7\frac{5}{8}$ (e) $8\frac{8}{15}$ (f) $8\frac{7}{20}$ (g) $7\frac{1}{12}$ (h) $13\frac{1}{16}$ (i) $8\frac{8}{21}$ (j) $10\frac{17}{20}$

Exercise 3.5 (a) $\frac{3}{8}$ (b) $\frac{1}{10}$ (c) $2\frac{1}{5}$ (d) $1\frac{11}{12}$ (e) $2\frac{5}{12}$ (f) $2\frac{29}{32}$ (g) $4\frac{13}{14}$ (h) $2\frac{3}{4}$ (i) $5\frac{3}{4}$ (j) $6\frac{33}{40}$

Exercise 3.6 (a) $\frac{1}{2}$ (b) $\frac{7}{24}$ (c) $\frac{3}{10}$ (d) $\frac{5}{24}$ (e) $2\frac{1}{2}$ (f) $4\frac{1}{4}$ (g) $7\frac{1}{2}$ (h) $\frac{11}{18}$ (i) 36 (j) $7\frac{5}{7}$

Exercise 3.7 (a) $\frac{5}{6}$ (b) $\frac{7}{8}$ (c) $\frac{8}{15}$ (d) $\frac{15}{16}$ (e) $\frac{2}{3}$ (f) $2\frac{1}{2}$ (g) $1\frac{1}{4}$ (h) $4\frac{1}{2}$ (i) $2\frac{2}{5}$ (j) $4\frac{4}{5}$

Exercise 3.8

1 (a) $\frac{7}{20}$ (b) £69,300 (gilt edged) £43,312 (equities) and £60,638 (investment account)

2 (a) $\frac{5}{48}$ to reserves (b) £2,920m £365m £1,460m £487m and £608m

3 (a) $\frac{7}{40}$ at the bank (b) (i) £51,090 (ii) £34,060 (iii) £27,248 and (iv) £23,842

Exercise 3.9 (a) $1\frac{1}{10}$ (b) $\frac{15}{16}$ (c) $1\frac{3}{10}$ (d) $\frac{7}{20}$ (e) $1\frac{2}{43}$ (f) $\frac{25}{44}$ (g) $5\frac{7}{33}$ (h) $25\frac{2}{3}$ (i) $\frac{2}{11}$ (j) 2

4 More about decimals

OBJECTIVES

At the end of this chapter you should:
1 Be able to add up decimals including decimal fractions;
2 Be able to subtract decimals including decimal fractions;
3 Be able to multiply numbers which have decimal fractions;
4 Be able to divide numbers which have decimal fractions;
5 Understand recurring decimals;
6 Be able to correct up to a given number of decimal places;
7 Be able to change vulgar fractions to decimal fractions and vice versa.

1 ADDITION OF DECIMALS

We have really already added up decimals, because when we were adding up money the pence were expressed as decimal fractions of £1. However, as decimal fractions can be expressed in smaller values than hundredths (there are 100 pence in a £1) it is just worth making sure everyone is quite clear on the four rules of decimals. Consider the number below:

    42.7135

It is read as 42 point 7135. The whole numbers 42 are separated from the fractions by the decimal point which is usually written slightly above the line, but in text books is usually printed on the line. The fractional part is made up of 7 tenths, 1 hundredth, 3 thousandths and 5 ten-thousandths of a whole unit so that the idea of place value under the decimal system: hundreds, tens and units is simple repeated below the decimal point but with 'th' to show it is a fraction – i.e. tens becomes 'tenths', hundreds becomes 'hundredths', thousands becomes 'thousandths' etc.

    The rule for adding up decimals is to put the decimal points under one another and all the different place values fall into correct alignment. For example $17.15 + 129.385 + 1,756.494 + 83.7216$ is written down:

```
      17.15
     129.385
    1756.494
 +    83.7216
    ─────────
    1986.7506
    ─────────
```

The alignment of the decimal points automatically aligns all the other place values, units under units, tens under tens, tenths under tenths etc. We can then add up easily.

Of course, if we use the calculator we do not need to set the sum down in this way, but as we press the decimal point key the calculator takes note of the decimal fraction that is being keyed in and when instructed to add up the numbers it takes the position of the decimal point into account. The sum above, done on the calculator, would proceed as follows:

CALCULATION: $17.15 + 129.385 + 1,756.494 + 83.7216$

SEQUENCE   ©   17.15   ⊞   129.385   ⊞   1,756.494   ⊞   83.7216   ⊟

DISPLAY   0   17.15   17.15   129.385   146.535   1,756.494   1,903.029   83.7216   1,986.7506

ANSWER   1,986.7506

■ EXERCISE 4.1

Set down these sums and complete them, or use the calculator and write down the answer only.

(a) $2.1 + 3.25 + 4.735 + 2.68$ (b) $17.15 + 193.2 + 15.1785 + 26.5984$

(c) $161.375 + 24.895 + 162.73856 + 42.985 + 15.6525$

(d) $816.7342 + 21.7 + 3.8658 + 14.6721 + 8,815.623$

(e) $71.586 + 492.3865 + 7.1056 + 0.00598 + 1.542$

2 SUBTRACTION OF DECIMALS

The rule for subtraction of decimals is exactly the same as for addition of decimals. You keep the decimal points aligned and this means all the place values on either side are also aligned correctly. For example:

$$\begin{array}{r} 27.595 \\ -\ 13.38642 \\ \hline 14.20858 \\ \hline \end{array}$$

The two hundred thousandths have no figure above them in the 'ten thousandths' column so we must borrow from the next column. However, there is no figure there either so we must borrow from the thousandths column. At the end we can check the result by adding the answer to the number subtracted – this should give us the number we started with. Check this now.

Once again – if we use the calculator it will remember the decimal points as we enter them and do the subtraction bearing those positions in mind.

CALCULATION: $27.595 - 13.38642$

SEQUENCE   ©   27.595   ⊟   13.38642   ⊟

DISPLAY   0   27.595   27.595   13.38642   14.20858

ANSWER   14.20858

■ **EXERCISE 4.2**

Set down these sums and complete them, or use the calculator and write down the answers only.

(a)   5.95 – 3.864   (b)   71.26 – 19.575
(c)   1.683 – 0.9565   (d)   253.7 – 19.655
(e)   137.865 – 19.718   (f)   425.65 – 137.488

3   MULTIPLICATION OF DECIMALS

The rule for setting down a multiplication of decimals sum is to disregard the decimal points altogether to begin with and only sort out the position of the decimal point at the end of the calculation. Consider 2.85×1.9. Set the sum down as though it was 285×19 – in other words ignore the decimal points – and do the multiplication sum.

```
   285
 × 19
 ─────
  2565     (multiplying by 9)
  2850     (multiplying by 10)
 ─────
  5415
 ═════
```

We now place the decimal point in the answer by the following method. Count up the figures after the decimal point in both the multiplier (1.9) and the multiplicand (2.85). The multiplicand is the number we are multiplying. There will be the same number of figures after the decimal point in the answer. There is one figure after the decimal point in the multiplier and two figures after the decimal point in the multiplicand. That means there will be three figures after the decimal point in the answer. So the answer is not 5415, but 5.415.

We can see why this is so if we think of the sum as a multiplication of fractions sum.

$$2.85 = \frac{285}{100}$$
$$1.9 \; = \frac{19}{10}$$

Multiplying we get

$$\frac{285}{100} \times \frac{19}{10} = \frac{5415}{1000} = \underline{5.415}$$

The answer we get is not 5415, but 5415 thousandths, which is 5.415.

Using the calculator we have no difficulty; the calculator itself decides where the decimal point will be. For example

CALCULATOR: 2.85×1.9

SEQUENCE   Ⓒ   2.85   ☒   1.9   ⊟

DISPLAY   0   2.85   2.85   1.9   5.415

ANSWER   5.415

■ EXERCISE 4.3

Set down these sums and complete them, or use the calculator and write down the answers only.

(a)	2.35×1.4	**(b)**	3.89×4.6
(c)	72.385×1.7	**(d)**	959.65×2.7
(e)	425.368×13.4	**(f)**	725.65×9.5
(g)	1.523×7.6	**(h)**	42.759×1.8
(i)	425.6×3.85	**(j)**	4.75×2.55

3.1   Multiplying numbers by 10, 100, 1000 etc.

It frequently happens in business calculations that we need to multiply numbers by 10, or 100, or 1000. With whole numbers it is easy; we simply add a nought, or two noughts, or three noughts. Thus:

$$16 \times 10 = 160$$
$$27 \times 100 = 2,700$$
$$156 \times 1,000 = 156,000$$

With numbers that involve a decimal fraction when we multiply by ten we need to move the number one place to the left, through the decimal point, so that each figure in the number has moved up one place and becomes ten times as big.

Thus $1.5 \quad \times 10 = 15$ (pushing the number through the decimal
and $1.342 \times 10 = 13.42$ point one place in each case)

Some teachers say move the decimal point one place to the right, but it is really better to regard the decimal point as immovable – it is the barrier between the units and the decimal fractions. If we push the number through the decimal point we can see it getting ten times bigger as we do so. If we multiply by 100 we push the number through the decimal point two places, and to multiply by 1000 we push it three places.

$$1.342 \times 10 \quad = 13.42$$
$$1.342 \times 100 \quad = 134.2$$
$$1.342 \times 1000 = 1,342.$$

4   DIVISION OF DECIMALS

When we divide numbers with decimals it does present some problems in setting the sum down, although of course if we use an electronic calculator the program built into the calculator solves the difficulty for us. Consider the division sum $275.32 \div 1.6$. It would be quite difficult to tell where the decimal point would go in the answer if we tried to divide by 1.6 so the usual way out of the difficulty is to make the divisor into a whole number 16. To do this we have to multiply it by 10. $1.6 \times 10 = 16$. This makes the divisor ten times bigger, which would give us a wrong answer, but to compensate we make the dividend (the number we are dividing up) ten times bigger too. So the rule for doing a division sum like $275.32 \div 1.6$ is:

(a)   Make the divisor a whole number.

(b)   Whatever you did to the divisor, do the same thing to the dividend.

$275.32 \div 1.6$

Make the divisor a whole number; 16. To do that we had to multiply it by 10.
Do the same to the dividend $275.32 \times 10 = 2753.2$
So we have:

$$275.32 \div 1.6$$
$$= 2753.2 \div 16$$

```
        172.075
16 | 2,753.2
      16
      ──
      115
      112
      ──
       33
       32
      ───
      120
      112
      ───
       80
       80
       ──
```

Are you weak at long division? The reasoning goes like this. 16 into 27 hundreds goes once. Put 1 in the answer, and put the 16 under the 27 and take away. The 11 hundreds are now turned into tens with the 5 tens already available. That makes 115 tens. 16 into 115 tens goes 7 tens (for each of the 16 sharers). This uses up $7 \times 16 = 112$ tens and leaves only 3 tens left over. This 3 tens becomes 30 units. With the three units already available it makes 33 units. 16 into 33 units goes 2, etc. etc.

Notice that the sum goes on until it works out exactly, but in some cases it might never work out exactly and we usually have to work only to a given number of decimal places. We will look at this problem using the calculator – to save a lot of space doing long division sums.

Using the calculator for the sum above we have:

CALCULATION: $275.32 \div 1.6$

SEQUENCE	Ⓒ	275.32	⊞	1.6	⊟
DISPLAY	0	275.32	275.32	1.6	172.075
ANSWER		172.075			

The calculator itself decides where the decimal point should go in the answer.

4.1   Correcting up and the decimal system

This has already been mentioned in Chapter 2, Section 7.1, but we need to look at it with decimal fractions. For example, consider the answer to the example used above: 172.075.

Had we wished to have this answer correct to the nearest whole number the answer would have been 172 – for the 0 tenths is clearly less than half.

Had we wished to have the answer correct to one decimal place we need to look at the second decimal place – the 7 hundredths. This is more than half of a tenth (for 5 hundredths is half a tenth). So the answer would be 172.1 correct to one decimal place.

Had we wished to have the answer correct to two decimal places we need to look at the third decimal place. This is a 5, exactly half way. Remember that the rule is 'Anything below 5, round down; 5 and above, round up.' The answer is therefore 172.08.

4.2 Recurring decimals

In many division sums the answer does not work out exactly and the calculator gives an answer which uses up the whole display. For example:

$$2.6 \div 1.7 = 1.5294117$$

We must give this answer correct to a specified number of decimal places. If no such number of decimal places is specified we choose a number of decimal places which is sensible for the degree of accuracy required in real life.

Sometimes the display results in a recurring decimal. For example

$$2.75 \div 0.3 = 9.1666666$$

The figure 6 recurs endlessly. This can be written as $9.1\dot{6}$. The dot over the top indicates that the 6 is a recurring figure. Sometimes more than one number occurs. For example

$$6.5 \div 0.7 = 9.285714285$$

A series of numbers is now recurring. This answer could be written

$$9.\dot{2}8571\dot{4}$$

The dots over the top indicate that all the figures between them recur endlessly. However, such degrees of accuracy are unlikely to be of much importance in banking.

■ EXERCISE 4.4

Set down these sums and complete them, or use the calculator and record the answers only. Unless an answer works out exactly in less places of decimals give the answers correct to two places of decimals in each case.

(a) $61.56 \div 1.9$ (b) $414.7 \div 3.25$

(c) $471.65 \div 1.15$ (d) $358.27 \div 14.3$

(e) $6.06 \div 2.9$ (f) $15.97 \div 0.25$

(g) $217.65 \div 4.28$ (h) $194.8 \div 3.3$

(i) $472.6 \div 1.8$ (j) $47.954 \div 2.1$

5 CHANGING VULGAR FRACTIONS TO DECIMALS

Any vulgar fraction consists of a numerator and a denominator. For example $\frac{1}{2}$, $\frac{2}{3}$, $\frac{3}{5}$, etc. To change a vulgar fraction into a decimal fraction we simply set down the numerator, put a decimal point after it and divide by the denominator.

Example 1

$\frac{1}{2}$ expressed as a decimal

Set down the 1 and put a decimal point after it (i.e. 1.)

Now divide by the denominator 2

$$\begin{array}{r} 0.5 \\ 2\overline{\smash{\big)}\,1.0} \end{array}$$ (2 into 1 unit won't go – so there are 0 units in the answer.)
(Change the 1 whole one into 10 tenths. 2 into 10 tenths goes 5. So the answer is 5 tenths.)

Example 2

$\frac{3}{5}$ expressed as a decimal

$$\begin{array}{r} 0.6 \\ 5\overline{\smash{\big)}\,3.0} \end{array}$$ (5 into 3 unit won't go – so there are 0 units in the answer.)
(Change the 3 whole ones into 30 tenths. 5 into 30 tenths goes 6.)

Example 3

Express $\frac{24}{25}$ as a decimal

$$\begin{array}{r} 0.96 \\ 25\overline{\smash{\big)}\,24.000} \\ \underline{225} \\ 150 \\ \underline{150} \\ \cdots \end{array}$$

This is of course very easy using the calculator.

CALCULATION: Express $\frac{24}{25}$ as a decimal

SEQUENCE	C	24	÷	25	=
DISPLAY	0	24	24	25	0.96
ANSWER	0.96				

■ EXERCISE 4.5

Express the following vulgar fractions as decimal fractions. If you use a calculator just set down the answer. If necessary give the answer correct to three decimal places.

(a) $\frac{3}{8}$ (b) $\frac{7}{12}$

(c) $\frac{5}{9}$ (d) $\frac{7}{16}$

(e) $\frac{3}{7}$ (f) $\frac{47}{48}$

(g) $\frac{12}{25}$ (h) $\frac{19}{40}$

6   CHANGING DECIMAL FRACTIONS TO VULGAR FRACTIONS

Decimal fractions can always be expressed as tenths, hundredths, thousandths, etc.
Thus:

$$0.25 = \frac{25}{100}$$
$$0.375 = \frac{375}{1000}$$
$$0.4127 = \frac{4,127}{10,000}$$

Note that there are always as many noughts in the denominator as there are figures
after the decimal point in the original decimal fraction. So to turn a decimal fraction
into a vulgar fraction we set it down as a fraction and cancel if we can, until we have
the fraction in its lowest terms – for example:

$$0.75 = \frac{75}{100} = \frac{3}{4} \quad \text{(cancelling by 25)}$$
$$0.18 = \frac{18}{100} = \frac{9}{50} \quad \text{(cancelling by 2)}$$
$$0.355 = \frac{355}{1000} = \frac{71}{200} \quad \text{(cancelling by 5)}$$

■ EXERCISE 4.6

Express the following decimal fractions as vulgar fractions in their lowest terms:

(a)   0.85   (b)   0.64
(c)   0.425   (d)   0.1375
(e)   0.325   (f)   0.375
(g)   0.4255   (h)   0.3752

■ ANSWERS

Exercise 4.1   (a) 12.765   (b) 252.1269   (c) 407.64606   (d) 9,672.5951
(e) 572.62608

Exercise 4.2   (a) 2.086   (b) 51.685   (c) 0.7265   (d) 234.045   (e) 118.147
(f) 288.162

Exercise 4.3   (a) 3.29   (b) 17.894   (c) 123.0545   (d) 2,591.055
(e) 5,699.9312   (f) 6,893.675   (g) 11.5748   (h) 76.9662   (i) 1,638.56
(j) 12.1125

Exercise 4.4   (a) 32.4   (b) 127.6   (c) 410.13   (d) 25.05   (e) 2.09
(f) 63.88   (g) 50.85   (h) 59.03   (i) 262.56   (j) 22.84

Exercise 4.5   (a) 0.375   (b) 0.583   (c) 0.556   (d) 0.438   (e) 0.429
(f) 0.979   (g) 0.48   (h) 0.475

Exercise 4.6   (a) $\frac{17}{20}$ (b) $\frac{16}{25}$ (c) $\frac{17}{40}$ (d) $\frac{11}{80}$ (e) $\frac{13}{40}$ (f) $\frac{3}{8}$ (g) $\frac{851}{2000}$ (h) $\frac{469}{1250}$

5 Percentages

OBJECTIVES

At the end of this chapter you should:
1 Understand the meaning of 'percentage';
2 Know the common percentage groups;
3 Understand the relationship between percentages, decimal fractions and vulgar fractions, and be able to convert each into the others;
4 Be able to find a percentage of any quantity;
5 Be able to express one quantity as a percentage of another quantity;
6 Understand cash discounts, settlement discounts and trade discounts;
7 Understand VAT fractions.

1 WHAT IS A PERCENTAGE?

A percentage is a way of expressing fractions by relating them to 100. *Centum* is the Latin for 100 and *per* may be translated for our purposes as 'out of' so that percentage means 'out of 100'. 100 is a nice round number, which is fairly easy to envisage; we talk of scoring a century at cricket, we live in the 20th Century and will shortly be moving into the 21st Century. Many countries have coins called 'cents', like the Americans with 100 cents to the dollar, and so on. Although it is easy to understand the fraction $\frac{1}{2}$ it is just as easy to imagine '50 per cent' – 50 out of 100 – as being $\frac{1}{2}$ too. Similarly $\frac{1}{4}$ can easily be understood as 25 per cent – 25 out of 100, and $\frac{3}{4}$ as 75 per cent – 75 out of 100. The number 100 is not too hard to imagine (1,000 would be more difficult and 1,000,000 would by quite impossible to imagine).

To save writing the words 'per cent' every time we mention a percentage figure, the symbol % has been adopted as the sign for a percentage. So 50%, 45%, 95%, 3% and 17% mean '50 per cent', '45 per cent' etc.

2 THE COMMON PERCENTAGE GROUPS

There are certain percentage groups which are related to one another and we should be familiar with them. They are:

$$\frac{1}{4} = \frac{25}{100} = 25\% \qquad\qquad \frac{1}{3} = \frac{33\frac{1}{3}}{100} = 33\frac{1}{3}\%$$

$$\frac{1}{2} = \frac{50}{100} = 50\% \qquad\qquad \frac{2}{3} = \frac{66\frac{2}{3}}{100} = 66\frac{2}{3}\%$$

$$\frac{3}{4} = \frac{75}{100} = 75\%$$

$$\frac{1}{5} = \frac{20}{100} = 20\%$$

$$\frac{2}{5} = \frac{40}{100} = 40\% \qquad\qquad \frac{1}{6} = \frac{16\frac{2}{3}}{100} = 16\frac{2}{3}\%$$

$$\frac{3}{5} = \frac{60}{100} = 60\% \qquad\qquad \frac{5}{6} = \frac{83\frac{1}{3}}{100} = 83\frac{1}{3}\%$$

$$\frac{4}{5} = \frac{80}{100} = 80\%$$

$$\frac{1}{8} = \frac{12\frac{1}{2}}{100} = 12\frac{1}{2}\% \qquad\qquad \frac{1}{10} = \frac{10}{100} = 10\%$$

$$\frac{3}{8} = \frac{37\frac{1}{2}}{100} = 37\frac{1}{2}\% \qquad\qquad \frac{3}{10} = \frac{30}{100} = 30\%$$

$$\frac{5}{8} = \frac{62\frac{1}{2}}{100} = 62\frac{1}{2}\% \qquad\qquad \frac{7}{10} = \frac{70}{100} = 70\%$$

$$\frac{7}{8} = \frac{87\frac{1}{2}}{100} = 87\frac{1}{2}\% \qquad\qquad \frac{9}{10} = \frac{90}{100} = 90\%$$

$$\frac{1}{20} = \frac{5}{100} = 5\%$$

$$\frac{1}{40} = \frac{2\frac{1}{2}}{100} = 2\frac{1}{2}\%$$

$$\frac{1}{80} = \frac{1\frac{1}{4}}{100} = 1\frac{1}{4}\%$$

3 THE RELATIONSHIP BETWEEN PERCENTAGES, FRACTIONS AND DECIMALS

Since a percentage is really a fraction which has 100 as the denominator (e.g. $17\% = \frac{17}{100}$, $29\% = \frac{29}{100}$) there is a clear link between percentages, fractions and decimals and we can easily change each into the other. The link between them is 100. In business we frequently need to convert one type of fraction into the other. The rules are simple and are given in turn below.

3.1 Changing fractions into percentages

To change a fraction into a percentage the rule is:

Write down the fraction and multiply it by $\frac{100}{1}$

Example 1

$$\frac{1}{\cancel{2}_1} \times \frac{\cancel{100}^{50}}{1} = \underline{\underline{50\%}} \quad \text{(Cancelling by 2)}$$

$$\frac{2}{3} \times \frac{100}{1} = \frac{200}{3} = \underline{\underline{66\frac{2}{3}\%}}$$

$$\frac{17}{\cancel{24}_6} \times \frac{\cancel{100}^{25}}{1} \quad \text{(Cancelling by 4)}$$

$$= \frac{425}{6}$$

$$= \underline{\underline{70\frac{5}{6}\%}}$$

The same rule can be used if a mixed number is involved, each whole number being 100%

$$1\tfrac{3}{4} \times \tfrac{100}{1}$$
$$= \tfrac{7}{4} \times \tfrac{100}{1}$$
$$= \tfrac{700}{4}$$
$$= 175\%$$

Most calculators have a % key which will convert any fraction or mixed number to a percentage straight away, without entering $\times \tfrac{100}{1}$.

CALCULATION: $\tfrac{7}{12}$ to be expressed as a percentage (correct to one decimal place).

SEQUENCE   C   7   ÷   12   %

DISPLAY   0   7   7   12   58.333333

ANSWER   58.3%

3.2 Changing decimals into percentages

To change decimal fractions into percentages the rule is:

Multiply the decimal fraction by 100 and put in the % sign

Example 2

Changing .75 to a percentage. Multiplying by 100 we push the number through the decimal point two places and put in the percentage sign.
   .75 = 75.% (the decimal point can be discarded in this case)
   .635 as a percentage becomes 63.5%
1.55 becomes 155%
   .7925 becomes 79.25%

■ EXERCISE 5.1

Change the following fractions to percentages. If necessary give the answer correct to one decimal place.

(a) $\tfrac{3}{8}$ (b) $\tfrac{5}{8}$ (c) $\tfrac{2}{3}$ (d) $\tfrac{3}{4}$ (e) $\tfrac{3}{10}$ (f) $\tfrac{5}{12}$ (g) $\tfrac{17}{20}$

(h) $\tfrac{9}{25}$ (i) $\tfrac{4}{9}$ (j) $\tfrac{7}{11}$ (k) $\tfrac{3}{14}$ (l) $\tfrac{7}{9}$

■ EXERCISE 5.2

Change the following mixed numbers to percentages. If necessary give the answer correct to two decimal places.

(a) $1\tfrac{5}{8}$ (b) $7\tfrac{1}{3}$ (c) $6\tfrac{3}{4}$ (d) $2\tfrac{2}{3}$ (e) $5\tfrac{7}{16}$ (f) $9\tfrac{1}{4}$ (g) $13\tfrac{1}{2}$

(h) $2\tfrac{11}{12}$

■ **EXERCISE 5.3**

Change these decimal fractions to percentages.

(a) 0.95   (b) 0.73   (c) 0.625   (d) 0.4955 (e) 0.375

(f) 1.62   (g) 1.85   (h) 3.755

3.3   Changing percentages into fractions

To change a percentage into a fraction the rule is:

Write down the percentage as the numerator of the fraction and put 100 as the denominator. Then cancel if you can.

Example 3

$$36\% = \frac{\overset{9}{\cancel{36}}}{\underset{25}{\cancel{100}}} = \frac{9}{25} \quad \text{(Cancelling by 4)}$$

$$75\% = \frac{\overset{3}{\cancel{75}}}{\underset{4}{\cancel{100}}} = \frac{3}{4} \quad \text{(Cancelling by 25)}$$

$$87\tfrac{1}{2}\% = \frac{87\tfrac{1}{2}}{100} = \frac{\overset{7}{\cancel{175}}}{\underset{8}{\cancel{200}}} = \frac{7}{8} \quad \text{(Cancelling by 25)}$$

3.4   Changing percentages into decimals

To change a percentage into a decimal the rule is:

Write down the percentage with any fractions given in decimal form. Then put a decimal point in if there isn't one already, and push the number through the decimal point two places to the right to divide it by 100.

Example 4

$$42\% = \tfrac{42}{100} = 0.42$$

$$77\tfrac{1}{2}\% = 77.5\% = \tfrac{77.5}{100} = 0.775$$

$$150\% = \tfrac{150}{100} = 1.5$$

■ **EXERCISE 5.4**

Change the following percentages to vulgar fractions in their lowest terms.

(a) 40%   (b) 45%   (c) 24%   (d) 85%   (e) 42%   (f) $37\tfrac{1}{2}\%$

(g) $42\tfrac{1}{2}\%$ (h) 65%   (i) $83\tfrac{1}{3}\%$ (j) $58\tfrac{1}{3}\%$

■ **EXERCISE 5.5**

Change the following percentages to decimal fractions. If necessary give the answer correct to three decimal places.

(a) 15%   (b) $22\tfrac{1}{2}\%$ (c) $41\tfrac{2}{3}\%$ (d) $1\tfrac{1}{4}\%$ (e) $28\tfrac{2}{3}\%$ (f) $91\tfrac{2}{3}\%$

(g) $77\tfrac{1}{2}\%$ (h) $66\tfrac{2}{3}\%$ (i) $13\tfrac{3}{4}\%$ (j) $97\tfrac{1}{2}\%$

4 FINDING PERCENTAGES OF A QUANTITY

It is often necessary to find a percentage of a given quantity, in any unit of measure –
for example length, weight, capacity, etc. In banking it is usually a percentage of a sum
of money that needs to be discovered.

Example 5

Farmer Brown had died and left 35% of his estate to his nephew John Brown, who is a
customer. How much should the bank expect from administrators if the total estate is
£132,800?

35% is of course $\frac{35}{100}$. We can therefore expect

£132,8$\emptyset\emptyset \times \frac{35}{1\emptyset\emptyset}$ (Cancelling by 100)

= £1,328 × 35

= £46,480

In each case of this type we simply set down the quantity concerned and multiply it
by the percentage expressed as a vulgar fraction.

Example 6

What is $28\frac{1}{2}$% of £45,000?

£4$\overset{225}{5,\emptyset\emptyset\emptyset} \times \frac{57}{\underset{1}{2\emptyset\emptyset}}$ (Cancelling by 100 and then by 2)

= £225 × 57

= £12,825

On the calculator it would be very simple, but the $28\frac{1}{2}$ would be entered as 28.5 and
we must remember to divide by 100.

CALCULATION: $28\frac{1}{2}$% of £45,000

SEQUENCE	C	45,000	×	28.5	÷	100	=	
DISPLAY	0	45,000	45,000	28.5	1,282,500	100	12,825	
ANSWER	£12,825							

■ EXERCISE 5.6

Calculate the following percentage parts:

(a) 60% of £1,240   (b) 75% of £2,600

(c) $33\frac{1}{2}$% of £12,810   (d) 40% of £5,000

(e) 95% of £2,760   (f) 15% of £1,400

(g) $2\frac{1}{2}$% of £3,860   (h) $62\frac{1}{2}$% of £1,280

(i) $16\frac{2}{3}$% of £7,260   (j) 35% of £12,000

■ **EXERCISE 5.7**

Calculate the following percentage parts. Answers correct to the nearest penny (i.e. two decimal places):

(a)   14% of £8,000   (b)   32% of £19,720

(c)   48% of £11,125   (d)   23% of £18,500

(e)   16% of £63,640   (f)   84% of £27,240

(g) $63\frac{1}{2}$% of £36,000   (h) $19\frac{1}{4}$% of £42,500

(i) $22\frac{1}{2}$% of £72,000   (j) $18\frac{1}{3}$% of £100,000

5   PERCENTAGES AND DISCOUNTS

There are three main types of discount: trade discounts, cash discounts and settlement discounts. The last two are very similar. None of these discounts is terribly important for banking itself. Their importance lies in our need to understand what goes on in the affairs of our business customers. For example, nearly all publishers have to give at least 45% trade discount to leading retailers in the book-selling field, and in some cases as much as 70%. It drastically changes our appreciation of the profitability of a 'best-selling' publisher if we know that only 30% of the published price of a best-seller is going to be available to the publisher to cover royalties, design, production and promotion expenses. The first question to ask any manufacturer who tells you how much his goods sell for in the shops is 'What proportion of that do you get as producer?'. In other words 'What percentage of trade discount do you have to give the wholesalers or retailers?'

5.1   Trade discount

Trade discount is the discount given by producers to the wholesalers or retailers who actually market their products to the consumer. It is convenient to talk of a product, such as a bicycle, at the retail price, or the recommended retail price. If we think of a model as 'our £100 machine' meaning that the final consumer pays £100 for it, it is obvious that the retailer cannot pay £100 for it, but must get it at a 'trade' discount. The retailer will usually hope to get the item at about 25% or $33\frac{1}{3}$% less, and the wholesaler will consequently need a higher discount than that. 45% or 50% is probably about the right trade discount for most manufactured goods. Trade discount does vary from product to product – slow moving items need a higher trade discount than fast-selling items because they have to carry a bigger share of the overheads. Large wholesalers can usually demand a larger trade discount than those placing only small orders.

Example 7

A wholesaler orders 60 bicycles @ £120 each less 45% trade discount. What will be the amount payable on the invoice?

$$\text{Value of goods} = £120 \times 60 = £7,200$$
$$\text{Trade discount} = £7,200 \times \tfrac{45}{100}$$
$$= £3,240$$
$$\text{Amount payable} = £7,200 - £3,240$$
$$= \underline{\underline{£3,960}}$$

5.2   Cash discount

Cash discount is discount given to a customer who pays cash. It is usually not more than 5%, or in some cases $2\frac{1}{2}$%. It is an inducement to pay cash rather than taking the goods on account, with the possible result for the seller that the debt will prove to be a bad debt should the customer's situation change for any reason.

Example 8

A customer purchases an item valued at £38.50 less a cash discount of 5%. What is the purchase price? Answer correct to the nearest penny (i.e. correct to two decimal places).

$$
\begin{aligned}
\text{Retail price} &= £38.50 \\
\text{Discount at } 5\% &= £38.50 \times \tfrac{\cancel{5}^{1}}{\cancel{100}_{20}} \quad \text{(Cancelling by 5)} \\
&= £1.925 \\
&= £1.93 \\
\text{Purchase price} &= £38.50 - £1.93 \\
&= \underline{\underline{£36.57}}
\end{aligned}
$$

5.3   Settlement discount

Settlement discount is very similar to cash discount. It is a discount offered on a monthly statement as an inducement to the customer to pay promptly. It may read 'Terms, $2\frac{1}{2}$% discount cash 30 days; 5% discount cash 7 days.' Settlement discounts improve the supplier's cash flow, perhaps reducing the need for expensive borrowed funds. Often a poor payer will be more likely to pay a bill which has a settlement discount offered than one which offers no inducement.

Example 10

Grovelands (Cambridge) Ltd trade on terms which allow account customers to deduct $7\frac{1}{2}$% discount on settlement within seven days and $2\frac{1}{2}$% on settlement within 30 days of the statement date. What will a customer, who elects to pay immediately, pay on a statement totalling £1,347.50? Answer correct to the nearest penny (i.e. correct to two decimal places).

$$
\begin{aligned}
\text{Statement value} &= £1,347.50 \\
\text{Discount at } 7\frac{1}{2}\% &= £1,347.50 \times \tfrac{7.5}{100} \\
&= £101.06 \\
\text{Amount due} &= £1,347.50 - £101.06 \\
&= \underline{\underline{£1,246.44}}
\end{aligned}
$$

■ EXERCISE 5.8

1   The Motor Transport Co (Girton) Ltd, orders eight motor vehicles for sale at the recommended price of £7,240 each. The trade discount is 35%. What will the final invoice value be if delivery charges of £240 are included on it, and are payable in full?

2   Home Cedar Products buys 20 sheds to retail at £148.50 each. Trade discount is 40% and delivery charges added to the invoice and payable in full are £168.00. What will be the invoice value?

3   A shop sells four items at the following prices: **(a)** £108   **(b)** £96.80   **(c)** £75.50 and **(d)** £68. A cash discount of 5% is available. What will be the actual amounts paid by the purchasers of the items?

4   What will be the amount actually paid on a statement of £3,756.80 if a $2\frac{1}{2}$% settlement discount is claimed?

5   What will be the actual amount paid on a statement totalling £856.30 if a $7\frac{1}{2}$% settlement discount is claimed?

6   VAT PERCENTAGES AND FRACTIONS

Before leaving the subject of percentages it is worthwhile mentioning a topic which sometimes puzzles our customers and gets them into difficulties with the VAT authorities. We will use the standard rate of VAT at the time of writing (15%) to illustrate the problem. Every VAT registered trader who supplies goods or services is required to add 15% value added tax to every supply, made as a tax on the supply. This tax is called output tax and must be accounted for to HM Customs and Excise. The amount of the VAT is easy to calculate if we supply an invoice.

Example 11

Goods sold at £89.56. VAT rate = 15%. Using a calculator this is easy and even mentally it gives no problems. It is 10% (£8.956) + half of 10% (£4.478) = £13.434 = £13.43.

The £13.43 will appear on the invoice as an addition to the £89.56 giving a total of £102.99.

The calculator would be used as follows:

CALCULATION: What is 15% of £89.56?

SEQUENCE	$\boxed{\text{C}}$	89.56	$\boxed{\times}$	15	$\boxed{\div}$	100	$\boxed{=}$
DISPLAY	0	89.56	89.56	15	1343.4	100	13.434
ANSWER	£13.43						

The difficulty arises when a trader who does not issue tax invoices to customers tries to calculate the VAT on the daily takings, or on the total takings for the month or the quarter. Such retailers have to account for their VAT under one of the twelve *Special Schemes for Retailers*. The problem is to know what part of the total sales is VAT.

Example 12

A Trader's quarterly sales total £56,274.95. What part of this is VAT output tax?

The tendency is for the trader to say 15% of it is output tax. This is not so. The figure of £56,274.95 is the trader's normal selling price + 15% VAT. If we call the selling price 100% and the VAT 15% this makes 115%. Therefore the VAT element is not $\frac{15}{100}$ but $\frac{15}{115}$, which cancels down to $\frac{3}{23}$. This is called, in VAT law, the *VAT fraction*.

Therefore the VAT element is:

> VAT output tax = £56,274.95 × $\frac{3}{23}$
> = £7,340.21

(Check: If the VAT element is deducted from £56,274.95, we get:

> £56,274.95
> − 7,340.21
> £48,934.74

This is the trader's selling price, without VAT.

> 15% of £48,934.74 =   4,893.474
> + 2,446.737
> £7,340.211 = £7,340.21

This proves we have found the correct VAT figure.)

The calculator display would be as follows:

> CALCULATION: What is $\frac{3}{23}$ of £56,274.95?
>
> SEQUENCE   Ⓒ   £56,274.95   ☒   3   ⊞   23   ⊟
>
> DISPLAY   0   56,274.95   56,274.95   3   168,824.85   23   7340.21
>
> ANSWER   £7340.21

If several such calculations are being done it is better to use the memory of the calculator. First set up $\frac{3}{23}$ as a fraction in the memory.

> CALCULATION: What is $\frac{3}{23}$ as a fraction in the calculator?
>
> SEQUENCE   Ⓒ   3   ⊞   23   ⊟   M+
>
> DISPLAY   0   3   3   23   0.1304347   0.1304347

This fraction is now in the memory.

> CALCULATION: What does a trader whose VAT inclusive sales total is £52,789.16 have
>   to pay in VAT output tax?
>
> SEQUENCE   Ⓒ   52,789.16   ☒   RM   ⊟
>
> DISPLAY   0   52,789.16   52,789.16   0.1304347   6,885.5382
>
> ANSWER   £6,885.54

You could use this method when doing Exercise 5.9 below.

■ EXERCISE 5.9

Six VAT registered traders make out VAT invoices (exclusive of VAT) as shown below. Each adds 15% of VAT to the invoice. Work out the final invoice total in each case.

(a)   £180   (b)   £240

(c)   £366.80   (d)   £429.72

(e)   £526.60   (f)   £795.50

■ EXERCISE 5.10

Six VAT registered traders have total sales including VAT as follows during the quarter. What amount of VAT is included in each total if the VAT rate is 15%?

(a) £16,245.50   (b) £27,256.65

(c) £97,505.84   (d) £136,540.65

(e) £727,625.68   (f) £1,494,156.32

(g) Work out the VAT fraction if VAT is set at 10%.

(h) Work out the VAT fraction if VAT is set at 25%.

(i) Work out the VAT fraction if VAT is set at $12\frac{1}{2}$%.

(j) Work out the VAT fraction if VAT is set at $18\frac{3}{4}$%.

■ ANSWERS

Exercise 5.1   (a) 37.5%   (b) 62.5%   (c) 66.7%   (d) 75%   (e) 30%   (f) 41.7%
(g) 85%   (h) 36%   (i) 44.4%   (j) 63.6%   (k) 21.4%   (l) 77.8%

Exercise 5.2   (a) 162.5%   (b) 733.33%   (c) 675%   (d) 266.67%   (e) 543.75%
(f) 925%   (g) 1350%   (h) 291.67%

Exercise 5.3   (a) 95%   (b) 73%   (c) 62.5%   (d) 49.55%   (e) 37.5%   (f) 162%
(g) 185%   (h) 375.5%

Exercise 5.4   (a) $\frac{2}{5}$ (b) $\frac{9}{20}$ (c) $\frac{6}{25}$ (d) $\frac{17}{20}$ (e) $\frac{21}{50}$ (f) $\frac{3}{8}$ (g) $\frac{17}{40}$ (h) $\frac{13}{20}$ (i) $\frac{5}{6}$
(j) $\frac{7}{12}$

Exercise 5.5   (a) 0.15   (b) 0.225   (c) 0.417   (d) 0.013   (e) 0.287   (f) 0.917
(g) 0.775   (h) 0.667   (i) 0.138   (j) 0.975

Exercise 5.6   (a) £744   (b) £1,950   (c) £4,270   (d) £2,000   (e) £2,622   (f) £210
(g) £96.50   (h) £800   (i) £1,210   (j) £4,200

Exercise 5.7   (a) £1,120   (b) £6,310.40   (c) £5,340   (d) £4,255   (e) £10,182.40
(f) £22,881.60   (g) £22,860   (h) £8,181.25   (i) £16,200   (j) £18,333.33

Exercise 5.8   1 £37,888   2 £1,950   3 (a) £102.60   (b) £91.96   (c) £71.73
(d) £64.60   4 £3,662.88   5 £792.08

Exercise 5.9   (a) £207   (b) £276   (c) £421.82   (d) £494.18   (e) £605.59
(f) £914.83

Exercise 5.10   (a) £2,118.98   (b) £3,555.,21   (c) £12,718.14   (d) £17,809.64
(e) £94,907.64   (f) £194,902.87   (g) $\frac{1}{11}$ (h) $\frac{1}{5}$ (i) $\frac{1}{9}$ (j) $\frac{3}{19}$

6 Simple interest

OBJECTIVES

At the end of this chapter you should be able to:

1 Appreciate the meaning of the word 'interest' and the terms 'principal', 'rate' and 'term';
2 Use the simple interest formula $I = PRT/100$ (sometimes written as $I = PRN/100$);
3 Calculate the simple interest on a sum of money for any number of days and to find out the number of days that a bill of exchange has to run;
4 Rearrange the simple interest formula to find the rate, or the time, or the principal as required.

1 WHAT IS INTEREST?

Interest is a payment for the use of money. Those who have money to spare and are prepared to lend it to others charge interest to the borrower for the use of their money. Those in need of funds, who borrow money, pay interest on it to the lender. Banks are heavily involved in the business of lending funds to those in need of money. They act as an intermediary, taking money as deposits from those who have funds and lending it out to those in need of funds. They may pay interest to those who deposit funds (but some deposits are non-interest bearing). They will charge interest to all who borrow funds, whether they borrow by way of overdraft, or as a personal loan, or mortgage loans, or in any other way. It stands to reason that bankers must charge more to borrowers than they pay to depositors, and rates of interest do vary considerably from one class of business to another. Bankers may be in an intermediary position, but they do not act as agents, merely putting those in funds in touch with those who need funds. They act always as principals, taking money from depositors and being responsible for its availability, with interest if necessary, at any future time. Similarly they act as principals when lending money; the borrower becomes the debtor of the banker, and has no relationship at all with anyone who supplied the funds originally.

There are several pieces of vocabulary associated with interest payments. They are:

(a) **The principal** This is the sum loaned (or borrowed) or in the case of money being placed at a bank's disposal it is the sum deposited.

(b) **The rate** This is the percentage rate of interest payable and is almost always expressed per annum. Thus 12% per annum, or 16% per annum, are quite common rates of interest. One rate that is often met today is the **annual percentage rate** (APR) used in consumer credit transactions, but this is not simple interest, and must be left until a later chapter.

(c) The **term** This is the period that a loan is to run, and is usually expressed in years, but it may be in fractions of a year, for example months, or days. A month is expressed as 1/12 of a year and a day is expressed as 1/365 of a year, leap year being ignored in simple cases. However when banks calculate days they do count every day, including the 29 February, when it occurs.

2 SIMPLE INTEREST ON LOANS MADE FOR 1 YEAR

Since the UK coinage is decimalised simple interest calculations for a single year are very easy.

Example 1

What is the simple interest on £3,800 for one year at 12% per annum. The easy way to calculate this is to find the interest at 1% per annum and then multiply by 12.

$$
\begin{aligned}
\text{Principal} &= £3,800.00 \\
\text{Interest at 1\% p.a.} &= £38 \quad \text{(pushing the number through the decimal point two} \\
&\qquad\qquad\quad \text{places to the right, to divide it by 100)} \\
\text{Interest at 12\% p.a.} &= £38 \times 12 \\
&= £456
\end{aligned}
$$

We could of course do this type of calculation more easily on the calculator.

CALCULATION: What is the simple interest on £4,200 at $12\frac{3}{4}$%?

SEQUENCE	4,200	÷	100	×	12.75	=
DISPLAY	4,200	£4,200	100	42	12.75	535.5
ANSWER	£535.50					

■ EXERCISE 6.1

1 Using a manual calculation find the simple interest on these loans for one year at the rates of interest shown.

(a) £2,000 at $12\frac{1}{2}$% (b) £3,500 at 11%

(c) £1,500 at $9\frac{1}{2}$% (d) £5,000 at $13\frac{1}{2}$%

(e) £2,800 at $10\frac{1}{4}$% (f) £6,500 at $14\frac{1}{4}$%

2 Using the calculator find the simple interest on these loans for one year at the rates of interest shown.

(a) £5,000 at 14% (b) £4,800 at $15\frac{1}{2}$%

(c) £8,500 at 9% (d) £5,600 at $16\frac{1}{2}$%

(e)   £3,500 at $8\frac{3}{4}$%   (f)   £16,500 at $23\frac{1}{2}$%

(g)   £8,750 at $17\frac{1}{2}$%   (h)   £19,760 at 26.8%

(i)   £10,750 at $12\frac{3}{4}$%   (j)   £27,850 at 27.6%

3   SIMPLE INTEREST FOR LONGER THAN ONE YEAR

With simple interest it is usual for the interest to be paid each year. A more difficult system of interest, called **compound interest**, is dealt with later in this book (see Chapter 9). Even though simple interest is paid each year, a person who arranges a loan for a term longer than one year may wish to know what the total interest payable will be. Clearly, it simply means that the interest for one year will be payable for each year, or part of a year. Extending Example 1 to a situation where the term is longer than one year we have the following.

Example 2

What is the simple interest on £3,800 for three years at 12%? The calculations are:

$$\begin{aligned}
\text{Principal} &= £3,800.00 \\
\text{Interest at 1\% p.a.} &= £38 \\
\text{Interest at 12\% p.a.} &= £38 \times 12 \\
&= £456 \\
\text{Interest for 3 years} &= £456 \times 3 \\
&= £1,368
\end{aligned}$$

Using the calculator a typical calculation would be

CALCULATION: What is the simple interest on £4,200 at $8\frac{1}{4}$% for $2\frac{1}{2}$ years?

SEQUENCE	4,200	÷	100	✕	8.25	✕	2.5	=
DISPLAY	4,200	£4,200	100	42	8.25	346.5	2.5	866.25
ANSWER	£866.25							

■ EXERCISE 6.2

1   Using manual calculations find the simple interest on the following sums borrowed at the rate shown for the term specified.

(a)   £2,000 at 14% for 3 years

(b)   £4,500 at 9% for 2 years

(c)   £5,000 at 11% for $3\frac{1}{2}$ years

(d)   £8,000 at 16% for $4\frac{1}{2}$ years

(e)   £10,000 at 24% for $6\frac{1}{4}$ years

2   Using the calculator find the simple interest on the following sums borrowed at the rate shown for the term specified.

(a) £1,500 at 14% for $2\frac{1}{2}$ years

(b) £3,250 at $15\frac{1}{2}$% for $3\frac{1}{4}$ years

(c) £7,500 at $16\frac{3}{4}$% for $5\frac{1}{2}$ years

(d) £10,800 at 23.4% for $3\frac{3}{4}$ years

(e) £12,500 at 28.6% for $7\frac{1}{4}$ years

4 SIMPLE INTEREST BY THE FORMULA METHOD

In mathematics a formula is a method of expressing a relationship in a general form, using letters instead of actual figures. We can then solve any problem by substituting in the real figures for the letters in the formula. For example, the simple interest on any principal, at any rate for any term, can be written down as the formula:

$$I = \frac{PRT}{100}$$

This says:

$$\text{Simple interest} = \frac{\text{Principal} \times \text{Rate} \times \text{Term (in years)}}{100}$$

Note that the 100 is the fractional part of the rate per cent – for example:

$$8\% \text{ is } \tfrac{8}{100}$$

Many schools help pupils to remember the formula by saying PRT stands for 'Please Remember This'.

Since the term is always expressed in years, interest for less than a year must be expressed as a fraction of a year – thus three months is entered as $\frac{1}{4}$ of a year, seven months is entered as 7/12 and 185 days would be entered as $\frac{185}{365}$ of a year.

Formulas such as

$$I = \frac{PRT}{100}$$

are very simple examples of *algebra* (Arabic for the joining together of broken parts). Where set down in this way, with the separate parts all joined together, we are expected to know that the letters written side by side have multiplication signs between them really.

$$\text{So } I = \frac{PRT}{100} \text{ really means } I = \frac{P \times R \times T}{100}$$

Using the formula we have a quick shorthand way of doing a simple interest calculation.

This formula is sometimes written $I = PRN/100$, the N standing for 'number of years'. Obviously this alternative symbol makes no difference to the calculation.

Example 3

What is the simple interest on £4,750 at $13\frac{1}{2}$% for $3\frac{1}{2}$ years. We always start with the formula and then substitute in the real figures in place of the letters.

$$1 = \frac{PRT}{100}$$

$$= \frac{£4,750 \times 13\frac{1}{2} \times 3\frac{1}{2}}{100}$$

$$= \frac{£4,75\cancel{0} \times 27 \times 7}{10\cancel{0} \times 2 \times 2} \quad \text{(Cancelling by 10)}$$

$$= \frac{£89,775}{40}$$

$$= £2,244.38$$

$$
\begin{array}{r}
475 \\
\times 27 \\
\hline
3,325 \\
9,500 \\
\hline
12,825 \\
\times 7 \\
\hline
89,775 \\
\hline
\end{array}
$$

$$
\begin{array}{l}
4|8977.5 \quad \text{(Cancellling by 10 again)} \\
2244.375
\end{array}
$$

Doing this on the calculator we have

SEQUENCE	4,750	⊠	13.5	⊠	3.5	⊞	100	⊟
DISPLAY	4,750	4750	13.5	64,125	3.5	224,437.5	100	2,244.375
ANSWER	£2,244.38							

You can see that the manual calculations are so lengthy that in practice we should always use a calculator, but there is one advantage about this formula which is very useful and also leads on rather well to compound interest – which is very important for bankers. Therefore it is worthwhile doing a few manual calculations using the formula before we go on to discuss these other points.

■ EXERCISE 6.3

Work out the following simple interest calculations using the formula I = PRT/100. Then check your answers using the calculator.

(a) Find the simple interest on £4,200 at $12\frac{1}{2}$% for $2\frac{1}{2}$ years

(b) Find the simple interest on £8,500 at $11\frac{1}{4}$% for $4\frac{1}{2}$ years

(c) Find the simple interest on £3,850 at $14\frac{1}{2}$% for $3\frac{1}{4}$ years

(d) Find the simple interest on £4,500 at $11\frac{3}{4}$% for $4\frac{1}{2}$ years

(e) Find the simple interest on £25,000 at $12\frac{1}{4}$% for $1\frac{1}{3}$ years

5   INTEREST ON BILLS OF EXCHANGE

A bill of exchange is an important financial document, and since a cheque is defined in the Bills of Exchange Act, 1882, as: 'A cheque is a bill of exchange, drawn on a banker, payable on demand' it is obvious that millions of bills of exchange are drawn (written out) every day.

We need not bother here with the full definition of a bill of exchange (banking students will learn this on their Elements of Banking course) but it is worthwhile mentioning the interest aspects here. A bill of exchange is an order to someone to pay someone else a sum of money. Where the sum of money is payable on demand (as with a cheque) there is no question of interest being involved, but where the drawer (the person writing out the bill) gives the drawee (the one ordered to pay the money) time to pay, there is an element of interest in the bill.

For example, suppose a bill reads 'Ninety days after date pay me the sum of £5,000' the drawee of the bill has 90 days to pay the money. If the drawee accepts the obligation to pay he/she writes 'accepted' on the bill and signs it (even just the signature alone will do) and from that moment the drawee becomes the **acceptor** of the bill, having accepted a legal obligation to pay it on the due date. The accepted bill is returned to the drawer, who now has a valuable negotiable instrument. The drawer may do three things with the bill:

(a)   It can be left until maturity, 90 days from now, and presented to the acceptor, who will pay the £5,000, the full value.

(b)   It can be discounted at a bank – i.e. sold to a bank for its present value.

(c)   It can be endorsed on the back (signed on the back with instructions to pay someone else) and used to pay a debt, to the extent of its present value.

In both (b) and (c) above, the question arises 'What is its present value?'

5.1   The value of a bill of exchange

If a bill is worth £5,000 in 90 days' time it is worth less than £5,000 today. Anyone taking it will not give £5,000 for it, because if he/she did they would be losing 90 days' interest on £5,000. If a bill is discounted to a bank, or if it is taken in settlement of a debt, the person taking it will only give its face value less the number of days interest that it has to run to maturity.

Example 4

What is the interest on a £5,000 bill of exchange which has 90 days to run, the agreed rate of interest being $11\frac{3}{4}\%$ per annum?

Starting with the formula $I = PRT/100$ and substituting in the values for P, R and T we have:

$$I = \frac{£5,000 \times 47 \times 90}{400 \times 365}$$

Table 6.1　A ready reckoner for days

January	February	March	April	May	June	July	August	September	October	November	December
1	32	60	91	121	152	182	213	244	274	305	335
2	33	61	92	122	153	183	214	245	275	306	336
3	34	62	93	123	154	184	215	246	276	307	337
4	35	63	94	124	155	185	216	247	277	308	338
5	36	64	95	125	156	186	217	248	278	309	339
6	37	65	96	126	157	187	218	249	279	310	340
7	38	66	97	127	158	188	219	250	280	311	341
8	39	67	98	128	159	189	220	251	281	312	342
9	40	68	99	129	160	190	221	252	282	313	343
10	41	69	100	130	161	191	222	253	283	314	344
11	42	70	101	131	162	192	223	254	284	315	345
12	43	71	102	132	163	193	224	255	285	316	346
13	44	72	103	133	164	194	225	256	286	317	347
14	45	73	104	134	165	195	226	257	287	318	348
15	46	74	105	135	166	196	227	258	288	319	349
16	47	75	106	136	167	197	228	259	289	320	350
17	48	76	107	137	168	198	229	260	290	321	351
18	49	77	108	138	169	199	230	261	291	322	352
19	50	78	109	139	170	200	231	262	292	323	353
20	51	79	110	140	171	201	232	263	293	324	354
21	52	80	111	141	172	202	233	264	294	325	355
22	53	81	112	142	173	203	234	265	295	326	356
23	54	82	113	143	174	204	235	266	296	327	357
24	55	83	114	144	175	205	236	267	297	328	358
25	56	84	115	145	176	206	237	268	298	329	359
26	57	85	116	146	177	207	238	269	299	330	360
27	58	86	117	147	178	208	239	270	300	331	361
28	59	87	118	148	179	209	240	271	301	332	362
29		88	119	149	180	210	241	272	302	333	363
30		89	120	150	181	211	242	273	303	334	364
31		90		151		212	243		304		365

Using the calculator we find this to be

$$= £144.86$$

Therefore the bill's present value is £5,000 − £144.86 = £4,855.14

The bank will credit the customer's bank account with £4,855.14, the value deposited, and add the bill of exchange to its portfolio of short-term investments.

It may keep the bill until maturity and present it on the due date for payment. This will mean the bank receives £5,000 and has earned the sum of £144.86 by discounting the bill for the customer.

(*Note* Alert students may notice that although the bank discounted the bill at $11\frac{3}{4}\%$ on its face value, in strict business calculations terms it actually earned rather more than $11\frac{3}{4}\%$. This is because it only actually loaned the customer £4,855.14 for 90 days. What rate of interest earns us £144.86 on £4,855.14 in 90 days? To do this we have to rearrange the formula − which is explained later in this chapter. Actually, when re-arranged to find the rate, the formula becomes:

$$R = \frac{100\ I}{PT}$$

$$= \frac{100 \times £144.86 \times 365}{£4,855.14 \times 90}$$

Using the calculator for this we get the answer 12.1%. So the bank actually got a slightly better rate than $11\frac{3}{4}\%$).

5.2 Working out the days to run on a bill

Bankers who handle bills of exchange regularly have to work out how many days the bill has to run to maturity. A ready reckoner for days shown in Table 6.1 is helpful. It shows all the days of the year, added cumulatively to give 365 days. February 29th is ignored, but in a leap year one extra day would be added if the bill ran through February 29th.

To use the ready reckoner consider the following example.

Example 5

A customer asks you to discount a bill on the 4th April which will mature on 21 July. How many days has the bill to run? Looking at 4th April we see it is the 94th day of the year, whereas 21 July is the 202nd day of the year. Taking 94 away from 202 we have:

$$\begin{array}{r} 202 \\ -\ 94 \\ \hline 108 \end{array}$$

so the bill has 108 days to run.

■ EXERCISE 6.4
Find out how many days to run on each of these bills.

(a) A bill discounted on January 15 which matures on 28 February
(b) A bill discounted on 12 March which matures on 31 May
(c) A bill discounted on 15 August which matures on 29 September
(d) A bill discounted on 7 February in a leap year which matures on 29 April
(e) A bill discounted on 28 November which matures on 27 January the following year. (Careful, you have to go through the 365th day of the year.)

■ EXERCISE 6.5

In each of the cases below work out how much a bank will pay a customer who discounts a bill of exchange with the number of days to run as shown, at the discount rate shown.

	Value of the bill	Days to run	Discount rate %
(a)	£850	36	$13\frac{3}{4}$
(b)	£1,650	42	$12\frac{1}{2}$
(c)	£3,800	29	$14\frac{1}{2}$
(d)	£5,500	84	$13\frac{3}{4}$
(e)	£6,850	56	$11\frac{3}{4}$

■ EXERCISE 6.6

In each of the cases below work out the number of days the bill has to run to maturity and then calculate the amount the bank will give a customer who discounts the bill at the rate shown.

	Value of the bill	Discounted on	Matures on	Discount rate %
(a)	£1,000	13 March	31 May	$11\frac{1}{2}\%$
(b)	£2,500	15 June	19 August	$12\frac{1}{4}\%$
(c)	£3,650	11 August	26 October	$13\frac{5}{8}\%$
(d)	£5,950	19 September	5 November	$14\frac{1}{4}\%$
(e)	£12,750	30 November	Jan 29 of the following year	$14\frac{1}{2}\%$

6 REARRANGEMENT OF FORMULAE

The formula $I = PRT/100$ enables us to calculate the simple interest on a known principal, at a known rate, for a known term of years. Suppose we need to know P, or R or T, instead of I. For example we could ask these questions:

(a) What principal will earn £1,837.50 simple interest in $3\frac{1}{2}$ years at $10\frac{1}{2}\%$ per annum?

(b) What rate of simple interest will give £4,375 interest in $2\frac{1}{2}$ years on a capital sum of £12,500?

(c)   How long will it take a principal of £8,000 to earn £3,315 at a rate of $12\frac{3}{4}\%$ per annum?

To work out the answers to these questions we need to rearrange the formula so that it is in the form $P =$, or $R =$, or $T =$. How can we do this? The answer is we need to obey the **rules of equations**.

The formula $I = PRT/100$ is an equation, that is to say it is an expression where one thing is said to be equal to another thing. The rules about equations can be illustrated by a more simple equation, for example $3 = 2 + 1$. The rules about equations say:

(a)   You can add anything to both sides of an equation and the equation will still be true, e.g. $3 + 1 = 2 + 1 + 1$ (i.e. $4 = 4$).

(b)   You can subtract anything from both sides of an equation and the equation will still be true, e.g. $3 - 2 = 2 + 1 - 2$ (i.e. $1 = 1$).

(c)   You can multiply both sides of an equation by the same thing and the equation will still be true, e.g. $3 \times 3 = (2 + 1)3$ (i.e. $9 = 9$).

(d)   You can divide both sides of an equation by the same thing and the equation will still be true, e.g. $3 \div 2 = (2 + 1) \div 2$ (i.e. $1\frac{1}{2} = 1\frac{1}{2}$).

(e)   You can raise both sides of an equation to a power and the answer will still be true, e.g. $3^2 = (2 + 1)^2$ (i.e. $9 = 9$).

(f)   You can take the square root of both sides of an equation and the answer will still be true.

Using the calculator for this we have $\sqrt{3} = \sqrt{(2 + 1)}$ (i.e. $1.73 = 1.73$).

We could sum up these rules by saying that *You can do anything you like to an equation and it will still be true, so long as you do the same to both sides.*

To rearrange our formula all we need to do is to get the expression $1 = PRT/100$ in the form $P =$, or $T =$, or $R =$.

Take P first. To find the principal we need to have P on one side of the equation and everything else on the other side.

$$I = \frac{PRT}{100}$$ we can get the 100 on the other side if we multiply both sides by 100

$$I \times 100 = \frac{PRT}{1\cancel{00}} \times 1\cancel{00}$$ cancelling the 100s we have changed the formula to $100I = PRT$

$$100\,I = PRT$$ to get R over to the other side we divide both sides by R

$$\frac{100\,I}{R} = \frac{P\cancel{R}T}{\cancel{R}}$$ the Rs cancel out on the right hand side

$$\frac{100\,I}{R} = PT$$ to get the T over to the other side we divide both sides by T

$$\frac{100I}{RT} = \frac{P\cancel{T}}{\cancel{T}}$$ the Ts cancel out on the right hand side

$$\frac{100I}{RT} = P$$ if we now turn the equation round for convenience we have:

$$P = \frac{100I}{RT}$$

Similarly we could rearrange $I = PRT/100$ to give us:

$$R = \frac{100I}{PT}$$

and

$$T = \frac{100I}{PR}$$

We are now ready to solve the three problems set out at the start of Section 6.

Example 6

What principal will earn £1,837.50 simple interest in $3\frac{1}{2}$ years at $10\frac{1}{2}\%$ per annum?

$$P = \frac{100I}{RT}$$

$$= \frac{100 \times £1,837.50}{10\frac{1}{2} \times 3\frac{1}{2}}$$

$$= \frac{100 \times £1,837.50 \times 2 \times 2}{21 \times 7} \quad \text{(the twos from } \tfrac{21}{2} \text{ and } \tfrac{7}{2} \text{ come up above the line)}$$

$$= \frac{100 \times £\cancel{1,837.50} \times 2 \times 2}{\cancel{21} \times \cancel{7,}} \quad \text{(cancelling by 7, 7 and 3)}$$

$$= £5,000$$

Example 7

What rate of simple interest will give £4,375 interest in $2\frac{1}{2}$ years on a capital sum of £12,500?

$$R = \frac{100I}{PT}$$

$$= \frac{100 \times £4,375}{£12,500 \times 2\frac{1}{2}}$$

Using the calculator this time we have

SEQUENCE	100	⊠	4,375	⊞	12,500	⊞	2.5	⊟
DISPLAY	100	100	4,375	437,500	12,500	35	2.5	14
ANSWER	14%							

(*Note* Be careful! Where we have to divide something by £12,500 $\times 2\frac{1}{2}$ it becomes ÷ £12,500 and ÷ $2\frac{1}{2}$ when we put it on the calculator.)

Example 8

How long will it take a principal of £8,000 to earn £3,315 simple interest at a rate of $12\frac{3}{4}\%$ per annum?

$$T = \frac{100I}{PR}$$

$$= \frac{100 \times £3,315}{£8,000 \times 12\frac{3}{4}}$$

Using the calculator again we have

SEQUENCE	100	$\times$	3,315	$\div$	8,000	$\div$	12.75	$=$
DISPLAY	100	100	3,315	331,500	8,000	41.4375	12.75	3.25
ANSWER	$3\frac{1}{4}$ years							

■ EXERCISE 6.7

In each of the following cases you have to find either the principal, or the rate % per annum or the term of years for which the money was invested, from the information provided. A question mark indicates the item to be found. You may use either manual calculation, or the calculator, as you choose. (*Answers correct to two decimal places where necessary.*)

	Simple interest earned	Principal	Rate per annum	Term in years
(a)	£4,500	?	$12\frac{1}{2}\%$	$4\frac{1}{2}$
(b)	£1,227.19	£2,750	?	$3\frac{1}{2}$
(c)	£1,898.44	£6,250	13.5%	?
(d)	£552	?	$11\frac{1}{2}\%$	5
(e)	£5,217.19	?	$13\frac{1}{4}\%$	$1\frac{3}{4}$
(f)	£3,729.69	£3,850	?	$6\frac{1}{4}$
(g)	£4,250.39	£11,250	$11\frac{5}{8}\%$	?
(h)	£8,662.50	£8,400	$13\frac{3}{4}\%$	?
(i)	£2,649.88	?	$10\frac{3}{4}\%$	$4\frac{1}{4}$
(j)	£2,746.56	£4,250	?	$5\frac{1}{2}$
(k)	£3,023.48	£7,500	?	$3\frac{3}{4}$
(l)	£2,012.03	£8,150	$9\frac{7}{8}\%$	?

7 TREASURY BILLS AND THE TREASURY BILL RATE

In order to ensure that central government can never be starved of funds the Treasury, through the Bank of England, offers Treasury bills for tender each week. Anyone may tender (put in a bid) for the bills which are issued in amounts from £5,000 to £250,000. Although the Government's requirements vary, an average offer would be of about £40 million of bills per week. The bills run for 91 days, and are redeemed at par – i.e. a £50,000 bill is redeemed for £50,000. It follows that anyone tendering for the bills offers less than their face value, so that when the bill is redeemed the tenderer (who is lending money to the Government) will have something extra for interest. Suppose there are three tenders for a £50,000 bill of £49,000, £48,750, and £48,250. The Bank of England will accept the highest bid, which is £49,000. The tenderer will therefore, one week after the offer was made, lend the government £49,000 and in 91 days will receive back £50,000. Viewed from the simplest point of view £1,000 out of £50,000 is 2%, which for a quarter of a year is 8% per annum interest

$$R = \frac{100\,I}{PT}$$

$$= \frac{100 \times 1,000}{50,000 \times \frac{1}{4}}$$

$$= \frac{100 \times 1,000 \times 4}{50,000} \quad \text{(cancelling the 0s)}$$

$$= \frac{40}{5}$$

$$= \underline{\underline{8\%}}$$

Viewed more strictly the actual return to the tenderer is a little better, for he/she really only invested £49,000.

$$R = \frac{100I}{P\,N}$$

$$= \frac{100 \times 1,000}{49,000 \times \frac{1}{4}}$$

Using the calculator this is $= \underline{\underline{8.16\%}}$

(*Note* The student might wonder whether there is ever a time when nobody wishes to lend money to the Government. This problem is overcome by an undertaking by the Discount Houses to buy all the Treasury Bills nobody else wants. In return for this undertaking, the Bank of England extends to the Discount Houses the 'lender of last resort' facilities which ensure that a Discount House which has lent unwisely can always balance its books by borrowing from the Bank of England – while it takes steps to recover from its illiquid situation.)

8   SIMPLE INTEREST BY PRODUCTS

The 'products method' of calculating simple interest is one which is now used in computerised form to do simple interest calculations on most bank accounts. It began as long ago as the 18th Century as a way of keeping account of interest between two parties either of which might at anytime be in debit or in credit with the other. An extra column was added to the ledger account on either side, and the products were calculated and inserted in this column. A product is simply a sum of money, multiplied by the number of days. For example: Peter Green deposits £1,000 in an account, the agreed rate of interest from the bank to be $8\frac{1}{4}\%$. The money is left in the bank for 30 days. If we multiply the £1,000 by 30 days we get 30,000 £ days. The interest will be calculated not on £1,000 for 30 days but on £30,000 for one day. The answer will come out the same.

Method 1   £1,000 for 30 days at $8\frac{1}{4}\%$

$$I = \frac{PRT}{100}$$

$$= \frac{£1,000 \times 8\frac{1}{4} \times 30}{100 \times 365}$$

$$= \frac{£1,000 \times 33 \times 30}{4 \times 100 \times 365}$$

$$= \underline{\underline{£6.78}}$$

Method 2   £30,000 for 1 day at $8\frac{1}{4}\%$

$$I = \frac{PRT}{100}$$

$$= \frac{£30,000 \times 33 \times 1}{400 \times 365}$$

$$= \underline{\underline{£6.78}}$$

Today the computer is programmed to do this calculation each time the balance changes on an account. The products do not appear on the customer's statement; the final result only being credited to the account if the customer is entitled to the interest, or debited to the account if the customer is liable to pay the interest. In a traditional Current Account where interest is not given to the customer any interest calculation must be on an overdraft situation, and the interest will always be debited to the account. In a Deposit Account, by contrast, the interest will always be credited to the account. In some modern Current Accounts, where interest is given to the customer who is in credit, but charged when the account is overdrawn, there may be two entries, as interest will be credited in respect of the credit balances and debited in respect of the overdraft. These entries may be 'netted' by some banks, to give only a single entry, as shown in Example 9 overleaf.

Consider the simple examples overleaf, where an extra column has been inserted to show the products. Note that the product has been inserted on the line where the balance changed, and it refers to the number of £ days for which the customer is owed interest (or the bank is owed interest if the sign is a − sign). This product is the result of multiplying the previous balance by the number of days it was on the books. The products column would not of course appear on a real statement. The interest has been shown for convenience as if it was added monthly.

Example 9

A. Customer's Account on which credit balances are to earn $6\frac{1}{2}\%$ reads as follows.

Date	Details	Products £	Dr £	Cr £	Balance £
Jan 1	Balance	—			1,342.60 C
Jan 18	Cheque	22,824.2	520.65		821.95 C
Jan 31	Balance	10,685.35			821.95 C
Jan 31	Interest			5.97	827.92 C

Notes

1   The balance of £1,342.60 was in the bank from 1–18 Jan and is entitled to 17 days' interest. The product of £1,342.60 × 17 = 22,824.2 £ days.

2   The balance of £821.95 was in the bank from 18 Jan to 31 Jan which entitles it to 13 days' interest. The product of £821.95 × 13 = 10685.35 £ days.

3   The result is the bank owes the customer interest on the equivalent of:

$$\begin{array}{r} 22,824.2 \\ + 10,685.35 \\ \hline £33,509.55 \end{array}$$ for one day at $6\frac{1}{2}\%$

$$I = \frac{PRT}{100}$$

$$= \frac{33,509.55 \times 13 \times 1}{2 \times 100 \times 365}$$

$$= £5.97$$

4   This interest has been added to the account at the end of the month but this might not be the bank's practice for all customers, the products simply being accumulated and added at quarterly or half yearly periods.

Example 10

R. Whiteside's Account, on which interest on debit balances is payable by Whiteside at $11\frac{1}{2}\%$ and interest is earned on credit balances at $6\frac{1}{2}\%$ reads as follows:

Date	Details	Products	Dr	Cr	Balance
Jan 1	Balance	—			279.65 C
12	Cheque	3,076.15	850.50		570.85 D
26	Sundries	−7,991.90		2,465.00	1,894.15 C
31	Balance	9,470.75			1,894.15 C
31	Interest		0.29		1,893.86 C

Notes:

1   The product figures were found as follows: £279.65 × 11; £570.85 × 14 (but this is an overdraft so the product has a minus sign) and £1,894.15 × 5.

2   Since the interest charged is at a different rate from the interest given to the customer the computer works out £7,991.90 for one day at $11\frac{1}{2}\%$ and £12,546.90 for one day at $6\frac{1}{2}\%$. (This is £3,076.15 + £9,470.75 for one day at $6\frac{1}{2}\%$.)

3   The result is that the customer owes the bank £2.52 interest for the time he/she was overdrawn, and the bank owes the customer £2.23 for the time the customer was in credit. The result is that the customer is charged 29 pence interest.

Example 11

Megabank Plc has a credit balance on its Current Account with Helpful Bank of £327,590.90 on 1 Jan. The arrangement is that debit balances will be charged interest at $13\frac{1}{4}\%$ and credit balances will earn interest at the same rate. The account reads:

Date	Details	Products	Dr	Cr	Balance
Jan 1	Balance				327,590.90 C
13	Cheque	3,931,090.80	554,272.10		226,681.20 D
19	Sundries	− 1,360,087.20		300,500.00	73,818.80 C
29	Sundries	738,188.00		148,665.50	222,484.30 C
31	Balance	444,968.60			222,484.30
31	Interest	3,754,160.20		1,362.81	223,847.11

Notes
1   The products total 3,754,160.20
2   Since the interest is the same whether the account is in debit or credit we only have to work out the interest on £3,754,160.20 at $13\frac{1}{4}\%$ for one day.
3   This is £1,362.81 which is credited to the account.

8.1   Products and interest tables

Once the products figures have been arrived at, a 'products and interest table' can be drawn up for use as a ready reckoner. Such a table for $13\frac{1}{4}\%$ is shown in Fig. 6.1.

We examine this table to work out the interest on any account, such as the one shown in Example 11. The method is shown in Example 12.

Example 12

The account in Example 11 shows products of 3,754,160.20 to be calculated at $13\frac{1}{4}\%$. Using the ready reckoner we have

Products	Interest
3,000,000 =	1,089.04
700,000 =	254.11
50,000 =	18.15
4,000 =	1.45
100 =	0.04
60 =	02
	1,362.81

This is the same answer as we arrived at by calculation in Example 11, but it is a fact that the last figure may sometimes be one penny out.

With the widespread use of computerised calculations it is unlikely that there will be much call for the use of products and interest tables any longer.

	£		£		£		£		£		£
1,000	0.36	26,000	9.44	51,000	18.51	76,000	27.58	200,000	72.60	20	.01
2,000	0.73	27,000	9.80	52,000	18.87	77,000	27.95	300,000	108.90	30	.01
3,000	1.09	28,000	10.16	53,000	19.24	78,000	28.32	400,000	145.21	40	.01
4,000	1.45	29,000	10.53	54,000	19.60	79,000	28.68	500,000	181.51	50	.02
5,000	1.82	30,000	10.89	55,000	19.97	80,000	29.04	600,000	217.81	60	.02
6,000	2.18	31,000	11.25	56,000	20.33	81,000	29.40	700,000	254.11	70	.03
7,000	2.54	32,000	11.62	57,000	20.69	82,000	29.77	800,000	290.41	80	.03
8,000	2.90	33,000	11.98	58,000	21.05	83,000	30.13	900,000	326.71	90	.03
9,000	3.27	34,000	12.34	59,000	21.42	84,000	30.49	1,000,000	363.01	100	.04
10,000	3.63	35,000	12.71	60,000	21.78	85,000	30.86	2,000,000	726.03	200	.07
11,000	3.99	36,000	13.07	61,000	22.14	86,000	31.22	3,000,000	1,089.04	300	.11
12,000	4.36	37,000	13.43	62,000	22.51	87,000	31.58	4,000,000	1,452.05	400	.15
13,000	4.72	38,000	13.79	63,000	22.87	88,000	31.95	5,000,000	1,815.07	500	.18
14,000	5.08	39,000	14.16	64,000	23.23	89,000	32.31	6,000,000	2,178.08	600	.22
15,000	5.45	40,000	14.52	65,000	23.60	90,000	32.67	7,000,000	2,541.09	700	.25
16,000	5.81	41,000	14.88	66,000	23.96	91,000	33.03	8,000,000	2,904.11	800	.29
17,000	6.17	42,000	15.25	67,000	24.32	92,000	33.40	9,000,000	3,267.12	900	.33
18,000	6.53	43,000	15.61	68,000	24.68	93,000	33.76	10,000,000	3,630.13		
19,000	6.90	44,000	15.97	69,000	25.05	94,000	34.12	20,000,000	7,260.27		
20,000	7.26	45,000	16.34	70,000	25.41	95,000	34.49	30,000,000	10,890.40		
21,000	7.62	46,000	16.70	71,000	25.77	96,000	34.85	40,000,000	14,520.54		
22,000	7.99	47,000	17.06	72,000	26.13	97,000	35.21	50,000,000	18,150.67		
23,000	8.35	48,000	17.42	73,000	26.49	98,000	35.58	60,000,000	21,780.80		
24,000	8.71	49,000	17.79	74,000	26.86	99,000	35.94	70,000,000	25,410.94		
25,000	9.08	50,000	18.15	75,000	27.32	100,000	36.30	80,000,000	29,041.07		

Fig. 6.1   A products and interest table for $13\frac{1}{4}$%

(*Note* In writing this section on the use of computerised calculations for products it became clear that some banks work the figures in '£ days' and some in 'pence days'. It makes no difference to the calculations at all, of course, but it does mean the products are 100 times as large if the figures are worked in pence.)

■ EXERCISE 6.8

1 A customer of the Helpful Bank Plc has a current account which is sometimes in debit and sometimes in credit. It is agreed that each shall pay the other interest at 15% per annum when the account is adverse, the calculations to be done by products on a daily basis. On 31 December the customer, Able Finance Plc, has a favourable balance of £285,626.50. The next entry on the account is a credit of £38,750.60 on 18 January and there is a further entry, a debit of £600,000 on 27 January. Work out the interest on 31 January. Is it a debit or a credit on the account of Able Fiance Plc?

2 Tom Jones is a customer of Helpful Bank Plc who earns interest on credit balances of $7\frac{1}{2}$%, but pays interest on debit balances of $14\frac{1}{4}$%. On 31 May he has a credit balance of £722.80. On 11 June there is a cheque paid out of £1,560.50 and on 26 June a credit for £3,245.65 Work out the A/c showing the products, and the net interest entered on 30 June.

3 Using the products and interest table in Fig. 6.1 work out the interest payable to J. Shaw, whose products balance at $13\frac{1}{4}$% comes to +4,720,056 £ days of interest.

4 Using the products and interest table in Fig. 6.1 work out the interest payable to Lowland Finance (Kew) Plc whose account with Helpful Bank Plc earns, or pays, interest at $13\frac{1}{4}$%. They were overdrawn on 31 December by £160,242.50 but paid in a cheque for £342,756.95 on 23 January. Work out the interest payable on 31 January. Who is paying whom?

■ ANSWERS

Exercise 6.1
1 (a) £250 (b) £385 (c) £142.50 (d) £675 (e) £287 (f) £926.25
2 (a) £700 (b) £744 (c) £765 (d) £924 (e) £306.25 (f) £3,877.50
(g) £1,531.25 (h) £5,295.68 (i) £1,370.63 (j) £7,686.60

Exercise 6.2
1 (a) £840 (b) £810 (c) £1,925 (d) £5,760 (e) £15,000
2 (a) £525 (b) £1,637.19 (c) £6,909.38 (d) £9,477 (e) £25,918.75

Exercise 6.3 (a) £1,312.50 (b) £4,303.13 (c) £1,814.31 (d) £2,379.38
(e) £4,083.33

Exercise 6.4 (a) 44 days (b) 80 days (c) 45 days (d) 82 days (e) 60 days

Exercise 6.5 (a) £838.47 (b) £1,626.27 (c) £3,756.22 (d) £5,325.96
(e) £6,726.51

Exercise 6.6 (a) £975.11 (b) £2,445.46 (c) £3,546.45 (d) £5,840.82
(e) £12,446.10

Exercise 6.7   **(a)** £8,000   **(b)** 12.75%   **(c)** $2\frac{1}{4}$ years   **(d)** £960   **(e)** £22,500.01
(f) 15.5%   **(g)** $3\frac{1}{4}$ years   **(h)** $7\frac{1}{2}$ years   **(i)** £5,800.01   **(j)** $11\frac{3}{4}$%   **(k)** $10\frac{3}{4}$%
(l) $2\frac{1}{2}$ years

Exercise 6.8
1   Able Finance has earned £2,859.53 interest, which appears as a credit on their A/c.
2   Interest earned on credits £3.61; interest payable on debit balances £4.91. Net interest charged to Jones £1.30.
3   Shaw has earned £1,713.44 interest.
4   Lowland Finance is debited with £807.88 Lowland Finance (Kew) Plc is paying Helpful Bank Plc.

7 Simple algebra

OBJECTIVES

At the end of this chapter you should understand:
1 The general nature of algebra;
2 How to collect together like terms;
3 How to substitute true values for symbols;
4 What a simple equation is and how to solve simple equations;
5 How to manipulate equations to re-arrange them into any desired form;
6 The importance of formulae in banking situations.

1 THE GENERAL NATURE OF ALGEBRA

Most of us are familiar with arithmetic, the science of numbers. We can add up, take away, multiply and divide. Most of us can square a number (multiply it by itself) and know that 12^2 is 144 and 20^2 is 400. Not so many of us can find the square root of a number (the number which, when multiplied by itself, gives us the number we started with). For example we may know that the square root of 144 is 12 (because 12 is the number which, when multiplied by itself, gives us $144 (12 \times 12 = 144)$. Asked what is the square root of 374 very few of us perhaps would know how to work it out – though we can see that it is less than 20 because $20 \times 20 = 400$ and 374 is smaller than 400. Fortunately we don't need to bother to learn that bit of arithmetic because we can go to any calculator which has a $\sqrt{}$ key, put 374 on it, press the $\sqrt{}$ key and it tells us the answer

> Calculation: What is the square root of 374?
> Sequence   374 $\sqrt{}$
> Display   374   19.339079
> Answer   19.34 correct to two decimal places

Algebra is **generalised arithmetic**. It simply applies the principles of arithmetic to any body of knowledge, in an abstract way, which will always be true whatever the body of knowledge may be. It uses symbols instead of numbers, and as the easiest symbols to use are letters, we keep referring to a, b, c, x, y and z etc as if they were real quantities. Sometimes, for a change, we use Greek letters like π (pie) and Σ (sigma), but they are just symbols. We could have drawn giraffes' heads, or petrol pumps, but letters are easier to use. If we are told $2a = b$ it is a generalised statement. It doesn't mean much until we are told what either a or b is in real life. If we are told that $a = 5$ then $2 \times 5 = 10$ so b must be 10. If we are told that $a =$ pints then $2a = 2$ pints $= 1$ quart so b must be quarts.

Learning elementary algebra is really a question of learning to manipulate symbols, without worrying too much what these symbols mean in real life. When we get round to using the pure mathematics for practical purposes we shall have to say what the symbols mean, as we did with simple interest.

$$I = \frac{PRT}{100}$$

We said what the symbols stood for: I = simple interest; P = principal (the sum of money loaned, or borrowed); R = the rate per cent per annum; T = the term for which the money was borrowed, in years.

Once we know what the symbols mean we can make a lot of use of algebra – in fact mathematics is often called the 'Queen of the Sciences' because it reigns over them all. Practically everything can be expressed in mathematical terms and manipulated to experiment with the figures and see how we can get the best results – a stronger bridge, a faster chemical reaction, a purer water system or a more profitable investment. For the present, don't worry about algebra making sense. All we have to learn is some sensible processes – how to handle and manipulate symbols.

2   THE BASIC RULES OF ALGEBRA

The basic rules of algebra are:

1   We can use any symbol we like.
2   If we want to talk about a single term, we use the symbol itself, for example a, b or c.
3   If we want to talk about more than one of the items represented by the symbol we put a number in front of it. So we could write $2a$, $3a$, $5a$, $19a$, or $26a$. The number in each case is called the **coefficient** of a, and it tells us how many times we have a. For example, $3a$ means we have a three times, and $26a$ means we have a 26 times. If we have a statement:

> $3a + 5a$

we can simplify it by adding them together. This means we add the coefficients together: $3 + 5 = 8$, so $3a + 5a = 8a$. We don't know what a means, it is just a symbol – it stands for something – but we do know that if we had three of them and then another five of them, we'd have eight of them altogether.

Suppose we had a statement $a + b$. We can't add them together because they are different things. If we have $3a + 5b$ we can't add them together, because they are still different things. But if we have a statement:

> $a + b + 3a + 5b + 4a + 2b + 5a + 7a + 6b$

we can do something to simplify the statement. We can at least **collect the like terms;**

put all the a's together and all the b's. The result is (adding the coefficients – and don't forget the coefficient of a by itself is 1, i.e. $1a$):

$20a + 14b$

■ EXERCISE 7.1

Simplify the following statements by collecting like terms

(a) $2x + 3x + x + 5x$ (b) $y + 3y + 4y + 2y$

(c) $5m + 3m + m + 2m + m$ (d) $7c + 3c + 4c + c$

(e) $a + 2b + 3a + 4b + 5a + 7b$

(f) $2c + d + 3c + d + 4d + 5c + c$

(g) $3f + 4f + 2g + g + f + 2g + g$

(h) $5x + 3y + 2z + x + 2y + 3z + y + 5x + 2z$

(i) $3m + 2t + 4m + 3t + 5t + m + 3t$

(j) $9x + 3y + 3z + 4y + 2z + 3x + z$

Naturally if a term is preceded by a minus sign and not a plus sign we subtract that term as we would with ordinary numbers. So $6a - 4a = 2a$ and $3x - x = 2x$.

■ EXERCISE 7.2

Simplify the following statements by collecting like terms

(a) $9c + 3c - 6c$ (b) $7m + 3m - 2m - 4m$

(c) $5a + 3b - 2a - b$ (d) $7c - 3x + 4c + 5x - d$

(e) $3x + 2y - z + 4x - 3y - 3z$ (f) $5m - 3n - 2m + n$

Continuing the rules of algebra we may say: if we want to multiply like terms together we do so by indicating that the symbol has been raised to a power. We know that 5×5 may be written 5^2 and $5 \times 5 \times 5$ may be written 5^3. Similarly $a \times a = a^2$ and $a \times a \times a = a^3$. If there is a coefficient involved as well we multiply the coefficient in the usual way. Therefore

$2a \times 4a = 8a^2$

$3a \times 3a = 9a^2$

Suppose in the last example $a = 6$

$3a \times 3a = 18 \times 18 = 324$

$9a^2 = 9 \times 36 = 324$

This shows that multiplying $3a \times 3a$ to give us $9a^2$ is perfectly correct because when we substitute in a value for a in both expressions we get the same answer.

If we multiply unlike terms we simply write the symbol parts down adjacent to one another. For example $a \times b = ab$ and $m \times n = mn$. In these two examples the coefficient of the symbols was 1 in each case. If there are coefficients greater than 1 we multiply the coefficients first and then write the symbols adjacent to one another. So

$5x \times 2y = 10xy$

Also

$$3m \times 2n = 6mn \text{ and } 5a \times 3b = 15ab$$

We can again prove that the answers are correct by substituting in values for the unknown symbols. Suppose $a = 2$ and $b = 4$, in the last example.

$$5a \times 3b = (5 \times 2) \times (3 \times 4) = 10 \times 12 = 120$$
$$15ab = 15 \times 2 \times 4 = 120$$

Finally, when we multiply like terms with indices we add the indices. Thus $a^2 \times a^3 = a^{2+3} = a^5$. This must be so, for if we write a^2 and a^3 down in extended form

$$a^2 = a \times a$$
$$a^3 = a \times a \times a$$

When we write these down and multiply them we have

$$a \times a \quad a \times a \times a$$

Inserting the multiplication sign we have

$$a \times a \times a \times a \times a = a^5$$

Remember – when we multiply numbers with indices we add the indices. So

$$b^2 \times b^4 = b^6 \text{ and } 2b^2 \times 3b^4 = 6b^6$$

■ EXERCISE 7.3

Do the following multiplication sums:

(a)	$c \times c \times c$	**(b)**	$d \times 2d \times 3d^2$
(c)	$5x \times 3y$	**(d)**	$4m \times 3n$
(e)	$5a^2 \times 3a^3$	**(f)**	$7x^3 \times 3x^3$
(g)	$4a \times 3b \times 2c$	**(h)**	$7a \times 2b \times 3c^2$
(i)	$5m \times 2n \times 3p$	**(j)**	$11a \times 5a^2 \times 3bc$

3   DIVISION IN ALGEBRA

When we divide in algebra there is no shorthand way of writing down the numbers as there is in multiplication, where we write the numbers down side by side. $a \times b = ab$ but $a \div b$ cannot be written any more simply, unless we are given values for a and b, and can work out a final answer. Of course we could write $a \div b$ as a/b, but that is really the same thing. Notice that a division sum in algebra means exactly the same as it does in arithmetic. For example $18 \div 2$ means 'if we divide up 18 items between 2 people what will each get? The answer is 9. Similarly $a \div a$ means 'if we divide up a items between a people what will each get? The answer is 1. Thus if $a = 9$ then 9 items divided among 9 people gives them 1 each. So $a \div a = 1$; $b \div b = 1$; etc., etc.

We could look on this in the same way as if we were dealing with fractions

$$\frac{\cancel{a}1}{\cancel{a}1} \quad \text{the } a\text{'s will cancel and give us } \frac{1}{1} = 1$$

Similarly

$$2a \div a = \frac{2\not{a}}{\not{a}1} = 2 \text{ (the } a\text{'s cancel out)}$$

$$3b \div b = \frac{3\not{b}}{\not{b}} = 3$$

$$6b \div 2b = \frac{\not{6}\not{b}^3}{2\not{b}_1} = 3$$

When we divide numbers with indices we **subtract** the indices

$$a^4 \div a^2 = a^{4-2} = a^2$$

or we could write this down as:

$$a^4 \div a^2 = \frac{\not{a} \times \not{a} \times a \times a}{\not{a} \times \not{a}} = a^2 \text{ (two of the } a\text{'s cancel out)}$$

Note what happens where the index powers are the same:

$$a^3 \div a^3 = a^{3-3} = a^0 = 1$$
$$b^4 \div b^4 = b^{4-4} = b^0 = 1$$

Anything to the power $0 = 1$. We can see this must be so if we set the sum down in another way

$$a^3 \div a^3 = \frac{\not{a}^1 \times \not{a}^1 \times \not{a}^1}{\not{a}^1 \times \not{a}^1 \times \not{a}^1} \text{ (all the } a\text{'s cancel out and leave 1)}$$

■ EXERCISE 7.4

Do the following division calculations. If there is no simpler way of expressing the answer say 'no simpler way'

(a) $p \div p$ (b) $p^4 \div p^2$

(c) $8c^2 \div 4c$ (d) $a^2 \div b^2$

(e) $25c^2d \div 5c$ (f) $72a^4b^2 \div 12a^3b$

(g) $15c \div 8d$ (h) $9r^3 \div 3r^2$

(i) $14cde \div 7d$ (j) $15b^2c^2d^5 \div 3bcd^2$

4   THE RULES OF INDICES

These rules tell us what to do when we multiply numbers with indices, divide numbers with indices, raise numbers with indices to a power and find a square root or a cubed root of a number with indices. The rules are:

Rule 1

When we are multiply numbers with indices we **add** the indices.

Example 1

$$a^2 \times a^3 = a^{2+3} = a^5$$
$$b^4 \times b^3 = b^{4+3} = b^7$$
$$x^2 \times x^5 = x^{2+5} = x^7$$

Rule 2

When we divide numbers with indices we **subtract** the indices.

Example 2

$$a^4 \div a^2 = a^{4-2} = a^2$$
$$m^3 \div m = m^{3-1} = m^2$$
$$y^8 \div y^4 = y^{8-4} = y^4$$

Rule 3

When a number with an index figure is raised to a further power we multiply the indices. We can illustrate this with an example.

$$(a^3)^2$$

Here we have a^3 to multiply by itself (i.e. it is to be squared) $a^3 \times a^3 = a^6$ (by rule 1 above).
This is the same result as we get if we multiply the indices.

$$(a^3)^2 = a^{3 \times 2} = a^6$$

Example 3

$$(a^4)^3 = a^{4 \times 3} = a^{12}$$
$$(m^2)^3 = m^{2 \times 3} = m^6$$
$$(z^3)^5 = z^{3 \times 5} = z^{15}$$

Rule 4

When we find the root of a number with an index figure we divide the index by 2 (for a square root) or 3 (for a cubed root).

Remember that when we find a square root we are looking for a number which, when multiplied by itself, gives the number we started with. Therefore if the number we start with has an index figure, we find the square root by dividing this figure by 2.

Example 4

$$\sqrt{a^6} = a^{6 \div 2} = a^3$$

(Check: If we have the right answer, a^3 when multiplied by a^3 will give us the number we started with – which was a^6.

$$a^3 \times a^3 = a^{3+3} = a^6$$

so our answer is correct.

More examples – find:

$$\sqrt{a^8} = a^{8 \div 2} = a^4$$
$$\sqrt[3]{x^9} = x^{9 \div 3} = x^3$$
$$\sqrt{y^{10}} = y^{10 \div 2} = y^5$$

■ **EXERCISE 7.5**

Simplify the following:

(a) $m^3 \times m^4$ **(b)** $n^2 \times n^3$

(c) $p^3 \times p^5$ **(d)** $p^8 \div p^5$

(e) $c^6 \div c^3$ **(f)** $(d^2)^2$

(g) $(d^9)^2$ **(h)** $\sqrt{a^4}$

(i) $\sqrt{y^{16}}$ **(j)** $\sqrt[3]{m^{12}}$

5 SOME SPECIAL POINTS

(a) $2a^2$ and $(2a)^2$

Be quite clear that these are not the same.

$2a^2$ is 'two a-squared'.

$(2a)^2$ is 'two-a all-squared'.

To see the difference we must substitute in some value for a.

Suppose a is 7.

$$2a^2 \text{ is } 2 \times 7^2 = 2 \times 49 = 98$$
$$(2a)^2 \text{ is } (2 \times 7) \times (2 \times 7) = 14 \times 14 = 196$$

Notice that 196 is twice 98 – in other words $(2a)^2 = 4a^2$. Everything inside the bracket has to be squared.

(b) The difference between $(ab)^2 + (ab^2)^3$ and $(ab)^2 \times (ab^2)^3$

The first is simplified as follows:

$$(ab)^2 + (ab^2)^3 = a^2b^2 + a^3b^6$$

We cannot simplify the expression any further because we are asked to add them up and they are not like terms.

The second is simplified as follows:

$$(ab)^2 \times (ab^2)^3 = a^2b^2 \times a^2b^6$$

As the sign between the two terms is a multiply we can add the indices to give us a^4b^8.

■ **EXERCISE 7.6**

Simplify the following:

(a) $(3b)^2$ (b) $(4c)^3$

(c) $(5cd)^2$ (d) $(7mn^2)^2$

(e) $(ab)^2 \times (a^2b)^3$ (f) $(mn^2)^2 \times (mn)^3$

(c) The meaning of x^0

Consider $x^2 \div x^2 = x^{2-2} = x^0$.

What does x^0 mean? We can use common sense and say $x^2 \div x^2$ means 'I have x^2 things and I divide them up among x^2 people. How much will each person get?'

The answer must be 1. So $x^0 = 1$.

We could prove this another way. Consider $x^0 \times x^3$.

The answer is $x^{3+0} = x^3$. In other words x^0 when multiplied by x^3 leaves x^3 unchanged. Therefore x^0 must be 1 because 1 is the only number which when multiplied by anything leaves it unchanged.

For example $1 \times 10 = 10$, $1 \times 12 = 12$, $1 \times 99 = 99$.

So $x^0 = 1$ and any number to the power $0 = 1$.

$a^0 = 1$; $b^0 = 1$; $c^0 = 1$ etc.

The rule is *Any number to the power nothing is equal to 1.*

(d) The meaning of a^{-1}, a^{-2} and a^{-3}

Consider $a^2 \div a^3 = a^{2-3} = a^{-1}$

Now set the sum down a different way:

$$a^2 \div a^3 = \frac{a \times a}{a \times a \times a} = \frac{1}{a}$$

So

$$a^{-1} = \frac{1}{a}$$

Similarly

$$a^2 \div a^4 = a^{2-4} = a^{-2}$$

But

$$\frac{a^2}{a^4} = \frac{a \times a}{a \times a \times a \times a} = \frac{1}{a^2}$$

So

$$a^{-2} = \frac{1}{a^2}$$

Similarly by the same reasoning process

$$a^{-3} = \frac{1}{a^3}$$

Remember then

$$a^{-1} = \frac{1}{a} \quad a^{-2} = \frac{1}{a^2} \quad \text{and} \quad a^{-3} = \frac{1}{a^3} \quad \text{etc.}$$

(e) The meaning of $a^{1/2}$

What can $a^{1/2}$ mean?

Let us start by saying $a^{1/2} \times a^{1/2} = a^{1/2+1/2} = a^1 = a$

So $a^{1/2}$ when multiplied by itself gives us a.

Therefore $a^{1/2}$ must be the square root of a, because every square root, when multiplied by itself gives us the number we started with. For example – suppose we start with 9. The square root of 9 is 3 $(3 \times 3 = 9)$. So as $a^{1/2} \times a^{1/2} = a$.

$$a^{1/2} = \sqrt[2]{a^1}$$

Of course $\sqrt[2]{a^1}$ is usually written $\sqrt{a}$ because by convention we never bother to show the power 1 and we also take it for granted that the square root sign means a square root and only higher powers need be inserted, like $\sqrt[3]{}$ and $\sqrt[4]{}$. So $a^{1/2} = \sqrt{a}$

Similarly

$$a^{1/3} = \sqrt[3]{a} \quad \text{and} \quad a^{1/4} = \sqrt[4]{a}$$

Now consider $a^{2/3}$.

$$a^{2/3} \times a^{2/3} \times a^{2/3} = a^{2/3+2/3+2/3} = a^{6/3} = a^2$$

Therefore $a^{2/3}$ must be the cubed root of a^2 (i.e. $a^{2/3} = \sqrt[3]{a^2}$)

Remember then

$$a^{1/2} = \sqrt{a}; \ a^{1/3} = \sqrt[3]{a}; \ a^{2/3} = \sqrt[3]{a^2}; \ a^{3/4} = \sqrt[4]{a^3} \quad \text{etc.}$$

(f) The meaning of $a^{-1/2}$

Since $a^{-1} = \frac{1}{a}$ and $a^{1/2} = \sqrt{a}$

$$a^{-1/2} = \frac{1}{\sqrt{a}}$$

Similarly

$$a^{-2} = \frac{1}{a^2} \quad \text{and} \quad a^{2/3} = \sqrt[3]{a^2}$$

Therefore

$$a^{-2/3} = \frac{1}{\sqrt[3]{a^2}}$$

Similarly

$$a^{-3/4} = \frac{1}{\sqrt[4]{a^3}} \quad \text{and} \quad a^{-2/5} = \frac{1}{\sqrt[5]{a^2}}$$

Remember then

$$a^{-1/2} = \frac{1}{\sqrt{a}}; \quad a^{-1/3} = \frac{1}{\sqrt[3]{a}}; \quad a^{-2/3} = \frac{1}{\sqrt[3]{a^2}}; \quad a^{-3/4} = \frac{1}{\sqrt[4]{a^3}}$$

■ **EXERCISE 7.7**

Simplify the following: (note: In (o)–(r) you will need to find the 3rd, 4th and 5th roots by trial and error.)

(a)	16^0	**(b)**	a^0	**(c)**	$(a^2b^2)^0$
(d)	x^{-1}	**(e)**	y^{-2}	**(f)**	$m^{-3} \times m^{-2}$
(g)	$a^{1/2}$	**(h)**	$m^{1/3}$	**(i)**	$n^{2/3}$
(j)	$x^{3/4}$	**(k)**	$a^{-1/2}$	**(l)**	$a^{-1/3}$
(m)	$a^{-3/4}$	**(n)**	$16^{1/2}$	**(o)**	$27^{2/3}$
(p)	$27^{-2/3}$	**(q)**	$81^{-1/4}$	**(r)**	$32^{-2/5}$

6 SIMPLE EQUATIONS

In Chapter 6 we learned that any mathematical statement which includes an = sign is called an equation.

$$I = \frac{PRT}{100}$$

For example

Where I means simple interest

   P means principal

   R means rate per cent per annum

and T = the term in years.

We also learned that, with any equation, it will still stay true if we do the same thing to both sides. So, an equation will still be true if:

(a) We add the same quantity to both sides.

(b) We subtract the same quantity from both sides.

(c) We multiply both sides by the same amount.

(d) We divide both sides by the same amount.

(e) We raise both sides to the same power.

(f) We find the square root of both sides or the cube root of both sides, etc.

These are called the **rules of equations**.

6.1 Transposition and the rules of equations

Many mathematical statements are made in the form of equations and we can use the rules of equations to rearrange the formulae. This is called **transposition** of formulae – because we move the position of various unknown items across to the opposite side – but always by keeping to the rules as we do so. The effect of the rules is to move things over to the opposite side, changing the sign as we do so to its opposite sign.

Note that transposition is not a separate rule. It is the result of applying the rules. For example:

  $x - 4 = 6$

To get the x on its own on one side and eliminate the 4 which is in the way we say: I need to get rid of the 4 on the left hand side (LHS) by adding 4 to the LHS. Since what I do to the LHS I must do to the right hand side (RHS), I must add 4 to the RHS.

$$x - 4 + 4 = 6 + 4$$

Therefore $x = 6 + 4$
Therefore $x = 10$
   We can abbreviate this to say:

$$x - 4 = 6 \quad \text{(transpose the 4 − take it over to the other side and change the sign)}$$
$$x = 6 + 4$$
$$= 10$$

Transposition is just a quick way of stating the rule, it is not a rule in itself.

Example 5

$$y - 3 = 8$$
$$y = 8 + 3$$
$$y = 11$$

(Check: To check our solution to any equation we substitute the value we have found for the unknown item into the original equation to see if it makes sense.)
Substituting 11 for y we have $11 - 3 = 8$. This is correct, so our answer is correct.

Example 6

$$p + 8 = 20$$
$$p = 20 - 8$$
$$p = 12$$

(Check: Substituting 12 for p we have $12 + 8 = 20$. This is correct.)

Example 7

$$27x = 81$$
$$x = \frac{81}{27}$$

The 27 (which is multiplied by x) comes over to the other side and the sign is changed to $\div$, which brings the 27 down below the line. 27 cancels with 81. Therefore $x = 3$.
(Check: $27x = 81$ becomes $27 \times 3 = 81$, which is correct.)

Example 8

$$\frac{x}{7} = 8$$
$$x = 8 \times 7$$
$$= 56$$

The 7, which is a divisor, is transposed above the line to become a multiplier.
(Check: $\frac{x}{7} = 8$ becomes $\frac{56}{7} = 8$ which is correct. The 7 cancels with 56 to give us $8 = 8$.)

Example 9

$$x^2 = 64$$

To get x by itself we need to take the square root of x^2. If we take the square root of the LHS we must take the square root of the RHS.

$$x^2 = 64$$
$$\sqrt{x^2} = \sqrt{64}$$
$$x = 8$$

(Check: In the original equation we substitute 8 for x. $x^2 = 64$ becomes $8^2 = 64$, which is correct.)

Example 10

$$\sqrt{x} = 32$$

To get rid of a square root we must multiply it by itself (in other words we must square it). If we square the LHS we must square the RHS.

$$\sqrt{x} \times \sqrt{x} = 32^2$$
$$x = 32 \times 32$$
$$= 1,024$$

The final point to make about equations is that we can turn them round completely and they are still true. Thus:

$$9 = 6 + 3 \text{ is the same as } 6 + 3 = 9$$
$$3x + 4 = 13 \text{ is the same as } 13 = 3x + 4$$

7   SOLVING SIMPLE EQUATIONS

A simple equation is one that does not have any unknowns which are raised to a power. It may have additions, subtractions, multiplication and division signs but it will not have powers or roots. We are usually asked to 'solve' such equations, which means 'find the values of the unknown symbols contained in the equation'. We can usually solve the equation by transposing terms to get the unknown symbols on one side and the known values on the other side. We usually get the unknown terms to the LHS and the known values on the RHS.

Where a term has a bracket in it we can remove the bracket if we multiply every term inside the bracket by the number outside the bracket. For example, if we have $3(x + 4)$, the removal of the bracket is as follows: $3(x + 4) = 3x + 12$.

Example 11

$$3(m + 1) = 2(m + 5) + 8$$
$$3m + 3 = 2m + 10 + 8$$
$$3m - 2m = -3 + 10 + 8$$
$$m = 15$$

(Taking the unknowns to the LHS and the known terms to the RHS.)
Check: substituting $m = 15$ in the original we have

$$3(15 + 1) = 2(15 + 5) + 8$$
$$3(16) = 2(20) + 8$$
$$48 = 40 + 8$$
$$= 48$$

This is correct, so our solution to the equation is correct.

■ **EXERCISE 7.8**

Solve the following simple equations.

(a) $5x - 8 = 12$

(b) $9b - 17 = 37$

(c) $9y + 4 = 3y + 22$

(d) $5m + 11 = 3m - 7$

(e) $14y - 36 - 3y = 5y + 12$

(f) $7(b - 4) = 3(b + 8)$

(g) $5(p - 3) = 4(p - 2)$

(h) $9(x + 6) = 6(x + 7)$

(i) $6(t - 2) = 3(t + 5)$

(j) $5(2r - 8) = 7(5 + r)$

■ **EXERCISE 7.9**

Solve the following simple equations.

(a) $7y + 11 = 25$

(b) $5h + 5 = 3h + 19$

(c) $4(x + 3) = 5(2x - 3)$

(d) $3(2t + 2) = 3(t + 4)$

(e) $8(2x - 4) = 4(x + 7)$

(f) $5(m + 5) = 7(3m + 7)$

(g) $2(3s - 5) = 2(5s - 2)$

(h) $7(y + 3) = 2(2y - 3)$

(i) $8(3t - 8) = 2(3t + 4)$

(j) $5(n - 8) = 10(2n - 7)$

8 SOLVING SIMPLE EQUATIONS WITH FRACTIONS

Consider the following equation:

$$\frac{6m + 4}{10} - \frac{2m + 8}{4} = 8$$

Here we have fractions to complicate the solution of the equation, but it is quite simple if we stick to our 'rules for equations'. First, though, one or two special points.

(a)   Where an expression includes a fraction the line of the fraction which separates the numerator from the denominator is a special kind of bracket. It is actually called a

vinculum, from the latin words 'to bind together' and it means exactly the same as an ordinary bracket. For clarity it is usual to put ordinary bracket signs in, so that the equation would be rewritten as:

$$\frac{(6m + 4)}{10} - \frac{(2m + 8)}{4} = 8$$

(b)   Also, any number that has no denominator in a fraction sum is understood to have a denominator of 1, so that 8 could be rewritten $\frac{8}{1}$.

(c)   Now, to eliminate the denominator 10 (which of course really means ÷ 10) we have to multiply throughout by 10, that is both sides of the equation have to be multiplied by 10. As there are two parts to the LHS each of them must be multiplied by 10. Similarly to eliminate the 4 we have to multiply both sides by 4. To eliminate both the 10 and the 4 we must multiply both sides by a common denominator of 10 and 4. 40 would be all right, but the lowest common denominator of 10 and 4 would be easier still, and that is 20. We therefore have, when multiplying thoughout by 20:

$$\frac{20(6m + 4)}{10} - \frac{20(2m + 8)}{4} = \frac{8}{1} \times 20$$

Cancelling we have:

$$2(6m + 4) - 5(2m + 8) = 160$$
$$12m + 8 - 10m - 40 = 160$$
$$2m = 160 - 8 + 40$$
$$2m = 192$$
$$m = 96$$

Check: Substituting in the original formula $m = 96$ we have

$$\frac{(6 \times 96 + 4)}{10} - \frac{(2 \times 96 + 8)}{4} = \frac{8}{1}$$

$$\frac{576 + 4}{10} - \frac{200}{4} = \frac{8}{1}$$

$$58 - 50 = 8$$
$$8 = 8$$

which is correct.
A slightly quicker way of doing the multiplication by 20 is as follows:

$$\frac{(6m + 4)}{10} - \frac{(2m + 8)}{4} = \frac{8}{1}$$

Multiplying throughout by 20, we say as we approach each term:

First term 20 ÷ 10 = 2; so we have 2(6m + 4)
Second term 20 ÷ 4 = 5; so we have 5(2m + 8)
Third term 20 ÷ 1 = 20; so we have 8 × 20 = 160

This brings us straight to

$$2(6m + 4) - 5(2m + 8) = 160$$

and from that point on the working is the same as that shown above.

Where there is only a single fraction each side of the equation we can shorten the procedure by what is known as cross-multiplying. This is just a special case of the ordinary rule. For example:

$$\frac{3x}{2} = \frac{9}{4}$$

The normal rule is to multiply both sides by the lowest common denominator which is 4. This would give us:

$$2(3x) = 9$$
$$6x = 9$$
$$x = 1\tfrac{1}{2}$$

The slightly quicker way is to cross-multiply, i.e. multiply $3x$ by 4, the denominator of the other side of the equation and the 9 by 2, the denominator of the other side. This is really the same as the transposition we saw earlier. We move the number across the $=$ sign and change the sign to the opposite one. So a $\times$ sign becomes a $\div$ sign and vice versa, i.e. $\div 4$ on one side becomes $\times 4$ on the other and $\div 2$ on one side becomes $\times 2$ on the other.

$$\frac{3x}{2} = \frac{9}{4}$$

$$4(3x) = 9 \times 2$$
$$12x = 18$$
$$x = 1\tfrac{1}{2}$$

■ EXERCISE 7.10
Solve the following equations.

(a) $\dfrac{x}{15} = \dfrac{4}{5}$

(b) $\dfrac{3m}{14} = \dfrac{12}{7}$

(c) $\dfrac{6t}{10} = \dfrac{27}{5}$

(d) $\dfrac{x+3}{5} = \dfrac{2x}{8}$

(e) $\dfrac{3m+5}{4} + \dfrac{4m+3}{5} = \dfrac{20m-4}{10}$

(f) $\dfrac{4x+8}{3} - \dfrac{3x+6}{4} = \dfrac{4x+2}{6}$

(g) $\dfrac{5a+6}{3} - \dfrac{3a-3}{2} = \dfrac{4a+4}{8}$

(h) $\dfrac{r-7}{12} + \dfrac{3r+5}{4} = \dfrac{5r-9}{4}$

(i) $\dfrac{2y+5}{7} + \dfrac{5y+4}{3} = \dfrac{13y-1}{3}$

(j) $\dfrac{m+2}{5} + \dfrac{m-7}{4} = \dfrac{10m+3}{10}$

■ ANSWERS
Exercise 7.1 (a) $11x$ (b) $10y$ (c) $12m$ (d) $15c$ (e) $9a+13b$ (f) $11c+6d$
(g) $8f+8g$ (h) $11x+6y+7z$ (i) $8m+13t$ (j) $12x+7y+6z$

Exercise 7.2   (a) $6c$ (b) $4m$ (c) $3a + 2b$ (d) $11c - d + 2x$ (e) $7x - y - 4z$
(f) $3m - 2n$

Exercise 7.3   (a) c^3 (b) $6d^4$ (c) $15xy$ (d) $12mn$ (e) $15a^5$ (f) $21x^6$ (g) $24abc$
(h) $42abc^2$ (i) $30mnp$ (j) $165a^3bc$

Exercise 7.4   (a) 1 (b) p^2 (c) $2c$ (d) no simpler way   (e) $5cd$ (f) $6ab$ (g) no
simpler way   (h) $3r$ (i) $2ce$ (j) $5bcd^3$

Exercise 7.5   (a) m^7 (b) n^5 (c) p^8 (d) p^3 (e) c^3 (f) d^4 (g) d^{18} (h) a^2
(i) y^8 (j) m^4

Exercise 7.6   (a) $9b^2$ (b) $64c^3$ (c) $25c^2d^2$ (d) $49m^2n^4$ (e) a^8b^5 (f) m^5n^7

Exercise 7.7

(a) 1 (b) 1 (c) 1

(d) $\dfrac{1}{x}$ (e) $\dfrac{1}{y^2}$ (f) $\dfrac{1}{m^5}$

(g) $\sqrt{a}$ (h) $\sqrt[3]{m}$ (i) $\sqrt[3]{n^2}$

(j) $\sqrt[4]{x^3}$ (k) $\dfrac{1}{\sqrt{a}}$ (l) $\dfrac{1}{\sqrt[3]{a}}$

(m) $\dfrac{1}{\sqrt[4]{a^3}}$ (n) 4 (o) 9

(p) $\dfrac{1}{9}$ (q) $\dfrac{1}{3}$ (r) $\dfrac{1}{4}$

Exercise 7.8   (a) $x = 4$ (b) $b = 6$ (c) $y = 3$ (d) $m = -9$ (e) $y = 8$ (f) $b = 13$
(g) $p = 7$ (h) $x = -4$ (i) $t = 9$ (j) $r = 25$

Exercise 7.9   (a) $y = 2$ (b) $h = 7$ (c) $x = 4\frac{1}{2}$ (d) $t = 2$ (e) $x = 5$ (f) $m = -1\frac{1}{2}$
(g) $s = -1\frac{1}{2}$ (h) $y = -9$ (i) $t = 4$ (j) $n = 2$

Exercise 7.10   (a) $x = 12$ (b) $m = 8$ (c) $t = 9$ (d) $x = 12$ (e) $m = 5$ (f) $x = 10$
(f) $x = 10$ (g) $a = 9$ (h) $r = 7$ (i) $y = 1$ (j) $m = -3$.

8 Ratios and proportions

OBJECTIVES

At the end of this chapter you should:
1 Understand what a ratio is, and be able to express a ratio in its simplest form (i.e. its lowest terms);
2 Understand the sorts of ratios that might be used in banking situations;
3 Understand proportional parts and their practical applications in such things as inheritance.

1 WHAT IS A RATIO?

A ratio is a relationship between two quantities expressed in the same units, which enables us to compare the two quantities. For example vehicle A, travelling at 60 mph could be compared with another, B, travelling at 30 mph in the following way:

A : B :: 60 : 30

This is read 'A is to B as 60 is to 30'.

The two things being compared have a colon between them, which we read as 'is to' and the two parts of the statement are separated by a double colon, which we read by the word 'as'.

So A is to B as 60 is to 30:

A : B :: 60 : 30

It is usual to express a ratio in its simplest form, which means in its lowest terms. This means that we cancel the two numbers down very much like a fraction, and in this case they cancel down to 2 and 1.

A : B :: 60 : 30

A : B :: 2 : 1

Note that we can only compare things if they are in the same units. Suppose we compare the speeds of two vehicles, one of which – A – is going at 60 mph and the other – B – at 32 kilometres per hour. Clearly, we cannot compare them directly because the units are different. We must either convert 60 mph to kilometres per hour or 32 kilometres per hour into miles per hour. Since 8 kilometres = 5 miles we can say that 32 kilometres ($4 \times 8 = 32$) is the same as $4 \times 5 = 20$ miles. Now we can compare their speeds.

    A : B :: 60 : 20 (cancelling by 20)

    A : B :: 3 : 1

Sometimes the figures will not cancel down easily until one side is 1.

For example suppose two banks make loans as follows: Bank A £350,000 in the week; Bank B £400,000.

    A : B :: 350,000 : 400,000 (cancelling by 10,000)

    = 35 : 40

    = 7 : 8

This gives some idea of the ratios of their respective lending, but it is not terribly clear, and we may feel we should go on until one side is 1. If we divide both sides by 7 we have:

    7 : 8

    $= 1 : 1\frac{1}{7}$ or 1 : 1.1428 etc.

Probably we would discuss this ratio as 'A is to B as 1 is to 1.14.'

When we have reduced a ratio to the point where one side is 1 we cannot express the ratio any more clearly.

Finally, notice that the actual ratio in the end is an abstract idea, the actual units we are talking about also cancel out, because both sides of the ratio are in the same units.

So we do not say that the ratio 60 mph : 30 mph cancels down to finish as 2 mph : 1 mph.

The mph cancels too, and the ratio is left as an abstract relationship, 2 : 1.

Example 1

One lorry is a 32 tonne lorry and another is a 16 tonne lorry. What is the ratio of their two loads?

    A : B :: 32 tonne : 16 tonne

    = 2 : 1

Example 2

One lorry is a 44 tonne lorry and the other a 32 tonne lorry. What is the ratio of their two loads?

    A : B :: 44 tonne : 32 tonne

    = 44 : 32

    = 11 : 8

Dividing both sides by 8 we have:

    A : B :: 1.375 : 1

■ EXERCISE 8.1

1 Express the following ratios as simply as possible in the form a : b :: 1 : ? (Answer correct to one decimal place where necessary.)

(a) £10 : £100

(b) £450 : £500

(c) 25 Ffrancs : 200 Ffrancs

(d) 40 mph : 100 mph

(e) 30 cm : 120 cm

(f) 45 seconds : 3 minutes

(g) 15 minutes : 1 day

(h) 2 tonnes : 32 tonnes

(i) £1,000 : £1 billion

(j) $7\frac{1}{2}\%$: 30%

2 Express the following ratios in the form a : b :: 1 : ? (Answers correct to one decimal place where necessary).

(a) The ratio between two bags of coins, one weighing 8 kilograms and one weighing 35.2 lbs (Use 1 kg = 2.2 lbs).

(b) The ratio between 64 kilometres per hour and 85 mph. (Use 5 m = 8 km)

(c) The ratio between a rate of interest of 16% and one of 30%.

(d) The ratio between National Income of the UK at £6,500 per citizen per annum and the USA at $18,560 per citizen per annum. (Use £1 = 1.60 dollars)

(e) The ratio between the lending by one bank of £640 million in a month and another bank lending £704 million in the same month.

2 THE USE OF RATIOS IN BUSINESS AND BANKING

Ratios are widely used in business and banking, because they show the relative importance of figures rather than the absolute figures. An absolute figure is one that is actually found, without any relationship with any other figure. It is true, and meaningful, but whether what it tells us is significant or not we cannot say until we start calculating a relative figure (a ratio).

Consider the following case: Plausible, a garage proprietor who applies for an overdraft, tells you that his prospects for the future are excellent. His recent price-cutting competition with other garages in the area has increased his sales by 12,000 gallons per week. On further enquiries you find that average weekly sales in the previous year were 430,000 gallons per week and the increase therefore is in the ratio:

$$430,000 : 442,000$$
$$430 : 442$$
$$1 : 1.028$$

The absolute increase of 12,000 gallons sounds quite impressive, but the ratio of the increase to the previous level of trade is much less impressive and as an argument for granting an overdraft is therefore less sound than implied by Plausible.

Four of the commonest ratios we can calculate when dealing with business customers are the **working capital ratio**, the **liquid capital ratio** (sometimes called the **acid test ratio**), the **return on capital employed** and the **return on capital invested**. These are explained more fully in Chapter 16.

3 PROPORTIONAL PARTS

It is common in business life to have to share things out proportionally. For example profits in partnership businesses may be shared equally but alternatively may be shared in proportions which reflect the contribution made to the business by the various partners. Thus a partner with specialised knowledge or many years' experience may deserve a higher reward than a less knowledgeable or less experienced member of the firm.

Example 3

A, B and C share profits in the proportions $5:4:1$. The total profits for the year are £92,750. What will each partner get?

Shared $5:4:1$ there are 10 shares altogether, of which A gets $\frac{5}{10}$, B $\frac{4}{10}$ and C $\frac{1}{10}$.

	£
Since $\frac{1}{10}$ of £92,750 is £9,275: C's share is	9,275
B's share is four times C's share. B's share is	37,100
A's share is five times C's share. A's share is	46,375
	£92,750

Check to ensure the total allocated is the same as the total profit.

Of course, since A's share was $\frac{5}{10} = \frac{1}{2}$ and B's share was $\frac{4}{10} = \frac{2}{5}$ we could have arrived at the same answer using $\frac{1}{2}$, $\frac{2}{5}$ and $\frac{1}{10}$ as the proportions for sharing out the total.

Similar calculations occur in the executorship branches of banking where an inheritance has to be shared out among a number of beneficiaries.

Example 4

Farmer Giles, who has no close relatives, leaves a will which says that after his death all assets are to be sold and the money realised, after paying inheritance tax, is to be shared between three nephews and seven nieces in the proportion of their ages (in completed years) on the day of his death. The assets fetch £498,265. Inheritance tax is agreed at £125,000, legal and other charges are £12,850. The nephews are aged 18, 16, and 9 respectively and the nieces 27, 23, 15, 14, 11, 9 and 7 respectively. What will the eldest nephew receive? What will the youngest niece receive?

$$\text{Funds available for distribution} = £498,265 - (£125,000 + £12,850)$$

	£498,265
=	£498,265
−	137,850
	£360,415

Number of shares $= 18 + 16 + 9 + 27 + 23 + 15 + 14 + 11 + 9 + 7$
$= 149$ shares
The eldest nephew gets $\frac{18}{149}$ of £360,415
$= £43,540.07$
The youngest niece gets $\frac{7}{149}$ of £360,415
$= £16,932.25$

■ EXERCISE 8.2

1 Share the following sums of money in the proportions shown:

(a) £18,255 in the proportions 2 : 1
(b) £16,295 in the proportions 2 : 2 : 1
(c) £45,960 in the proportions 8 : 7
(d) £58,728 in the proportions 3 : 1
(e) £96,525 in the proportions 4 : 4 : 1
(f) £224,718 in the proportions 6 : 4 : 3

2 Profits are shared among three partners A, B and C such that A has twice as much as B who has three times as much as C. The total profits are £78,000. What will each partner get? (Hint: Give C 1 share.)

3 Profits are shared among three partners A, B and C in the ratios 3 : 3 : 2. C, who is young, energetic and doing most of the heavy work, is allowed a salary of £10,000 out of profits before the share-out takes place. If the profits of the partnership are £86,000 how much will each partner receive?

4 A reward for information leading to the arrest of bank robbers is set at £50,000 – the division to be made 'in such a fashion as our insurers shall deem to be fair'. A gang of eight dockers who are suspicious of two persons known to have been dishonest when working with them at an earlier date are persuaded by one of them to give information. The insurers agree that all shall share equally in the reward, except that the person who showed the initiative shall receive a double share. What will each receive? (Answers correct to the nearest £1, the award being adjusted to make this possible.)

5 Prize money at a sponsored golf tournament is to be shared up as follows. Forty golfers only will be allowed to proceed to the 3rd and 4th days of the tournament. The first ten will each get a major prize. The first prize will be 18 shares, the second 9 shares, the next three 7, 6 and 5 shares respectively and the next five will get 4 shares each. The remaining 30 will each receive 2 shares of the prize money. The total prize money is £500,000. How much will each person receive?

■ ANSWERS
Exercise 8.1
1 (a) 1 : 10 (b) 1 : 1.1 (c) 1 : 8 (d) 1 : 2.5 (e) 1 : 4 (f) 1 : 4 (g) 1 : 96
(h) 1 : 16 (i) 1 : 1,000,000 (j) 1 : 4
2 (a) 1 : 2 (b) 1 : 2.1 (c) 1 : 1.9 (d) 1 : 1.8 (e) 1 : 1.1

Exercise 8.2
1 (a) £12,170; £6,085 (b) £6,518; £6,518; £3,259 (c) £24,512; £21,448
(d) £44,046; £14,682 (e) £42,900; £42,900; £10,725 (f) £103,716; £69,144; £51,858
2 A's share = £46,800; B's share = £23,400; C's share = £7,800.
3 A and B get £28,500 each and C gets £29,000.
4 Ordinary members will take one ninth = £5,556. The one who showed initiative gets £11,112.
5 Winner gets £72,000; 2nd gets £36,000; 3rd £28,000; 4th £24,000; 5th £20,000; 6, 7, 8, 9 and 10 get £16,000 each and the rest get £8,000 each.

9 Compound interest

OBJECTIVES

After studying this chapter you should:
1 Appreciate the nature of compound interest and its difference from simple interest;
2 Be able to do easy compound interest calculations involving only a few years;
3 Know the compound interest formula and be able to do compound interest calculations using it;
4 Understand the effect of compounding more frequently than once a year.

1 THE NATURE OF COMPOUND INTEREST

When interest is calculated as simple interest, and paid over to the lender of the money each year, the capital sum (the principal) remains unchanged from year to year. If the interest is not paid over, but is added to the principal annually, the sum effectively placed at the disposal of the borrower increases each year by the amount of the interest left with the borrower, and in its turn is entitled to interest. **Compound interest may therefore be defined as a system of interest where any interest earned is added to the original principal and the lender not only earns interest on the original sum deposited, but interest on the interest accumulated over the years**.

Compound interest adds considerably to the value of any investment. For example, interest added at 10% causes money to double in about seven years. Banks, life assurance companies and other financial institutions are vitally concerned with compound interest, which lies at the root of most pension funds, finance for industry and commerce and the general prosperity of the nation.

Perhaps it should be mentioned here that the Mohammedan faith does not allow the charging of interest as a matter of religious principle. Some banks are adopting alternative arrangements with Moslem customers who need finance. The usual alternative is a joint venture approach, the bank having a share in the profits of the venture financed by its funds. Such participation is not a breach of the Mohammedan faith. Regrettably the author is not an authority on such schemes, which do vary from bank to bank, and students who meet with this problem are advised to consult Head Office for guidance.

2 COMPOUND INTEREST BY THE '1%' METHOD

Where compound interest is to be calculated without a calculator, it is simplest to use this method, which is based on the fact that 1% is an easy calculation, and from that any other percentage can easily be derived. Consider the following example.

Example 1

A bank loans a customer £850 at $9\frac{1}{2}\%$ compound interest, over two years, the interest being added annually. What will be the total amount to repay?

	£	
Principal =	850.00	
1% interest for one year =	8.50	(dividing £850 by 100)
plus 8% interest for one year =	68.00	(multiplying 1% by 8)
plus $\frac{1}{2}$% interest for one year =	4.25	(dividing 1% by 2)
Position at end of year 1	930.75	
1% interest in Year 2 =	9.3075	
plus 8% interest in Year 2 =	74.4600	
plus $\frac{1}{2}$% interest in Year 2 =	4.65375	
	£1019.17125	
Amount to repay =	£1,019.17	

By taking 1% and then 8% and then $\frac{1}{2}$% we arrive at $9\frac{1}{2}$% to add on to the original principal, and then using the revised principal we add on a further $9\frac{1}{2}$% for the second year. Interest can be calculated at any percentage by this method. For example $14\frac{3}{4}$% would be found by 10%, 1%, 3% and then $\frac{3}{4}$% could be done either as $\frac{1}{2}$% and $\frac{1}{4}$% or, more subtly, as one quarter of the 3% line.

■ EXERCISE 9.1
Calculate correct to the nearest penny the amount to be repaid on the following loans borrowed at $13\frac{1}{2}$% over two years.

(a) £1,000   (b) £2,500

(c) £3,800   (d) £4,200

(e) £5,500   (f) £8,250

■ EXERCISE 9.2
The details are given overleaf of ten loans made at compound interest. Work out the total amount to be repaid at the end of the loan period. Calculations correct to the nearest penny.

	Principal	Rate of interest per annum	Terms of loan in years
(a)	£500	10%	2
(b)	£780	$11\frac{1}{2}$%	2
(c)	£1,000	$12\frac{1}{2}$%	2
(d)	£1,250	$14\frac{1}{2}$%	2
(e)	£1,800	$16\frac{1}{4}$%	3
(f)	£2,500	$14\frac{3}{4}$%	3
(g)	£3,250	$16\frac{1}{2}$%	3
(h)	£4,800	$17\frac{1}{2}$%	3
(i)	£7,600	$14\frac{3}{4}$%	4
(j)	£14,400	$15\frac{1}{4}$%	4

Using the calculator for these calculations is very simple, but we need to think clearly about what the calculator needs to know to work out the answer. The reasoning is as follows:

(a) The calculator needs to know the rate of interest so that it can work out the interest to be added each year at that rate. For example in question 9.2(j) above the rate of interest was $15\frac{1}{4}$% i.e. 15.25% when keyed into the calculator.

(b) However each year the principal is different because the interest is added to the principal at the start of the year to give a new principal for the next year.

(c) That means that at the end of the first year, the new principal is the original principal + the interest in the year. We can go straight to this figure by multiplying the principal, not by the interest rate alone, but by 1 plus the interest rate, i.e. in 9.2(j) we multiply the original principal by 1.1525. Keying in £14,400 × 1.1525 we get £16,596 for the amount of the investment after one year.

(d) As we need to work this out for several years all we need to do is to put 1.1525 in the memory and keep multiplying by it using the memory recall key for the number of years in question. The procedure is therefore as shown below.

CALCULATION: What is the final amount to be repaid when £14,400 is borrowed at $15\frac{1}{4}$% for four years?

SEQUENCE	1.1525	M+	14 400	☒	RM	☒	RM
DISPLAY	1.1525	1.1525	14,400	14,400	1.1525	16,596	1.1525

SEQUENCE (continued)	☒	RM	☒	RM		⊟
DISPLAY (continued)	19,126.89	1.1525	22,043.74	1.1525		25,405.41

ANSWER   £25,405.41

Your calculator may also have a function key for multiplying by a constant, in which case you could use that method instead. For this feature refer to the instruction leaflet supplied with your calculator.

■ **EXERCISE 9.3**

Use the calculator to calculate the total amount to be repaid when the following sums are borrowed at the rates of interest shown, for the period of years indicated.

(a) £1,500 for three years at $14\frac{1}{4}\%$

(b) £3,500 for three years at $16\frac{1}{2}\%$

(c) £7,500 for four years at $15\frac{3}{4}\%$

(d) £8,250 for four years at $11\frac{3}{4}\%$

(e) £15,000 for five years at $14\frac{1}{2}\%$

3 COMPOUND INTEREST BY THE FORMULA METHOD

The calculation of compound interest can be reduced to a formula which follows the reasoning given above when using the calculator. The formula is

$$A = P \times \left(1 + \frac{r}{100}\right)^{n}$$

where A is the total amount to be repaid
P is the original principal (the sum borrowed or deposited)
r is the rate of interest per annum
n is the number of years

Using this formula with the example already used on the calculator, we have:

Example 2

What is the final amount to be repaid when £14,400 is borrowed at $15\frac{1}{4}\%$ for four years.

Substituting in on the formula we have

$$A = P \times \left(1 + \frac{r}{100}\right)^{n}$$

$$= £14,400 \times \left(1 + \frac{15.25}{100}\right)^{4}$$

$$= £14,400 \times (1.1525)^{4}$$

$$= £14,400 \times 1.7642645$$

$$= \underline{\underline{£25,405.41}}$$

The calculation of $(1.1525)^{4}$ involves us multiplying 1.1525 by itself three more times, and would be very laborious to do by hand. It is simple enough on the calculator provided we use the memory. We work out $(1.1525)^{4}$ first, and then multiply the answer to that by the principal sum of £14,400.

CALCULATION: What is the total amount repayable if £14,400 is borrowed at $15\frac{1}{4}\%$ for four years?

SEQUENCE	1.1525	M+	×	RM	×	RM
DISPLAY	1.1525	1.1525	1.1525	1.1525	1.3282562	1.1525

SEQUENCE (continued)	×	RM	×	14400	=
DISPLAY (continued)	1.5308152	1.1525	1.7642645	14400	25,405.408

ANSWER   £25,405.41

■ EXERCISE 9.4

Using the formula method find the total amount repayable on the loans made below at the rates of interest shown for the term of years indicated.

(a) £1,800 at $14\frac{3}{4}\%$ for three years

(b) £3,000 at $15\frac{1}{2}\%$ for three years

(c) £4,750 at $13\frac{3}{4}\%$ for four years

(d) £5,950 at $16\frac{1}{4}\%$ for five years

(e) £12,000 at $12\frac{1}{8}\%$ for ten years

4   COMPOUND INTEREST TABLES

Although calculators have now made compound interest calculations relatively simple many people still use compound interest tables which show the way in which a sum of £1, if invested at various rates of interest, increases over a period of years. An extract from a table is shown in Fig. 9.1 below.

Table 9.1   The amount of £1 at the rate of interest shown, for the number of years shown.

Years	12%	$12\frac{1}{2}\%$	13%
1	1.12000	1.125000	1.13000
2	1.25440	1.26563	1.27690
3	1.40493	1.42383	1.44290
4	1.57352	1.60181	1.63047
etc	etc	etc	etc
10	3.1058	3.24732	3.39457
11	3.4785	3.65324	3.83586
12	3.8960	4.10989	4.33452
etc	etc	etc	etc
20	9.6463	10.54509	11.52309

Since the tables are based on £1 only, the figure found from the table must be multiplied by the number of pounds invested.

Example 3

What will £4500 invested at 13% for four years amount to by the end of the investment period? From the table we see that £1 becomes £1.63047 at 13% in four years.

$$\text{Therefore £4,500 will become £1.63047} \times £4,500$$
$$= £7,337.115$$
$$= \underline{\underline{£7,337.12}}$$

Example 4

What will be the compound interest on £5,275 invested at $12\frac{1}{2}$% for ten years?

$$\text{£1 becomes £3.24732}$$
$$\text{Therefore £5,275 becomes £3.24732} \times 5,275$$
$$= \underline{\underline{£17,129.61}}$$

The interest earned will be this answer less the original principal
$$= £17,129.61 - £5,275$$
$$= \underline{\underline{£11,854.61}}$$

■ EXERCISE 9.5

Work out the final amount that will be available if the sums mentioned below are invested at the rate of interest shown for the time indicated. Use the table provided to find the amount of £1 in each case.

	Principal	Rate	No. of years
(a)	£1,500	12%	3
(b)	£5,000	$12\frac{1}{2}$%	4
(c)	£7,800	13%	10
(d)	£20,000	13%	20

■ ANSWERS

Exercise 9.1 (a) £1.288.23 (b) £3,220.56 (c) £4,895.26 (d) £5,410.55
(e) £7,085.24 (f) £10,627.86

Exercise 9.2 (a) £605 (b) £969.72 (c) £1,265.63 (d) £1,638.78 (e) £2,827.82
(f) £3,777.44 (g) £5,138.79 (h) £7786.73 (i) £13,177.24 (j) £25,405.41

Exercise 9.3 (a) £2,236.97 (b) £5,534.08 (c) £13,463.10 (d) £12,866.01
(e) £29,520.16

Exercise 9.4 (a) £2,719.76 (b) £4,622.40 (c) £7952.42 (d) £12,632.28
(e) £37,688.22

Exercise 9.5 (a) £2,107.40 (b) £8,009.05 (c) £26,477.65 (d) £230,461.80

10 The accounts of customers

OBJECTIVES

At the end of this chapter you should:
1 Understand these terms: ledger, account, folio number, account number, debit and credit;
2 Understand the three classes of account: personal, nominal and real accounts;
3 Understand the banker-customer relationship as a debtor-creditor relationship with no special 'trustee' status;
4 Be able to open a Current Account for a customer, and also a loan account;
5 Be thoroughly familiar with a Current Account, able to understand every entry on it and explain it to a customer if necessary;
6 Be able to do a Bank Reconciliation Statement from the customer's point of view.

1 WHAT IS AN ACCOUNT?

An account is a page in the chief book of account, which is called the **ledger**. Although today banks keep their customers' accounts in the memory bank of their computers, and not in a ledger, the traditional wording is still used. Every customer has a numbered account, which shows the customer's place in the ledger. The account number is the first thing we give a customer when an account is opened and it is embossed in magnetic ink on every cheque and paying-in slip. The ledger, in medieval times, lay open on a ledge under the window in the counting house and that is how it got its name. Each customer, and each item of expense, had an account opened all to itself. The account was actually a leaf, i.e. both sides of a page, and every item affecting that person, or that expense was entered into the account. The account was divided down the middle, and entries were made either on the left hand side (called the debit side) or on the right hand side (called the credit side). The rule was: **Debit the account if it receives goods, or services, or money. Credit the account if it gives goods, or services, or money.**

The double-entry system gets its name from the fact that whenever any transaction takes place it always affects two accounts, one account being debited and another credited. Thus if I pay T Smith £50, T Smith's account has to be debited (he has received £50) but my Cash Account has to be credited, it has given £50. The idea of double-entry is explained more fully in Chapter 11.

There is a story of the painter Rembrandt that he was so hard up he had to beg a local shopkeeper for a shilling. The shopkeeper grudgingly gave him the shilling, which Rembrandt promised to repay, but the shopkeeper knew that it would be a waste of a page in his ledger to open an account for Rembrandt − since he was always poor. 'Debit', he said, 'one shilling to Charity Account.'

Since Rembrandt had received one shilling he should have been debited in a personal account with that amount, and have become a debtor on the books. Instead the money was debited to Charity Account, which is a **Nominal Account**. A nominal account is one where the money is there in name only − we haven't got the money − Rembrandt is using it to buy groceries. A nominal account is a loss we have recorded, and it will have to be written off the profits at the end of the year.

It helps us to look at one or two traditional accounts just to get the idea of debits and credits. Actually banks don't use traditional accounts for ordinary customers, but the more convenient 'running balance accounts' which are so easily kept by computers. These are illustrated later in this chapter.

2   THE THREE CLASSES OF ACCOUNTS

Note that there are three kinds of accounts. They are:

1   *Personal accounts* − the accounts of persons we deal with. They are either debtors (they owe us money) or creditors (we owe them money):

2   *Nominal accounts* − accounts where the money recorded is there 'in name only'. It has either been lost (an expense of the business) or gained (a profit of the business). Losses are debited and profits are credited. Examples are Rent Account, Telephone Account and Interest Received Account.

3   *Real accounts* − accounts where we record the assets of the business; the real things we own. Examples are Typewriters Account, Furniture and Fittings Account, Premises Account, etc.

You should now study Figs. 10.1, 10.2, 10.3, 10.4 and 10.5 carefully. Figure 10.1 is a personal account.

Tom Bell A/c. 2047 High Street, Ipswich, Suffolk Tel. (0473) 579614									L19	
Dr										Cr
Date		Details	F	£	p	Date	Details	F	£	p
19..						19..				
Oct	1	Balance	b/d	27	50	Oct 9	Sales returns	SRB1	5	—
	7	Sales	SDB1	210	35	15	Bank	CB5	21	38
	29	"	SDB6	59	50	15	Discount allowed	CB5	1	12
						31	Balance	c/d	269	85
			£	297	35			£	297	35
Nov	1	Balance	b/d	269	85					

Fig. 10.1   A Debtor's Account

Notes

1   The debtor is a debtor at the start of the month, because there is a debit balance on the account.
2   The month is only written once on each side (Oct.).
3   The dates then run down the page in the column provided.
4   Wherever possible to save time ditto marks are used (as under Sales).
5   When balancing off, the totals are written on the same line. In this example one line was left blank on the left hand side. To prevent mistakes (someone might try to write figures on this line) it is filled up with a neat Z.
6   It is usual to use red lines for underlining totals, and for the Z lines.
7   When we carry down the balance we write c/d in the 'carried down' folio column and b/d in the 'brought down' folio column.
8   Although the Z entries are used to fill up the gaps between sides as shown in the example these are difficult to insert in a printed book and will not be inserted in future exercises.
9   The cross references in the Folio (F) columns stand for Sales Day Book page 1, etc, Sales Returns Book, page 1 and Cash Book, page 5.

Figure 10.2 is really in exactly the same style as Fig. 10.1 except that the person dealt with is a creditor, not a debtor. However, for ease of printing, it is presented in the way such accounts are usually shown in text books, with just the central line. These are called T accounts.

Mohammed Haji, 27, Zanzibar Street, Dodoba, Tanzania.   L84

19..		F	£	19..		F	£
Mar 5	Bank		4,081.01	Mar 1	Balance	b/d	4,185.65
5	Discount			13	Purchases		4,250.50
	Received		104.64	27	Purchases		3,827.70
16	Purchases returns		426.32				
31	Balance	c/d	7,651.88				
			£12,263.85				£12,263.85
				19..		F	£
				Apr 1	Balance	b/d	7,651.88

Fig. 10.2   A Creditor's Account

Notes

1   On 1 March Haji is a creditor for £4,185.65.
2   On 5 March we pay him his money (but we deduct discount of £104.64).
3   On 13 March we purchase more goods – credit Haji – the giver of the goods.
4   On 16 March we have returns of £426.32. It is very unlikely we would return anything all the way to Tanzania. What probably happened was that we complained to Haji by telex about the quality of the goods received. He sent us a document (called a credit note) saying he would make an allowance on the price of £426.32. This reduces our debt to him, so it must be debited on his account – we pretend he has received back some of the goods.
5   On 27 March we purchased more goods – credit the giver – Haji.
6   On 31 March the account is balanced off and the balance brought down.
7   Of course, in a real office the folio columns would have been completed with the cross references showing the source of each entry to the account. These have to be ignored in practice exercises, but you can invent sensible ones if you like – like CB11 for 'Cash Book, page 11' on 5 March – since the Bank Account is actually kept in the Cash Book.

Figure 10.3 is a Nominal Account, Light and Heat Account, one of the expenses (i.e. losses) of the business. It will be totalled up and written off the profits at the end of the year. Figure 10.4 is another Nominal Account, but this time it is a profit.

Light and Heat Account   L79

19..				£
Mar	7	Gas Board	L23	127.56
	17	Electricity Board	L27	179.23
	29	Calor Gas Co.	L56	84.62

Fig. 10.3   A Nominal Account (an expense, i.e. loss, of the business)

Notes

1   In each case the Light and Heat Account is debited because it has received money from the business (but in name only). The actual money has gone to the Board or Company concerned.

2   All expenses (losses) of the business are debited in this way and at the end of the year are deducted from the profits earned in the year.

3   The folio numbers indicate the ledger pages where we will find the other half of the double-entry.

Commission Received Account   L80

19..				£
Mar	15	Cash	CB27	125.50
	24	Bank	CB34	1524.40

Fig. 10.4   A Nominal Account (a profit)

Notes

1   Once again this is a Nominal Account, where the money is recorded in name only. Commission Received has given money to the firm, but the actual money is in the cash box, or the Bank Account. All profits are credit entries and will be added to the profits at the end of the year when we work out the profits for the year.

2   The other halves of these double entries are in the Cash Book, on the pages shown.

Figure 10.5 is a Real Account. The assets of the business are recorded in Real Accounts. The things represented on the account are real, they can actually be touched and used, like typewriters or plant and machinery.

Plant and Machinery Account   L66

19..			£
Jan	1 Balance	b/d	12,745.00
	17 Press Moulders Ltd	L159	4,295.60

Fig. 10.5   A Real Account

Notes

1   This is an asset account. The purchase of an asset is always debited in the asset account, because that department of our activities has received a new piece of equipment.

2   The account of the firm that supplies the asset will be credited, and eventually the firm will be paid – but that will be another transaction.

3   THE RELATIONSHIP BETWEEN THE CUSTOMER AND THE BANK

Now that we know something about the three types of account we are in a position to understand more clearly the relationship between the customer and the bank. Of course there can be numerous relationships, and they vary from situation to situation, but if we think for the moment simply of the Current Account of a customer, the relationship is quite clear in law, and is called a **debtor-creditor relationship,** with the bank being the debtor owing back any money deposited, and the customer the creditor to whom the balance on the account is owed. Of course, should the customer become overdrawn at the bank the situation reverses, and the customer becomes the debtor (with a debit balance on the account) and the bank becomes the creditor, who is owed the money outstanding. There is no question of that particular money being the depositor's money, held in trust by the bank for the depositor. It is just general cash, and disappears into the bank's general funds. The bank does not have to retain that money and account for it – but it does have a duty to ensure that a depositor who needs to use the funds will have funds made available to him/her to the same value.

3.1   Opening a Current Account

Picture the situation of a college student, Mary Jones, who applies to the reception desk at a branch of the Hearing Bank Plc to open an account, on 1 September 19.., using the grant cheque she has just received of £850. Naturally the bank is happy to open an account for Mary (having confirmed her identity) and accepts the cheque as her initial deposit. At this moment Mary is giving the Bank £850 and we must credit the giver, as the rules about double-entry say. We shall pass the cheque on to Head Office to collect, so it is Head Office that is receiving the money really, and it will eventually merge in with all the rest of the bank's funds, as a debit entry in an asset account. As mentioned earlier it is no longer Mary's money, she has given it to the bank to use exactly as the bank likes, not as a trustee accountable for how the money is used. The right Mary has is to use the funds as she wishes, by writing cheques to pay bills or to draw cash, but it will not be the particular funds the bank received from Mary – they have been merged in the bank's general funds. It is up to the bank where they find the funds for Mary to use when she draws a cheque for any reason.

As far as Mary is concerned the account in her name appears as follows, and the running balance is a credit balance:

Mary Jones Account   A/c No 12345678

	Withdrawals (Dr)	Deposits (Cr)	Date	Balance
				Credit C Debit D
	£	£	19..	£
Initial deposit		850.00	1 Sept	850.00 C

Fig. 10.6   Opening a customer's account

Notes

1   We are still using the double-entry system, and we still have two sides to the account, a debit side and a credit side, but these now lie alongside one another.

2   The balance is a credit balance, and has a C alongside it to indicate this.

3 Mary Jones is a creditor of the bank (a person to whom the bank owes money).
4 The bank has received £850 which is now an asset of the bank (or will be once the cheque has been cleared and the funds have been collected from the authority that gave Mary a grant).

A special note for young bankers – are you confused about debits & credits? Many young bankers spend all day debiting accounts which appear to be giving money away, in cheques, standing orders, direct debits or transfers to another account. They think to themselves: 'When people's accounts are debited they are givers of money to someone else.' If you think like that you have got the double-entry idea totally wrong.

All those customers are not giving away the money – at least not as far as the bank is concerned. They are all people who did have money in their Current Accounts but are now receiving it back again and using it for some other purpose, to pay someone by cheque, or to pay a standing order etc. We debit them because they are receiving back the use of their money, and as a result have less to their credit in the bank. The fact that, instead of them actually receiving the money, they ask the branch to pay it to someone else, does not mean they are not receiving back the use of it.

So do be clear; when we debit a customer with any amount it is because they are receiving the use of their money – debit the receiver. We only credit them when they pay in cash or cheques and give the money to the bank for safe keeping (and as a result increase the balances available to them on their current accounts). The bank now owes them more money – they are creditors of the bank for a greater amount.

3.2 Opening a Loan Account

Now suppose that on 2 September the bank agrees to make Mary a loan of £1,000. This may be done in different ways in different banks, but if we disregard the interest for the moment and simply deal with the principal of £1,000, the double entry will be as follows:

Debit the £1,000 in a Mary Jones Loan Account especially opened for the purpose since Mary Jones is receiving the loan.

Credit the £1,000 in her Current Account, because she is virtually depositing it in her account at the same moment. No actual funds move of course, but she now has a credit balance of £1,850.00, which is offset by the new debt recorded in the Loan Account. The accounts would now read as follows (not fully displayed here however):

Mary Jones Current Account				A/c No. 12345678
	Dr	Cr	Credit C	Debit D
	£	£	Date	£
Initial deposit		850.00	1 Sept	850.00C
Loan Account		1,000.00	2 Sept	1,850.00C

Mary Jones Loan Account				A/c No. 987654
	Dr	Cr	Credit C	Debit D
	£	£	Date	£
Current Account	1,000.00		2 Sept	1,000.00D

Fig. 10.7 Mary's new accounts

Notes

1   Mary's credit balance has increased by the amount of the loan, now available in her Current Account.

2   It is offset by the debit of £1,000 in the Loan Account.

3   Interest will be calculated on a daily basis and each month it will be added to the Loan Account, increasing Mary's debt.

4   However, each month Mary will pay the agreed amount of repayment from her Current Account to the bank, to reduce the loan.

■ EXERCISE 10.1

(a)   Tom and Mary Brown approach the Hearing Bank Plc on 1 January 19.. for assistance in opening a new business under the Enterprise Allowance Scheme. They need funds of £2,000.00 as initial capital. They agree to open a Current Account with their personal savings of £650.00 and to repay the loan of £2,000 over two years. The two year period will be covered by a loan insurance policy at a premium of £113.09, which will be loaned to them in addition to the £2,000.

Show, in the same style as Fig. 10.9, the Current Account and the Loan Account of Tom and Mary Brown on 1 January 19...

(b)   On 28 February 19.., the account of Thomas Howard is overdrawn by £895. The bank manager calls him in to discuss this. Tom is a student in his final degree year and estimates that he needs another £500 before starting work in four months' time. The manager suggests that Tom resolves his difficulties by a loan of £2,000 repayable over three years. This will clear the overdraft, give him some current funds and enable him to meet the first few repayments. The loan will be covered by an insurance policy at a premium of £149.75 which will be loaned to Tom in addition to the £2,000. Show Tom's Current Account and Loan Account at the end of the day, after these matters have been attended to.

(c)   On 5 April 19.. Maira Malik, who has been in partnership with Abdul Kadarr and has £3,800.55 in a Deposit Account approaches the Hearing Bank Plc with a proposal. Her partner has died and it is necessary to purchase his share of the business, valued at £15,725.00. She proposes to take her sister Ayesha Malik into partnership, and trade as Maira Malik and Partner. She proposes:

(i) That the Deposit Account be closed and the balance transferred to a new Current Account in the partnership name.

(ii) That she will contribute a further £5,000 and Ayesha will bring in a further £1,000 as capital to this Current Account.

(iii) That the Bank should lend the partnership £10,000, repayable over five years, covered by an insurance policy for the full period at a premium of £240 per annum. The first of these premiums to be deducted by the bank from the Current Account, and not regarded as a further loan.

(iv) To ensure that the funds are used for the purpose intended the bank is to debit the account with the amount payable to the heirs of Abdul Kadarr, and to pay this amount to their solicitor, Patel and Partners, against a receipt recognising the purchase of Abdul Kadarr's share in the previous business.

The bank accepts the proposal and all the matters are put into effect on 15 April 19.., it also being agreed that the bank shall receive £100 for its services in making these arrangements, which will be debited to the account as charges.

Show the Deposit Account, the Current Account and the Loan Account at the close of business on 15 April 19...

4 MORE ABOUT RUNNING-BALANCE ACCOUNTS

We have now seen how to open the book-keeping entries for simple running-balance accounts, but it is very important to become thoroughly familiar with these accounts, and understand every entry. Consider the account shown in Fig. 10.9.

Hearing Bank PLC R T Jones Esq Rowhedge Burslem AB4 2KQ	Cambridge Branch			Account No 12756498
Details	Withdrawals (debits)	Deposits (credits)	Date	Balance
				Credit C Debit D
	£	£	19..	£
Balance Forward			9 Dec	727.36 C
Cheque 108246	786.25		12 Dec	58.89 D
Cheque 108245	20.00		14 Dec	78.89 D
Deposit A/c transfer		500.00	15 Dec	421.11 C
Counter credit		326.50	21 Dec	747.61 C
Cheque 108247	36.50		21 Dec	711.11 C
Economics Asscn DDR	6.50		23 Dec	704.61 C
Cash till Cambridge 2	40.00		27 Dec	664.61 C
Fixed charge	1.50		30 Dec	663.11 C

Fig. 10.8   A customer's Current Account

Notes
1   The rule for double entries is:
   Debit the account that receives goods or services or money
   Credit the account that gives goods or services or money
2   This is the account of R T Jones who on 9 December had £727.36 in his Current Account. This is a credit balance because Jones gave the money to the bank some time ago.
3   All the entries in the debit column are entries where Jones received back some of his money on the account (so the balance of the account falls). He used the money in three cases to pay someone with a cheque. In one other case he drew cash from a cash till for

personal use and in another the Economics Association asked for a direct debit (DDR) to be made to pay R. T. Jones' annual subscription.

4   One of the cheques was so large that the account became overdrawn, in other words Jones drew out more money than he had as a balance on his account. The letter D draws attention to this overdrawn balance, which is a debit balance (in other words Jones became a debtor of the bank for £58.89).

5   Notice that once an account has been overdrawn any further cheques drawn increase the debit balance on the account, because Jones is receiving even more money than he has deposited in the past. The cheque of £20 drawn on 14 Dec. increases his debt to £78.89.

6   The only other debit entry is a debit of £1.50, which is a charge made by the bank for marking an overdraft temporarily to assist Jones in paying the £786.25 cheque.

7   In order to clear the overdraft and restore the account to a credit balance Jones transferred £500 from his Deposit Account, and he later paid in £326.50. These are both amounts given by Jones to the bank, and are therefore credited in the account.

8   One important point in following such accounts is to get the procedure clear in your mind. This is an account in the bank's ledger. To see what is happening you read the name of the account holder and ask yourself 'What happened to Jones on ....?' or 'What was Jones's position on ....?'. For example: What happened to Jones on 12 December? Answer: He received back some of his funds from the bank (debit the receiver), used them to pay someone £786.25 and as a result became overdrawn to the tune of £58.89. Or again: What was Jones's position on 30 December? Answer: He had a credit balance at the bank of £663.11, in other words he was a creditor of the bank which owed him £663.11.

■ EXERCISE 10.2

To develop familiarity with running-balance accounts you should try the following exercises. Rule up pieces of paper in the same style as Fig. 10.8 and make the entries required.

(a)   R T Jones, whose account is shown in Fig. 10.8, continues into February with the following transactions:

 1 Feb Balance on current account £663.11
 3 Feb Paid away a cheque (No. 108248) for £76.56
 5 Feb Direct debit from Urban District Council for Community Charge £146.50
11 Feb Paid in over the counter £736.59
16 Feb Cash till Cambridge 2 Withdrawal £100.00
17 Feb Paid a cheque (No. 108250) £848.60
28 Feb Bank giro credit (salary) £725.60
28 Feb Bank giro credit (dividend warrant) £38.56

What is the final balance?

(b)   The Hearing Bank Plc has a customer, B Mullins, of 3172 Hills Road, Cambridge CB5 17PT, account number 14991746. On 1 January 19.. his balance was £1,386.56, a credit balance. The following transactions took place in January:

1 Jan Cheque drawn 172652 £850.58
4 Jan Direct debit (charity) £5.50

5 Jan Cheque drawn 172654 £642.65

8 Jan Overdraft marked (fixed charge) £3.50

11 Jan Transfer from deposit account £1,000.00

17 Jan Cheque drawn 172653 £48.50

19 Jan Direct debit (subscription) £16.50

23 Jan Bank giro credit (dividend) £34.20

24 Jan Cheque drawn 172655 £137.50

27 Jan Bank giro credit (salary) £825.68

30 Jan Cheque drawn 172656 £42.60

31 Jan Direct debit (loan account) £158.60

What is the balance on 31 January 19..?

(c) The Hearing Bank has a customer J Travis (Tarpots) Ltd, of 2475 Crescent Bypass, Great Tarpots, Cambridge CB22 1QW, account number 42957164. On 1 March the company's balance was overdrawn by £3,856.54. Open the account and make the following entries:

1 Mar Paid by cheque No. 523368 £47.25 (careful – it increases the overdraft)

3 Mar Loan credited to account £5,000

4 Mar Paid by cheque No. 523369 £63.75

11 Mar Direct debit (rates) £425.60

12 Mar Bank giro credit transfer (A. Customer) £136.50

13 Mar Paid by cheque No. 523372 £1,427.20

16 Mar Direct debit (subscription) £23.50

21 Mar Bank giro credit transfer £148.52

23 Mar Paid by cheque No. 523371 £149.65

24 Mar Bank giro credit (A. Debtor) £14,265.26

26 Mar Paid by cheque No. 523370 £875.80

28 Mar Debit transfer – loan repaid £5,000.00

30 Mar Interest charged £23.16

31 Mar paid by cheque No. 523373 £38.19

What is the balance on 31 March 19..?

5 EXPLAINING RUNNING-BALANCE ACCOUNTS TO A CUSTOMER

Figure 10.9 shows Mary Jones's current account after a full month's entries. Below it is a series of questions with answers given on the next line below. Cover up the page with a sheet of paper except for Question 1. Answer it by looking at Fig. 10.9. Then slide the paper down to check your answer with the explanation given. Then try Question 2 and repeat the process.

Hearing Bank PLC	Cambridge Branch			Account No
Mary Jones (Miss)				123456789
Rowhedge				
Burslem				
AB4 2KQ				

Details	Withdrawals (debits)	Deposits (credits)	Date	Balance
				Credit C Debit D
	£	£	19..	£
Initial deposit		850.00	1 Sept	850.00 C
Personal loan		1,000.00	2 Sept	1,850.00 C
Cheque 175001	45.20		4 Sept	1,804.80 C
Counter credit		55.00	5Sept	1,859.80 C
Students' Union DDR	6.25		8 Sept	1,853.55 C
Cheque 175002	36.18		11 Sept	1,817.37 C
Cheque 175005	7.50		12 Sept	1,809.87 C
Cheque 175007	2,000.00		17 Sept	190.13 D
Bank giro cr		2,500.00	19 Sept	2,309.87 C
AA DDR	39.50		23 Sept	2,270.37 C
Guardian Insurance DDR	152.50		24 Sept	2,117.87 C
Cheque 175004	17.25		25 Sept	2,100.62 C
S/O, Personal Loan	95.40		30 Sept	2,005.22 C

Fig. 10.9   Mary's account after one month

Questions and answers on Mary's account (see Fig. 10.9)

Answers	*Questions*
————	1 What does it mean if an entry is made in the Deposits (credits) column?
1 It means Mary has deposited more funds with the bank. We credit Mary (credit the giver of goods, or services or money) as she gives her funds to the bank.	2 What does an entry in Withdrawals (debits) column mean?
2 It means Mary has received back the use of some of the money she had previously deposited. (Debit the receiver of goods or services or money.)	3 Did Mary receive the £45.20 on 4 September herself?
3 We can't tell. We would have to look at the cheque. If it was made out 'Pay Cash' then she did receive the money herself. If it was made out 'Pay College Bursar' it would be the bursar that received the money – but Mary has still received back the use of her money, and has to be debited.	4 What does DDR mean?

Answers *Questions*

4   Direct Debit. Mary has authorised the Students' Union to claim her subscription direct from the bank. She has received back the use of her money, but the SU actually received the cash.

5   What happened on 17 September?

5   It looks as if Mary purchased a car – and went into debt doing so. The balance is an overdraft. (She joined the AA a few days later.)

6   What is unusual about this overdraft?

6   Most banks won't let you have an overdraft if you have a loan out at the same time. They may have sanctioned it specially.

7   How did Mary get over that difficulty?

7   She quickly deposited £2,500. Perhaps a doting parent restored her finances for her.

8   What does the entry S O Personal Loan mean?

8   It is the standing order for Mary's personal loan repayment for the month of September. She has received back the use of some of her funds, which were used to pay the monthly amount due.

9   Would you say Mary was a good customer of the bank?

9   Yes – apart from that one slip of going into debt, but possibly this was sanctioned beforehand and was therefore perfectly proper. Since banks exist to lend money to customers by way of overdraft or loans, and make profits by charging interest and fees for doing so the appearance of an overdraft on an account is a perfectly normal occurrence.

10   Go over the page again if you are not clear on the reasoning behind each entry

6   BANK RECONCILIATION STATEMENTS

Most business customers who keep a record of their transactions in a proper Cash Book, or on some computerised system, will ask for a bank statement once a month, and all customers must occasionally be sent a bank statement. Some banks send them out regularly on the same day each month – but those receiving a statement do not necessarily receive it on the last day of the month. That would overload the system and instead the banks prefer to use a system known as 'cyclical billing' with about 4% of statements being sent out each working day. Despite this many people ask for their statements to be sent just after pay day, and this means a heavier workload in the first few days of the month.

For a number of reasons the customer's records rarely agree with the bank's records, and customers who are not very sophisticated financially may complain that their figures do not tally with the bank's figures as given on the statement. The explanations are as follows:

(a)   Neither party knows exactly what the other party is doing during the course of a month's transactions. For example, the customer is drawing cheques to pay for all sorts of expenses. Sometimes these cheques will be presented at once (as where a customer draws cash at the counter) and the bank then knows what the customer has done. Sometimes the cheques will be sent to the customer's creditors many miles away, and may not be presented for payment for several days, or even for several weeks. They may get lost in the post and never be presented. All such outstanding cheques are called 'time-lag' or outstanding items.

Similarly the bank may receive bank giro credit transfers in favour of the customer which the customer is not aware of. For example: salary payments, enterprise allowance payments, pension payments, annuities, dividends, gilt-edged interest, etc., all arrive by bank giro to be credited to the customer's account. By contrast direct debits authorised by the customer for rates, community charges, annual subscriptions to professional bodies, charitable covenants, etc., may have been presented by the bodies authorised and debited to the customer's account. Standing orders may be similarly deducted from the customer's balance. The customer may be unaware of all these matters until the statement arrives.

(b)   Either party can make mistakes, and records which have mistakes in them will never agree.

It follows that the customer must take the following actions to ensure that there is no problem on the banking arrangements:

(a)   Work through the bank statement checking it against his/her personal records (whether kept in a full system of book-keeping records or just in his/her cheque book).

(b)   Record in the accounting records (or on the cheque book) any items the bank has recorded on the statement but which are not yet entered in the trader's own records because he/she did not know about them until the statement arrived.

(c)   Finally a statement called a bank reconciliation statement must be drawn up which takes account of any cheques not yet presented or paid in for some reason at another branch or another bank, and not yet received by the account holding branch.

To follow this situation consider Fig. 10.10 opposite. The top half shows the bank account of T Morgan in his Ledger. The lower part shows T Morgan's Current Account at the bank. Before studying it, and the notes below it, notice one important point. Whenever Morgan puts money in his bank account he debits the bank account – the bank account as far as Morgan is concerned is receiving money. However, in the Current Account at the bank the Current Account is credited, because as far as the bank is concerned Morgan is giving the bank the money. So the two records are kept from the opposite point of view. A customer who has a credit balance on his Current Account is in funds, which means that in his own books there is a debit balance – he has an asset (money at the bank) and all assets are debit balances. Be quite sure you understand this point as you look at Fig. 10.10. The debits in the customer's records are credits on the bank statement, and the credits in the customer's records are debits on the bank statement.

T Morgan Cash Book (Bank Columns Only)

Dr 19..		£	Cr 19..		£
June 20	Balance b/d	595.20	June 21	Abel	19.78
25	Charles	105.38	23	Baker	51.86
30	Ewart	23.80	29	Dodds	88.52
			30	Balance c/d	564.22
		£724.38			£724.38
		£			
July 1	Balance b/d	564.22			

T Morgan Statement in account with Hearing Bank Plc

19..	Details	Dr	Cr	Balance £
June 20	Balance			595.20
23	Cheque	19.78		575.42
25	Sundries		105.38	680.80
29	Cheque	88.52		592.28
30	Charges	13.95		578.33
30	Bank giro (dividend)		52.65	630.98

Fig. 10.10 Figures for a bank reconciliation

Notes

1 On 20 June both the accounts started the same at £595.20 of cash in the bank.

2 On June 25 Charles paid Morgan £105.38 which he paid into the bank and we can see on the bank statement that it was cleared and the money was added to the account.

3 The cheque Ewart paid to Morgan for £23.80 has been received on the cash book, but not yet paid into the bank. The bank does not yet know Morgan has received these funds. It is a 'time-lag' item. It will get sorted out later. It will have to go on the bank reconciliation statement.

4 On the bank statement there is an item £52.65 which is a bank giro credit transfer. Morgan did not know this money had been received and he must enter it in his cash book.

5 On the credit side of the cash book Morgan has paid out three cheques to Abel, Baker and Dodds. Abel and Dodds have presented their cheques for payment and they appear in the Dr column of the bank statement but Baker's cheque has not yet been presented and the bank do not know about it. It will be sorted out later, but in the meantime it must go in the bank reconciliation statement. It is a 'time-lag' item.

6 Finally, on the bank statement the bank has passed a debit of £13.95 charges for operating the account. Morgan does not know about these charges and must enter them in his cash book.

6.1 How the customer gets the bank account right in his/her cash book when the bank statement arrives

The first thing to do is to get the bank account in the customer's cash book right. This requires us to start with the balance of £564.22 and enter the bank giro item and the bank charges. This will give us a new balance on the cash book of £602.92, now that we know about these items, but it still does not agree with the bank statement balance of £630.98, because of the time-lag items.

T Morgan Cash Book (bank columns only)

19..		£	19..		£
July 1	Balance b/d	564.22	July 1	Bank charges	13.95
1	Dividend received	52.65	1	Balance c/d	602.92
		£616.87			£616.87
19..		£			
July 1	Balance b/d	602.92			

6.2 Drawing up the bank reconciliation statement

We are now ready to do the bank reconciliation statement. We start with the revised cash book figure of £602.92.

Bank Reconciliation Statement
as at 1 July 19..

£

Balance as per revised Cash Book   602.92

As we can see on the bank statement the bank thinks we have £630.98. We have to reconcile the two statements by showing that it is reasonable for the bank to show a balance of £630.98.

We now look at each of the time-lag items. We have to ask ourselves: 'What does the bank think about each item?'

Well, what does the bank think about the cheque we paid Baker (£51.86)? The cash book knows we've paid Baker, and has deducted the cheque from the bank account in Morgan's records but the bank doesn't know about it, and thinks Morgan still has the money. We must add back the £51.86 to get what the bank thinks is the correct situation.

What does the bank think about the cheque Ewart paid us, and which we have added on to our bank figure? The bank doesn't know about it. We have only just received the cheque and have not yet paid it in. So our branch does not know that we have the money. Therefore the full reconciliation reads:

Bank Reconciliation Statement
as at 1 July 19..

	£
Balance as per revised Cash Book	602.92
Add back the cheque drawn, but not yet presented (Baker) (*because the Bank thinks T Morgan still has this money*)	51.86
	654.78
Deduct the cheque received but not yet paid in (Ewart) (*because the bank does not yet know T Morgan has received this cheque*)	23.80
Balance as per Bank Statement	£630.98

We can see that the two figures have been successfully reconciled. Bank reconciliation statements, once they have confirmed that our books are correct, are simply filed away for safe-keeping.

■ EXERCISE 10.3

(a) M Carlisle's bank statement reads as follows for March 19..:

Date	Details	Dr £	Cr £	Balance Debit D Credit C £
1.3.19..	Balance C/fwd			1,427.40C
3.3.19..	Cheque	31.30		1,396.10C
5.3.19..	Sundries		300.00	1,696.10C
12.3.19..	DDr Urban District Council	181.50		1,514.60C
14.3.19..	Sundries		400.00	1,914.60C
14.3.19..	DDr AA Services	28.80		1,885.80C
15.3.19..	Sundries		250.00	2,135.80C
19.3.19..	Sundries		350.00	2,485.80C
26.3.19..	Cheque	346.24		2,139.56C
29.3.19..	Sundries		350.00	2,489.56C
30.3.19..	Charges	12.50		2,477.06C
30.3.19..	Bank of England (bank giro)		33.80	2,510.86C

For the same month his Bank Account according to his Cash Book reads:

Cash Book (bank columns only)

19..		£	19..		£
Mar 1	Balance b/d	1,427.40	Mar 2	H Balfour	31.30
	Cash sales	300.00	17	T Lucas	85.40
14	" "	400.00	24	R Moore	346.24
15	R. Ajakaiye	250.00	29	K Ahura	75.80
19	Cash sales	250.00	31	Balance	2,438.66
29	" "	350.00			
		£2,977.40			£2,977.40
19..		£			
Apr 1	Balance	2,438.66			

You are required:

(i) To draw up the revised Cash Book based on any figures you discover in comparing the two sets of figures. In particular the figure in the bank statement on 19 March is found to be correct (£350.00) but it has been entered incorrectly as £250.00 in the Cash Book. An extra £100 Cash Sales is therefore to be recorded.

(ii) To draw up the Bank Reconciliation Statement reconciling this new figure with the bank statement figure of £2,510.86.

(b) The following statement was received from the bank indicating R Walker's position during January:

Bank Statement (as at 31 January 19..)

Date	Details	Dr	Cr	Balance
Jan		£	£	£
1	Balance			411.55
3	Sundries		1,380.00	1,791.55
5	DDR General Assurance	104.50		1,687.05
9	Credit Transfer (J Jones)		38.50	1,725.55
10	Cheque	221.65		1,503.90
13	Cheque	1,139.25		364.65
17	Sundries		1,584.50	1,949.15
20	SO HP Finance Ltd	60.05		1,889.10
22	Cheque	48.35		1,840.75
25	Cheque	72.64		1,768.11
29	Cheque	384.26		1,383.85

The Bank Account in his Cash Book showed the following entries:

Cash Book (Bank columns only)

19..		£	19..		£
Jan	1 Balance b/d	189.90	Jan	5 B Lord	495.15
	3 Cash sales	1,380.00		13 M Deacon	1,139.25
17	" "	1,584.50		14 P Lark	48.35
31	" "	1,580.00		17 M Gross	198.24
				19 J Gorman	72.64
				29 Urban District Council	384.26
				31 Balance c/d	2,396.51
		£4,734.40			£4,734.40
19..		£			
Feb	1 Balance b/d	2,396.51			

Note: The opening balances on 1 January do not agree, but this is put right on 10 January when the cheque for £221.65 (drawn in early December) was cleared. You are asked:

(i) To draw up a revised Cash Book figure for R Walker taking account of matters you discover when comparing the two sets of figures.

(ii) To draw up a Bank Reconciliation Statement as at 1 February 19.. starting with the revised Cash Book figure you have discovered.

(c) Here is the bank statement as supplied by Hearing Bank Plc to M Tyler on 31 January 19..:

Bank Statement
in account with Hearing Bank Plc

Date	Details	Dr £	Cr £	Balance £
1.1.19..	Balance c/fwd			1,508.40
3.1.19..	Cheque	114.16		1,394.24
5.1.19..	Sundries		362.80	1,757.04
12.1.19..	"		475.00	2,232.04
14.1.19..	SO HP Finance Ltd	130.50		2,101.54
14.1.19..	Sundries		412.56	2,514.10
15.1.19..	Cheque	560.00		1,954.10
19.1.19..	Sundries		335.00	2,289.10
26.1.19..	"		385.00	2,674.10
29.1.19..	Cheque	248.00		2,426.10
30.1.19..	Charges	14.55		2,411.55
30.1.19..	International Inventors (bank giro)		112.80	2,524.35

The bank columns of his Cash Book read:

Cash Book (Bank columns only)

19..		£	19..		£
Jan 1	Balance b/d	1,394.24	Jan 13	R Mellor	560.00
5	Cash sales	362.80	25	T Sorrell	248.00
12	" "	475.00	27	A B Supplies	878.56
14	" "	412.56	31	Balance c/d	2,150.79
19	" "	335.00			
26	" "	385.00			
31	" "	472.75			
		£3,837.35			£3,837.35
19..		£			
Feb 1	Balance b/d	2,150.79			

Note: The original balances do not agree but this is sorted out when the first cheque is cleared on the bank statement on 3 January 19...

You are required:

(i) To draw up a revised Cash Book balance taking into account any items discovered when comparing the two sets of figures, of which M Tyler would have been unaware until the arrival of the statement.

(ii) To draw up a Bank Reconciliation Statement as at 1 February 19.., reconciling the revised Cash Book figure with the balance on the bank statement of £2,524.35.

■ **ANSWERS**

Exercise 10.1 (a) Tom and Mary Brown's Current Account credited with £650.00 and £2,000.00. Their Loan Account debited with the loan £2,000.00, and the insurance premium £113.09 **(b)** Thomas Howard's Current Account overdrawn at £895 (a debit balance). Then credited with £2,000, leaving a balance of £1,105. His Loan Account is debited with the loan of £2,000 and the insurance premium of £149.75 **(c)** The accounts would appear as shown in Fig. 10A

Maira Malik Deposit Account

		Dr	Cr	Balance
		£	£	£
15 April	Balance b/d			3,800.55Cr
15 April	To Current A/c	3,800.55		NIL

Account closed

Maira Malik and Partner Current Account

		Dr	Cr	Balance
19..				
15 April	Per M. Malik Deposit A/c		3,800.55	
15 April	Sundries		1,000.00	
15 April	Sundries		5,000.00	
15 April	Per Loan A/c		10,000.00	
15 April	Insurance Premium	240.00		
15 April	Patel & Partners	15,725.00		
15 April	Arrangement Fee	100.00		3,735.55Cr

Maira Malik and Partner Loan Account

		Dr	Cr	Balance
19..				
15 April	To Current Account	10,000		10,000Dr

Fig. 10A

As can be seen Maira Malik's Deposit Account with its credit balance of £3,800.55 has been debited with £3,800.55 to leave a balance of £0.00 and marked Account Closed. Maira Malik and Partner's Current Account has been credited with £3,800.55 (transfer from deposit account) and also with Sundries £1,000 (Ayesha's deposit) and £5,000 (Maira's deposit). It has also been credited with a loan of £10,000. It has then been debited with £15,725 (the payment to the solicitors), £240 (the insurance premium) and £100 (bank charges). The final balance will therefore be a credit balance of £3,735.55. Maira Malik and Partner's Loan Account has been debited with £10,000.

Exercise 10.2 (a) R T Jones: Balance in hand £992.20 credit **(b)** B Mullins: Balance in hand £1,340.51 credit **(c)** J Travis (Tarpots) Ltd: Balance in hand £7,619.64 credit.

Exercise 10.3 (a) *Books of M Carlisle* Revised balance £2,349.66 (reconciliation arrived at by adding back two cheques not yet presented) **(b)** *Books of R. Walker* Revised balance £2,270.46 (reconciliation arrived at by (i) adding back two cheques not yet presented and (ii) deducting the cash takings received on 31 Jan. and not yet paid in) **(c)** *Books of M Tyler* Revised balance £2,118.54 (reconciliation achieved by adding back one cheque not yet presented and deducting the cash takings for 31 January which have not yet been paid in).

11 Double-entry book-keeping

OBJECTIVES

At the end of this chapter you should:

1 Understand the principles of double-entry book-keeping and appreciate where every type of transaction fits into the double-entry system;

2 Appreciate the fact that every transaction starts with a business document, and the importance of the slip or voucher system of documentation to bankers;

3 Understand books of original entry, and why they are of less interest to bankers than to ordinary traders because of the sophistication of bank computerised systems;

4 Appreciate the meaning of the words 'Trial Balance' and understand the make-up of a typical Trial Balance, such as a customer might prepare from his/her books;

5 Appreciate the term 'Final Accounts' and be aware of the terms Gross Profit and Net Profit;

6 Understand the Balance Sheet as a snapshot of the affairs of a business at the time stated in the heading of the Balance Sheet. The usual moment chosen is the last moment of the financial year, after the Final Accounts of the business have been prepared.

1 DOUBLE-ENTRY BOOK-KEEPING

Double-entry book-keeping is a system of book-keeping first developed in Northern Italy by the Lombards, the celebrated bankers of the Middle Ages who gave their name to Lombard Street – still the banking centre of the City of London.

Much of the work banks do for their customers is keeping Current Accounts for them, in running-balance form as described in Chapter 10. However, the true function of banks is wider than this and includes lending surplus funds to both personal and business customers. Banks also market a host of specialist services which meet the financial needs of customers. In order to do this bankers must understand the customer's financial position, and the key to this is to understand double-entry book-keeping. This is a separate study from business calculations really, but we will touch upon it here, using the illustration in Fig. 11.1 to make the ideas clear.

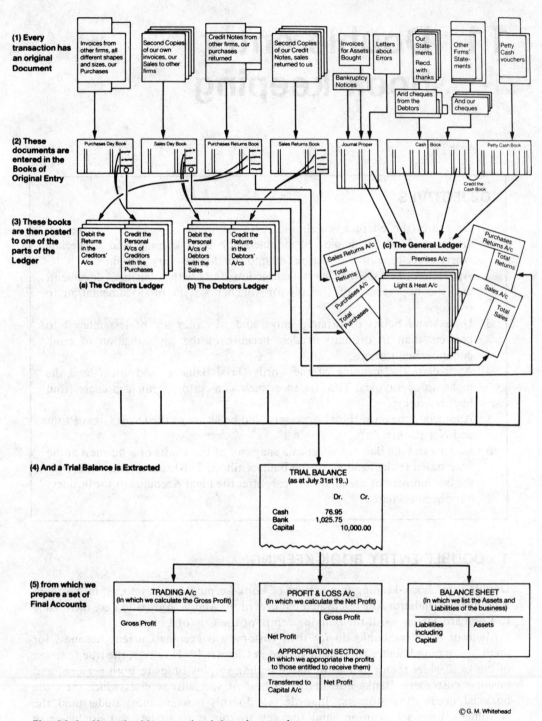

Fig. 11.1 How double-entry book-keeping works

Note: Study the diagram carefully, and then read the notes in the main text referring to the diagram again as you read each note. (*Reproduced by courtesy of G M Whitehead*)

2   A DETAILED DESCRIPTION OF DOUBLE ENTRY BOOK-KEEPING

(1)   Every transaction has its original document

Every business uses documents. The chief ones are:

(a)   Invoices, which we make out whenever we supply goods or services;

(b)   Credit notes, which we make out when we return goods or give an allowance for services which have been overcharged;

(c)   Statements (the monthly summary of an account, requesting payment of the balance on the account). In banks we often send out statements monthly, but merely to acquaint customers with their financial position at the bank on the date concerned;

(d)   Cheques – a method of payment. A cheque is an order to a banker to pay money to a named individual, the payee;

(e)   Petty cash vouchers – which prove that small sums of money have been paid for some valid business purpose;

(f)   Some businesses rely for many of their transactions on the use of slips or vouchers, such as paying in slips, debit slips for debit transfers, credit slips for bank giro credits, etc. These lend themselves easily to coding and 'batching up' for computerised data processing;

(g)   More formal documents such as deeds, leases, insurance policies, etc.

(2)   Documents are entered in books of original entry (but see (b) below)

(a)   To give a more permanent record of a transaction documents are often recorded in books of original entry. The most common are the Sales Day Book, the Purchases Day Book, the Sales Returns Book, the Purchases Returns Book, the Cash Book and the Petty Cash Book. Because these books are used every day, with records kept in chronological order as they happen, they are often called **Journals** and one of them, the **Journal Proper**, is used for all the more important items that do not happen every day, such as the purchase of premises and other assets. The Journal Proper sweeps up all awkward transactions and puts them into the double-entry system (for example bad debts, depreciation, issue of stocks and shares, etc.).

(b)   To save a lot of effort some firms use the documents themselves as books of original entry (usually providing a hard cover binder in which they can be kept). The document itself is entered directly into the books of account, or more likely these days is batched up with similar documents and coded, before the information on it (the data) is keyed into the computer. This is called the slip system of accounting, and is particularly useful for banks, where cheques, paying-in slips etc., can be used to keep computerised accounts.

(3)   The Ledger

(a)   The Ledger is the main book of account, and it is really this book which is kept on the double-entry principle. Every page in the Ledger is called an account, and keeps records of one thing only. Thus the Rent Account keeps records of rent paid, and the

Plant and Machinery Account keeps records of machines purchased and disposed of at the end of their useful lives. We have already seen that there are three classes of accounts: **personal accounts**, **nominal accounts** and **real accounts**.

Personal Accounts are the accounts of the persons we deal with. The word 'persons' includes 'legal persons' as well as humans, so Helpful Bank Plc's Account is a personal account and so is Cambridgeshire County Council Account. Since all the people we deal with are either debtors or creditors, we may say that personal accounts are always found in the Debtor's Ledger or the Creditors' Ledger. Since these are usually large parts of the Ledger they are often sectioned off from the other two classes of accounts, which are usually kept together in the General Ledger.

Real Accounts are the accounts where we keep a record of all the things we really own – the assets of the business. They include Land and Buildings, Plant and Machinery, Fixtures and Fittings, Office Equipment, Stock, Cash at Bank and Cash in hand. Real accounts always have debit balances, because they have received a certain amount of the business's wealth – debit the receiver. Of course they do gradually lose value (depreciate) so that normally an asset declines in value over the years of its useful life. A few assets (notably Land and Buildings) increase in value, and are said to 'appreciate'.

Nominal Accounts are accounts where the money is there in name only; we are just keeping a record of it. Thus if we have paid £560 in rent, the landlord has the actual money. The Rent Paid Account is debited with £560 (it has received £560 of the business's money) but the landlord really has the money and Rent Paid Account is one of the losses of the business. Similarly Commission Received Account has a record of any commission received, on the credit side. Its activities have given money to the business, but the actual cash is in the Cash Account; it is a nominal record only – it is a profit of the business.

One further point is that the Capital Account, or in limited companies the various Capital Accounts such as the Ordinary Share Capital Account and the 8% Preference Share Capital Account are special cases of personal accounts. The proprietors of the business are really just one further group of creditors but they are usually recorded in the General Ledger and not in the Creditors' Ledger. In some businesses they are sectioned off into a special ledger called the Private Ledger.

Confusing use of terms It is regrettable that different names are used in different banks for various accounts and if they are loosely used it can be confusing. Remember there are only three classes of accounts, personal, nominal and real. The personal accounts are often kept in the Debtors' Ledger or the Creditors' Ledger and the General Ledger is only used for the impersonal accounts, or non-personal accounts, in other words the nominal accounts and the real accounts. A nominal account is either a loss or a profit; a real account is always an asset.

Finally a word about capital letters. All accounts are unique – there is only one of them. They are proper nouns. Do not write them with small letters, they need capital letters: Cash Account, Bank Account, J. Smith's Account, etc.

(b)   As mentioned, the ledger is often split into separate parts for convenience. Thus we have a Debtors Ledger, a Creditors Ledger, and a General Ledger; while partnerships often have a Private Ledger to keep the partners' affairs private from other members of staff. Every transaction that takes place in a business results in a double entry in the ledger as we have seen, with one account being debited and one being credited.

(4) The Trial Balance

At any moment, although it is usually only done once a month, we can take out a Trial Balance of the Ledger. Since every ledger entry has a debit entry and a matching credit entry, if we have done our book-keeping without any errors we should find that the total of the balances on all the accounts with debit balances exactly equals the total of the balances on all the accounts with credit balances. If the Trial Balance does in fact balance we can say that it is highly likely that our book-keeping has been correctly done, though it is possible to have a few errors still present (for example compensating errors – where we have made the same mistake on both the debit and credit sides). The Trial Balance is examined in greater detail in Chapter 12.

(5) The Final Accounts of the business, and the Balance Sheet

From the Trial Balance we can take out what are called the Final Accounts of the business: a **Trading Account** and a **Profit and Loss Account**. The Trading Account enables us to find our **gross profit on trading** (the difference between the cost price and the selling price of our goods). The Profit and Loss Account starts with this gross profit, and by deducting all the overhead expenses, leaves us the **net profit** (clean profit) of our business.

Finally we can take out a Balance Sheet of the business after working out the profits for the year. It takes the form of a list of the assets of the business set against a list of the liabilities of the business. The assets are divided into two main groups, the **fixed assets** and the **current assets**. Fixed assets are purchased for use in the business, and include premises, plant and machinery, office equipment, motor vehicles, etc. They have a long life (more than a year) although they do depreciate in the end and are finally disposed of. Current assets have a life of less than one year and eventually turn into cash. For example stock is sold and becomes cash, or stock is sold and becomes debtors who eventually pay and the asset 'debtors' turns into cash.

Liabilities are what the business owes to outsiders, either trade creditors (suppliers) or financial creditors, such as banks and building societies. Among these outsiders we must include the owner or owners of the business, to whom the capital they have supplied must one day be returned, together with any balances of profits left in the business over the years. Remember capital is not an asset; it is a liability. It is what the business owes to the owner of the business.

3   THE DOUBLE-ENTRY SYSTEM AND BANKERS

Modern banking uses advanced computerised methods and it might seem that there is little relationship between the traditional double-entry system as illustrated in Fig. 11.1 and the type of accounting records we are keeping in our branches today. In fact, the link is much closer than at first appears, and an ability to be able to think in double entries, and see the way any particular transaction with a customer will be dealt with in the double-entry system is a tremendous advantage to a banker. To be able to see the accounts from the customer's point of view is also very important, since many of them will be using less sophisticated systems than the bank, and even very rudimentary systems which are short cuts on double-entry – like the Simplex System. (*Note*: Any lecturer in business calculations who thinks his/her students would benefit from seeing this very simple system of accounting can obtain a specimen exercise and working papers for every student by applying to George Vyner Ltd, Freepost, Holmfirth, Huddersfield, HD7 1BR – or phone Brian Senior on (0484) 685221. There is no charge and an Answer Booklet is supplied.)

The chief points to note as far as bankers are concerned, when thinking of double-entry systems are these:

(a) *The actual double entries*   Every branch is running a specialised set of accounts for its customers, in which slips of various sorts are the original documents. They may be:

(i) deposits by the customer, which are credited to the customer (credit the giver) and debited to Cash Account as the money is merged with the bank's cash funds.

(ii) any withdrawal by the customer is debited to the customer and credited to Cash Account as the funds are paid out.

(iii) any cheque used by the customer is debited to the customer's account (they have received back the funds for their own private purposes) but the credit is made somewhere in the accounts of another bank customer, either in our own bank, or in any other bank, after inter-bank adjustments, through the clearing system.

(iv) interest may be credited to a customer's account (if it is a type of account that earns interest) and it will be debited in Interest Payable Account – a Nominal Account at the Head Office (as one of the losses (i.e. expenses) of the bank).

(v) all charges and interest payable by the customer on loans, overdrafts, etc., will be debited in the customer's account and credited in Head Office's accounts as Charges Receivable or Interest Receivable. These are nominal accounts and profits of the bank.

(b) *Branch accounts*   The branch is also running Head Office Accounts which deal with all the many transactions between the branch and Head Office. For example we might have transactions for assets purchased, salaries of branch staff, overhead expenses like rent, rates, lighting, heating, etc. These may involve invoices, credit notes, debit notes and other documents. These are dealt with more fully in Chapter 15.

(c) *The books of original entry*   As far as books of original entry go the computerised system virtually does away with them, because the documents themselves are retained long enough to be turned up if needed, and a laborious recording of documents is avoided. Instead, all the entries are made, under the guidance of the computer programs, direct into the various accounts.

(d) *The Ledger*   The computer stores a vast ledger of accounts split up into sections which probably vary from bank to bank. We shall all have our Debtors and our Creditors, by the million. We shall also have a General Ledger, with its memory packed with nominal accounts which are losses (like Rent Account, Discount Allowed

Account, Wages Account, etc.) and Nominal Accounts which are profits (like Interest Received, Discount Received, Profit on Foreign Exchange, etc.). We will also have all the Asset Accounts for all the branches. To make sense of these millions of accounts we shall have various Control Accounts, which will in the end all fall into place as part of the bank's Trial Balance.

(e) *The Trial Balance* The Trial Balance of an ordinary business is illustrated in Chapter 12. It is simply a list of all the balances on the accounts of any firm. With millions of accounts to worry about a Bank's Trial Balance would be a fantastically long print-out, and it has to be shortened by grouping the accounts together in some sensible way. Fortunately for our syllabus we do not need to study the Final Accounts of the bank, but we should understand the Final Accounts of sole traders, partnerships and limited companies since these are the customers with whom we are dealing every day. The starting point is the Trial Balance – which tells us the book-keeping has been properly done, in double entries which exactly balance one another. From a correct Trial Balance we can begin to draw up the Final Accounts of any business, and hence find the profit.

(f) *The Trading Account* The Trading Account is the first part of the Final Accounts of all trading businesses – though where a business manufactures the things that it trades in it will be necessary to draw up a Manufacturing Account first. The Manufacturing Account then passes on the manufactured goods to the Sales Department which actually handles the sales side of the business. Profit in a trading firm is the difference between the cost price of something and the selling price. By using five accounts – the Stock Account, the Purchases Account, the Purchases Returns Account, the Sales Account and the Sales Returns Account – we shall see in Chapter 12 that we can work out the profit on trading. This profit is called the gross profit – so called because 'gross' means 'fat' and this profit has not been reduced by having the overheads deducted from it. The final result of the Trading Account therefore is the 'Gross Profit on Trading'.

(g) *The Profit and Loss Account* The gross profit is now taken into the Profit and Loss Account and any further bits of profit not made by trading are added to it.

For example Interest Received Account will have some profits tucked away in it, and so will Charges Receivable Account. Set against these will be the much more numerous overhead expenses of the business, such as Light and Heat, Salaries, Advertising, etc. When all these are deducted from the total profits we find the net profit, or clean profit. The word 'net' comes from the French word 'nettoyer' – to clean. The net profit belongs to the owners of the business, either the sole trader, or the partners, or the shareholders if it is a limited company. The sole trader and partners get the profits at once. The shareholders only get the profit if the directors recommend a dividend.

(h) *The Balance Sheet* The final part of any set of Final Accounts is the Balance Sheet. What is a Balance Sheet? It is a list of balances still left on the books of a business after all the losses of the business and all the profits have been cleared into the Trading Account and Profit and Loss Account. All that is left of all those accounts is one final figure – the net profit. All the Nominal Accounts are clear and only the assets, the liabilities and the personal accounts are left. Of course, with a bank there are millions of them, but all the customers can be lumped together in one figure – creditors of the bank. Of course some may have overdrafts, or loans, and they can be lumped together as debtors. We have a number of asset accounts, Premises, Plant and

Machinery, Furniture and Fittings, etc. and we have a number of liabilities – including the capital owed to the shareholders.

All these items are set down on the Balance Sheet, with assets on one side and liabilities on the other. The two sides should balance. What is a Balance Sheet? It is a snapshot picture of a business, taken at a given moment in time – the last second of the last day of the financial year which has just ended. It shows us what the business owns, and what the business owes, and the profit it has made during that year.

We shall see examples of these in Chapters 12, 13 and 14.

4 A REVISION TEST ON DOUBLE-ENTRY BOOK-KEEPING

It is impossible to set an exercise on double-entry book-keeping. Instead you are invited to check your knowledge by this test exercise, which covers the syllabus subject matter. Cover the page with a sheet of paper, and slide it down to reveal the first question. Answer this question and then slide the page down to read the correct answer and the next question.

Answers	*Questions*
——	1 Who invented double-entry book-keeping?
1 The Lombards from Northern Italy, the first real bankers.	2 What is the principle behind double-entry book-keeping?
2 Every transaction that ever takes place affects two persons, or two accounts in book-keeping. There is always a giver, who gives goods or services or money, and there is always a receiver, who receives goods or services or money.	3 What is the basic rule of double-entry book-keeping?
3 Debit the account that receives goods or services or money; credit the account that gives goods or services or money.	4 A. Customer deposits £1,000 in cash. What is the double entry?
4 Debit Cash Account, which receives £1,000. Credit A. Customer who gives £1,000.	5 A. Customer is granted a loan of £5,000. What is the double entry?
5 Debit the Customer's Loan Account, which has received £5,000. Credit the customer's Current Account – the customer has in effect deposited the money borrowed in his/her Current Account.	6 A local factory manager sends the bank a list of 5,000 employees who are to receive the sums of salary indicated against their names. He also sends a cheque drawn on the factory's Current Account for the full amount. What is the double entry?

| *Answers* | *Questions* |

6   Debit the factory's Current Account – it has received back the use of money formerly deposited with the bank. Credit the individual accounts of the employees, who have effectively deposited their salaries with the bank.

7   The Bank buys 12 ATMs from Flashcash Plc at a price of £15,000 each. What is the double entry?

7   Debit Electronic Machinery Account which has received £180,000 of machinery. Credit Flashcash Plc who are creditors of the bank, awaiting payment in due course.

8   What are the three classes of account?

8   Personal accounts, nominal accounts and real accounts.

9   What happens to a personal account at the end of the year?

9   It appears on the Balance Sheet, either as a debtor or a creditor.

10   What happens to a nominal account at the end of the year?

10   Nominal accounts are accounts where the money is there 'in name only'. The amount recorded is either a profit or a loss. They get cleared into the Trading Account if they are trading items, or into the Profit and Loss Account if they are overhead expenses or non-trading profits. They are used to work out the profits of the business.

11   What happens to a real account at the end of the financial year?

11   Real Accounts are assets. They appear on the Balance Sheet as assets of the business.

12   What is the final result of the Trading Account?

12   We find the gross profit.

13   What is the final result of the Profit and Loss Account?

13   We find the net profit.

14   Who gets the net profit?

14   The sole trader, or the partners, or the shareholders of a company (but only if the directors recommend a dividend at the AGM of the company).

15   What is the final element in a set of final accounts?

15   The Balance Sheet

16   What is a Balance Sheet?

16   It is a snapshot of the state of affairs of a business, taken at any time, but usually at the last second of the last day of the financial year.

17   Go over the test if you are not sure of all the answers.

12 The Final Accounts of small businesses

OBJECTIVES

At the end of this chapter you should:
1 Understand the Trial Balance as the starting point for the Final Accounts of a business;
2 Be able to find the **gross profit** of a business by drawing up a Trading Account;
3 Be able to find the **net profit** of a business by drawing up a Profit and Loss Account;
4 Understand the Balance Sheet as a residue of the Trial Balance, and as a snapshot of the affairs of a business, usually a snapshot taken after business closes on the last day of the financial year;
5 Be able to draw up the Balance Sheet of a small business and a full set of Final Accounts from a Trial Balance.

1 THE TRIAL BALANCE OF A BUSINESS'S BOOKS

We saw in Chapter 11 that simple book-keeping leads to a set of accounts, some of which are personal accounts, some nominal accounts (profits and losses of the business) and some real accounts (assets that the business really owns). Every month, if we are keeping a full set of double-entry books, we extract a Trial Balance from these accounts to see if the Trial Balance balances, and if it does we assume that the books have been carefully kept and are correct. From this Trial Balance we can now draw up a set of Final Accounts, which consist of a Trading Account, a Profit and Loss Account and a Balance Sheet of the business. To make this clear let us first look at a reasonably detailed Trial Balance. This is shown in Fig. 12.1. Two columns of notes are given alongside the Trial Balance, which indicate whether the item listed is a trading item (which will come in the Trading Account), or a profit (or loss) item, which will come in the Profit and Loss Account, or a Balance Sheet item. A Balance Sheet item is one that is not concerned only with this year's trading activities, but has to be carried over to next year. This means that the item is either an asset, for long-term use in the business, or a liability, owing to someone at the end of the year and due for settlement either in the short-term (next year) or in the long-term (such as a mortgage repayable

Trial Balance of T Marshall's books as at 31 December 19..

Accounts	Dr £	Cr £	Notes (Dr)	Notes (Cr)
Purchases	26,800.00		Trading A/c	
Sales		71,868.50		Trading A/c
Purchases Returns		1,460.00		Trading A/c
Sales Returns	1,568.50		Trading A/c	
Stock (as at 1 Jan 19..)	4,200.00		Trading A/c	
Salaries	16,600.00		Loss	
Office Expenses	2,256.00		Loss	
Light and Heat	2,188.50		Loss	
Redecorations	465.80		Loss	
Rent (warehouse)	3,450.00		Loss	
Discount Allowed	248.80		Loss	
Discount Received		232.80		Profit
Commission Received		432.60		Profit
Land and Buildings	88,750.00		Asset	
Furniture and Fittings	14,250.00		Asset	
Motor Vehicles	16,500.00		Asset	
Sundry Debtors	4,680.80		Asset	
Sundry Creditors		6,430.80		Liabilities
Plant and Machinery	12,880.00		Asset	
Cash	764.25		Asset	
Bank	12,047.85		Asset	
Drawings (T. Marshall)	7,620.00		Special asset	
Mortgage on Premises		62,000.00		Liability
Loan (Finance Co.)		11,000.00		Liability
Capital (T. Marshall)		62,175.80		Special liability
Carriage out	330.00		Loss	
	£215,600.50	£215,600.50		

The closing stock was found to be worth £10,300.00 (Trading Account item)

Fig. 12.1 A Trial Balance (with notes)

over many years). The longest-term liability of all is the capital which is owed back to the proprietor when the business ceases to trade, which may be many years later.

Figure 12.1 shows a typical Trial Balance, prepared on 31 December 19.., after T Marshall has been in business for one year. Note that a Trial Balance is always made out 'as at a certain date'. This is because it is only really valid at that moment in time – the close of business on a given date. The next morning things will start to change and the Trial Balance will have to be altered too. Study the notes to the items carefully. You will notice that a summary of the notes reveals that the debit and credit columns contain the following types of item:

Dr	Cr
3 Trading Account items	2 Trading Account items
Loss items	Profit items
Assets	Liabilities
A special asset	A special liability
(drawings of the proprietor)	(capital of the proprietor)

To make the picture complete, we should point out that outside the Trial Balance, not yet recorded on the books of the business, is the closing stock figure found by taking stock at the end of the trading period. This, like the opening stock shown, is a Trading Account item.

The procedure for taking out a set of final accounts is explained later in this chapter. Briefly the five Trading Account items, together with the 'Closing Stock' figure referred to, are used to draw up a Trading Account, which enables us to find the profit on trading. This is called the *gross profit* in accountancy. From that gross profit figure which is taken into the Profit and Loss Account, we have to deduct all the losses (the expenses of the business) and add any other profits (such as commission received). This gives us the *net profit*. The items left are then marshalled into the Balance Sheet, which starts the new year, and all its activities.

Before going into all this, try drawing up some Trial Balances from the exercises given in Exercise 12.1.

■ EXERCISE 12.1

(a) Prepare a Trial Balance from the following accounts, which appear in Philip Mayne's books on 31 December 19..:

Discount Allowed £226.45; Capital £52,806.30; Rates £2,250.00; Office Expenses £3,142.50; Loan from M Louth £25,000.00; Stock in hand (at 1 Jan 19..) £8,600.00; Sundry Creditors £2,845.00; Cash at Bank £2,876.85; Plant and Machinery £14,750.00; Returns Inwards £845.50; Selling Expenses £8,248.50; Sales Account £71,860.00; Purchases £26,880.50; Cash in hand £465.50; Freehold Property £82,000.00; Sundry Debtors £4,225.50; Returns Outwards £1,200.00; Commission Received £800.00.

(b) The following accounts in J Shannahan's books have balances on them at 30 April 19... You are asked to arrange them in Trial Balance form:

	£
Sundry Debtors' A/cs	2,516.50
Sundry Creditors' A/cs	4,826.50
Land and Buildings A/c	63,000.00
Plant and Machinery A/c	41,550.00
Furniture and Fittings A/c	3,825.00
Opening Stock at 1 April 19..	13,266.00
Cash A/c	175.00
Bank A/c	2,475.00
Purchases A/c	26,875.00
Purchases Returns A/c	175.00

Sales A/c	96,365.00
Sales Returns A/c	1,365.00
Office Salaries A/c	33,265.50
Light and Heat A/c	604.40
Telephone A/c	476.70
Warehouse Expenses A/c	14,595.50
General Expenses A/c	3,295.50
Community Charges A/c	2,462.90
Insurance A/c	380.50
Rent Received A/c	1,650.00
Drawings A/c (J Shannahan)	12,228.00
Loan A/c (Helpful Bank Plc)	11,000.00
Commission Received A/c	28,340.00
Capital A/c	80,000.00

(c) Prepare a Trial Balance as at 31 December 19.. from the following ledger accounts of Peter Trench, exporter of manufactured goods.

Account	£
Premises	75,000.00
Bad Debts	1,426.00
Commission Received	4,288.00
Motor Vehicles	16,750.00
Furniture	23,950.00
Drawings (P Trench)	23,800.00
Warehouse Wages	21,150.00
Discount Received	324.50
Creditors	4,284.00
Debtors	2,562.00
Carriage In	382.00
Returns In	2,141.00
Returns Out	460.50
Cash in hand	268.00
Machinery	31,250.00
Office Salaries	42,376.00
Sales	197,989.00
Stock at 1 January	24,450.00
Postage	1,656.50
Office Expenses	4,275.50
Bank Loan	60,000.00
Capital	61,640.90
Insurance	2,450.50
Community Charges	3,250.00
Light and Heat	3,276.80
Purchases	48,572.60

2   FINDING THE GROSS PROFIT IN THE TRADING ACCOUNT

In any profit calculation we first find the gross profit, for which we need to know the cost price of the goods sold and the selling price. Gross profit is the difference between the cost price and the selling price. Since, in real life, some of the things we buy (purchases) are returned for various reasons, and some of the things we sell are subsequently returned as unsuitable, the net purchases figure (purchases less returns) and the net sales figures (sales less returns) are the figures that really interest us. Net sales is usually called **net turnover**, and is an important figure, taken into account when buying and selling businesses. (Banking students should be careful not to confuse a company's net turnover (sales less returns for the period) with the turnover on the company's Bank Account.

Besides these returns there is one other aspect that is important when drawing up a Trading Account. It is the question of stock. In every trading period we start off with a certain amount of stock on the shelves. This is called Opening Stock and is later sold, perhaps in the first few days of the next trading period. It has to be replaced by more purchases, and so on throughout the year, but when the end of the trading period arrives we shall have some unsold stock on the shelves. This is called Closing Stock. We count and value this stock (valuing it **at cost price, or net realisable value, whichever is lower**). Thus most of our stock is valued at cost price, but stock which has deteriorated below cost value is only valued at what it will fetch on stock-taking day. Using the figures from the Trial balance in Fig. 12.1 we have a Trading Account as shown in Fig. 12.2. The result is a gross profit of £51,060.00. Study this Trading Account and the notes below it.

Trading Account for Year ending 31 December 19..

		£			£
Opening Stock		4,200.00	Sales		71,868.50
Purchases	26,800.00		*Less* Returns		1,568.50
Less Returns	1,460.00		Net Turnover		70,300.00
Net Purchases		25,340.00			
Total stock available		29,540.00			
Less Closing Stock		10,300.00			
Cost of Stock Sold		19,240.00			
Gross Profit					
(To Profit and Loss A/c)		51,060.00			
		£70,300.00			£70,300.00

Fig. 12.2   Finding the gross profit

Notes

1   The Trading Account is always headed 'for year ending' or something similar to show the period to which it refers – in this case one year.

2   For convenience the Sales Returns figure is deducted from the Sales figure to bring out the net sales figure, which is usually called the Net Turnover.

3   The same thing applies to the Purchases and Purchases Returns figures, but we also have the Stock figures to take into account. This is best understood if we look at the line reading 'Cost of Stock Sold'. What did the stock we sold for £70,300.00 actually cost us? The answer is that we sold the stock on the shelves at the start of the year (Opening Stock) plus what we purchased – less the returns – giving a total stock of £29,540.00. As we still had Closing Stock that we had not sold we must deduct this, leaving the Cost of Stock Sold at £19,240.00.

4   Taking this from the Sales figure we find we made a gross profit of £51,060.00

5   The gross profit figure is then taken to the Profit and Loss Account to begin that Account.

You should now try one or two exercises in finding the gross profit, as in Exercise 12.2 below.

■ EXERCISE 12.2

(a)   At the end of her trading year, on 31 December 19.., Nina Hewson has the following balances on her account: Opening Stock £4,276.50; Purchases £37,295.80; Sales £95,387.50; Purchases returns £1,295.80; Sales Returns £1,887.50. A check on her stock in hand gives a total for Closing Stock of £3,875.55. Prepare her Trading Account and discover the gross profit.

(b)   At the end of his trading year, on 30 June 19.., R Markowitz has the following balances on his accounts: Sales £97,350.00; Purchases £28,550.00; Sales Returns £1,050.00; Purchases Returns £1,550.00. Opening Stock had been £12,500.00 on 1 July the previous year. Stock-taking revealed a Closing Stock figure of £10,370.00. Prepare his Trading Account and hence calculate his gross profit for the year.

(c)   When M Olaleye closes her books for the year on 31 March 19.. she has the following balances on her accounts: Purchases £89,875.60; Sales £224,060.40; Purchases Returns £1,675.60; Sales Returns £4,246.50; Opening Stock £19,286.60. Stock-taking revealed a Closing Stock figure of £14,286.60. Prepare her Trading Account and thus find her gross profit.

(d)   On 31 March 19.. Abdul Shaik has the following balances on his books: Opening Stock £12,800.00; Purchases £126,560.00; Sales £195,800.00; Sales Returns £4,760.00; Purchases Returns £3,868.00. The Closing Stock is found to be £16,908.60. Prepare his Trading Account and find the gross profit of his business.

3   FINDING THE NET PROFIT IN THE PROFIT AND LOSS ACCOUNT

Having found the gross profit we can now carry this into the Profit and Loss Account and find the net profit by adding to the gross profit any other profits made, and deducting any losses such as the various overhead expenses. Again using the figures from Fig. 12.1 we have the Profit and Loss Account in Fig. 12.3.

Profit and Loss Account for year ending 31 December 19..

	£		£
Salaries	16,600.00	Gross profit	51,060.00
Office Expenses	2,256.00	Discount Received	232.80
Light and Heat	2,188.50	Commission Received	432.60
Repairs	465.80	Total profits	51,725.40
Rent	3,450.00		
Discount Allowed	248.80		
Carriage Out	330.00		
Total expenses	25,539.10		
Net profit	26,186.30		
	£51,725.40		£51,725.40

			£
		Net profit (to Capital Account)	26,186.30

Fig. 12.3   Finding the net profit

Notes

1   The gross profit is transferred in from the Trading Account.

2   To this are added any other profits made, in this case Discount Received and Commission Received.

3   The expenses (losses) of the business are transferred in on the debit side, and when totalled come to £25,539.10.

4   Taking these losses from the total profits we find that the net profit (clean profit) is £26,186.30.

5   To whom does this profit belong? Answer: to the proprietor, and in a sole trader business it would be transferred to the credit side of his/her Capital Account. Why the credit side? Because the business owes the profits to the owner of the business, who is a creditor for the amount due.

Now try some of the exercises below.

■ EXERCISE 12.3

(a)   Prepare the Profit and Loss Account from Peter Parkinson's books for the year ending 31 December 19... Figures are as follows: Trading Account balance (gross profit) £38,288.60; Rent Paid Account £2,880.00; Light and Heat Account £1,380.50; Office Salaries Account £14,945.00.

(b)   Prepare the Profit and Loss Account of Marie Tinderman, for the year ending 31 March 19... Her Trial Balance shows: gross profit £48,685.60; Business Rates Account £2,860.00; Light and Heat Account £486.60; Commission Received Account £3,895.50; Office Salaries Account £23,956.60; Rent Received Account £1,240.80; Telephone Expenses Account £637.59; Sundry Expenses Account £8,132.45; Postage Account £1,425.65.

(c)   Prepare from the following list of balances the Profit and Loss Account of R Matlock for the year ending 30 June 19...

	£
Gross profit	78,562.85
Rent Paid A/c	2,965.70

Rent Received A/c   2,525.25
Office Salaries A/c   19,389.75
Office Expenses A/c   12,541.00

Office Light and Heat A/c   2,454.60
Advertising Expenses A/c   7,365.85
Interest Paid A/c   615.75
Discount Allowed A/c   220.00
Discount Received   225.65

(d) From the following figures, prepare Valerie Burton's Profit and Loss Account for the year ending 31 December 19..:

	£
Gross profit	52,840.75
Business Rates A/c	2,870.24
Office Expenses A/c	11,490.95
Lighting and Heating A/c	670.38
Discount Received A/c	256.60
Commission Received A/c	3,458.60
Interest Paid A/c	420.00
Salaries A/c	15,674.59
Discount Allowed A/c	436.58
Advertising Expenses A/c	2,816.65
Transport Charges A/c	2,176.60
Rent Received A/c	3,850.25

4 THE RESIDUE OF THE TRIAL BALANCE

We are about to move on to the last part of the Final Accounts of a business, the Balance Sheet. Before we do so there is one point we need to make clear. We drew up the Trading Account and the Profit and Loss Account by transferring figures into them from the ordinary accounts. Thus we transferred the purchases figure of £26,800.00 from the debit side of Purchases Account to the debit side of the Trading Account. Of course we can't make a debit entry like that unless we make a credit entry somewhere else. This entry is made on the credit side of Purchases Account, and as a result it leaves the Purchases Account clear (and ready to start a new financial year). The two accounts would therefore look like this:

Purchases Account

19..	£	19..	£
Jan 1			
to			
Dec 31 Numerous entries totalling	26,800.00	Dec 31 Transfer to Trading A/c	26,800.00
	£26,800.00		£26,800.00

Continued

Trading Account for year ending 31 December 19..

19..	£	
Dec 31 Purchases	26,800.00	

Fig. 12.4   Closing off the Purchases Account

Notes

1   The action of transferring the purchases for the year to the Trading A/c closes off the Purchases A/c.

2   It has no balance on it, and therefore disappears from the Trial Balance.

3   This will be true of all the expense accounts and all the profit accounts, leaving only a residue of the Trial Balance, which is shown in Fig. 12.6 below.

4   The only account that is different is the Stock Account, because this account is not only closed off as the stock at the start of the year is transferred to the Trading Account, but is immediately reopened with a debit balance as the closing stock figure for the year is debited to bring it onto the books. The Stock Account therefore looks as shown in Fig. 12.5.

Stock Account

19..		£	19..		£
Jan 1	Opening Stock	4,200.00	Dec 31	Transfer to Trading A/c	4,200.00
19..		£			
Jan 1	Opening Stock	10,300.00			

Fig. 12.5   Closing the Stock Account and re-opening it

Figure 12.6 shows the residue of T Marshall's Trial Balance, based on Fig. 12.1 but leaving out all the items cleared off into the final accounts we have prepared.

Trial Balance of T Marshall's books as at 31 December 19..

Accounts	Dr £	Cr £	Notes (Dr)	Notes (Cr)
Land and Buildings	88,750.00		Asset	
Furniture and Fittings	14,250.00		Asset	
Motor Vehicles	16,500.00		Asset	
Sundry Debtors	4,680.80		Asset	
Sundry Creditors		6,430.80		Liabilities
Plant and Machinery	12,880.00		Asset	
Cash	764.25		Asset	
Bank	12,047.85		Asset	
Mortgage on Premises		62,000.00		Liability
Loan (Finance Co)		11,000.00		Liability
Stock (at close)	10,300.00		Asset	
Capital (T Marshall)		62,175.80		Liability
Drawings (T Marshall)	7,620.00		Special asset	
Profit and Loss balance		26,186.30		Special liability
	£167,792.90	167,792.90		

Fig. 12.6   The residue of the Trial Balance

5 THE BALANCE SHEET IDEA

Balance Sheets were invented in 1536, when Simon Stevin of Bruges was teaching his royal patron double-entry book-keeping. After drawing up the Trading Account and Profit and Loss Account from his Trial Balance, a procedure which as we have seen leaves all the loss accounts and all the profit accounts clear (and therefore removed from the Trial Balance), he had only a few accounts left. They were nearly all assets and liabilities but they did include the balance of profit left on the Profit and Loss Account, and the Drawings Account which recorded the sums drawn by the proprietor during the year. He arranged these in what he called a 'Statement of Affairs' – a name still used today in bankruptcy cases, but replaced by the name 'Balance Sheet' for ordinary businesses, partnerships and companies.

When he arranged these assets and liabilities in a Balance Sheet Stevin actually made a mistake and listed them with the assets on the right hand side and the liabilities on the left hand side. This error has been perpetuated down to the present day in the UK, even though Simon Stevin's own country long ago corrected the error. Fortunately the Companies Act of 1985 now says that for company accounts assets should be on the left and liabilities on the right, as is done in the rest of Europe. For many small businesses the old method is still used so we shall find many of our customers presenting sets of final accounts where the Balance Sheet is in Simon Stevin's original form. The style of layout is quite important and is illustrated in Fig. 12.7 and explained in the notes below the Balance Sheet.

Balance Sheet of T Marshall as at 31 December 19..

	£	£		£	£
Fixed assets:			*Capital*:		
Land and Buildings		88,750.00	At start of year		62,175.80
Plant and Machinery		12,880.00	Add Net profit	26,186.30	
Furniture and Fittings		14,250.00	Less Drawings	7,620.00	
Motor Vehicles		16,500.00			18,566.30
		132,380.00			80,742.10
Current assets:			*Long-term liabilities*:		
Stock	10,300.00		Mortgage on premises	62,000.00	
Sundry Debtors	4,680.80		Loan A/c (Finance Co)	11,000.00	
Cash at bank	12,047.85				73,000.00
Cash in hand	764.25				
		27,792.90	*Current liabilities*:		
			Creditors		6,430.80
		£160,172.90			£160,172.90

Fig. 12.7   *T Marshall's Balance Sheet*

Notes
1 The assets are listed in the order of permanence, with the most permanent asset (Land and Buildings) stated first.
2 Fixed assets are assets which are used in the business over several years and cannot be disposed of without seriously affecting the profit-making capacity of the business.

3   Current assets are assets which can be disposed of, and indeed that is the whole idea. Stock is sold either for cash or on credit to debtors who eventually pay and yield a profit. The most liquid item (cash) is shown last.

4   The liabilities side is also arranged in order of permanence. Capital is the most permanent liability – it is not repaid until the proprietor ceases to trade. Notice that the amount owing to the proprietor year by year grows, as profits (if they are not shown as drawings) are added to the capital at the start of the year. Mortgages and loans are repaid over a number of years and are called long-term liabilities but creditors are current liabilities repayable in less than a year – usually within one month.

You should now practice drawing up some Balance Sheets using the exercises below.

■ EXERCISE 12.4

(a)   Prepare Peter Marlow's Balance Sheet in the order of permanence from the abbreviated Trial Balance given below.

Trial Balance (Peter Marlow) as at 31 December 19..

Accounts	Dr £	Cr £
Cash	150	
Bank	6,880	
Stock (at Close)	14,800	
Debtors	1,660	
Motor Vehicles	15,600	
Land and Buildings	60,000	
Office Equipment	12,060	
Plant and Machinery	33,600	
Capital (at start)		81,050
Net profit		38,600
Mortgages on Premises		35,000
Creditors		4,850
Drawings	14,750	
	£159,500	159,500

(b)   Prepare Anna Fordson's Balance Sheet from the Trial Balance given below, arranging the items in the order of permanence.

Trial Balance (Anna Fordson) as at 31 December 19..

Accounts	Dr £	Cr £
Cash	136.50	
Bank	12,848.56	
Sundry debtors	4,036.50	
Stock (at close)	11,245.00	
Investments (Current Asset)	7,400.00	

cfwd 35,666.56

	B/fwd 35,666.56	
Motor Vehicles	13,800.78	
Furniture and Fittings	2,515.85	
Plant and Machinery	24,400.00	
Land and Buildings	83,000.00	
Creditors		3,997.20
Mortgages on Premises		50,000.00
Capital (at start)		77,415.99
Bank Loan		13,600.00
Drawings	24,880.60	
Net profit for year		39,250.60
	£184,263.79	184,263.79

(c) Prepare Peter Dorrit's Balance Sheet in the order of permanence from the figures given below in his Trial Balance.

Trial Balance (Peter Dorrit) as at 31 March 19..

Accounts	Dr. £	Cr. £
Cash	488.56	
Bank	14,780.50	
Debtors and creditors	4,484.85	2,949.25
Closing stock	12,500.00	
Motor Vehicles	17,675.80	
Furniture and Fittings	2,865.80	
Land and Buildings	79,000.00	
Mortgages on Premises		51,940.00
Capital		36,555.00
Drawings	14,500.00	
Profit and Loss A/c		54,851.26
	£146,295.51	146,295.51

■ EXERCISE 12.5 PREPARING A FULL SET OF FINAL ACCOUNTS

In each of the exercises below you are asked to prepare a full set of final accounts, Trading Account, Profit and Loss Account and Balance Sheet for the sole trader concerned, from the Trial Balance provided.

1 Books of Mary Simpson, who runs a hair dressing salon. Her closing stock was valued at £894.60. Her final Trial Balance was as follows:

Trial Balance of M Simpson's books as at 31 December 19..

Accounts	Dr £	Cr £
Purchases	9,236.50	
Sales		48,254.75
Purchases Returns		136.50
Sales returns	12.25	
Stock (as at 1 Jan 19..)	429.50	
Salaries	15,245.50	
Office Expenses	127.30	
Light and Heat	585.65	
Redecorations	195.20	
Laundry Expenses	525.75	
Rates	1,124.20	
Discount Received		248.55
Commission Received		820.50
Land and Buildings	38,500.00	
Furniture & Fittings	1,850.00	
Motor Vehicles	5,800.00	
Sundry Debtors	126.50	
Sundry Creditors		485.50
Salon Equipment	3,850.00	
Cash	424.65	
Bank	5,850.60	
Drawings (M Simpson)	12,284.00	
Mortgage on premises		25,000.00
M Vehicles Expenses	425.00	
Capital (M Simpson) at 1 Jan		21,646.80
	£96,592.60	96,592.60

2   Books of M Shah, who runs a retail computer outlet. His final Trial Balance reads as follows:

Trial Balance of M Shah's book as at 31 December 19..

Accounts	Dr £	Cr £
Purchases	86,844.50	
Sales		186,252.50
Purchases Returns		324.80
Sales returns	4,225.60	
Stock (as at 1 Jan 19..)	8,715.80	
Salaries	29,214.85	
Office Expenses	13,826.75	
Light and Heat	876.20	
Motor Expenses	1,868.58	
Rent (Warehouse)	4,500.00	
Discount Allowed	865.50	
Discount Received		424.25
Repair Fees Received		8,475.60
Land and Buildings	61,000.00	
Furniture & Fittings	13,825.00	
Motor Vehicles	12,260.00	
Sundry Debtors	124.50	
Sundry Creditors		828.60
Rates	4,640.50	
Cash	926.25	
Bank	27,926.80	
Drawings (M Shah)	19,650.20	
Mortgage on premises		38,560.00
Loan (Finance Co)		20,000.00
Capital (M Shah)		36,425.28
	£291,291.03	291,291.03

Closing stock was valued at £9,250.27.

■ ANSWERS

Exercise 12.1   (*Exercise (c) is shown in full*)   **(a)** Trial Balance agrees at £154,511.30 **(b)** Trial Balance agrees at £222,356.50   **(c)** Trial Balance agrees at £328,986.90. The full working is shown above.

Book of Peter Trench
Trial Balance as at 31 December 19..

Account	Dr £	Cr £
Premises	75,000.00	
Bad Debts	1,426.00	
Commission Received		4,288.00
Motor Vehicles	16,750.00	
Furniture	23,950.00	
Drawings (P Trench)	23,800.00	
Warehouse Wages	21,150.00	
Discount Received		324.50
Creditors		4,284.00
Debtors	2,562.00	
Carriage In	382.00	
Returns In	2,141.00	
Returns Out		460.50
Cash in hand	268.00	
Machinery	31,250.00	
Office Salaries	42,376.00	
Sales		197,989.000
Stock at 1 January	24,450.00	
Postage	1,656.50	
Office Expenses	4,275.50	
Bank Loan		60,000.00
Capital		61,640.90
Insurance	2,450.50	
Rates	3,250.00	
Light & Heat	3,276.80	
Purchases	48,572.60	
	£328,986.90	328,986.90

Note: When working out which accounts would normally have debit balances and which would have credit balances remember the rule:

    Assets and losses (expenses) have debit balances.

    Liabilities and profits have credit balances.

Exercise 12.2 **(a)** N Hewson: Gross Profit £57,099.05; totals of Trading A/c £93,500.00. **(b)** R Markowitz: Gross Profit £67,170.00; totals of Trading A/c £96,300.00 **(c)** M Olaleye: Gross Profit £126,613.90; totals of Trading A/c £219,813.90. **(d)** A Shaik: Gross Profit £72,456.60; totals on Trading A/c £191,040.00.

Exercise 12.3 **(a)** Peter Parkinson: net profit £19,083.10; totals of Profit and Loss A/c £38,288.60 **(b)** Marie Tinderman: net profit £16,323.01; totals of Profit and Loss A/c £53,821.90 **(c)** R Matlock: net profit £35,761.10; totals of Profit and Loss A/c £81,313.75 **(d)** Valerie Burton: net profit £23,850.21; totals of Profit and Loss A/c £60,406.20.

Exercise 12.4 The answer to (a) is as follows:

Books of Peter Marlow
Balance Sheet as at 31 December 19..

Fixed Assets	£			£
Land and Buildings	60,000	Capital at Start		81,050
Plant and Machinery	33,600	*Add* Net Profit	38,600	
Office Equipment	12,060	*Less* Drawings	14,750	
Motor Vehicles	15,600			23,850
	121,260			104,900
Current Assets		*Long-term Liabilities*		
Stock	14,800	Mortgage		35,000
Debtors	1,660			
Bank	6,880	*Current Liabilities*		
Cash in hand	150	23,490	Creditors		4,850
		£144,750			£144,750

(b) Anna Fordson: Fixed Assets £123,716.63; Current Assets £35,666.56; Total £159,383.19; Capital at end £91,785.99; Long Term Liabilities £63,600.00; Current Liabilities £3,997.20.
(c) Peter Dorrit: Fixed Assets £99,541.60; Current Assets £32,253.91; Total £131,795.51; Capital at end £76,906.26; Long-term Liabilities £51,940.00; Current Liabilities £2,949.25.

Exercise 12.5 **1** Books of M Simpson: Gross Profit £39,607.60; Trading Account totals £48,242.50; Net Profit £22,448.05; Profit and Loss Account totals £40,676.65; Fixed assets £50,000.00; Current Assets £7,296.35; Capital at close £31,810.85; Balance sheet totals £57,296.35
2 Books of M Shah: Gross Profit £96,041.67; Trading Account totals £182,026.90; Net Profit £49,149.14; Profit and Loss Account totals £104,941.52; Fixed assets £87,085.00 Current Assets £38,227.82; Capital at close £65,924.22; Long-term liabilities £58,560.00; Balance sheet totals £125,312.82.

13 Partnership Accounts

OBJECTIVES

After studying this chapter you should:

1 Know what a partnership is and understand the special arrangements that banks need to make when opening accounts for a partnership.
2 Understand the special accounts necessary for a set of Final Accounts for Partnership, including the fixed nature of Capital Accounts, the Current Accounts of Partners, the Appropriation Account and the layout of a Partnership Balance Sheet.
3 Know of (a) the Partnership Act of 1890 and (b) the residual arrangements it lays down to deal with the accounting affairs of partners.

Note: Detailed questions on partnership accounts will not be set in the Business Calculations examination but this chapter will give you some understanding of the concepts involved.

1 WHAT IS A PARTNERSHIP?

A partnership is defined in the Partnership Act of 1890 as 'the relationship which subsists between persons carrying on a business in common with a view to profit? There are many reasons for forming a partnership, for example to provide greater capital for an enterprise; to bring different kinds of expertise to the business; to give a marriage between youth and experience; to avoid difficulties through illness, vacations, etc which a sole trader cannot overcome and so on.

From the bank's point of view there are certain difficulties about partnerships. The initial arrangements for opening a partnership account must include a clear mandate for operating the account with regard to the signing of cheques, and about joint and several liability. This should be admitted in the mandate, which should be signed by all the partners. It simply means that all the partners jointly and each of the partners individually are liable for any overdrafts or loans made to the partnership. In the ordinary course of business each partner is the agent of the other partners and the actions of any one are binding on all the others. It is made clear in the Partnership Act of 1890 that borrowing money is not in 'the ordinary course of business', and therefore loans made to a partnership need the agreement of all the partners. This difficulty is usually overcome by a clear statement in the mandate that it is agreed that loans shall be regarded as 'in the ordinary course of business' and therefore a loan made to one party does bind all partners.

This is not an 'Elements of Banking' book, and therefore the full details of arrangements with partners need not concern us here – where we are concerned only with the financial accounts of partnerships, and not their current accounts, loan accounts, etc.

2   THE FINANCIAL ACCOUNTS OF PARTNERSHIPS

Ordinary book-keeping entries are no different for partnerships from similar entries for sole traders, but there are a few areas which do need special attention. These are:

(a)   The partners' Capital Accounts
(b)   The partners' Current Accounts (which are nothing to do with banking)
(c)   The partners' Drawings Accounts
(d)   The Appropriation Account (where the profits of the business are shared up in accordance with any **partnership agreement** which may, or may not, be in force)
(e)   The Balance Sheet of a partnership.

We must deal with each of these in turn. Before doing so, a word about partnership agreements (sometimes called **partnership deeds** if they have been drawn up formally by a solicitor). Many partnerships have no such formal deed, and no written agreement of any sort. They often begin with a handshake. It follows that later the partners may disagree about things they should have discussed before entering into the partnership. The Act of 1890 is said to be a residual Act in that its rules in many instances can be totally ignored by partners who have made their own rules in a written agreement or a deed. The Act only applies in a residue of cases where partners did not discuss a particular point before starting up in partnership. The rules then are:

(a)   Profits are shared equally.
(b)   No partners may have interest on capital.
(c)   Where a partner makes loans to the partnership, such loans bear interest. The original Act says at 5%, but in fact the prevailing rate of interest is promulgated from time to time for all such statutory rules and is considerably more than 5% at the time of writing.
(d)   No partner may have a salary.

There are many situations when partners will not want these rules to apply – for example a young partner is often given a salary out of the profits to assure him/her of a basic income. Such arrangements must be clearly agreed between partners, and preferably be put in writing or in a formal deed. Even if this is not done and the partners only made a verbal agreement, the points on which they agreed will still apply, and the act will be over-ridden. The difficulty is that if a dispute arises over what was agreed verbally you can only prove what was agreed if a witness was present when the agreement was made, or by a course of dealing over several years. Thus if it was agreed that Partner B should have a salary of £5,000 per annum and it could be shown that such a salary was in fact paid for several years the Courts would deem it proved by a course of dealing over the years.

3   THE CAPITAL ACCOUNTS OF PARTNERS

If there is more than one proprietor to a business each of them will need a separate capital account. It will rarely be the case that the balances on their capital accounts are the same. They often start off at quite different figures: Mr A contributing £20,000 and Mr B £5,000 for example. For this reason the partnership agreement often specifies that partners will be allowed interest at an agreed rate on their capital as a prior claim on the profits. For this reason it is usual to regard the capital as fixed – the accounts being retained on the books at their original values.

A typical set of Capital Accounts for partners might therefore look as shown in Fig. 13.1.

Capital Account Mr A Smith

19..			£
Jan 1	Opening Balance		15,000.00

Capital Account Mrs B Smith

19..			£
Jan 1	Opening Balance		15,000.00

Capital Account Miss C Smith

19..			£
Jan 1	Opening Balance		10,000.00

Fig. 13.1   The Capital Accounts of partners

Notes
1   Capital Accounts nearly always have a credit balance, because they are a liability of the business – they are what the business owes back to the owner(s) of the business.
2   As the Capital Accounts of a partnership are fixed at the original value, they will remain on the books at the figures shown during the lifetime of the partnership – although just occasionally, if a revision of affairs between the partners becomes necessary (for example by the admission of a further partner) the old balances will be cleared off and the revised arrangements recorded.

4   THE CURRENT ACCOUNTS OF PARTNERS

Banking students be careful here. The term 'current accounts' in partnership affairs does not refer to a current account at a bank, but to a new account opened for each partner to which any profits due can be transferred and from which the total drawings for the year can be deducted. Since the capital accounts are fixed, partners must have an account which can be varied as profits are received and drawings are withdrawn. Fig. 13.2 shows a typical Current Account – in this case for the youngest of the partners referred to in Fig. 13.1.

Current Account Miss C Smith

19.1		£	19.1		£
Dec 31	Drawings	8,500.00	Jan 1	Balance b/d	185.00
31	Balance c/d	2,410.00	Dec 31	Salary	5,000.00
			31	Interest on Capital	800.00
			31	Share of residue of profit	4,925.00
		£10,910.00			10,910.00
			19.2		
			Jan 1	Balance b/d	2,410.00

Fig. 13.2   A Current Account in a partnership business

Notes

1   At the start of year 19.1 Miss Smith had a balance of £185.00 on her Current Account.

2   At the end of the year the partnership agreement allowed her to have a salary of £5,000; interest on capital of £800 (8% on £10,000) and a share of the residue of the profits ($\frac{1}{5}$) which came to £4,925.00. Profits were shared in the ratio $2:2:1$.

3   Her drawings, which had been drawn in cash monthly, and collected together in her Drawings Account, were transferred to the debit side of the Current Account, to be offset against the profits.

4   The balance due to her is £2,410, which she leaves in the business.

5   THE PARTNERS' DRAWINGS ACCOUNTS

Each partner has a Drawing Account to which drawings are posted as they are taken out, either in cash or by cheque from the bank account. The double entry would be Debit Drawings Account (the proprietor is receiving the money) and credit Cash Account, or Bank Account as the case may be.

At the end of the year there will be a number of debit entries on the Drawings Account and no entries at all on the credit side, until the last day of the financial year, when the whole sum drawn will be cleared from the account (by crediting it) and instead it will be debited on the partner's Current Account, as shown in Fig. 13.2. It is hardly worth illustrating the Drawings Account at this stage.

6   THE APPROPRIATION ACCOUNT OF A PARTNERSHIP BUSINESS

As the name of the account implies, an Appropriation Account is one where we appropriate funds for the purpose for which they were intended. The funds in this case are the profits of the business, which of course are found by preparing a Trading Account and a Profit and Loss Account. The final profit figure is the net profit found in the Profit and Loss Account, and this is transferred into the Appropriation Account for distribution according to the partnership agreement. We can best understand how this works by considering the Trial Balance of a partnership business after the profits have been worked out. At this stage we only have a residue of the original Trial Balance; all the losses and profits having disappeared from it as the Trading and Profit and Loss Accounts were worked out. Such a Trial Balance is shown below.

Example 1

M Brown and P Green conduct a trading business in partnership on the following terms:

- Interest to be allowed on partners' Capital Accounts at 10% per annum.
- Green to be credited with a partnership salary of £8,000 per annum.
- The balance of profit in any year is to be shared by the partners in the ratio $\frac{3}{4}$ to Brown $\frac{1}{4}$ to Green.
- After preparing their Trading and Profit and Loss Accounts for the year ended 31 March 19.. but before making any provision for interest on capital or for partnership salary, the following balances remained on the books:

	Dr £	Cr £
Capital Accounts:		
M Brown (as on 1 April previous year)		20,000
P Green (as on 1 April previous year)		4,000
Current Accounts:		
M Brown (as on 1 April previous year)		1,800
P Green (as on 1 April previous year)	500	
Drawing Accounts:		
M Brown	16,500	
P Green	9,200	
Profit and Loss Account—net profit for year		33,920
Stock at end of year	5,950	
Goodwill Account	1,500	
Plant and Machinery	10,800	
Office Equipment	3,050	
Fixtures and Fittings	2,850	
Hire Purchase loans		2,400
Trade debtors and creditors	650	1,450
Loan from Helpful Bank Plc		5,800
Cash in hand	226	
Insurance unexpired at 31 March (current asset)	142	
Cash at bank, Current Account	7,352	
Cash at bank, Deposit Account	10,650	
	£69,370	69,370

- It is agreed by the partners to reduce the book value of goodwill by writing off £500 at 31 March 19.. (to be charged to the Appropriation Account).
- You are asked to prepare the Appropriation Section of the firm's Profit and Loss Account and the partners' Current Accounts for the year ended 31 March, 19.., together with the Balance Sheet on that date.

The Appropriation Account, Current Accounts and Balance Sheet of the business would then appear as shown in Figs 13.3, 13.4 and 13.5.

Appropriation Account for year ending 31 March 19..   L121

19..		£	19..		£
Mar 31	Goodwill reduction	500	Mar 31	Net Profit	33,920
Mar 31	Salary (Green)	8,000			
Mar 31	Interest on Capital				
	Brown 2,000				
	Green 400				
		2,400			
Mar 31	Share of residue:				
	Brown ($\frac{3}{4}$) 17,265				
	Green ($\frac{1}{4}$) 5,755				
		23,020			
		£33,920			£33,920

Fig. 13.3   The Appropriation Account of a partnership

Notes
1   The goodwill reduction is made first – £500 of the profits used to reduce the goodwill.
2   Then the younger partner is paid the salary due.
3   Then each partner receives the interest on the capital at the start of the year – because it has been used in the business all that time.
4   Finally we find out what is left of the profits (£33,920 – £10,900) and this is shared up $\frac{3}{4}$ Brown, $\frac{1}{4}$ to Green.
5   All the sums are taken into the partners' Current Account, on the credit side, except the Goodwill which is credited in Goodwill Account to reduce the balance on the account to £1000.

Current Account (M Brown)

19..		£	19..		£
Mar 31	Drawings	16,500	April 1	Balance b/d	1,800
31	Balance c/d	4,565	Mar 31	Interest on Capital	2,000
			31	Share of Residue	17,265
		£21,065			£21,065
			19..		
			April 1	Balance b/d	4,565

Current Account (P Green)

19..		£	19..		£
April 1	Balance b/d	500	Mar 31	Salary	8,000
Mar 31	Drawings	9,200	31	Interest on Capital	400
31	Balance c/d	4,455	31	Share of Residue	5,755
		£14,155			£14,155
			19..		
			Apr 1	Balance b/d	4,455

Fig. 13.4   The Current Accounts of the partners

Notes

1   At April 1 when the financial year began Brown had a credit balance on the Current Account but Green had a debit balance (an overdrawn Current Account) where more profit had been taken out than had actually been earned.

2   The various allocations of profit made in the Appropriation Account are credited in the partners' Current Accounts.

3   The drawings taken by each partner in the year are debited to their respective Current Accounts – leaving the Drawings Accounts clear.

4   When the accounts are balanced off both the partners are found to have credit balances – meaning that the business still owes them some of the profits – they have not been fully drawn out.

Balance Sheet as at 31 March 19..

Fixed Assets		£	*Capital at Start*		£
Goodwill	1,500		Brown		20,000
Less amount written off	500		Green		4,000
		1,000			24,000
Plants & Machinery		10,800	*Current Accounts*	£	
Office Equipment		3,050	Brown	4,565	
Fixtures & Fittings		2,850	Green	4,455	
		17,700			9,020
Current Assets	£		*Long-term Liabilities*		
Stock	5,950		Hire purchase loans	2,400	
Debtors	650		Loan from Helpful Bank	5,800	
Cash on deposit	10,650				8,200
Cash at Bank	7,352				
Cash in hand	226				
Insurance	142				
		24,970			
			Current Liabilities		
			Creditors		1,450
		£42,670			£42,670

Fig. 13.5   The Balance Sheet of the partnership

Notes to Fig. 13.5

1   The Balance Sheet has been drawn up in modern Europe style with the assets on the left and liabilities on the right.

2   The partners' Current Accounts are fixed at the starting figure, and simply added together.

3   The residue of profits owed to the partners appears on their Current Accounts and these are again added together.

4   Apart from that the rest of the figures are displayed just as they would be in the accounts of a sole trader.

■ EXERCISE 13.1   THE FINAL ACCOUNTS OF PARTNERSHIP

1   Cain and Abel conduct a trading business in partnership on the following terms:

- Interest is to be allowed on partners' Capital Accounts at 8% per annum.
- Abel is to be credited with a partnership salary of £5,000 per annum.
- The balance of profit in any year, after the above arrangements have been met, is to be shared by the partners in the ratio 3 : 2; Cain getting the larger share.

After preparing their Trading and Profit and Loss Accounts for the year ended 31 March 19X9, but before making any provision for interest on capital or for partnership salary, the following balances remained on the books:

	Dr £	Cr £
Capital Accounts:		
Cain (as on 1 April 19X8)		30,000
Abel (as on 1 April 19X8)		5,000
Current Accounts:		
Cain (as on 1 April 19X8)		2,426
Abel (as on 1 April 19X8)		1,524
Drawing Accounts		
Cain	10,250	
Abel	8,465	
Profit and Loss Account − net profit		37,895
Cash in hand	425	
Stock at end of year	5,925	
Goodwill Account	3,000	
Plant and Machinery	11,250	
Office Equipment	11,600	
Fixtures and Fittings	3,800	
Hire Purchase Loans		2,500
Trade debtors and creditors	825	1,675
Loan from Helpful Bank Plc		4,000
Rent owing (current liability)		240
Insurance unexpired at 31 March (current asset)	380	
Cash at bank, Current Account	11,874	
Cash at Bank, Deposit Account	17,466	
	£85,260	85,260

It is agreed by the partners to reduce the book value of goodwill by writing off £500 at 31 March 19.. (to be charged to the Appropriation Section of the Profit and Loss Account).

You are asked to prepare the Appropriation Account and the partners' Current Accounts for the year ended 31 March, 19X9, together with the Balance Sheet on that date.

2   Malvern and Worcester conduct a trading business in partnership on the following terms:

● Interest is to be allowed on partners' Capital Accounts at 10 per cent per annum.
● Worcester is to be credited with a partnership salary of £9,000 per annum.
● The balance of profit in any year is to be shared by the partners in the ratio 2 : 1, with Malvern taking the larger share.

After preparing their Trading and Profit and Loss Accounts for the year ended 31 December 19.. but before making any provision for interest on capital or for partnership salary, the following balances remained on the books:

	Dr £	Cr £
Capital Accounts:		
Malvern (as on 1 Jan 19..)		25,000
Worcester (as on 1 Jan 19..)		8,000
Current Accounts:		
Malvern (as on 1 Jan 19..)		4,560
Worcester (as on 1 Jan 19..)	2,300	
Drawing Accounts:		
Malvern	22,560	
Worcester	12,250	
Profit and Loss Account – net profit		49,257
Cash in hand	380	
Stock at end of year	12,056	
Motor Vehicles Account	8,540	
Plant and Machinery	27,295	
Office Equipment	3,650	
Fixtures and Fittings	4,927	
Hire Purchase Loans		3,850
Trade debtors and creditors	626	1,274
Loan from Helpful Bank Plc		20,000
Rent owing from tenant (current asset)	160	
Cash at bank, Deposit Account	13,272	
Cash at bank, Current Account	3,925	
	£111,941	111,941

You are asked to prepare the Appropriation Section of the firm's Profit and Loss Account and the partner's Current Accounts for the year ended 31 Dec 19.., together with the Balance Sheet on that date.

■ ANSWERS
Exercise 13.1   1   Books of Cain and Abel: shares of residue of profit. Cain £17,757; Abel £11,838; Current Account balances: Cain £12,333; Abel £10,297; Balance Sheet

totals: Fixed assets £29,150; Current Assets £36,895; Capitals £35,000; Current Accounts £22,630; Long-term liabilities £6,500; Current liabilities £1,915; Grand Totals of Balance Sheet £66,045.

2 Books of Malvern & Worcester: Shares of residue of profit: Malvern £24,638; Worcester £12,319; Current Account balances: Malvern £9,138; Worcester £7,569; Balance Sheet totals: Fixed Assets £44,412, Current Assets £30,419; Capitals £33,000; Current Accounts £16,707; Long-term liabilities £23,850; Current liabilities £1,274. Balance Sheet grand total £74,831.

14 The accounts of limited companies

OBJECTIVES

At the end of this chapter you should be able:
1 To appreciate the special features of company accounts;
2 To understand the appropriation of profits at the end of a company's financial year;
3 To prepare the Balance Sheet of a limited company;
4 To understand the vertical style of Balance Sheets.

1 THE ACCOUNTS OF LIMITED COMPANIES

The accounts of limited companies are largely the same as the accounts of other businesses except that they are subject to more rigorous control. Accounts must be audited properly by professional accountants and the professional bodies have laid down a number of *Statements of Standard Accounting Practice (SSAPs)* which give guidance on the correct methods for treating controversial parts of the accounts. These are too difficult for study at this stage.

All we need to do here is look at two aspects of company accounts:

(a) The sharing of profits amongst the shareholders.
(b) The company Balance Sheet.

1.1 Sharing profits amongst the shareholders

A company's capital is usually subscribed by many people, each of whom becomes a **shareholder** of the company. Most of the shareholders hold **ordinary shares**, and are called **ordinary shareholders**. They join the company hoping to gain an equal share of the profits, but must also stand by to bear an equal share of any losses should losses occur. For this reason ordinary shares are called **equity shares**, and because of the risk are also called **risk shares**. Other shareholders, of a nervous disposition perhaps, do not wish to run all the risks run by equity shares. They take **preference shares**, which get a known rate of dividend (say 7% or 8%), before any profits go to the ordinary shareholders, but the latter may get a much higher dividend in good years.

Another group of investors are the **debenture holders**. Debentures are securities recognising a loan to a company, as distinct from a share in the company's capital. The debenture has first claim on the assets in the event of a dissolution, and earn interest (not dividends). Interest is a charge against the profits (in the Profit and Loss A/c) not an Appropriation of profits (as explained below). Debentures are secured by a deed – either a fixed debenture secured on the fixed assets, or a floating debenture which floats over the stock, and only crystallises into a firm control if there is some sign of financial insecurity.

Although shareholders are the owners of the company and have a right to vote at meetings where the affairs of the company are discussed, power resides with the person or persons controlling 51% of the voting shares, and it is the Board of Directors which runs the company and alone can make recommendations about how the profits are to be used. They will usually recommend payment of any preference dividends, and a reasonable dividend for the ordinary shareholders, but they may also put considerable sums of money away as reserves. Thus a Plant Replacement Reserve would be designed to buy new machinery when required, and a General Reserve could be used in the future for any purpose. The commonest use of the General Reserve is to equalise the dividend over the years by transferring reserves put away in good years back into the

HTP Bolsover (Sawston) Ltd
Residue of Trial Balance as at 31 December, 19..

	Dr £	Cr £
Appropriation A/c (Balance at 1 January 19..)		23,759.50
Net profit for year		97,301.90
General Reserve		15,000.00
Land and Buildings (cost)	127,000.00	
Plant and Machinery (cost)	55,500.00	
7% Preference Shares of £1 (Authorised £100,000)		100,000.00
7% Debentures of £100 each		20,000.00
Ordinary Shares of £1 (Authorised £100,000)		60,000.00
Motor Vehicles (cost)	24,285.60	
Depreciation on Plant & Machinery		13,875.00
Depreciation on Motor Vehicles		8,095.20
Trade Investments (Market value £39,200)	35,500.00	
Fixtures and Fittings	30,000.00	
Depreciation on Fixtures and Fittings		5,000.00
Stock	9,255.00	
Investments (current asset)(Market value £42,750)	40,000.00	
Debtors and creditors	1,726.50	13,250.60
Cash in hand	824.25	
Cash at Bank	32,190.85	
	£356,282.20	356,282.20

Notes

1 The directors have decided to make a Reserve for Corporation Tax of £32,000.
2 They will also set up a Plant Replacement Reserve of £20,000.
3 They will put a further £30,000 in General Reserve.
4 They will pay the dividend on the Preference Shares.
5 They will pay a dividend of 25% on the Ordinary Shares.

Fig. 14.1   The residue of a company's Trial Balance

HTP Bolsover (Sawston) Ltd
Profit and Loss Account for the year ending 31 December 19..
Appropriation Section

19..		£	19..		£
31 Dec	Reserve for Corporation Tax	32,000.00	1 Jan	Balance b/d	23,759.50
	Plant Replacement Reserve	20,000.00	31 Dec	Net profit	97,301.90
	General Reserve	30,000.00			
	Preference dividend	7,000.00			
	Ordinary dividend	15,000.00			
	Balance c/d	17,061.40			
		£121,061.40			£121,061.40
			19..		
			1 Jan	Balance b/d	17,061.40

Fig. 14.2   The Appropriation Account of a limited company

Notes

1   The opening balance on the account is that part of last year's profit which was not distributed to the shareholders or put away into reserves for any particular purpose.

2   The net profit for the present year is transferred into the Appropriation Section to be appropriated to particular uses as the directors recommend.

3   First claim on the profits is the Government's share, but as this is not fully calculated at this time it is usual to put away an adequate sum into a Reserve for Corporation Tax Account.

4   After this the Plant Replacement Reserve and the General Reserve were put away.

5   Then the preference shareholders were given their 7% dividend.

6   Then the ordinary shareholders were given a reasonable dividend, in fact 25% on 60,000 Ordinary Shares of £1 each.

7   This left a balance of £17,061.40 to be carried forward to next year.

8   An interesting point in all this is – to whom do all these profits belong? The answer is that apart from the preference shareholders, who are entitled to the dividend specified in their original contract to buy shares, all the profits belong to the ordinary shareholders, who are entitled to share them equally. So the various reserves, the ordinary dividend and the balance on the Appropriation Account all belong to the ordinary shareholders, although the only bit they can draw is the actual dividend recommended by the directors. The rest of the reserves are 'ploughed back' into the business, which consequently increases in value. Therefore the shares rise in value on the Stock Exchange, because they represent a share in a bigger company.

9   One final point. Where would the double-entries be for the various reserves set aside? Answer: On the credit side of General Reserve Account, for example, as a liability. Why a liability? Because really we owe the money to the ordinary shareholders (and if the company was dissolved tomorrow they would share it all). If the company keeps in business the reserves will be used to expand the business and make even more profit in the future.

ordinary accounts in bad years to give the shareholders a dividend even though profits have not been made. This distribution of profits is made in an account called the Appropriation Account, sometimes called the Appropriation Section of the Profit and Loss Account. If we start with a Trial Balance (after the Trading and Profit and Loss Accounts have been completed) we can extract the Appropriation Account and then prepare the Balance Sheet. Such a residue of a Trial Balance is shown in Fig. 14.1. The Appropriation Account is shown in Fig. 14.2 and explained in the notes below it. When you have studied this figure draw up some simple Appropriation Accounts from those given in Exercise 14.1 below.

■ EXERCISE 14.1

(a)   Supergas (Royston) Ltd is a company making excellent profits in the bottled gas industry. Draw up its Appropriation Account from the following figures for the year ending 31 December, 19..

Balance on the Appropriation Account 1 January £1,875; net profit from the Profit and Loss Account £288,226; Reserve to be created for Corporation Tax £75,000; Plant Replacement Reserve £40,000 and General Reserve £60,000 to be created out of the profits; the Preference Dividend (8% on 80,000 £1 shares) is to be paid and a dividend of 20% on the Ordinary Shares (160,000 £1 shares) is to be paid. The balance is to be carried forward to next year.

(b)   Easter Bonnets Ltd is a company making excellent profits in the clothing trade. Draw up its Appropriation Account from the following figures for the year ending 31 December 19..

Balance on the Appropriation Account 1 January £2,498; net profit from Profit and Loss Account £122,714.45; Reserve to be created for Corporation Tax £25,000; Machinery Replacement Reserve £16,000 and General Reserve £48,000 to be created out of the profits; the Preference Dividend (7% on 20,000 £1 shares) is to be paid, and a dividend of 35% on the Ordinary Shares (45,000 £1 shares) is to be paid. The balance is to be carried forward to next year.

(c)   Supersonic Flight (Duxford) Ltd is a company making excellent profits in the aviation industry. Draw up its Appropriation Account from the following figures for the year ending 31 December 19..

Balance on the Appropriation Account 1 January £17,859; net profit from Profit and Loss Account £1,886,525; Reserve to be created for Corporation Tax £540,000; Plant Replacement Reserve £250,000 and General Reserve £425,000 to be created out of the profits; the Preference Dividend (8% on 250,000 £1 shares) is to be paid together with a dividend of 25% on the Ordinary Shares (2 million £1 shares). The balance is to be carried forward to next year.

2   THE BALANCE SHEET OF A LIMITED COMPANY

When a company's Appropriation Account has been used to share out the profit for the year, or place it into the various reserves, we have only to draw up a Balance Sheet of the remaining items. The format of the Balance Sheet is laid down in the Companies Act 1985, but the detailed requirements are too numerous for a full discussion at this point. The student will study these matters more fully in the 'Introduction to Accounting' course. There are two ways of marshalling the Balance Sheet, in the horizontal style or the vertical style. The horizontal style is the logical style, for any 'balance' must be horizontal. In this style the assets and liabilities are shown in the correct manner (sometimes called the European style) with the assets on the left and the liabilities on the right. In the vertical style the assets are shown first and the liabilities below them. A typical Balance Sheet in horizontal style is shown in Fig. 14.3, using the information given in Figs. 14.1 and 14.2. The vertical style is then shown in Fig. 14.4. Study both figures carefully, and read the notes below them.

HTP Bolsover (Sawston) Ltd
Balance Sheet as at 31 December 19..

	At Cost £	Less Depr to date £	Value £
Fixed Assets			
Intangible Assets			
None (in this example)			
Tangible Assets			
Land & Buildings	127,000.00	—	127,000.00
Plant & Machinery	55,500.00	13,875.00	41,625.00
Fixtures & Fittings	30,000.00	5,000.00	25,000.00
Motor Vehicles	24,285.60	8,095.20	16,190.40
	£236,785.60	£26,970.20	209,815.40
Trade Investments (market value £39,200)			35,500.00
Current Assets	£		
Stock	9,255.00		
Investments (Market value £42,750)	40,000.00		
Debtors	1,726.50		
Cash at Bank	32,190.85		
Cash in hand	824.25		
		83,996.60	
Less:			
Current Liabilities			
Creditors	13,250.60		
Preference Dividend	7,000.00		
Ordinary Dividend	15,000.00		
		35,250.60	
Net current assets			48,746.00
			£294,061.40

	Authorised £	Issued £
Ordinary Shareholders' Interest in the Co		
Ordinary shares of £1	100,000.00	60,000.00
Capital Reserves		
(None in this example)		
Revenue Reserves		
Plant Replacement Reserve (new)		20,000.00
	£	
General Reserves	15,000.00	
+ additions	30,000.00	45,000.00
Balance on Appropriation A/c		17,061.40
		82,061.40
		142,061.40
Ordinary Shareholders' Equity		
Preference Shareholders' Interest in the Co.	Authorised	
7% Preference Shares of £1	100,000.00	100,000.00
7% Debentures		20,000.00
Reserve for Corporation Tax		32,000.00
		£294,061.40

Fig. 14.3 The Balance Sheet of a company in correct horizontal 'European' style (as laid down in the Companies Act 1985, Schedule 4)

Notes on Fig 14.3

1   Dealing with the assets side first, note that they are on the left hand side in correct European style, and show the fixed assets at cost, less depreciation to date as required by the Companies Act 1985. Intangible assets (rights of ownership of patents, goodwill, etc) have to be shown separately from tangible assets (which can be physically touched).

2   Trade Investments are investments in subsidiaries. They can be sold, but if we do sell them we lose control of the subsidiary. They are sometimes called 'assets which are neither fixed nor current'. The Act requires that besides their value on the books, the accounts must reveal the market value of any investments. If the shares held are in a subsidiary which is not a public company, and therefore it is not possible to give a market price, the directors must give an estimate of their value.

3   The current assets are shown in the usual way, and if there are any investments their book value and their market value must be given. Such investments are not trade investments, but investments of cash not required at the moment, which can be realised when necessary.

4   Notice that the current liabilities are brought over from the liabilities side of the Balance Sheet and deducted from the current assets. This brings out the 'net current assets' which is the amount of assets that would be left if all the immediate debts were paid. This is often called the **net working capital**. It is the capital left to work the business after purchasing the fixed assets. Shortage of working capital is one of the chief reasons for the failure of businesses, and is often the point where a banker is approached for funds to keep the business going while it sorts out its cashflow problems.

5   On the liabilities side of the Balance Sheet the capital has been arranged to bring out the Ordinary Shareholders' Interest in the company. Note that the preference shareholders draw their agreed dividend in full each year. As the preference shareholders always draw out all the profit they are entitled to, all the reserves belong to the ordinary shareholders. The result is that any share held becomes more valuable than its original face value, because it really represents not only the money paid for it originally, but also a share of the profits ploughed back over the years.

6   The only amount which belongs to the preference shareholders is the amount of capital they originally contributed.

7   Debentures are loans to a company, usually repayable at a known date some years ahead. They are therefore a long-term liability.

8   Note that all the reserves and provisions made in the Appropriation Account must appear on the Balance Sheet somewhere. Follow these through from Fig. 14.2 to Fig. 14.3 and Fig. 14.4.

HTP Bolsover (Sawston) Ltd
Balance Sheet as at 31 December 19..

Fixed Assets	At Cost	Less Depreciation to date	Value
	£	£	£
Intangible Assets			
None (in this example)	—	—	—
Tangible Assets			
Land and Buildings	127,000.00	—	127,000.00
Plant and Machinery	55,500.00	13,875.00	41,625.00
Fixtures and Fittings	30,000.00	5,000.00	25,000.00
Motor Vehicles	24,285.60	8,095.20	16,190.40
	£236,785.60	£26,970.20	209,815.40
Trade Investments			
(market value £39,200.00)			35,500.00
Current Assets	£		
Stock	9,255.00		
Investments (Market value £42,750)	40,000.00		
Debtors	1,726.50		
Cash at Bank	32,190.85		
Cash in hand	824.25		
		83,996.60	
Current Liabilities			
Creditors	13,250.60		
Preference Dividend	7,000.00		
Ordinary dividend	15,000.00		
		35,250.60	
Net current assets			48,746.00
Total assets less current liabilities			£294,061.40

Financed by:		Authorised	
Reserve for Corporation Tax			32,000.00
7% Debentures			20,000.00
Preference Shareholders' Interest in the Co			
7% Preference Shares of £1		100,000	100,000.00
Ordinary Shareholders' Interest in the Co			
	Authorised	Issued	
Ordinary shares of £1 fully paid	£100,000.00	60,000.00	
Capital Reserves			
None in this example			
Revenue Reserves			
Plant/Replacement Reserve (new)		20,000.00	
General Reserve	15,000.00		
+ additions	30,000.00		
		45,000.00	
Balance on Appropriation Account		17,061.40	
Ordinary Shareholders' Equity			142,061.40
			£294,061.40

Fig. 14.4   A Balance Sheet in vertical style, as laid down in Schedule 4 of the Companies Act 1985

Notes

1 The two halves of the Balance Sheet are shown one above the other, and the assets shown first. There is no change from the horizontal Balance Sheet, shown in Fig. 14.3, as far as the assets are concerned.

2 The second part shows the liabilities, but these are in reverse order to the order given in the horizontal Balance Sheet. There is absolutely no reason for this – it is a Parliamentary slip really. The liabilities are not listed in the order of permanence, with the most permanent liabilities first, but in the order of liquidity, with the least permanent items first. However this slip need not concern us.

3 The words 'Financed by' are not included in the Act's requirements, but really should have been. They tell anyone studying the Final Accounts that the assets held in the top half of the Balance Sheet were financed by the investors mentioned in the bottom half of the Balance Sheet. The debenture holders provided loan finance, and capital was subscribed by both the preference shareholders and the ordinary shareholders.

■ EXERCISE 14.2

(a) The following residue of the Trial Balance was extracted from the books of Andrews Ltd on 31 December 19.. after the Trading and Profit and Loss Accounts had been prepared. You are asked to prepare the Appropriation Account and the Balance Sheet in horizontal style.

Residue of Trial Balance as at 31 December, 19..

	£	£
Share capital, authorised and issued:		
200,000 ordinary shares of £1 each		200,000
Motor Vehicles (at cost)	17,255	
Freehold properties at cost	172,000	
Furniture and fittings at cost	12,000	
Trade Debtors	17,950	
Trade Creditors		12,530
Renewal of Properties Reserve (revenue reserve)		5,400
Investments (current asset)	46,260	
Stock	20,470	
Rates in advance (current asset)	75	
Depreciation on Motor Vehicles to date		3,240
Depreciation of Furniture and Fittings		6,600
Wages due (current liabilities)		240
Balance on Profit and Loss Account 1 January		3,251
Net Profit for year		53,380
Cash in hand	386	
Cash at Bank	39,845	
8% Debentures		40,000
Debenture interest due (current liability)		1,600
	£326,241	326,241

Notes

1 The directors have decided to provide a Reserve for Corporation tax of £20,000.
2 They have also decided to increase the Renewal of Properties Reserve by £2,600 and to put £10,000 in a new General Reserve Account.
3 A dividend will be paid of 10% on the ordinary shares.

(b) The following residue of the Trial Balance of R T Norman (Stevenage) Plc was left at 31 December 19.. after the Trading and Profit and Loss Accounts were worked out. You are asked to draw up the Appropriation Account and the Balance Sheet in vertical style.

R T Norman (Stevenage) Plc
Residue of Trial Balance as at 31 December 19..

	Dr £	Cr £
Appropriation Account (Balance at 1 January 19..)		6,262
Net profit for year		76,255
Plant Replacement Reserve		4,000
Land and Buildings (cost)	84,500	
Plant and Machinery (cost)	38,760	
Furniture and Fittings (cost)	18,284	
Motor Vehicles (cost)	19,716	
Depreciation on Plant & Machinery		9,690
Depreciation on Furniture & Fittings		4,571
Depreciation on Motor Vehicles		9,858
8% Debentures		20,000
Trade Investments (Market value £89,200)	186,425	
Investments (current asset)	10,000	
Stock	27,355	
Debtors and Creditors	1,784	5,268
General Reserve		8,500
Cash at Bank	57,155	
7% Preference Shares of £1 (authorised £100,000)		100,000
Cash in hand	425	
Ordinary Shares of £1 (authorised £200,000)		200,000
	£444,404	444,404

Notes

1 The directors have decided to make a Reserve for Corporation Tax of £28,000.
2 They will put a further £4,000 in Plant Replacement Reserve and £10,000 in General Reserve.
3 They will pay a dividend of $12\frac{1}{2}$% on the Ordinary Shares, and the 7% dividend on the Preference Shares.

(c) The balances appearing below were those remaining on the books of Microdots Ltd after the Trading Account and Profit and Loss Account had been completed. You

are asked to draw up the Appropriation Account for the year ended 31 Decemer 19..
and the Balance Sheet at that date, in vertical style.

	£	£
Ordinary Share capital: authorised, 80,000 shares of £1 each:		
issued 60,000 shares of £1 each		60,000
7% Preference Share Capital (authorised and issued)		100,000
Cash in hand	855	
Premises at cost	142,000	
Machinery at cost	29,000	
Depreciation on machinery		5,000
Investments (current asset)	35,750	
8% Debentures		9,000
Creditors		7,430
Debtors	14,900	
Stock in trade	22,920	
Machinery Replacement Reserve		4,000
Profit and Loss Account balance (1 January)		10,620
General Reserve		18,000
Fixtures at cost	3,200	
Depreciation on fixtures		1,000
Wages due (current liability)		500
Cash at bank	50,755	
Net Profit for year		78,750
Motor Vehicles	18,650	
Depreciation on Motor Vehicles		3,730
Mortgage on premises		20,000
	£318,030	318,030

Notes

1   The directors recommend a dividend of 30% on the ordinary shares, and will pay the preference dividend in full.
2   The Machinery Replacement Reserve to be doubled.
3   The General Reserve is to be increased by £20,000.
4   A Reserve for Corporation Tax is to be set aside £35,000.

■ ANSWERS

Exercise 14.1   (a) Books of Supergas (Royston) Ltd: Balance on Appropriation Account £76,701; totals of Appropriation Account £290,101;   **(b)** Easter Bonnets Ltd: Balance on Appropriation Account £19,062.45; totals of Appropriation Account £125,212.45;   **(c)** Supersonic Flight (Duxford) Ltd: Balance on Appropriation Account £169,384; totals of Appropriation Account £1,904,384.

Exercise 14.2 **(a)** New balance on Appropriation Account £4,031; Fixed Assets less depreciation £191,415; Net current assets £90,616; Ordinary Shareholders' Equity £222,031; Balance Sheet totals £282,031.
(b) New balance on Appropriation Account £8,517; Fixed Assets less depreciation £137,141; Net Current Assets £59,451; Ordinary Shareholders' Equity £235,017; Balance Sheet totals £383,017.
(c) New balance on Appropriation Account £5,370; Fixed Assets less depreciation £183,120; Ordinary Shareholders' Equity £111,370; Balance Sheet totals £275,370.

15 The use of ratios in analysing accounts

OBJECTIVES

At the end of this chapter you should:
1 Appreciate the uses of the commonest accounting ratios;
2 Know how to work out each of these ratios and be able to calculate them for any customer's business if the necessary figures are available;
3 Appreciate the limitations of the ratios when assessing the viability of a business for loan purposes.

Note:
Although it is not necessary to memorise all these ratios for the Business Calculations examination, by working through this chapter you will understand how the theory of ratios is applied in the banking and business world.

1 INTRODUCTION TO RATIOS

A ratio shows the relationship of one thing with another, and brings out the relative importance of the figures under scrutiny. Thus to say a business is expanding may be true, even if the growth is quite small. To find out the ratio between the growth and the original size at the start, before the growth began to be measured, will bring out a much clearer idea of the expansion achieved. A ratio is made up to two parts, which are most easily expressed as a numerator and a denominator. Naturally this is a fraction, but since results are often expressed as decimal fractions we may find a ratio given in decimal form. For example:

$$\text{Stock to turnover ratio} = \frac{\text{stock}}{\text{turnover}} = \frac{\text{stock}}{\text{sales less returns}}$$

Suppose stock is on average £50,000, sales £256,000 and returns £6,000:

$$\text{Stock to turnover} = \frac{£50,000}{£256,000 - £6,000}$$

$$= \frac{£50,000}{£250,000}$$

$$= \tfrac{1}{5} \text{ or } 0.2$$

The accuracy of the figures used affects the accuracy of the ratio that is found from them and can never be more accurate than the least accurate figure used. If a ratio is worked out to several decimal places it is almost certain that the last two or three figures are meaningless. They give an impression of meticulous accuracy but actually they are no help at all. This is called **spurious accuracy**.

2   RATIOS AND THE BUSINESS

Ratios are of little value in the very early days of a business, until it has become established and a steady pattern of trading has emerged. Once that has happened, the figures which are used in the ratios accumulate and it becomes possible to evaluate the success of the business.

The most common ratios are:

2.1   Ratios to assess profitability

   (a)   The gross profit percentage
   (b)   The net profit percentage
   (c)   The rate of stock turnover
   (d)   The expense ratios
   (e)   The return on capital employed
   (f)   The return on capital invested

2.2   Ratios to assess liquidity

   (a)   The current ratio or working capital ratio
   (b)   The acid test ratio (liquid ratio)
   (c)   The borrowing ratio
   (d)   The average credit granted
   (e)   The average credit taken
   (f)   The repayment capacity ratio

Although the ratios have been grouped as shown above, the figures which are used in them are to be found in the final accounts of a business (in the case of a limited company in the audited accounts). As this is a simple text book we will use examples from a sole trader business, but where there is something extra to be learned by considering figures from a limited company, additional explanations will be given. Since the final accounts are the basis for the ratios, each ratio will be explained by reference to the place in the final accounts where the figures appear, and therefore will not be dealt with in the order given in 2.1 and 2.2 above.

3   RATIOS FROM THE TRADING ACCOUNT

To start, consider the Trading Account shown in Fig. 15.1.

Ken Perkins Trading Account for year ended 31 December 19..

	£		£
Opening stock	16,985	Sales	198,860
Purchases	87,900	*Less* sales returns	− 2,340
Add carriage in	855	Net turnover	196,520
	88,755		
Less purchases returns	2,155		
Net purchases	86,600		
Total stock available	103,585		
Less closing stock	19,254		
Cost of stock sold	84,331		
Gross profit			
(to Profit & Loss Account)	112,189		
	196,520		196,520

Fig. 15.1   A Trading Account for analysis

From the Trading Account shown in Fig. 15.1 we can calculate two ratios:

(a)   the gross profit percentage
(b)   the rate of stock turn.

3.1   The gross profit percentage

This ratio helps us understand how a customer's business is doing as far as the trading activities are concerned, and enables us to compare trading this year with last year, this quarter with last quarter, or this quarter with the same quarter last year. We may also compare the ratio with the average for this type of business.

First, the calculation is based on the formula:

$$\text{Gross profit percentage} = \frac{\text{gross profit}}{\text{turnover}} \times 100$$

When applied to Ken Perkins' Trading Account this gives us:

$$\text{Gross profit percentage} = \frac{\text{gross profit}}{\text{turnover}} \times 100$$

$$= \frac{112,189}{196,520} \times 100$$

$$= 57.1\%$$

This means that 57.1% of the cash actually taken on turnover is gross profit. This seems to be a good rate of gross profit, but in fact it is about average. Many businesses look for a much bigger mark up on stock than that (it is just over 100% mark up).

Remember that gross profit is profit before all the overhead expenses are deducted, and a 57.1% gross profit percentage means a much lower net profit percentage – say 15%–20%. Many businesses that get into financial difficulties do so because the proprietor just does not realise that he/she has to add on a really good mark up to come out with a decent net profit. You can't buy something for £10 and sell it for £11 and not finish up in the bankruptcy court.

So telling a customer to add on a good mark up for gross profit is good advice – 100% is quite common and 200%–300% is not unheard of.

Gross profit percentage – this year and last year

While the facts of life about gross profit percentage referred to in the last paragraph may be of great importance to some customers, the use of comparisons between accounting periods is more significant still. The reason is that, all things being equal, whatever the volume of trading is in one period or another, the gross profit percentage should be constant. We usually use the term K to indicate a constant (C having been commandeered by centigrade and celsius).

Consider if Ken Perkins doubles his sales next year, and all other things remain equal in other words disregard any economies or diseconomies of large scale that he might have achieved. Of course you can't sell twice as much goods unless you buy twice as much stock for resale, so we can expect purchases to double and gross profit to double. What is the gross profit percentage now?

$$\text{Gross profit percentage} = \frac{£224,378}{£393,040} \times 100$$

$$= 57.1\%$$

This is the same answer as before, the gross profit percentage is a constant (K).

Now, it follows that if we take the gross profit percentage this year and compare it with what the gross profit percentage was a year ago, we may find that it has not been constant. If not, why not?

Suppose that last year Ken Perkins' turnover was £155,274 and his gross profit was £97,823. Looking at these figures, Ken Perkins might be very happy with the results this year. Turnover is up, gross profit is up, give every one a bonus – all is well. However, if we work out the gross profit percentage we find:

$$\text{Gross profit percentage} = \frac{£97,823}{£155,274} \times 100$$

$$= 63\%$$

So, in fact, the gross profit percentage this year was only 57.1%, whereas last year it was 63%. Cancel the bonuses – all is not well. Why has the gross profit percentage fallen? There can be many reasons, and if you think them through in terms of Fig. 15.2 you will find it very instructive. For example:

(a)   Is someone stealing from the tills? Theft from the tills reduces the daily takings figure (the turnover figure is smaller) and that makes the gross profit smaller and the gross profit percentage smaller.

(b)   Is someone stealing the stock? Stolen stock makes the stock taking figure smaller and hence the cost of stock sold is greater and the gross profit is smaller.

(c)   Is Ken Perkins suffering other sorts of stock losses? We can lose stock in many other ways. Strawberries rot, bananas ripen apace, powders blow away, cooked meats deteriorate, newspapers don't sell, garments fade etc. These are all aspects of bad buying – mis-judgement of the market. The turnover is less than it should be if we sell off stock cheaply, while if we throw it away the closing stock figure is smaller. Many a buyer loses his/her job because of such mistakes. We shall see later that bad buying means a lower rate of stock turnover, and it is as stock turns over that we make a profit.

(d)   Are the costs of Ken Perkins' supplies (purchases) rising? If so, and he has been slow to pass these increases on to his customers, the gross profit will decline and so will the gross profit percentage.

(e)   It could be competition. If competition is tough, Ken Perkins may be forced to lower profit margins to meet it. This will mean a drop in gross profit percentage but Ken Perkins may not be able to do much about it. If this means he is short of cash because cash flows in are smaller than in former times the bank may need to be careful. It is no help to Ken Perkins to throw the bank's money into a deteriorating situation. We may need to make him face the reality of the situation.

(f)   Is expansion being achieved at the cost of tighter profit margins? We may need to take a 'marginal costing' view of Ken Perkins' activities. For example, if a customer is placing large orders he may be glad to do the extra business even though the customer is demanding more favourable treatment than other customers. Marginal costing is a method of costing which says we do not need to load every unit of our output with a fair share of the overheads of the business. If the present volume of output is carrying all the overheads, and we have a new customer offering to place a big order provided he/she gets more favourable terms, we might as well take the business. Ken Perkins may be right – the turnover is up, and the profits are up, and even though the gross profit percentage is down we are still better off. The extra turnover is not making what we would normally hope – but it is making something, and every little helps.

When gross profit percentage rises

When the gross profit percentage rises there is no cause for concern and Ken Perkins is pleased. It may be worth while finding out why the improvement has occurred. Has Ken Perkins tightened up on shoplifting, staff thefts, poor buying, breakages, etc? If he approaches us for a loan to expand after a series of increases in gross profit percentage over the years we can feel confident in lending to him. A rise in gross profit percentage indicates improved efficiency.

3.2   The rate of stock turnover

Profits are made at the moment when stock, whether goods purchased for re-sale or goods manufactured in a customer's factory, turn over – in other words, sell. Suppose goods costing £1,000 are sold for £2,000; we have a profit of £1,000. If we do that once a year the annual gross profit is £1,000. If we do it twice a year the annual gross profit is £2,000. If we do it monthly the gross profit is £12,000 and if we do it daily it is £365,000. It follows that any firm's prospects of profitability are closely tied to the rate of stock turnover. Any increase in the rate of stock turnover is beneficial, and any reduction in the role of stock turnover makes the business less reliable as a customer for loan purposes.

The rate of stock turnover can be found using either of two formulae:

$$\text{Rate of stockturn} = \frac{\text{cost of stock sold}}{\text{average stock at cost price}}$$

$$\text{Rate of stockturn} = \frac{\text{net turnover}}{\text{average stock at selling price}}$$

The point here is that the two figures used must be in the same form – either both at cost price or both at selling price. Using the cost price figures from Fig. 15.2 we have:

$$\text{Rate of stock turnover} = \frac{\text{cost of stock sold}}{\text{average stock at cost price}}$$

The best figure we can get for average stock from the figures Ken Perkins is providing is:

$$
\begin{aligned}
\text{Average stock} &= \frac{\text{Opening stock and closing stock}}{2} \\[6pt]
&= \frac{£16{,}985 + £19{,}254}{2} \\[6pt]
&= \frac{£36{,}239}{2} \\[6pt]
&= £18{,}119.50
\end{aligned}
$$

$$
\begin{aligned}
\text{So: Rate of stock turnover} &= \frac{£84{,}331}{£18{,}119.50} \\[6pt]
&= \underline{\underline{4.7 \text{ times}}}
\end{aligned}
$$

Whether this is a reasonable rate of stock turnover for the customer who is asking for a loan is a question of product. The stock is turning over 4.7 times a year. That doesn't sound too bad for washing machines or bicycles, because they don't deteriorate too much over time. It wouldn't do for new laid eggs or newspapers. We can get a little help on this if we turn the rate of turnover into a time period of months, weeks or days.
  Thus:

    12 months ÷ 4.7 = 2.5 months
    52 weeks ÷ 4.7 = 11.1 weeks
    365 days ÷ 4.7 = 77.6 days

If a refrigerator is in the warehouse for 77.6 days it isn't going to suffer much, but if the goods concerned are groceries or magazines they will certainly be unsaleable. These are extreme examples of course – but the number of days an average item is in stock is a useful figure to ask for when a customer wants a loan. Is he/she in fact asking us to finance stocks which really should be disposed of now at the best price possible while our customer concentrates on more saleable goods.

■ EXERCISE 15.1
ANALYSING THE TRADING ACCOUNT

These calculations should be done (where appropriate) correct to one decimal place. Calculators may be used.

1 Peter Clarke's Trading Account shows his turnover to be £179,655 and his gross profit to be £76,259. What is his gross profit percentage?

2 Anne Young trades as 'Wedding Bliss'. Sales in the year of bridal gowns, etc. total £92,560 and the gross profit is £21,250. What is the gross profit percentage?

3 Abdul Kadarr trades in computer equipment. His sales in the year are £1,795,626 and his gross profit is £729,755.

(a) What is his gross profit percentage?
(b) Last year the gross profit percentage was 44.3%. If his turnover was £2,104,299 what was his gross profit? (Answer correct to the nearest £ in this case.)

4 Steven Wakamba runs a music factory reproducing taped music under licence. His turnover is £728,500 in the year and his gross profit is £112,650.

(a) What is his gross profit percentage?
(b) In the following year both his turnover and gross profit rise by 20%. What happens to his gross profit percentage? Work out the figures to prove your answer is correct.

5 Robina Newcastle has an average stock of £7,219 and the cost of stock sold last year was £58,724.   **(a)** What was her rate of stock turnover?   **(b)** How many weeks was the average item in stock?

6 Charles Tremaine has an average stock of £12,295 in his grocery store, and the cost of stock sold last year was £163,725.   **(a)** What was the rate of stock turnover? **(b)** How long was the average item in stock? (Answer in days.)

7 Mrs A is thinking of buying two businesses. She has the following monthly figures about them:

	Business No.1	Business No.2
Monthly turnover	£27,524	£28,200
Gross profit	6,976	6,950
Opening Stock	3,381	6,365
Closing Stock	4,261	8,248
Cost of stock sold	19,348	21,250

(a) Find the gross profit percentage in each case.
(b) Find the rate of stock turnover in each case.
(c) Which business would you say was the better choice?

8 Trubright Ltd has expanded until it has four outlets A, B, C and D. The annual turnover and gross profit figures for the year just ended are:

	Turnover	Gross Profit
A	£38,000	£9,500
B	£26,000	£5,750
C	£27,000	£7,150
D	£49,560	£11,250

(a) Work out the gross profit percentage in each case.
(b) Which outlet is showing the best results based on these figures?

The Trading Account figures are required for other ratios in business use, and we shall return to Fig. 15.1, but in the meantime we will consider Fig. 15.2, Ken Perkins' Profit and Loss Account.

4   RATIOS FROM THE PROFIT AND LOSS ACCOUNT

The ratios we can find directly from the Profit and Loss Account are the **Net Profit Percentage** and **Expense Ratios**. First let us look at Ken Perkins' Profit and Loss Account, Fig. 15.2.

Ken Perkins
Profit and Loss Account for year ended 31 December 19..

	£		£
Carriage Out	160	Gross Profit	112,189
Rent and Rates	4,840	Commission Received	720
Light and Heat	270	Rent Received	2,080
Insurance	100	Discount Received	160
Salaries	49,240		
Advertising	1,480		
Bad Debts	60		
Discount allowed	144		
Postage	326		
Travelling Expenses	75		
	56,695		
Net Profit (to Capital A/C)	58,454		
	£115,149		£115,149

Fig. 15.2   A Profit and Loss Account

4.1   Net Profit Percentage

The formula for the net profit percentage is:

$$\text{Net Profit Percentage} = \frac{\text{net profit}}{\text{turnover}} \times 100$$

The turnover figure comes of course from the Trading Account (Fig. 15.1). In Ken Perkins' case this is:

$$\text{Net Profit Percentage} = \frac{£58,454}{£196,520} \times 100$$

$$= \underline{\underline{29.7\%}}$$

Once again we can't really answer the question 'Is this a satisfactory net profit percentage?' with any real certainty, but we can say that it doesn't look too bad. The net profit is the reward of the entrepreneur for showing enterprise. A person who does not show enterprise, but simply puts whatever savings they have away in National Savings, or perhaps in a bank Deposit Account, earns about 8–10%. We certainly wouldn't want to be in business, with all the worry and stress and risk involved and only get 8–10%, because we can get that even if we don't show enterprise. Customers who approach a bank with accounts that only show a 6% net profit percentage should be advised that the business is not really profitable and that they are wasting their time unless the non-monetary satisfactions of being in business are more important to them than the monetary rewards.

We shall see later that two other ratios – **return on capital employed** and **return on capital invested** throw a bit more light on the profitability of the business.

Notice the relationship between gross profit percentage and net profit percentage. Ken Perkins' gross profit percentage was 57.1% but by the time all the overheads had been deducted the net profit percentage was down to 29.7%.

Once again, all things being equal, the net profit percentage will tend to be a constant, whatever the turnover. If the turnover rises, the profit will rise, and the net profit percentage will be roughly the same. Suppose that last year the net profit percentage was 34%, but this year it is down to 29.7%. Of course this could have been due to a fall in the gross profit percentage, but if we assume that this figure was all right, the trouble must lie in the figures that appear on the Profit and Loss Account. It could be:

(a) the expenses have risen, or

(b) the profits have fallen (but not the gross profit because we are agreed that that is all right).

It may be obvious just by comparing this year's figures with last year's figures where the problem lies, but a more rigorous check is to work out an **expense ratio** for each item of expense. For example, suppose we work out an expense ratio for Salaries Account. The formula for an expense ratio is:

$$\text{Expense ratio} = \frac{\text{Items of expense}}{\text{Turnover}} \times 100$$

For salaries this is:

$$= \frac{£49,240}{£196,520} \times 100$$

$$= 25.1\%$$

Suppose last year the expense ratio for salaries was 21.5% of turnover, we have a serious increase in salaries. The number of staff has risen, or rewards to staff have risen without any increase in profits to match. There is a serious deterioration in the contribution made on average by each employee to the profits of the business. Has Perkins taken on staff he does not really need? Some people feel important if they have a little group of subordinates genuflecting in their direction; empire building is the term usually used.

By this type of analysis Perkins can detect weaknesses he did not appreciate before.

On the profits side, we can consider each item of profit and see whether it is up or down on last year. Has Perkins for some reason failed to earn this year an income that made a useful contribution to profits in the previous year. If so every attempt should be made to try to recover the business previously enjoyed.

■ **EXERCISE 15.2**

NET PROFIT PERCENTAGE AND EXPENSE RATIOS

Answers correct to one decimal place where appropriate.

1 Mark Yates has net profits of £28,724 on a turnover of £119,256. What is his net profit percentage?

2 Romola Sabbatini has a net profit from her salon of £41,275 on a turnover of £197,350 in the year. What is her net profit percentage?

3 Rachel Shaw has a net profit of £24,725 on a turnover of £146,520. Two of the expenses in the Profit and Loss Account are Salaries £37,526 and Power and Light £4,325. Calculate:

(a) the net profit percentage

(b) the salaries expense ratio

(c) the power and light expense ratio.

4 Callus Cabs is a cooperative of taxi cab drivers who share profits equally. They make a net profit of £94,295 on a turnover of £397,500. **(a)** What is their net profit percentage? Last year it was 27.5%. They suspect that the rise in the price of diesel during the year has been the largest single cause of their declining profitability. Last year diesel costs represented 19.1% of turnover. This year they were £73,935 **(b)** Calculate the expense ratio for diesel this year, and advise them about their problem.

5 **(a)** Fill in the missing parts to the following table. **(b)** Hence decide which of these businesses is the best candidate for a loan by your bank. Each is seeking to borrow £100,000.

	Turnover £	Gross Profit £	Overhead Expenses £	Net Profit £	Gross Profit % £	Net Profit % £
Tough Dealing Ltd	525,950	274,590	95,716	?	?	?
Easy-go Ltd	659,625	358,254	196,318	?	?	?

6 **(a)** Fill in the missing parts to the following table.

(b) Decide which of these businesses is the best candidate for a loan from your bank. Each is seeking to borrow £50,000.

	Turnover £	Gross Profit £	Overhead Expenses £	Net Profit £	Gross Profit % £	Net Profit % £
Beautiful Bonnets	186,525	97,254	54,254	?	?	?
Brighter Homes	157,325	105,636	22,762	?	?	?

5 RATIOS FROM THE BALANCE SHEET

The rest of the ratios listed at the start of this chapter depend upon figures to be found in the Balance Sheet. They enable us to assess the health and prosperity of the business we are asked to help. We will start by considering Ken Perkins' Balance Sheet, the figures for which are given in Fig. 15.3.

Ken Perkins
Balance Sheet as at 31 December 19..

Fixed Assets		£	Capital	£	£
Land and Buildings		66,345	At start		123,655
Plant and Machinery		26,500	Add net profit	58,454	
Furniture and Fittings		17,321	*Less* Drawings	19,600	
Motor Vehicles		15,250			38,854
		125,416	Net worth		162,509
Current Assets	£		Long term liabilities		
Stock at close	49,254		Mortgage		20,000
Sundry Debtors	6,171				
Bank	7,254				
Cash	2,350		Current liabilities		
		65,029	Sundry Creditors		7,936
		£190,445			£190,445

Fig. 15.3   A Balance Sheet for appraisal

When appraising a Balance Sheet there are certain key figures we should use which must be explained. Two essential points to realise first are these:

(a)   the two sides of the Balance Sheet, the assets and the liabilities must balance. That is what gives the Balance Sheet its name.

(b)   The items on the left hand side – the assets of the business – have been purchased with the funds made available by the other side. The liabilities are owed because the people named have provided the funds to finance the business. In this case there are three sources of funds. The proprietor Ken Perkins has provided the original capital and also ploughed back profits made in the year. The mortgagors have provided £20,000 and certain creditors have provided funds amounting to £7,936. With these funds the business has obtained certain assets. They are divided into two parts, fixed assets and current assets. The key figures are:

(a)   *Fixed Assets* These are assets purchased for use in the business, which last a long time and permanently increase the profit-making capacity of the business. Of course they do depreciate and have to be replaced and renewed from time to time. The dividing line between fixed assets and current assets is a lifetime of at least one year.

(b)   *Current Assets* are assets which are in the process of earning profits for the business. They are called current assets because they are 'courrant' the French word for 'running'. They run round in an endless cycle changing into cash and making profits as they do so. Ken Perkins buys stock which is sold to debtors who pay Ken Perkins either in cheque form (bank) or in cash. The cycle is endless and the faster it goes the happier Ken Perkins is. It is the turnover of the business and every time it turns over Ken Perkins makes a profit: stock – debtors – cash; stock – debtors – cash; etc.

(c)   *Current Liabilities* Some of those who provide finance to a business only do so for a short period – these are the current liabilities. The proprietor has to pay the creditors – usually within 30 days.

(d)   *Long-Term Liabilities* Other people who help finance the business make a longer-term arrangement. Mortgages often take years to repay.

(e)   *Net Worth* The proprietor makes the longest committment of all. The capital is injected into the business for as long as the proprietor continues to be the proprietor. Ken Perkins' share in the business is called the 'net worth' of the business. This means the worth of the business to the proprietor, net of all other liabilities. When everyone else has been paid, the proprietor owns all the rest.

(f)   *Working Capital* Some of the capital provided to finance a business is spent on fixed assets. The rest of the money is available to work the business and is called 'working capital'. It is of course largely the current assets, but as some items (the current liabilities) are repayable very shortly, we define working capital as follows:

$$\text{Working Capital} = \text{Current Assets} - \text{Current Liabilities}$$
$$= £65,029 - £7,936$$
$$= £57,093$$

5.1   The working capital ratio or current ratio

We can look at this working capital in a more meaningful way if we work it out as a ratio.

$$\text{Working capital ratio} = \frac{\text{current assets}}{\text{current liabilities}}$$
$$= \frac{£65,029}{£7,936}$$
$$= 8.2$$

This is more properly expressed as 8.2 : 1, a true ratio.

In other words Ken Perkins, with his present current assets, can repay all his current liabilities eight times over. This is a very good level of working capital. Bankers chiefly get asked for loans when their customers are short of working capital. If you haven't got enough working capital to work the business, that is to buy the raw materials and goods you want to manufacture or sell again, you are in a very poor way. It is easy to get into this position if a business buys too many fixed assets and hasn't got enough funds to work the business. It is usually held that the working capital ratio should always be at least 2 : 1. In other words Ken Perkins should be able to pay his current liabilities twice over to be safe. We can see that with a working capital ratio of 8.2 : 1 Ken Perkins' business is in a very healthy state.

5.2   The acid test ratio or liquid capital ratio

There is an even better test of a firm's position; so good that it is called the 'acid test' ratio. It measures the firm's situation by considering its **liquid capital**. Liquid capital is capital that is in liquid form (i.e. money form). Liquid capital is made up of cash, plus money in the bank plus debtors (because they are due to pay us in 30 days normally and we count that as being as good as money in the bank). If a business has readily realisable investments (not trade investments in subsidiary firms) these can also be included. Ken Perkins has none of these so we will disregard them for the moment.

Ken Perkins liquid capital is:

£6,171 + £7,254 + £2,350 = £15,775

The formula for the liquid capital ratio (acid test ratio) is

$$\text{Liquid Capital ratio} = \frac{\text{Liquid capital}}{\text{Current liabilities}}$$

$$= \frac{£15,775}{£7,936}$$

$$= 2.0 \text{ or } 2:1$$

So, even with just his liquid assets, Ken Perkins can pay up his current liabilities twice over. This is a very healthy position to be in. It is usually held that the liquid capital ratio should not be below 1. If it is above 1, then if all Ken Perkins creditors said 'Pay me at once' he could look cheerful and pay up. That is when a business is in good heart. No one can pull the rug from under the feet of a business that has liquid assets exceeding its current liabilities. A firm or company is only in real financial difficulties when its current liabilities exceed its liquid assets. That is the acid test for solvency.

The acid test ratio is sometimes called the 'quick ratio' because it only takes account of the current assets which can quickly be turned into cash. Stock is not a 'quick' asset because we cannot usually turn it into cash at a moment's notice. Of course, there may be debtors also who cannot pay but if we take it for granted that the firm is reviewing debtors regularly and dealing with bad debts firmly (by selling them for what they will fetch to a debt collector) the debtors' figure should be a reasonably liquid asset.

Other ratios of interest at this point are:

(a) **The borrowing ratio or gearing ratio** A business can be financed in two main ways. The proprietor, partners or shareholders can finance the business by putting up long-term capital, or the business can borrow from banks, debenture holders, etc.

The relationship between long-term capital (net worth) and borrowed money is called the borrowing ratio, or gearing ratio. The formula is.

$$\text{Borrowing Ratio} = \frac{\text{Total Borrowings}}{\text{Net Worth}}$$

Net worth is the funds provided by the proprietors and is usually easy to see. It is their capital and profits ploughed back, or in the case of companies it is the total shareholders' interest in the business, both ordinary shareholders and preference shareholders.

Total borrowing refers to long-term liabilities and current liabilities of a borrowing nature – such as overdrafts. It does not include trade creditors.

$$\text{Ken Perkins Borrowing Ratio} = \frac{\text{Total Borrowings}}{\text{Net Worth}}$$

$$= \frac{£20,000}{£162,509}$$

$$= 0.12$$

This is sometimes expressed as a percentage, i.e. 12% geared.

Anything below 1 is a low-geared business. It means that more than half the fiananance of the firm is being provided by the long-term funds of the proprietors. As we move above a Borrowing Ratio of 1 we have the business financing itself more than 50% by borrowing. For example:

Total borrowings £60,000, net worth £60,000

$$\text{Borrowing Ratio} = \frac{£60,000}{£60,000}$$

$$= 1$$

Total borrowings £90,000, net worth £60,000

$$\text{Borrowing Ratio} = \frac{£90,000}{£60,000}$$

$$= 1.5 \text{ or } 150\% \text{ geared.}$$

The point is that the higher the gearing the more the profits of the organisation are creamed off to pay the interest to the various banks, finance companies, etc and the less chance there is for any worthwhile reward to the equity shareholders – and also less chance of any capital gain, since there are less spare profits to plough back.

However we must not make too sweeping a condemnation of high gearing. High gearing is not bad if the company's type of business is such that liquidity can be recovered fairly easily and loans can be repaid. Thus a wholesaler dealing in a variety of goods in popular demand can turn the stock back into cash fairly quickly and (instead of re-stocking) repay the debts outstanding. By contrast a manufacturer in the capital goods industries, with a lot of specific assets (which are not much use to any other industry) cannot recover from an illiquid position quickly and should really be financed by equity capital not borrowing. The best equity capital for such firms comes from those with a genuine interest in the industry, and the aim is to plough back profits in good years to ensure that the plant is kept in good condition, without the need for overdrafts and borrowed money.

(b) **Average credit granted ratio** This ratio lets us know what sort of control is being exercised over debtors. Credit control limits should be established for every debtor when a business opens an account. The limit can be raised as the months go by but not too readily – it is not unknown for a series of small orders to be honoured on time, followed by a huge order for which there is no intention to pay.

The formula for this ratio is:

$$\text{Average Credit Granted (or Given)} = \frac{\text{Average debtors}}{\text{turnover}} \times \text{time period}$$

The time period may be months, weeks or days. Average debtors can be an average of opening and closing debtors if these are the only figures available, but if we have monthly figures for debtors available so much the better. Assuming we use days and the average debtors of Ken Perkins are £8,250 we have:

$$\text{Average Credit Granted} = \frac{£8,250 \times 365}{£196,520}$$

$$= 15.3 \text{ days}$$

Clearly, this seems to be a very satisfactory situation. The average period of credit granted is only 15 days. Probably a good deal of Ken Perkins' business is done on a cash basis and what debtors he does have pay promptly before their credit limits are reached.

Where a company has a good volume of export trade it is usual to safeguard payments by the use of one or other of the methods which have developed over the years. These are:

(i)   cash with order
(ii) letters of credit
(iii) documents against payment
(iv) documents against acceptance of a bill of exchange.

In such cases it is best to separate off export orders from home orders and find the Average Credit Granted Ratio for the home trade only.

(c) **Average credit taken ratio** It might be thought that taking extended credit is advantageous to the firm or company, since it is financing the business with the creditors' money. However, while a debtor can rarely threaten the existence of a business, legal action by a creditor may have dire consequences. Quite apart from the moral and contractual obligation to pay for goods according to the agreed terms, a reputation as a poor payer can lead to refusal of supplies, especially in times of shortage – when the supplier will naturally favour reputable traders.

The formula is similar to the one for debtors.

$$\text{Average credit taken} = \frac{\text{Average trade creditors}}{\text{Net Purchases}} \times \text{Time period}$$

The words 'trade creditors' are important. There is a tendency to lump all creditors together in a single figure – for example the VAT office and the Inland Revenue may be creditors. A trader will only get a clear picture if the creditors' figure relates only to the purchases made, just as the debtors' figure refers to the sales (turnover).

Suppose the average trade creditors figure is £7,236, Ken Perkins ratio will be:

$$\text{Average credit taken} = \frac{£7,236}{£86,600} \times 365 \text{ days}$$

$$= \underline{30.5 \text{ days}}$$

30.5 days is a fairly average figure for most businesses these days.

The Balance Sheet ratios already mentioned have been chiefly connected with liquidity and financial stability rather than with profitability. Although they tell us helpful things about a business they do not tell us much about the profitability of the business or the use the business is making of the funds made available to it. We must now consider ratios that deal with profitability.

6   RETURN ON CAPITAL EMPLOYED (ROCE)

Looking again at Fig. 15.3 we can see once again the fundamental nature of the Balance Sheet – that what has been obtained by way of funds on the liabilities side has been used to purchase the assets on the assets side.

Strictly speaking therefore we can say that the capital employed in the business is the total of the Balance Sheet £190,445. Speaking even more strictly, an economist would say that the true figure for the capital employed in this business is the total of the assets – debtors (i.e. £190,445 – £6,171 = £184,274). This is because the debtors are actually using Ken Perkins' capital in *their* businesses, just as he is using the creditors' capital to the extent of £7,936.

Disregarding these ideas, accountants regard the capital employed as being the total long-term funds available to the business, which means the net worth provided by the proprietor and the mortgage funds. We will set down the figures for a moment to consider them

		£
Capital at start		123,655
Add Net Profit	58,454	
Less Drawings	19,600	
		38,854
Net Worth		162,509
Long-term Liabilities		
Mortgage		20,000

The capital at the start has certainly been employed in the business all year, and so has the mortgage figure, presumably. However, the £38,854 profit has been earned during the year and gradually accumulated at the service of the business. It is therefore usual to assume that it accumulated at an even rate throughout the year, and therefore only half of it was available on average. We can therefore say:

Capital employed = Capital at start + half the addition + long-term liabilities
$$= £123,655 + £19,427 + £20,000$$
$$= £163,082$$

The return on this capital is the profit earned in the year, which is £58,454. However, this profit calculation was made after the interest on the mortgage has been paid, so that we must include the rewards paid to the mortgagor. Let us suppose the £20,000 mortgage earned interest of $12\frac{1}{2}\%$ = £2,500. Therefore the return on capital invested is £58,454 + £2,500.

Expressed as a ratio (or better still as a percentage) we have:

$$\text{Return on Capital Employed} = \frac{£60,954}{£163,082} \times 100$$
$$= 37.4\%$$

This seems to be a very satisfactory use of the resources placed at the disposal of the business.

7   RETURN ON CAPITAL INVESTED

A slightly more personal view of the business is given by the Return on Capital Invested. Here we view the business from the proprietor's point of view. An original investment of £123,655 earned the proprietor £58,454. What we must not forget though is that some of this income could have been obtained without going into business at all. For example the capital could have been left in a high interest deposit account and earned – say – 9.3% net of tax – or 12.4% gross. Similarly the proprietor, had he/she not been in business, could have earned an income elsewhere, in employment. Let us suppose Ken Perkins could have earned £9,500 in employment.

These alternative earnings were sacrificed to go into business; they are called the 'opportunity cost' of self-employment. By taking the self-employment opportunity Ken Perkins sacrificed these alternative opportunities. The formula for the true return on capital invested = net profit – opportunity cost. In Ken Perkins' case:

$$\text{Return on Capital Invested} = £58,454 - (£9,500 + £15,333)$$
$$= £58,454 - £24,833$$
$$= £33,621$$

$$\text{Return on Capital Invested} = \frac{£33,621}{£123,655} \times 100$$
$$= 27.2\%$$

By being in business Ken Perkins earned an extra 27.2% on his/her capital. It was clearly worth while being in business.

8 THE REPAYMENT CAPACITY RATIO

Finally, to bankers, especially, the repayment capacity ratio is important. There are a good many approaches to the problems of risk management, but this is an elementary book and we will only consider a simple formula for deciding whether a business will be able to repay the money that we lend to it. Clearly we should not lend funds to a business which manifestly will not be able to repay both the interest and the principal sum borrowed, according to the terms of the contract. Even if a bank likes to say 'Yes', it will often have to say 'No'. The simplest guide compares the profit available (before deductions have been made for interest and taxation) with the interest charges on outside borrowed money. Written as a formula this is:

$$\text{Repayment Capacity Ratio} = \frac{\text{Profit (before tax and interest charges)}}{\text{Interest charges on outside borrowed money}}$$

In Ken Perkins' case this was

$$\frac{\text{Net Profit} + \text{Interest on Mortgage}}{\text{Interest on Mortgage}}$$

$$= \frac{£60,954}{£2,500}$$

$$= 24.4$$

In other words Ken Perkins could cover the interest on borrowings 24.4 times at present.

Suppose he proposed borrowing £100,000 at 16%. The interest would be £16,000 per annum, which together with the mortgage interest gives us:

$$\text{Repayment Capacity Ratio} = \frac{£60,954}{£18,500}$$

$$= 3.3 \text{ times}$$

This does not take any account of the need to repay the capital sum over the lifetime of the loan, but clearly it puts quite a different complexion on the business, and Ken Perkins should not be encouraged to borrow so much. Some more limited form of expansion is desirable.

■ EXERCISE 15.3
Answers correct to 1 decimal place where appropriate.

1 Martin Gooch has current assets of £38,250, of which £9,560 is stock. His current liabilities total £14,256.

(a) Calculate his working capital ratio.
(b) Calculate his acid test ratio.

2 Elvira Bright has current assets of £86,524 of which stock is £63,580. Her current liabilities total £46,500.

(a) Calculate her working capital ratio.
(b) Calculate her acid test ratio.
(c) Do you consider her business sound, or not, from the liquidity point of view?

3 **(a)** Give another name for working capital ratio.
(b) Give two other names for the acid test ratio.
(c) Rajinder Shah has current assets of £16,254, of which £9,585 is stock. Current liabilities are £5,591. Calculate (i) the working capital ratio and (ii) the acid test ratio.
4 **(a)** What is gearing?
(b) Work out the gearing ratio for Trufinance Plc which has Ordinary Share Capital of £100,000; Preference Share Capital of £100,000 Debentures of £50,000 and an overdraft of £250,000.
5 **(a)** What is meant by a gearing ratio of 1.0?
(b) Abdul Ajakaiye has capital (including profits ploughed back) of £360,000. He has a mortgage of £50,000, secured loans from a finance company of £100,000 (secured on his stock) and an overdraft of £25,000. What is his gearing ratio?
(c) He tells you that most of his trade is with retailers who pay within 15 days' of delivery and on a turnover of £1,000,000 last year he had £17,200 of bad debts, which he sold to a debt recovery firm for £7,500. In view of this, what comment would you make on his gearing ratio, as found in (b) above.
6 Doberman and Airedale had average debtors of £7,250 and turnover last year of £117,295. What was the average credit period granted to debtors? (Answer in days.)
7 Landscaping Ltd had average debtors last year of £1,614. Turnover (work done) was £19,650. What was the average credit period granted to customers? (Answer in weeks.)

8 Wedded Bliss ordered wedding garments and accessories worth £14,295 in the year. Average creditors outstanding at any time were £756. What was the average credit period taken by the firm? (Answer in weeks.)

9 The Wilson Paper Group purchases stationery of various sorts in the year to a total value of £895,726. Average creditors outstanding at any time were £156,520. What was the average credit period taken? (Answer in months.)

10 Here is the Balance Sheet of T French. You are asked to answer the questions below it, with calculations correct to one decimal place if necessary.

Balance Sheet as at 31 December 19..

Fixed Assets		£	Capital		£
Premises		140,000	At start		111,000
Plant & Machinery		42,500	*Add* Net Profit	85,000	
Furniture and Fittings		13,800	*Less* Drawings	26,800	
Motor Vehicles		16,700			58,200
		213,000			169,200
Current Assets			Long-term liabilities		
Stock	15,725		Mortgage	60,000	
Debtors	3,875		Loan from bank	15,000	
Cash at bank	24,610				
Cash in hand	1,390				75,000
		45,600			
			Current Liabilities		
			Creditors	14,250	
			Wages due	150	
					14,400
		£258,600			£258,600

(a) What is the fixed capital?
(b) What is the working capital?
(c) What is the capital owned by the proprietor at the end of the year?
(d) What is the long-term capital employed in the business at 31 December?
(e) What is the return on the capital employed, assuming that profits ploughed back are available for use at an even rate throughout the year (i.e. use half the figure only of £58,200)? Interest paid on the mortgage and the loan totalled £11,250.

11 Here is K Shah's Balance Sheet. You are to answer the questions below (with calculations to 1 decimal place if needed).

Balance Sheet as at 31 December 19..

Fixed Assets			*Capital*		£
Goodwill		4,000	At start		40,000
Premises		44,000	Add Net Profit	23,000	
Plant and Machinery		22,000	Less Drawings	17,200	
Motor Vehicles		16,000			5,800
		86,000			45,800
Current Assets			*Long-term Liabilities*		
Stock	14,560		Mortgage	38,000	
Debtors	4,810		Loan from bank	30,000	
Cash at bank	14,370				68,000
Cash in hand	160				
		33,900			
			Current liabilities		
			Creditors	5,936	
			Accrued Charges	164	
					6,100
		£119,900			£119,900

(a)   What is the capital owned by the proprietor at the end of the year?
(b)   What is the long-term capital employed? (Assume profits earned at a steady pace.)
(c)   What is the working capital?
(d)   What is the liquid capital?
(e)   Work out the acid test ratio (correct to one decimal place).
(f)   Work out the return on capital invested assuming that Shah could earn £12,000 a year in an alternative position, with none of the responsibilities of a small businessman, and his capital would also have earned 8% if invested safely.

■ ANSWERS
Exercise 15.1
1   Gross profit percentage = 42.4%.
2   Gross profit percentage = 23.0%.
3   (a) Gross profit percentage = 40.6%   (b) £932,204.
4   (a) Gross profit percentage = 15.5%   (b) It stays the same. Turnover becomes £874,200; gross profit £135,180; % = 15.5% as before.
5   (a) 8.1 times a year   (b) Average period in stock = 6.4 weeks.
6   (a) 13.3 times a year   (b) 27.4 days.
7   (a) No.1: 25.3%   No.2: 24.6%   (b) No.1: 5.1 times a year   No.2: 2.9 times a year   (c) It appears that Business No.1 is the better, since it has both a higher rate of stock turnover and a higher gross profit percentage.
8   (a) Gross Profit Percentages are: A = 25%   B = 22.1%   C = 26.5%   D = 22.7%
(b) C is showing the highest gross profit percentage.

Exercise 15.2
1   Net Profit percentage = 24.1%

2 Net Profit percentage 20.9%

3 (a) 16.9% (b) 25.6% (c) 3.0%

4 (a) 23.7% (b) Expense ratio for diesel = 18.6%. It is not the cause of their problem. There must be some other aspect of their activities which is the cause of the problem. We need to work out all the other expense ratios.

5 Tough Dealing Ltd: Net Profit £178,874; Gross profit % = 52.2%; Net profit % = 34.0%

Easy-go Ltd: Net Profit £161,936; Gross profit % = 54.3%; Net Profit % = 24.5%

Tough Dealing Ltd seems to be the more sound, as the net profit percentage is higher, but in fact both are probably viable risks for £100,000. £100,000 is going to cost them about £20,000 (say) a year in interest and their net profit should be able to support this, but it depends upon their other commitments, which are not revealed by the figures available. We can't judge their ability to repay the capital sum until we know a bit more.

6 (a) Beautiful Bonnets: Net Profit £43,000; Gross Profit % = 52.1%; Net Profit % = 23.1%

Brighter Homes: Net Profit £82,874; Gross Profit % = 67.1%; Net Profit % = 52.7%

(b) There is no doubt Brighter Homes is the better prospect, but even Beautiful Bonnets might be able to support the repayments on a £50,000 loan. It depends upon their other commitments which we need to know before we can judge their ability to repay.

Exercise 15.3

1 (a) 2.7 (b) 2.0

2 (a) 1.9 (b) 0.5

(c) Not sound – she has too much stock and too little cash. The acid test ratio should be at least 1, and it is only 0.5. If asked to pay all her current liabilities she would be unable to do so.

3 (a) current ratio (b) quick ratio or liquidity ratio (c) (i) 2.9 (ii) 1.2

4 (a) Gearing is the relationship between long-term capital provided by the proprietors and external finance obtained by borrowing whether secured or unsecured. Low gearing means most of the finance is provided by the proprietors or shareholders (if a company). High gearing means most of the finance is provided by borrowing, either by debentures or in unsecured loans. (b) Gearing ratio = 1.5.

5 (a) A gearing ratio of 1.0 means that the finance of the company or firm is provided equally by long-term (proprietor's) capital and borrowing from external sources. (b) Gearing ratio = 0.49 (c) It is quite OK. It is a low gearing anyway, and as he deals in stock which is promptly turned into cash once it is ordered he is unlikely to be put into difficulties – he exercises good credit control procedures.

6 22.6 days.

7 4.3 weeks.

8 2.8 weeks.

9 2.1 months.

10 (a) £213,000 (b) £31,200 (c) £169,200 (d) £244,200 (e) 44.7%.

11 (a) £45,800 (b) £110,900 (c) £27,800 (d) £13,240 (e) acid test ratio = 3.2 (f) return on capital invested = 19.5%.

16 Branch accounts for banking

OBJECTIVES

At the end of this chapter you should:
1 Be able to pass correct double entries in your branch for the commoner accounting events affecting customers;
2 Be able to pass correct double entries in your branch for matters affecting the relationship between the branch and Head Office;
3 Understand the clearing systems used in UK banking.

1 DOUBLE ENTRIES IN BANKING

Banking activities are heavily computerised today, and the double entries that are essential for every banking transaction are largely effected by computerisation. There might seem little point in learning double entries for routine book-keeping matters, since the computers have all been programmed long ago and it is not the part of any relatively young and inexperienced person to make double entries other than by depressing some key which sends the various pieces of data on their way. However, this is not a good attitude. A better attitude is to know exactly what the computer is doing when you depress any key – to see the double entry being carried out as the computer does it, or even before. At the speed computers work perhaps we can't hope to think that fast ourselves, but we do have the advantage of being the one who depresses the key. If you hold up depressing the key long enough to think:

'Right – go on then – credit the customer and debit Branch Cash Account for me. Go!'...

... you will get a good deal of satisfaction from pressing the key.

In giving the account that follows, of all the common double-entries which occur in day-to-day banking, I have only been able to describe a typical system. Some banks may follow a slightly different pattern of activities, but I have endeavoured to illustrate the basic principles of double entry and I am sure you will be able to see the link between the explanations given and the system in use in your own bank.

2 ACCOUNT ENTRIES FOR CUSTOMERS

2.1 Deposits by a customer

Deposits by a customer place funds with the bank for a variety of reasons, either in a Current Account or in some sort of Deposit Account. Competition between the banks has produced in recent years a wide variety of different accounts, each of them with its own special features, but fundamentally there are only two real types of account, current accounts and deposit accounts. Whatever the marketing people in banking may do to attract customers, the accounts they propose must embody the main features of current accounts and deposit accounts.

In the first part of this chapter we will only refer to entries in a customer's Current Account. Entries in a Deposit Account are similar, but less numerous because it is not usual to have a cheque book facility with a Deposit Account and if such a facility is available it is usually limited in some way – for example cheques might only be permitted for a minimum of £250 at a time.

When a customer pays in money to a Current Account his/her reasons include:

(a) Safe keeping of the deposits made available to the bank.

(b) The convenience of using the bank payments systems: cheques, standing orders, direct debit authorisations, cheque cards, bank cards, credit cards, etc.

(c) The convenience of receiving money without handling cash, for example salaries paid direct to the bank and bank giro transfers – credit transfers – by such people as home agents in the mail order business.

The formalities for opening an account need not concern us here – that is part of an Elements of Banking course. We are concerned with the accounting entries. It is perhaps worth saying though that when a customer deposits funds they cease to be the customer's funds and become the bank's funds. The bank is not a trustee of the funds, held on behalf of the customer, and liable to account for every penny of them and the uses to which they are put. The funds merge with the bank's own funds and are entirely at the bank's disposal. All the bank has to do is to make the funds deposited available at any future time, to the same amount and as the customer may request.

Double entries for deposits

Example 1

A cash deposit A customer, Tom Smith, deposits £500 in cash. The double entry reasoning is as follows:

(a) Tom Smith has given the bank £500. Credit the giver. Tom is now a creditor of the bank (the bank owes him back £500).

(b) The £500 is in cash and becomes merged with the bank's cash funds. Cash is an asset. Whenever we obtain an asset we debit the asset account. However the computer only makes the entry in the Branch Cash Account once a day, and in the meantime it simply collects it all together in some general set of statistics in an account called 'Counter Suspense'. A Suspense Account is a name given to any account where we hold an item pending a final decision about where it should be entered, and this is done once a day when the branch has sorted out the whole day's work. The £500 paid in by Tom Smith will finish up as part of the Branch Cash Account, mixed in with all the other cash paid in during the day.

The double entry is therefore:
Debit Branch Cash Account with £500.00
Credit Tom Smith Account with £500.00.

Special note about cash deposits   Under recent legislation it is necessary for banks to report when customers pay in very large sums of money in cash. This is part of the attempts to control drug dealing. Cashiers should draw any such situations discreetly to the attention of their supervisors.

Example 2

A deposit that leads to a branch clearing   Maira Malik pays in a cheque for £180.50 to her branch, from her cousin Abdul Kadarr, who also banks at the same branch.

Here there is no new deposit of funds. Head Office is not affected, for all it means is that Abdul Kadarr, who already has funds on deposit at the bank, has received back the use of some of these funds and used them to pay Maira Malik a sum he owes her. The double entry is:

Debit Abdul Kadarr – he has received back the use of £180.50
Credit Maira Malik – she has deposited £180.50 with the bank – credit the giver.
Looking at this in account form we have the situation shown in Fig. 16.1.

Abdul Kadarr a/c			L24
	Dr	Cr	Bal
Balance			529.80C
Cheque 071625	180.50		349.30C

Maira Malik a/c			L17
	Dr	Cr	Bal
Balance			13.30Dr
Sundries		180.50	167.20C

Fig. 16.1   Double entries for a branch clearing

Notes
1   Since both parties bank at the same branch this matter is sorted out as a 'branch clearing'.
2   Kadarr is debited; he has received back the use of £180.50. This reduced the bank's indebtedness to Kadarr, but he is still a creditor for £349.30.
3   Maira Malik was overdrawn for a small amount, £13.30.
4   This new deposit of £180.50 extinguishes her overdraft and leaves her in credit for £167.20.

5 Head Office is not affected – it has the same amount of funds as before, but it is now responsible for them to different parties.

Example 3

A deposit that leads to a Head Office clearing As far as a branch is concerned, any clearing that is not a branch clearing is an 'out-of-house' clearing or a 'non-house' clearing and is a matter for Head Office. The usual case is where a customer is the payee named on a cheque which he/she pays in for collection.

Isaac Olaleye, whose premises have been damaged in a storm, receives a cheque for £680 from the Solicitous Insurance Co. It is drawn on the City of London branch of the Helpful Bank Plc. Isaac pays it into the Redhill branch of the Helpful Bank Plc.

This is going to result in a Head Office clearing – which is explained more fully later in this chapter.

Double-entry thinking of the Redhill branch The double entry thinking is: Isaac has deposited £680 in the Redhill branch. Credit Isaac's account, he is the giver of funds to the bank – credit the giver. However, no new money is involved. The £680 is to come from the account of the Solicitous Insurance Co, at the City of London branch. It will be necessary to debit their account, as they have received back the use of funds. We can't do this directly from Redhill – the cheque will have to be cleared by a Head Office clearing. We will pass the details of the cheque to Head Office for clearing. At the end of the day the total of the Remittances Outward will be debited to Head Office Account.

The double entry therefore is:
Debit Head Office Account £680.00
Credit Isaac Olaleye with £680.000.

If the Solicitous Insurance Co had banked with a different bank altogether this would have made no difference at all to the entries, but instead of Head Office clearing the money from its own branch in the City it would claim it through the clearing house mechanism from the other bank. This is explained more fully later.

We have now said enough about deposits to realise that whenever a deposit is made it results in a credit entry in the depositor's account and a debit entry in some other account. This may be Branch Cash Account or Head Office Account but in the case of a branch clearing it will be the account of the payer of the money (who is receiving back funds previously on deposit).

One final point. As mentioned in Chapter 9, the interest on accounts is only payable when the cheque paid in has been cleared. In a branch clearing the cheque has been cleared, since the payer also banks at our branch. When the payee is credited interest starts to run from that moment, and as the payer's account is debited at the same moment, interest ceases on that amount at once. With a cheque cleared out of house, the credit entry on the payee's account is **'uncleared effects'** and is not entitled to interest until the fourth day, when the cheque will have been cleared the day before and interest can start to run. Thus funds paid in on a Monday (Day 1) will be cleared on Wednesday, be available to the payee on Thursday morning and – if withdrawn on a Friday – will have earned one day's interest.

2.2 Dishonoured cheques

Example 4

A cheque value £50 paid in by Mary Thomas is from R Radcliffe, who banks at the same branch. Radcliffe is debited and Thomas is credited. Next day it is noticed that Radcliffe has insufficient funds. We make entries cancelling the previous day's entries, i.e. debit Thomas and credit Radcliffe. We now return the cheque to Mary Thomas asking her to 'refer to drawer; please re-present'. This request to re-present implies that we feel Radcliffe's lack of funds is purely an oversight on his part, or a temporary state only on his account.

Example 5

A cheque credited to P Marshall's account three days ago for £480, which was drawn on another bank, is returned unpaid (refer to drawer).

When a cheque which has been paid in by a customer is returned unpaid for some reason, the customer's account has to be debited at once. The credit entry we made a day or so ago when the cheque was paid in has to be cancelled by a debit entry as it has been found to be unjustified. The double entry is: debit the original payee, P Marshall, and return the cheque to him/her. It will have been marked by the returning bank to explain why it has not been honoured. Credit the Returns Account. This is a branch account where cheques which are being returned are recorded. As the returned cheque comes in the returning bank/branch will have debited the Branch Returns Account via Head Office with the value of the dishonoured cheque. When the branch removes the money from the payee's account and credits it to Returns Account it clears the Returns Account and acknowledges that the funds have been removed from the payee's account.

Example 6

A cheque made out by a customer P Turner for £560 arrives through the clearing inwards. He has only £120. Head Office has already debited the customer's account and credited the collecting bank, or the collecting branch if it is another branch. If we decide to dishonour the cheque, we credit the customer or minus the entry so that it is deleted from the account. This restores the account to the state it was in before Head Office debited it and we debit the collecting banker via Head Office. The cheque is then returned to the collecting branch direct by post, marked refer to drawer.

Note: To dishonour a cheque is a serious matter, and customers where cheques are wrongly returned may sue for damage to their good name and business status. Always check carefully

    (a) Is the account definitely out of funds?

    (b) Has any regular payment due to the customer not arrived for any reason?

    (c) Could such a credit have been wrongly credited to an account with a similar name?

    (d) Has an overdraft been sanctioned but not marked on the account for any reason?

(e)   Is it advisable to phone the customer and discuss the need to return the cheque?

(f)   Sometimes a cheque can be marked – 'Refer to drawer and re-present.' This implies that the cheque cannot be honoured at present but the bank feels fairly sure it will be honoured in a few days.

2.3   Standing orders, direct debits and bank giro credits

Example 7

A standing order from P Havers for £85.90 reaches the date of payment. The computer will feed through a debit to P Havers' Account and a credit to Head Office Account from the branch. We check that P Havers' Account can make the payment and if all is well allow the entry to proceed. If we cannot allow the payment to proceed we cancel the overnight debit by crediting or minusing the entry in P Havers' Account (thus restoring it to the original position) and debit Standing Order Recall Account to show that the standing order cannot be honoured.

Example 8

A local authority passes a direct debit request for £373.50 community charge to P Havers. We check the authorisation and the balance on the account. If all is well we debit P Havers Account (he is receiving back the use of his funds) and credit the Local Authority if it banks with us. If it banks elsewhere we credit Head Office Account and let the local authority get its funds through the clearing mechanism. If we do not wish the direct debit to proceed we credit P Havers, (or minus the entry so it does not appear on his Account) and debit Direct Debit Recall Account.

Example 9

Bank giro credits are used to transfer money directly into the accounts of customers, without the need to write cheques and send them to the payee, who must then pay them in. They are chiefly used

● to pay wages and salaries;
● to pay dividends and debenture interest – for example the Bank of England pays all interest on gilt-edged securities in this way;
● by mail order houses, whose home agents pay the sums collected from their customers over the counter of local banks for the credit of the mail order house's current account;
● to pay credit card accounts, bills for utilities such as water, gas and rates, etc.

(a)   List of credits arriving from a firm for payroll payments to employees.

(i) Debit the firm's Current Account with the total payroll figure – the firm is receiving back the use of its money formerly deposited with the bank.
(ii) Credit the accounts of local employees who bank with the branch.
(iii) Credit Head Office with the balance due to other employees – the Head Office is a creditor of the branch for this money now deducted from the firm's Current Account to be used in paying salaries elsewhere.

(b)   List of credits arriving through clearing inwards for the credit of employees etc, who bank at your branch.

(i) Credit the account of the employees who are to be paid their salaries.
(ii) Debit Head Office Account – it is a debtor of the branch for the money credited in the customer's individual accounts.

(c)   Cash paid over the counter by home agents, for the credit of mail order houses etc. elsewhere. The cash is debited in Branch Cash Account at the end of the day. The credit-entry is in Head Office Account at the end of the day along with all other remittances outwards.

(d)   Bills paid in cash are treated as in (c). If paid by cheque it will be the customer's A/c which is debited rather than Branch Cash Account.

2.4   Bank charges and interest due to the bank

These are profits of the bank. They will be debited to customers' accounts (the customers have used up some of their deposits in banking services and consequently may be regarded as receiving back some of their deposits and using them to pay the bank for its services.) The double entry will be profits of the branch. The interest will be credited in Branch Interest Account and the charges in Branch Charges Account, as profits of the branch. At the end of the year these profits will be transferred to Head Office and become part of the main profits of the bank.

2.5   Interest due to customers

These are expenses (i.e. losses) of the bank. They will be credited to the customers' account (net of basic rate tax for personal customers) and, there will be a debit in the branch's Interest Paid Account for the gross amount (the customer's net gain and the tax due). This leaves the double entry short by the amount of the tax due to Inland Revenue. This will be credited to Branch Inland Revenue Account along with all the other amounts affecting other customers, and the Inland Revenue will be paid the tax deducted from time to time.

Note that where a customer is a foreign national not subject to UK tax law the computer will be coded in such a way that it pays the interest gross. The double entry is then: debit Branch Interest Paid Account, credit the customer with the full amount.

2.6   Loans, interest on loans and loan repayments

Loans made to customers

Whenever a loan is made to a customer the amount of the loan is credited in a customer's Current Account. It is balanced by the opening of a Loan Account in the customer's name. Interest will sometimes be added to the loan at the start (though in other cases it is charged at intervals later) and often a one-off payment for insurance cover will be added as well. The entries therefore are:

(a)   Debit the Loan Account of the customer – specially opened for this purpose –

with the full charge for the loan, including interest and insurance premium if appropriate.

(b)   Credit the customer's Current Account with the net amount of the loan. This thus becomes available for normal spending.

(c)   Credit the interest to Branch Interest Account and the full premium to Head Office for the benefit of the insurance subsidiary of the bank. The insurance subsidiary will probably later pay the branch a commission for its work in arranging the policy, but pending this event the branch pays the whole premium over. Any such commission of course becomes a branch profit, to be transferred at the end of the year to Head Office.

Repayments of loans

Here the loan repayment is almost always in the form of a standing order. The double entry is:

(a)   Debit the customer's Current Account to remove the funds from the account.

(b)   Credit the Loan Account to reduce the balance owing now that the instalment has been paid.

Interest on loans added at intervals after arrangement of the loan

Here the double entry is very simple:

(a)   Debit the customer's Loan Account – the customer is a debtor for the extra interest.

(b)   ʼCredit Branch Interest Received Account. The interest is a branch profit, to be transferred at the end of the year to Head Office.

Sometimes the customer prefers to pay the interest straight away in which case it will be the customer's Current Account, rather than the Loan Account, which is debited.

3   A TABLE OF DOUBLE ENTRIES

To sum up the double entries for maintaining accounts of customers in branches they are as shown in Table 16.1.

Table 16.1   Double entries for Customers' Accounts

	Nature of Activity	Account to be debited	Account to be credited
1	A cash deposit	Branch Cash Account (at the end of the day)	Customer's Account
2	A cash withdrawal	Customer's Account	Branch Cash Account (at the end of the day)

(*Note*: On 1 and 2 until the end of the day the Branch Cash Account entries are collected in either debit or credit totals in a 'Counter Suspense' register)

Continued

Table 16.1 Continued

Nature of Activity	Account to be debited	Account to be credited
3 Cheque paid in (House item)	Account of the payer	Account of the payee

(*Note*: A house item is one where both payee and payer bank at the branch, so that the item can be cleared at once in house, without reference to Head Office.)

Nature of Activity	Account to be debited	Account to be credited
4 Cheque paid in as in (3) above (House item) but dishonoured next day	Payee's Account	Payer's Account

(Return cheque to payee, marked refer to drawer, after checking the account carefully to ensure it is not possible to honour the cheque.)

Nature of Activity	Account to be debited	Account to be credited
5 Cheque paid in (Non-house item)	Head Office Account (at the end of the day −remittances outwards)	Payee's Account
6 Remittance outwards returned dishonoured	Payee's Account	Returns Account

(*Note*: Head Office debits our Returns Account as the cheque is returned, making us a debtor for the sum already credited to the payee. When we remove the funds by debiting the Payee's Account we credit Returns Account to tell Head Office we have recovered the money).

Nature of Activity	Account to be debited	Account to be credited
7 Remittances inwards (Cheque made out by our customer and sent to someone, now reaching us through the clearing system)	Payer's Account	Head Office Account Remittances inwards
8 Remittances inwards (which we find we must dishonour)	Collecting banker (or collecting branch via HO truncation system)	Customer's Account to cancel HO's automated debit (to prevent the entry appearing at all on the customer's statement the computer will do a minus entry)
9 Standing orders	Payer's Account	Head Office Account (who will pass the payment to the beneficiary)
10 Direct debit	Payer's Account	Head Office Account for onward transmission
11 Bank giro credit (a) Wages payment from local firm	Firm paying wages	Payees' Accounts (if in-house) Head Office Account (for onward transmission otherwise)
(b) Wages payment arriving via Head Office	Head Office Account	Payee's Account

Table 16.1   Continued

	Nature of Activity	Account to be debited	Account to be credited
	(c) Cash payment by home agent, etc for credit of named payee	Branch Cash Account (at end of day)	Payee (if in-house) Head Office Account (for onward transmission if not in-house).
	(d) payment of a bill	Branch Cash Account (if cash) Payer's Account (if a cheque)	As for (c) above.
12	Bank charges	Customer's Account	Branch Charges Account (a branch profit)
13	Bank interest due from customers	Customer's Account	Branch Interest Received Account (a branch profit)
14	Bank interest due to depositors	Branch Interest Payable Account	Customer's Account
15	Loan to customer	Customer's Loan Account (with the full sum repayable)	(i) Customer's Current Account (with the net amount of the loan) (ii) Branch Interest Received Account (with the interest) (iii) Bank Insurance Subsidiary Co Account with the premium (if any)
16	Loan repayment	Customer's Current Account	Customer's Loan Account (reducing the balance owed)
17	Loan interest added from time to time	Customer's Loan Account (or Current Account if Customer wishes to clear the interest at once)	Branch Interest Received Account (a branch profit)

4   OTHER MATTERS AFFECTING THE BRANCH AND HEAD OFFICE

Head Office is interested not only in the day to day affairs of all the customers of each branch, but in evaluating each branch's performance. This is not an easy task – there may be many valid reasons why a branch cannot expand its activities in a particular locality, or which make it a 'high cost' branch compared with other branches. However there must be some uniform method of allocating costs to branches so that Head Office knows the situation and can achieve sound control of branch activities. Practices vary from bank to bank but some of the general rules are:

(a)   If costs are borne centrally by Head Office (which ensures bulk buying with the maximum opportunity to obtain good quality products at reasonable prices) branches will be charged a fair sum for the supplies they use. This could include consumable items (like stationery) or capital items, such as furniture and equipment. Branch Charges Account will be debited with these expenses of the branch, and Head Office Account will be credited. It has given the branch the items used.

(b) If costs are borne locally Branch General Charges Account will be debited and Branch Payments Account credited as the cheque goes out to the local supplier.

(c) Branch Salaries will be credited to the accounts of individual staff and debited to Branch Salaries Account, which will eventually be cleared to Head Office Account at the end of the year.

Although there are, no doubt, many transactions which will occur between the branch and its suppliers and between the branch and Head Office these entries are likely to be of two types only. Some will be kept within the branch as if it was a totally autonomous institution, until the end of the year arrives, when all the various branch accounts will be cleared off to Head Office leaving the branch to start a new financial year with 'nil' balances on all accounts. Others will be matters that Head Office wishes to handle immediately and a transaction with Head Office will clear it at once from the Branch's accounts.

We need not be too concerned here with the actual arrangements made for handling the millions of cheques and credits that are handled every day. An average day sees 15 million cheques worth − about £35,000 million − cleared. It is perhaps worth saying that the timetable goes as shown below, assuming that a paper system is being considered only. The speed-up which occurs when electronic systems short circuit paper movements is called **truncation** and is explained later.

Day 1 Cheques paid in by customers for collection are sorted by the branch of the **collecting bank**. Any branch clearings (cheques made out by one customer of the branch for payment to another customer of the branch) are cleared that day. All the other cheques are sent in bundles to the Clearing Office at Head Office to be dealt with on Day 2. This is the 'out' clearing. A typical day's remittances are shown in Fig. 16.2 (courtesy of Midland Bank Plc).

Day 2 The cheques have now arrived at the Clearing Office and those cheques which will be the subject of a Head Office clearing are removed. These are cheques drawn by a customer of one branch of our bank in favour of a customer at another branch of our bank. They are sorted into branches and sent off so that when they arrive at the branches (next day) the drawers of the cheques can be debited with the money which they have used out of their accounts.

The Clearing Office is left with the cheques drawn upon other banks. These are sorted into bundles for the other banks and each tray of cheques is totalled to give a total figure on a docket. They are then taken to the Clearing House to await collection by the other banks (the **paying bankers**). In return we collect our cheques from the other banks and take them back to Head Office. After listing the cheques to agree the totals, the cheques are sorted into branches and sent off to the branches for processing next day.

Day 3 The cheques arrive at the branches for clearing − the 'in' clearing. They are examined for the genuineness of the signature, the date, etc. and whether the account has the necessary funds. In most banks Head Office will already have debited the customer's account with the cheque through the automated clearing. Any 'returned

REMITTANCE AGREEMENT – DEBITS

Midland	181,061.31
Abbey National	4,498.50
Bank of England	41,003.41
Bank of Scotland	142.31
Barclays	681,320.60
Co-op	7,740.35
Lloyds	135,059.30
National Giro	3,694.74
National Westminster	450,073.79
Royal Bank of Scotland	14,563.87
TSB	6,426.77
Eurocheque	784.00
Sundry Banks	12,750.95

REMITTANCE AGREEMENT – CREDITS

Midland	126,319.20
Abbey National	1,304.20
Bank of England	0.00
Bank of Scotland	0.00
Barclays	9,493.73
Co-op	0.00
Lloyds	2,970.15
National Giro	168.75
National Westminster	3,619.99
Royal Bank of Scotland	9,786.73
TSB	926.24
Sundry Banks	1,489.71

Fig. 16.2   A day's branch remittances

unpaid' items are mailed to the collecting bank on Day 3 to arrive on Day 4. In the meantime we debit the collecting bank and credit the customer's account to restore it to the position it was in before Head Office debited it.

Payment will be made through the settlement at the Bank of England from the Paying Banker to the Collecting Banker on Day 3.

There will always be a few cheques which cannot be processed automatically. Perhaps they were torn, creased or rejected as indecipherable by the reader-sorter machines at Head Office which read the encoded numbers on the cheques. They must be debited individually to the relevant customers' accounts. The double entry is a credit to Head Office Account. These form the Manual Debit Clearing.

Day 4   The payee will be free to use the Funds on Day 4, although the cheque was cleared the day before.

The amount of interest is affected by the clearing procedure. This is explained later.

For certain major corporate customers whose accounts are of great value to the bank, and who issue and receive very large value cheques, a reduced two-day clearance cycle may be agreed instead of the standard 3-day cycle. This means that their funds are available to be drawn one day early, but this is only available to a very few customers.

4.1 Truncation

Truncation is the short-circuiting of a paper procedure by an electronic procedure. Since millions of cheques are on the move every day and it takes a great deal of labour to handle and move them, there is much to be said for leaving the cheques where they are and only sending a message about them. The system is not universal and the programs for implementing full truncation procedures are still being written, but most banks now have the system installed as far as their own branches are concerned, for cashed cheques, payment of which is guaranteed.

Details of cheques cashed are input over a computer terminal by the paying bank. The information is actually queued in a storage device during the day and transmitted overnight. The sorting process formerly carried out on the physical cheques now takes place electronically and the details are relayed to the branches who thus get, only one day after the cheques were cashed, a list of accounts to be debited.

Truncation can also be used for credit transfers – especially if the customer is an important customer whose goodwill it is desired to maintain. Also transactions such as ATM entries and EFTPOS entries which are initiated electronically anyway are all treated in the 'truncated' manner, which will no doubt, in due course, become universal for all inter-bank clearings. Table 16.2 shows a clearance schedule for most types of businesses.

5   THE CLEARING SYSTEMS

A clearing house is an organisation which simplifies the clearing procedures, and reduces the sums that need to be moved between banks to the 'net indebtedness' only. Before the clearing system was introduced (about 1770 AD) Bank A, which had a number of cheques drawn on Bank B, had to send a messenger round to present the cheques and ask for cash in exchange. Since Bank B almost certainly had cheques drawn on Bank A the messengers would often pass one another as they made their collections. The logical thing was to have a room where they could meet and exchange their cheques, and only the one who had the greater value of cheques needed to collect cash to the value of the difference between the two totals. This amount would be the net-indebtedness between them.

Today the system is even simpler, because all banks keep working balances at the Bank of England, and at the end of the working day all that is necessary is to transfer funds to the extent of the 'net indebtedness' between their accounts at the Bank of England. The original Clearing House was set up at 10 Lombard Street, where it is still situated, but the clearing banks do not now run the Clearing House themselves. In 1985 APACS, the Association of Payment Clearing Services was set up and thrown open to any financial institution that wished to participate. There are four main clearings.

(a)   The cheque and credit clearing, which deals with cheques and bank giro credit transfers. This is run by the Cheque and Credit Clearing Co Ltd.

(b)   CHAPS and the Town Clearing. CHAPS is the Clearing House Automated Payments System and the Town Clearing is a London clearing for interbank dealings. The minimum cheque is £100,000. These are run by the CHAPS and TOWN Clearing Co Ltd.

(c)   BACS is the Bankers' Automated Clearing Service, run by BACS Ltd.

Table 16.2 shows the clearance schedule that prevails at the time of writing.
  (d) The EFTPOS UK clearing.

Table 16.2 Clearance Schedule
Funds become available to payees on the days shown below

Day on which item paid in to collecting bank	Standard 3 day	2 day clearing cheques	Credit clearings (cash and cheques)	Truncation (Cash and cashed cheques – other cheques are not yet part of the truncation procedure)
Monday	Thurs	Wed	Wed	Mon
Tuesday	Fri	Thurs	Thurs	Tues
Wednesday	Mon	Fri	Fri	Wed
Thursday	Tues	Mon	Mon	Thurs
Friday	Wed	Tues	Tues	Fri

Note: This table becomes important when calculating the interest to which a customer is entitled.

5.1 The traditional clearing systems

There are four situations

  (a) Branch clearings
  (b) Head Office clearings
  (c) Clearing House clearings
  (d) Clearing House clearings of cheques paid in at another bank, which is neither the account holding bank of the payee or the paying bank.

There is also the modern computerised system of truncated clearings, as yet not fully developed and largely restricted to the clearing of cashed cheques, claims for unpaid items and certain credits for important customers by arrangement with Head Office.
    We may illustrate these clearings as shown in Figs. 16.3–16.6. Study these now, and the notes below them.

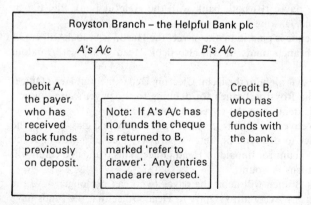

Fig. 16.3 A branch clearing

Notes

   (a)   Both payer (A) and payee (B) bank at the same branch of the same bank.

   (b)   The account of the payer is debited; he/she has received back the use of funds previously on deposit.

   (c)   The account of the payee is credited; he/she has deposited funds with the bank (they came from the payer's account).

   (d)   Head Office is not involved. There is no new money – all that has happened is that the Head Office now owes the funds transferred to a different depositor.

   (e)   If the payer has no funds to cover the cheque we will first of all make quite sure that the account cannot honour the cheque and if we find this is definitely the case we reverse the entries made and the cheque is returned to the payee marked 'refer to drawer'. We do not lightly dishonour a cheque, but if we must it is for the person who paid it in to take the matter up with the drawer.

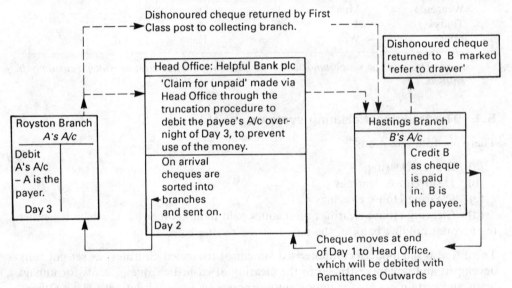

Fig. 16.4   A Head Office clearing

Notes

   (a)   The payer (A) and the payee (B) both bank with the Helpful Bank Plc, but at different branches (Royston and Hastings).

   (b)   On Day 1, when the cheque is paid in by the payee, the Hastings branch will credit the payee who has given the branch funds. It will also debit Head Office with random remittances.

   (c)   The cheque then moves overnight to the Debit Clearing Department at Head Office. On Day 2 it is forwarded to the Royston branch for debiting to the payer's account.

   (d)   On Day 3 the cheque is debited to the payer's account.

   (e)   If there are no funds to cover the cheque it will be returned by first class post to the collecting branch marked 'refer to drawer', or 'refer to drawer, please re-present'. The Royston branch will start off a claim for unpaid to Head Office. This truncated claim will debit the Hastings Branch Returns Account.

   (f)   On Day 4 the Hastings Branch will debit the payee (who can no longer have the money) and credit Branch Returns Account to signify to Head Office that the funds have been reclaimed.

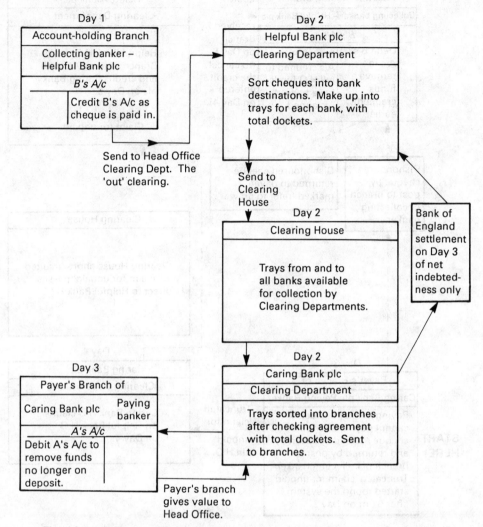

Fig. 16.5 A Clearing House clearing

Notes

(a)   The payer A and the payee B bank at different banks.

(b)   On Day 1 when the cheque is paid in the payee is credited and Head Office Account deibited with random remittances. The cheque is sent off to Head Office Clearing Department.

(c)   On Day 2 the cheques are sorted into bank destinations and each tray is listed to find the total.

(d)   The trays are taken round to the Clearing House for collection by the paying bankers.

(e)   The paying banker collects the tray and agrees the total. Then they are sorted and sent off to the paying branches.

(f)   On Day 3 the paying branches check the cheque, verify that funds are available and debit the payer's account. (What happens if funds are not available to cover the cheque is shown in Fig. 16.6.) The paying branch gives value to its Head Office for the cheque cleared on Day 3.

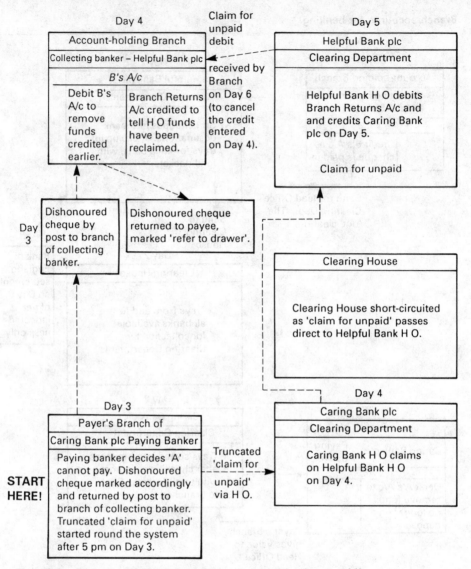

Fig. 16.6 Path of a dishonoured cheque, and 'claim for unpaid'

Notes

(a) Remember that 'claims for unpaid' are usually truncated. However they do take longer than a normal truncation to get right round the system.

(b) The dishonoured cheque is returned by post on Day 3 to reach collecting banker's branch on Day 4.

(c) The 'claim for unpaid' moves electronically via Head Office to debit Head Office of Collecting Banker on Day 4 and in turn the collecting branch a day or so later.

(d) On Day 4 the Collecting branch which has received back the dishonoured cheque debits the payee to reclaim the funds credited earlier and credits Branch Returns Account so Head Office knows funds have been reclaimed. The cheque is returned to the payee marked 'Refer to drawer', or in some other appropriate way.

(e) On Day 5 the Head Office of the Collecting Bank debits Branch Returns Account and credits the Head Office of the Paying Bankers, to re-imburse them with the money paid on Day 3.

(f) On Day 6 the debit sent by Head Office on Day 5 reaches the Collecting Branch to clear the credit made on Day 4 in Branch Returns.

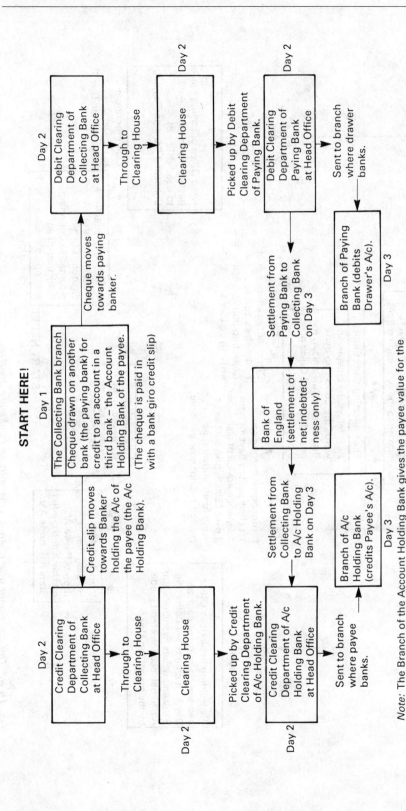

START HERE!

Day 1

The Collecting Bank branch

Cheque drawn on another bank (the paying bank) for credit to an account in a third bank – the Account Holding Bank of the payee.

(The cheque is paid in with a bank giro credit slip)

Credit slip moves towards Banker holding the A/c of the payee (the A/c Holding Bank).

Cheque moves towards paying banker.

Day 2

Credit Clearing Department of Collecting Bank at Head Office

Through to Clearing House

Day 2

Clearing House

Picked up by Credit Clearing Department of A/c Holding Bank.

Day 2

Credit Clearing Department of A/c Holding Bank at Head Office

Sent to branch where payee banks.

Day 3

Branch of A/c Holding Bank (credits Payee's A/c).

Settlement from Collecting Bank to A/c Holding Bank on Day 3

Bank of England (settlement of net indebtedness only)

Settlement from Paying Bank to Collecting Bank on Day 3

Day 2

Debit Clearing Department of Collecting Bank at Head Office

Through to Clearing House

Day 2

Clearing House

Picked up by Debit Clearing Department of Paying Bank.

Day 2

Debit Clearing Department of Paying Bank at Head Office

Sent to branch where drawer banks.

Day 3

Branch of Paying Bank (debits Drawer's A/c).

Note: The Branch of the Account Holding Bank gives the payee value for the cheque on Day 3 (one day earlier than if the cheque had been paid in at its own branch).

Fig. 16.7   Clearing a cheque drawn on one bank and paid in at another bank, for credit of an account at a third bank (see Notes on page 197)

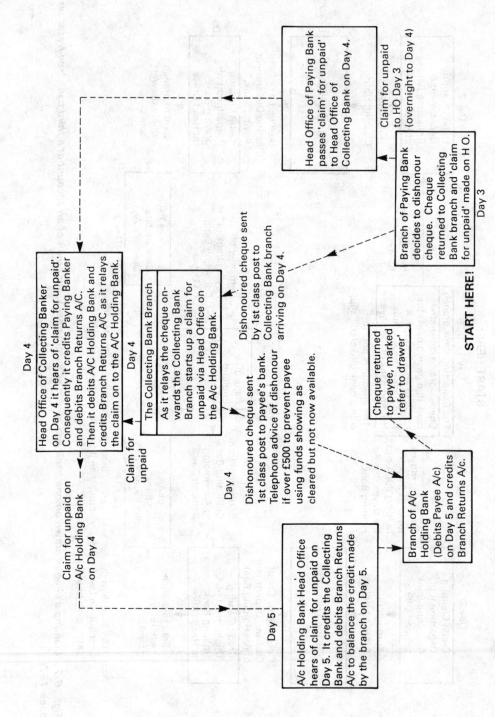

Fig. 16.8   The dishonour of a cheque where three banks are involved

Notes to Fig. 16.7 (see page 195)

(a)   The cheque is paid in at a bank, the Collecting Bank, to claim money from a payer (drawer) (banking at the Paying Bank) for the benefit of the payee, an account holder at a third bank (the Account-holding Bank).

(b)   The cheque is paid in together with a credit slip. The cheque moves towards the paying banker and the credit slip moves towards the account-holding banker.

(c)   The cheque goes via the Debit Clearing Department of the Collecting Bank to the Clearing House and then on to the Debit Clearing Department of the Paying Bank, which routes it through to the paying branch to debit the Payer's Account (the Drawer's Account).

(d)   The credit moves via the Credit Clearing Department of the Collecting Bank to the Clearing House and thence to the Credit Clearing Department of the Account-holding Bank which routes it through to the branch where the payee banks. The Payee's Account is credited. (What happens if the cheque cannot be honoured is shown in Fig. 16.8.)

(e)   The actual payment by the Paying Banker to the Collecting Banker will take place on Day 3, and the Collecting Banker will pay the money to the Account-holding Banker on Day 3, through the Bank of England at the Daily Settlement.

Notes to Fig. 16.8 opposite

(a)   On Day 3 when it discovers the cheque cannot be honoured, the drawers' branch of the Paying Banker sends the cheque by first class post to the branch of the Collecting Banker and starts a 'claim for unpaid' on its way via Head Office to the Collecting Banker.

(b)   On Day 4 the Collecting Banker's branch receive the dishonoured cheque and send it on again by first class post to the Account Holding Branch. They also start another 'claim for unpaid' via Head Office on the Account Holding branch.

(c)   On Day 5 the Account-Holding branch receives the cheque and debits the payee with the money that is no longer available and credits Branch Returns Account. It then returns the cheque to the payee marked 'refer to drawer'.

(d)   On Day 5 the Account Holding Banker credits the Collecting Banker and debits Branch Returns Account to balance the entry referred to in (c) above.
Bank.

Remember that a cheque may be returned for a number of reasons besides the fact that funds are not available to honour it. For example, it could be marked 'account closed' or 'drawer deceased'. If the payer has uncleared effects the cheque may be marked 'uncleared effects—please re-present'. This implies that the cheque may be honoured once the uncleared effects have been cleared.

5.2   Truncated clearings

Only a limited number of clearings are at present truncated (shortened). They include cashed cheques (payment of which will have been guaranteed either by the use of a cheque card or by a confirmatory call to the drawer's branch). Claims for unpaid, and credits approved by Head Office (to important customers only) may also be truncated.

Examples

1   A visitor cashes a cheque for £50 drawn on the branch where she normally banks. A cheque card is used to guarantee the cheque.

(a)   Credit Counter Suspense Account (it has given the customer the money).

(b)   Debit (via Head Office and the truncation procedure) the visitor's Branch with £50. This will be queued on the electronic system and sent overnight to arrive in the visitor's branch on Day 2.

2   A 'claim for unpaid' outwards – we dishonour our customer's cheque. Overnight our customer will have been debited with the amount of the cheque in the electronic system. If we don't do anything to stop it this debit will go through in the course of the day. If we want to dishonour the cheque we can 'minus' the entry (which is the same as crediting our customer to cancel the overnight debit), and we debit the Collecting Banker because he cannot have the money.

3   A 'claim for unpaid' inwards – our customer has paid in a cheque which has been dishonoured. In this situation the paying banker (who is unable to pay because his customer has no funds) debits our Branch Returns Account. We must now debit our payee (who was credited a few days ago with the money that is not now available) and credit Branch Returns Account to show Head Office that we have reclaimed the funds from the payee.

6   THE CLEARING SYSTEM AND INTEREST

We have seen that the modern clearing system is very sophisticated and highly computerised. Even so, it only amounts in the end to an endless succession of double entries performed at electronic speeds, which result in the running balances on customers' accounts rising or falling as they are credited or debited with the various entries.

Where an account earns interest, or pays interest, we have seen that the interest calculation is done by a method of products, so that each sum of money is multiplied by the number of days it is in the bank, or overdrawn. Any calculation of interest is therefore affected by the balance on the account and in this respect the clearing process is important.

Suppose a customer deposits a cheque for £1,000 in an interest-earning account, the money being paid by a person who also banks at the branch, the double entry will be an in-house matter, dealt with on Day 1. The £1,000 is credited to the depositor, and debited on the payer's account. So the £1,000 on the depositor's account is cleared, and the depositor can use it at once, while if it remains in the bank interest will be earned forthwith. By contrast the payer has been debited (he/she has received back the use of the money previously on deposit) and the entitlement to interest is lost at once on Day 1.

Taking the same situation which is not in-house. Although the depositor has been credited with the £1,000 he/she should not use this money without making special arrangements, for the £1,000 is **uncleared effects**. The bank cannot get the money from the payer until the end of Day 3, when the branch will be notified and the funds become available to the depositor at dawn on Day 4. The basic rule in banking is that interest is not payable on cheque deposits until the cheque has been cleared. Similarly an overdraft which is paid up in full with a cheque must pay interest until the cheque is cleared, because the overdraft is not cleared until that moment.

Similarly if an account is clear, and the account holder deposits a cheque (say for

£500) and starts to use these funds at once, the cleared balance of the account immediately becomes overdrawn until the cheque is cleared, although the account balance appears to be in credit. The customer must pay interest until the clearing of the cheque restores the true balance to a credit balance. When cash is paid in, it is of course cleared right away.

■ EXERCISE 16.1

(a) P Jones deposits a cheque from R Peters, his next-door neighbour, who has purchased his old car for £820. They both bank at the Bristol branch of Helpful Bank Plc. Explain the double entry.

(b) R Lark deposits a cheque for £2,000 from Rumpole and Rumpole in his Hastings branch of Caring Bank Plc. Explain:

(i) the double entry at the Hastings Branch
(ii) the double entry at Helpful Bank Plc, Strand branch in London, where Rumpole and Rumpole have their account.

(c) A cheque deposited at the Southampton branch of Caring Bank Plc is drawn on the Dover branch of Caring Bank Plc. Explain:

(i) the double entry at the Southampton branch
(ii) the situation at the Dover branch where it is discovered that the Payer's Account has been closed due to the Payer's death in a road accident. Dover branch have closed the account on the instructions of Mortmain and Death, Solicitors, who are handling the affairs of the deceased.

(d) What is meant by truncation? Explain what happens (if anything) on Day 1, Day 2, Day 3 and Day 4 after a cheque has been cashed in a branch in a different town from the customer's own home area.

(e) Mary Smith, who runs a home agency among her neighbours for Northern Traders Ltd pays cash over the counter of Helpful Bank Plc for the credit of Northern Traders Ltd's Account. Explain the double entry in the branch on receiving this money. Northern Traders Ltd's bank at another bank 200 miles away.

(f) What is a standing order? Explain:

(i) what is the double entry when a standing order becomes due for payment?
(ii) what is the action required if a customer who has made out the standing order has no funds to cover it?

(g) Explain the double entries when a personal loan for £1,000, on which interest of £160 has been agreed as payable, together with an insurance premium of £54, is processed.

(h) Explain the double entry when an instalment of £53.74 on this loan is deducted from the customer's Current Account balance.

(i) A customer of the Helpful Bank has a £500 overdraft on 31 December 19.. On Thursday 19th January he pays in a cheque for £750, which is not cleared until the following Tuesday. The rate of interest on overdrafts is $13\frac{1}{4}$% and no interest is given if the account is in credit. What will be the interest charged for the month, if no further overdraft occurs?

(j) A customer whose account is overdrawn to the extent of £680.00 on 31 December pays in a cheque for £2,000 on 11 January (a Wednesday) and on the same day cashes a cheque for £150. Interest on overdrafts is charged at 14% and credit balances are given interest at $6\frac{1}{2}$%. What will be the interest payable (or receivable) on the account for the month of January, if no further transactions take place?

■ ANSWERS
Exercise 16.1
Do not look at these answers until you have made a genuine attempt to give written answers to the questions. If you are totally unsure what the particular double entry is by all means look at the answer, but make a note to return to the exercise in seven days' time and see if you are clear on the answer and can remember the double entry. (*Note: It is possible that your own bank may use a slight variation on the system described. If that is so console yourself with the thought that we live in an intricate world. All sensible answers in the examination will be honoured with full marks.*)

(**a**) It is an 'in-house' entry. Credit Jones who has deposited funds (credit the giver) and debit Peters, who has received back the use of some of his funds previously on deposit.

(**b**) (i) It is a non-house clearing as far as the Hastings branch is concerned. Credit R Lark, the payee, with £2,000 of uncleared effects and debit Head Office Account with 'random remittances' at the end of the day.

(ii) At the Strand branch of the Helpful Bank Plc the account of Rumpole and Rumpole will be debited (they have received back the use of funds previously on deposit, and Head Office will be credited with remittances inwards).

(**c**) (i) It is a non-house clearing for the Southampton branch. Credit the payee with the amount of the cheque (uncleared effects) and debit Head Office with 'random remittances'.

(ii) Dover branch will have the cheque. The computer will have rejected the debit since the account is closed and it will be listed as an unapplied debit to the Dover branch. Dover branch will reverse the debit thus giving a credit voucher against a truncated debit to the collecting bank/branch. (Remember that claims for unpaid are truncated via Head Office.) The cheque is posted first class to the collecting bank so they can return it to the payee marked 'Drawer deceased'.

(**d**) Truncation is a procedure for inter-branch clearing which short-circuits Head Office and enables overnight data transmission to debit the accounts of drawers on Day 2. The rules are:

Day 1 The payee is credited and the electronic data queued for overnight sending.
Day 2 The payer (drawer) is debited.
Day 3 No activity.
Day 4 No activity.

(**e**) The funds will be held in Counter Suspense until the end of the day when they will be debited to Branch Cash Account (it has received the money). The credit entry will be credited in Head Office Account for onward transmission to the bank which handles Northern Traders Ltd's affairs.

(**f**)   A standing order is a payment to be made at regular intervals at the request of a customer, for hire purchase, loan repayments or some similar entry.

(i) The double entry is a debit by the computer to the account of the payer and a credit to Head Office account. The payment will then be made to the credit of the payee's account, wherever that is, either direct if the payee banks at the same bank – credit the payee and debit that branch's Head Office Account or, if it is to got to another bank, it will be credited to the other bank and debited to the originating bank.

(ii) The Branch will reject the debit, by crediting the payer's account (to cancel out the overnight debit) and debiting Standing Order Recall Account. A recall is sent to the beneficiary's bank branch.

(g) We shall have to:

(i) Debit the customer's Loan Account with the net amount and the Insurance Premium, (i.e. £1,054).

(ii) Credit the customer's Current Account with the net amount of the loan (£1,000).

(iii) Notify the computer of the agreed method for calculating interest. It will then debit the Loan Account with the interest payable and credit Branch Interest Receivable Account (a branch profit).

(iv) Credit the Insurance Subsidiary with the premium of £54.

(h) (i) Debit the Customer's Current Account with £53.74.

(ii) Credit the Customer's Loan Account with £53.74, to reduce the outstanding debt.

(i) The simple interest will be calculated as follows:

£500 overdrawn for 24 days (31 December–24 Jan) = 12,000 £ days

$$\text{Interest} = \frac{£12,000 \times .1325}{365}$$

$$= \underline{\underline{£4.36}}$$

(j) The cheque is cleared on Monday 16 January

£680 overdrawn for 16 days (31 Dec–16 Jan) = 10,880 £ days

£150 overdrawn for 5 days (11–16 Jan) =   750 £ days

$$\text{Interest payable} = \frac{£11,630 \times .14}{365}$$

$$= \underline{\underline{£4.46}}$$

$$\text{Interest receivable} = (£2,000 - £830) \times 15 \text{ days (16 Jan–31 Jan)}$$
$$= £1,170 \times 15$$
$$= 17,550 \text{ £ days}$$

$$\text{at } 6\tfrac{1}{2}\% \text{ interest receivable} = \frac{17,550 \times .065}{365}$$

$$= \underline{\underline{£3.12}}$$

The result is net interest payable is £4.46 – £3.12 = $\underline{\underline{£1.34}}$

17 Consumer credit and APR

OBJECTIVES

After studying this chapter you should:
1 Understand the legal requirements for those who sell goods or supply services on credit to state the **annual percentage rate (APR)** to their customers;
2 Know the exact meaning of annual percentage rate and the official definition;
3 Understand 'present value';
4 Be able to calculate APR by the three formulae, for simple examples;
5 Be able to read off the APR from the Consumer Credit Tables, as supplied by the Office of Fair Trading.

1 RATES OF INTEREST AND CONSUMER CREDIT

When consumers obtain goods or services on credit they usually pay by instalments. The interest on the money borrowed to buy the goods they require is usually calculated at a 'flat rate' per cent per annum and added to the purchase price, less any deposit paid. Let us imagine £200 borrowed at a flat rate of 10% per annum, repayable over two years. Millions of ordinary people borrow in this way to buy household appliances, motor cars, holidays abroad, etc. and there would seem to be no objection to the system, were it not that the flat rate of interest is quite untrue. Let us see why.

£200 borrowed for two years at 10% per annum, means 20% to be added to the purchase price, making a repayment of £240 altogether. Over 24 months this means a repayment of £10 per month.

Consider the first £10 repaid after one month. It paid two years' interest, but it was only borrowed for one month. Actually £1.67 of the £10 was interest, so to borrow £8.33 for one month cost £1.67 interest, which is a rate of 240% per annum (not 10%).

Consider the next £10 repaid after two months. It paid two years' interest, but it was only borrowed for two months. Actually £1.67 of the £10 was interest, so to borrow £8.33 for two months cost £1.67 interest, which is a rate of 120% per annum (not 10%).

The true rate of interest falls each month, until we get to the last payment of £10, which is £1.67 interest and £8.33 principal. To borrow £8.33 for two years cost £1.67 interest which is a rate of:

$$\frac{\pounds 1.67}{\pounds 8.33} \times 100 = 20\% \text{ for two years, or } 10\% \text{ per annum.}$$

So the 10% flat rate is only true for the last payment of the 24; for all the other payments it is higher than 10% and for the first payment it is as high as 240%.

Clearly the flat rate of 10% is misleading, and under the Consumer Credit Act 1974 Parliament enacted that anyone offering consumers credit must tell them the true average rate of interest per annum. This is called the **APR (annual percentage rate)** and you will see it mentioned in many different situations: in shops where hire purchase is a common method of dealing; in advertisements from finance houses which offer loans and in bank advertisements about credit cards.

2 ANNUAL PERCENTAGE RATE

Most consumers borrow money at some time, either by way of a hire purchase transaction, a personal loan or a running-balance loan on a credit card from a bank or a large store. The Act requires that they must all be told the true APR, the true annual percentage rate of interest, so that they can compare one source of credit with another and obtain the goods and services they require at a competitive rate. The APR should always be truncated, i.e. shortened, to one decimal place (not rounded).

Annual Percentage Rate is defined in the official regulations made under the Consumer Credit Act as follows:

APR is a rate per annum such that the sum of the present values of all repayments of credit and the total charge for credit is equal to the sum of the present values of all credits when calculated at that rate.

This rather complicated official definition simply means that the APR is the true rate of interest payable on a consumer credit transaction. This true rate of interest is found by a rather difficult calculation, which takes account of the present values of all the repayments made during the lifetime of the credit agreement. It is that rate of interest which makes the present value of all the repayments added together exactly equal to the amount of the original loan or loans. For practical purposes it is found by reference to the tables published by the Office of Fair Trading and based on the 'present value' method, which is explained later in this unit.

It is worthwhile learning by heart the definition of APR, which is in bold print above. It does make it much easier to follow the explanation of 'present value' given below and you may be asked to quote it in the examination.

3 THE PRESENT VALUE RULE

The present value rule is a rule that is used in accountancy, about the value of money. £100 in my wage packet today is worth £100 — that is its present value. Suppose my employer said 'I won't pay your wages today, I'll give you your £100 in one month's time.' How much is £100 in one month's time worth to me — what is its present value? If I had the money today I could invest it somewhere and earn interest for one month. Suppose the interest was at 10% per annum. In one month I would earn:

$$I = \frac{PRT}{100}$$

$$= \frac{£100 \times 10 \times 1}{100 \times 12} \text{ (the time is } \tfrac{1}{12} \text{ of a year)}$$

$$= £\frac{10}{12}$$

$$= £0.83$$

If my employer does not pay me the £100 today I shall lose 83 pence, so the present value of the money is not £100, it is £99.17.

Suppose I could invest the money at 20% not 10%. This time the calculation shows that in one month the interest I should earn would be £1.67, so that at a 20% rate of interest the present value of £100 in one month's time is £98.33.

There is a different present value for every possible rate of interest. There is a formula for calculating present values which is very useful (though in some cases you do have to make certain assumptions before your start to use it. In this simple chapter we will disregard that complication for the present).

The formula is:

$$\text{Present value} = \frac{A}{\left(1 + \dfrac{r}{100}\right)^t}$$

where PV = the amount loaned
  A = amount of the repayment
  r = rate of interest per annum
and t = time in years

Taking a simple example of £500 borrowed at 12% and repaid with interest in one lump (£560) exactly one year later we have:

$$\text{Present value} = \frac{A}{\left(1 + \dfrac{r}{100}\right)^t}$$

$$= \frac{£560}{(1.12)^1}$$

$$= \frac{£560}{1.12}$$

$$= £500$$

Clearly the formula does give the correct answer, since we know that £500 was borrowed on this occasion.

Now take the case of a person who borrows £800 to be repaid by a lump sum of £960 in exactly one year's time. We know the present value, we know the amount to be repaid. What we don't know is the rate of interest. We can find it with our formula.

$$\text{Present value} = \frac{A}{\left(1 + \dfrac{r}{100}\right)^{t}}$$

$$£800 = \frac{£960}{\left(1 + \dfrac{r}{100}\right)^{1}}$$

Transposing the formula we have:

$$\left(1 + \frac{r}{100}\right)^{1} = \frac{£960}{£800} \text{ (This cancels down to } \tfrac{6}{5} \text{ or } 1.20)$$

$$1 + \frac{r}{100} = 1.20$$

$$\frac{r}{100} = 1.20 - 1$$

$$\frac{r}{100} = .20$$

Transposing the formula again we have:

$$r = .20 \times 100$$
$$= \underline{\underline{20\%}}$$

The present value method may therefore be defined as a method for calculating the true rate of interest on a consumer credit transaction by finding that rate of interest which renders the total of the present values of the agreed repayments, to be made by a borrower in the future, exactly the same as the amount borrowed at the present moment when the credit transaction commences.

4 PRESENT VALUE AND THE APR

The formula for present value can be used to calculate the APR of any credit transaction, but it is not an easy thing to do and all we really need to understand is the principle behind the calculations, because in real life all we do is to read the Annual Percentage Rate from a table drawn up by the Office of Fair Trading. (These tables are often fed into a computer so that a simple enquiry to the bank's computer will produce the APR on any given transaction. This is almost certainly what happens in your own bank.)

The principle is this. When a lender makes money available to a borrower he runs a risk – the risk that he will not be repaid. He is giving up a present value (the amount of the loan) and getting in return the sum borrowed plus a certain rate of interest, and this rate of interest is high enough to compensate him for the risk being run. Now whatever the amount borrowed, and whatever the method of repayment (lump sum, monthly instalments, weekly instalments, etc.), there must be a rate of interest which exactly gives the lender his money back – that is the present values of the various repayments as they come in exactly equals the amount of the loan (the present value handed over to the borrower at the start of the scheme). What is this rate of interest? If we find that we've found the APR being charged. Consider the examples below.

Example 1

A loan of £120 is advanced and repaid one year later, together with all charges for credit, by a single repayment of £150. Using the formula:

$$PV = \frac{A}{\left(1 + \dfrac{r}{100}\right)^t}$$

We have:

$$120 = \frac{150}{\left(1 + \dfrac{r}{100}\right)^1}$$

Leaving out the power figure, which is not needed as it is only one year, we have:

$$120 = \frac{150}{\left(1 + \dfrac{r}{100}\right)}$$

$\left(\text{multiplying both sides by } \left(1 + \dfrac{r}{100}\right) \right.$

$\left. \text{in other words cross-multiplying}\right)$

$$120\left(1 + \frac{r}{100}\right) = 150$$

$$120 + \frac{120r}{100} = 150$$

$$12000 + 120r = 15,000 \text{ (multiplying both sides by 100)}$$

$$120r = 15,000 - 12,000$$

$$120r = 3,000$$

$$r = \frac{3,00\cancel{0}}{12\cancel{0}}$$

$$= \underline{\underline{25\%}}$$

This was a fairly simple example, but the calculation of APR using the Present Value rule is usually much more complicated, as the following example shows.

Example 2

Credit of £1,000 is to be advanced to a borrower on 1 January 19.. and repaid by four annual instalments of £400. What is the APR?

It will be the rate of interest that gives a present value of £1,000 from the four repayments to be received on 31 December for the next four years.

The present value of the first repayment will be:

$$PV = \frac{400}{\left(1 + \dfrac{r}{100}\right)^1}$$

The present value of the second repayment will be:

$$PV = \frac{400}{\left(1 + \dfrac{r}{100}\right)^2}$$

The present value of the other repayments will be similar, with three and four years as the time in years.

Since the whole of the repayments has to give the lender back his original present value of £1,000, we have for the whole group of repayments:

$$PV = \frac{400}{\left(1 + \dfrac{r}{100}\right)^1} + \frac{400}{\left(1 + \dfrac{r}{100}\right)^2} + \frac{400}{\left(1 + \dfrac{r}{100}\right)^3} + \frac{400}{\left(1 + \dfrac{r}{100}\right)^4}$$

As the PV has to be £1,000 we have:

$$£1,000 = \frac{400}{\left(1 + \dfrac{r}{100}\right)^1} + \frac{400}{\left(1 + \dfrac{r}{100}\right)^2} + \frac{400}{\left(1 + \dfrac{r}{100}\right)^3} + \frac{400}{\left(1 + \dfrac{r}{100}\right)^4}$$

We can only solve this question by trial and error. Let us choose 10% as a possible APR. This gives us:

$$£1,000 = \frac{£400}{1.10} + \frac{£400}{(1.10)^2} + \frac{£400}{(1.10)^3} + \frac{£400}{(1.10)^4}$$

$$= £363.36 + £330.58 + £300.53 + £273.21$$

$$= £1,267.68$$

Since £1,000 does not equal £1,267.68 it is clear that 10% is not the correct APR. The interest rate must be higher than this, so that the present values are lowered. We shall have to try again. Try 15%.

With 15% as the rate of interest we have:

$$£1,000 = \frac{£400}{1.15} + \frac{£400}{(1.15)^2} + \frac{£400}{(1.15)^3} + \frac{£400}{(1.15)^4}$$

$$= £347.83 + £302.46 + £263.01 + £228.70$$

$$= £1,142.00$$

Once again, as £1,000 does not equal £1,142 we conclude that 15% is too low a rate of interest.

By continual trial and error we come to a figure of interest at 21.9% APR. The calculations are:

$$£1000 = \frac{£400}{1.219} + \frac{£400}{(1.219)^2} + \frac{£400}{(1.219)^3} + \frac{£400}{(1.219)^4}$$

$$= £328.14 + £269.19 + £220.83 + £181.15$$

$$= £999.31$$

This is about as perfect as we can get. At a rate of interest of 21.9% the lender recovers from the payments the same amount as he borrowed, so this is the true APR of the loan.

The reader will see that this is a cumbersome calculation, and it only involved four repayments. Think how difficult it would be to repeat the exercise with 36 monthly repayments over three years, or 156 weekly repayments over three years. Fortunately the Office of Fair Trading has done it all for us in the Consumer Credit Tables it publishes.

5   THE CONSUMER CREDIT TABLES FOR APR

The Consumer Credit Tables published by the Office of Fair Trading are in 15 parts. A guidance booklet, available free on request from Office of Fair Trading, Bromyard Avenue, Acton, London, W3 7BB, explains that there are three sets of tables. They are:

(a)   Charge per pound lent tables (Tables 1–10)
(b)   Flat rate tables (Tables 11–14)
(c)   Period rate tables (Table 15)

A small extract fom one of the tables, from which you can read off the APR, is given below. Copies may be obtained from HMSO, PO Box 569, London, SE1 9NH.

Equal instalments: monthly intervals
Number of instalments (months)

Annual flat rate %	18	19	20	21	22	23	24
13.00	26.0	26.0	26.0	25.9	25.9	25.9	25.9
13.25	26.5	26.5	26.5	26.5	26.4	26.4	26.4
13.50	27.0	27.0	27.0	27.0	27.0	26.9	26.9
13.75	27.6	27.6	27.5	27.5	27.5	27.4	27.4
14.00	28.1	28.1	28.1	28.0	28.0	28.0	27.9
14.25	28.6	28.6	28.6	28.6	28.5	28.5	28.4
14.50	29.2	29.2	29.1	29.1	29.1	29.0	29.0
14.75	29.7	29.7	29.7	29.6	29.6	29.5	29.5
15.00	30.2	30.2	30.2	30.2	30.1	30.1	30.0
15.25	30.8	30.8	30.7	30.7	30.6	30.6	30.5
15.50	31.3	31.3	31.3	31.2	31.2	31.1	31.1
15.75	31.9	31.8	31.8	31.8	31.7	31.7	31.6

Fig. 17.1   Extract from Consumer Credit Tables Part 12 – Flat-rate Equal Monthly Instalment Tables (Courtesy of the Controller General, HMSO)

6   SINGLE REPAYMENT FORMULA

As stated above, the Present Value formula can be used for any type of credit agreement (as can the consumer credit tables) but it can be very cumbersome to work out.

There are two other formulae which can be used in certain circumstances and are a little simpler.

The first is the Single Repayment formula. As the name implies, this can only be used where an advance is repaid in a single amount (e.g. a bridging loan). The formula is:

$$\text{APR} = 100\left[\left(1 + \frac{c}{p}\right)^{1/t} - 1\right]\%$$

Where c = Total charge for credit.
p = Amount of credit
t = Time in years between advance and repayment

This is really just another way of expressing the PV rule but you may find it easier to use. You are strongly advised to learn this formula by heart.

Example 3

£200 is advanced for one year with a single repayment of £235 at the end of the period. Therefore the total charge for credit is £35. Amount of credit is £200. Time is one year.

$$\text{APR} = 100\left[\left(1 + \frac{c}{p}\right)^{1/t} - 1\right]\%$$
$$= 100\left[\left(1 + \frac{35}{200}\right)^{1/1} - 1\right]\%$$
$$= 100[1.175 - 1]\%$$
$$= 100[0.175]\%$$
$$= 17.5\%$$

Example 4

£500 is advanced for two years to be repaid in full at the end of the period by a single payment of £845.

$$\text{APR} = 100\left[\left(1 + \frac{345}{500}\right)^{1/2} - 1\right]\%$$

$= 100[(1.69)^{1/2} - 1]\%$ (Remember that any number to the power of $\frac{1}{2}$ is the square root of the number – *see* Chapter 7.)

$= 100[1.3 - 1]\%$ (The $\sqrt{1.69} = 1.3$ – find it on your calculator.)

$= 100[0.3]\%$

$= 30\%$

7 PERIOD RATE TRANSACTION FORMULA

The second formula for particular circumstances can be used for period rates, e.g. credit card accounts where the rate is quoted per month, per quarter etc.

The Period Rate Transaction formula is:

$$APR = 100\left[\left(1 + \frac{x}{100}\right)^y - 1\right]\%$$

Where x = period rate of charge as a percentage

y = number of periods in a year (e.g. for a monthly period rate $y = 12$).

Again, you are strongly advised to learn this formula by heart.

Example 5

A credit card company charges interest at 2.5% per month on an account – what is the APR?

$$APR = 100\left[\left(1 + \frac{x}{100}\right)^y - 1\right]\%$$

$$= 100\left[\left(1 + \frac{2.5}{100}\right)^{12} - 1\right]\%$$

$$= 100[(1.025)^{12} - 1]\%$$

$$= 100[1.34489 - 1]\%$$

$$= 100[0.34489]\%$$

$$= 34.4\% \text{ (truncated to one decimal place).}$$

If you find $(1.025)^{12}$ difficult to work out, remember that it is the same as: $(1.025)^6 \times (1.025)^6$ or $(1.025)^3 \times (1.025)^3 \times (1.025)^3 \times (1.025)^3$ and so on. (It is much easier using a calculator than by long multiplication!)

Working this type of calculation on a calculator

First note that most calculators will raise numbers to powers in the following way. Use 2 as the number to be raised to a power, and check your calculator to see if the method works for you. If not, consult your handbook to find out how to raise numbers to a power.

Enter the number to be raised to a power. **2**

Press the × key twice. **× ×**

Then press the = sign once for the square of the number, 4.

Again for the cube 8. Again for the 4th power 16, etc.

In the above example we have to multiply 1.025 by itself 12 times.

One of the twelve times is entered as we enter the number on the display 1.025. There are 11 more times to go.

Press the × sign twice. **× ×**

Press the equal sign 11 times.

This gives us 1.344884.

The working is now as shown above.

$APR = 100[1.34489 - 1]\%$

$$= 100[0.34489]\%$$

$$= \underline{34.4\%} \text{ (truncated to one decimal place)}$$

■ EXERCISE 17.1

1   Give the official definition of annual percentage rate (APR).

2   Give the formula for present value, and explain each symbol in the formula.

3   Give the single repayment formula, and explain each symbol in the formula.

4   What is the annual percentage rate if £1,000 is repaid with a lump sum repayment of £1,180 in 12 months' time? (Try using the present value rule, then the single repayment formula. You should get the same result!)

5   What is the annual percentage rate if £5,000 is repaid with a lump sum repayment of £6,000 in 12 months' time?

6   What is the APR if £1,000 is repaid with a lump sum repayment of £650 one year later and £650 one year after that? (Note: You will have to proceed by trial and error. Start with a guess and then try again until you get the right answer.) *Give the answer truncated to one decimal place.*

7   What is the APR if £2,500 is repaid with a lump sum repayment of £1,650 in one year's time and another £1,650 one year after that? *Answer truncated to one decimal place.*

8   A customer is granted a loan at a flat rate of $14\frac{3}{4}\%$ over two years, repayable in 24 monthly instalments. Using the extract of a table shown in Fig. 17.1, what is the APR of the transaction?

9   Give the period rate formula for APR, explaining each symbol in the formula.

10   A credit card company charges 1.75% per month as its 'period rate' charge to cardholders. What is the APR? (Use the period rate formula.) *Answer truncated to one decimal place.*

11   A credit card company charges a period rate charge of 2.2% per month to card holders. What is the APR?

12   A store's budget account has a period rate charge of 5.6% on the amount outstanding each quarter. What is the APR? (Use the period rate formula.)

■ ANSWERS
Exercise 17.1

1   APR is a rate per annum such that the sum of the present values of all repayments of credit and the total charge for credit is equal to the sum of the present values of all credits when calculated at that rate.

$$2 \quad PV = \frac{A}{\left(1 + \dfrac{r}{100}\right)^t}$$

Where PV is the amount loaned to the client, A is the amount of the repayments, r is the rate per annum interest and t is the time in years.

$$3 \quad APR = 100\left[\left(1 + \frac{c}{p}\right)^{1/t} - 1\right]\%$$

where APR means Annual Percentage Rate, c is the total charge for credit, p is the amount loaned and t is the time in years between the advance being made and the date of repayment.

4   APR = 18%.

5   APR = 20%.

6   APR = 19.4%.

7   APR = 20.7%.

8   APR = 29.5%.

9 $APR = 100\left[\left(1 + \dfrac{x}{100}\right)^{y} - 1\right]\%$

where x = period rate of charge as a percentage and y = number of periods in a year (i.e. for a monthly rate $y = 12$ and for a quarterly rate $y = 4$).

10   APR = 23.1%.

11   APR = 29.8%.

12   APR = 24.3%.

18 Introduction to computers

OBJECTIVES

After studying this chapter you should:
1 Know something about the development of computers;
2 Be aware of most of the components of a computer and the part they play;
3 Be aware of the commoner uses of computers in the business and banking fields.

1 THE DEVELOPMENT OF COMPUTERS

The first mechanical calculator was the 'Arithmetic Engine' devised by the Frenchman, Blaise Pascal, in 1642, but the engineering of its gear wheels proved unsatisfactory. The Englishman Charles Babbage is generally regarded as the father of modern computing. In 1833 he devised the concept of an 'analytical engine'. The concepts included were (a) an **input** mechanism to allow numbers to be fed into the machine; (b) **a store** to hold the numbers and a **program** of instructions; (c) a **'mill'** to perform the actual calculations; (d) a **control unit** to control the sequence of operations and (e) **output devices** to communicate the results. He postulated **punched cards** and **printed outputs** as possibilities. The reader will see how closely these ideas fit in with our modern ideas today, but it was over a hundred years before these ideas could be successfully achieved.

In the meantime the Hollerith Tabulator in America had successfully developed the punched card idea to analyse the American census of 1890. The information was recorded on punched cards and magnetic attraction caused rods to pass through the holes to complete an electrical circuit. The machine was so successful that a company was formed to exploit it and this became IBM – International Business Machines. An English company formed to exploit the Hollerith device in the UK eventually became ICL – International Computers Ltd.

It was 1950 before the first generation computers were developed, using thermionic valves (i.e. vacuum tubes) to act as semi-conductors, restricting the flow of electricity to one direction only. By the late 1950s valves were being replaced by transistors; in the 1960s the silicon chip was providing an even smaller semi-conductor, with the equivalent of a transistor on a chip of silicon. Called an 'integrated circuit' the tiny circuit on the silicon chip acted as a semi-conductor. Later it became possible to put more and more circuits on a silicon chip, a process called 'integration'. In 1971 the Intel Corporation produced the first micro-processor, a computer on a silicon chip. Miniaturisation had reached its logical conclusion, and what in 1950 had required special air-conditioned premises was reduced to the size of a thumb nail.

The use of silicon chips for memory storage illustrates the growth of integration, from 1K chips (with 1,024 bits per chip) to 4K, 16K, 64K, and 256K bit chips in use.

Today we talk about generations of computers:

- 1st generation computers had thermionic valves.
- 2nd generation computers had transistors.
- 3rd generation computers had integrated circuits instead of transistors.
- 4th generation computers are those with VLSI technology (very large scale integration).
- 5th generation computers are likely to arrive shortly.

The power of a computer lies in its ability to perform certain simple functions (basically, addition and subtraction) immeasurably faster and more accurately than a human being can. Because of this enormous speed of operation a computer can be programmed to do millions of calculations every second, and certain activities like book-keeping and accounting are made very simple as a result.

Today there are three main types of computers:

Mainframe computers are the largest, with enormous capacities able to handle all the computerised activities of even the biggest companies and government departments.

Mini-computers are of medium size, and a serious rival to mainframe computers. They cost around £50,000. They can handle the affairs of most companies, and even the largest firms might prefer to use two or three mini-computers in various areas rather than a single mainframe computer.

Micro-computers are small, very cheap, adaptable for many uses and their low cost means that a separate computer can be used for each aspect of work in a large firm, while for the small firm they are still large enough to handle all aspects of the work required: accountancy, costing, design, payrolls, etc. They bring computerised methods within the reach of even the smallest businesses.

2   HARDWARE AND SOFTWARE

A business that is thinking of buying a computer system has to consider both the machines required (the hardware) and the instructions or programs (software) that are needed to run them, and which tell the computer exactly what it has to do.

A wide range of computers is available to businesses, from microcomputers suitable for small to medium-sized firms to very large mainframe machines with enormous capacity and power. The rate of development in the computer industry is such that machines require updating or even replacing every few years. The underlying principles of the equipment remain the same, however. We have to feed numbers or facts (under the general term – **data**) into the machine by some sort of **input device**. This data then has to be processed (**data processing**) by means of a program of instructions. Finally

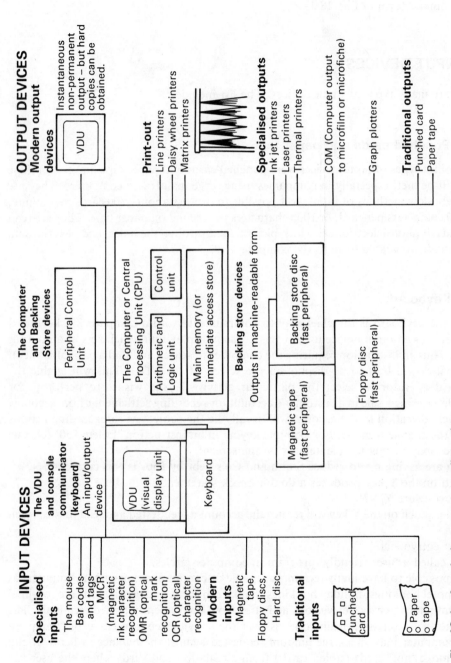

Fig. 18.1 A typical computer configuration

INPUT DEVICES

Specialised inputs

The mouse
Bar codes and tags
MICR (magnetic ink character recognition)
OMR (optical mark recognition)
OCR (optical character recognition)

Modern inputs

Magnetic tape, Floppy discs, Hard disc

Traditional inputs

Punched card

Paper tape

The VDU and console communicator (keyboard)
An input/output device

VDU (visual display unit)

Keyboard

The Computer and Backing Store devices

Peripheral Control Unit

The Computer or Central Processing Unit (CPU)

Arithmetic and Logic unit

Control unit

Main memory (or immediate access store)

Backing store devices

Outputs in machine-readable form

Magnetic tape (fast peripheral)

Backing store disc (fast peripheral)

Floppy disc (fast peripheral)

OUTPUT DEVICES

Modern output devices

VDU

Instantaneous non-permanent output – but hard copies can be obtained.

Print-out

Line printers
Daisy wheel printers
Matrix printers

Specialised outputs

Ink jet printers
Laser printers
Thermal printers

COM (Computer output to microfilm or microfiche)

Graph plotters

Traditional outputs

Punched card
Paper tape

the results have to be put out of the machine in readable form by some sort of **output device** (thus becoming useful information). The essential components are shown in diagrammatic form in Fig. 18.1.

3   INPUT DEVICES

There are many types of input devices. The list includes:

3.1   Punched cards and paper tape

The earliest types of input devices were punched cards and paper tape inputs and these may still be met, especially in companies using large mainframe computers. They are relatively slow methods of input. It is possible to process about 1500 cards per minute, with 80 characters per card, or 1000 characters per second on paper tape. They are read by bands of photo-electric cells which pick up light through the holes, and pass the data in a machine-readable form to the computer.

3.2   Keyboard

Today the keyboard is the chief way to communicate with a computer. A keyboard which acts as an input device usually has a visual display unit which acts as an output device. Thus an instruction requiring the computer to search and find a particular menu of activities will lead to its display on the screen of the VDU. This will enable the keyboard operator to select the particular activity he/she wishes to perform, for example entering a sale in a customer's account, or recording settlement of the account. Any such alteration to the account will usually be the subject of safeguarding actions before the change is made. For example keying in an instruction 'Delete £50' (cheque received) may be met by a statement on the screen:

'You are asking me to reduce Smith and Co's debt by £50. Is this correct Y/N?'

A touch on the Y key produces a double check statement

'Are you sure Y/N?'

A further touch on the Y key will reduce the account as requested and lead to the screen display

'Next entry please'

This is called a 'user-friendly' program in computer circles.

It is possible to have many terminals capable of communicating with a computer, as where hotel bookings, holiday bookings, bank cash cards and credit cards are 'on-line' to a computer to carry out various activities from conveniently placed terminals. The computer will exercise certain controls over the activities concerned – for example a bank computer may check the amount requested against the balance in hand. It can also remove 'hot' cards (stolen cards) from circulation and cards where the user has given an incorrect reference number more than twice. You will probably have to deal with irate customers at the enquiries desk, complaining that the cash dispenser has 'swallowed' their card for some reason.

3.3 Magnetic tape, disks and floppy disks

Magnetic tape and disks are modern fast input devices which enable information to be fed into a computer more quickly than with punched cards or punched tape. Tape consists of plastic tape coated with iron oxide which is magnetic. Each character is in coded form across the width of the tape, and the computer reads them in sequence as the tape passes. About 1600 characters are normally recorded per inch with about 45 million characters on a full tape, which can be read at about 180,000 characters per second. Higher densities and speeds are possible.

Disks (or hard disks) are actually packs of between one and twelve or more metal disks, up to a foot or more in diameter, which rotate continuously on a spindle. The flat surface of each disk is coated in magnetic iron oxide and covered with closely-packed, concentric tracks of magnetic spots – similar to the grooves on a record – which are read or written to by read/write heads mounted on arms, which move radially across the disk to select the required track. The capacity of such a disk pack will be many hundreds of thousands of bytes, i.e. many megabytes – a megabyte being a million bytes – or even gigabytes – thousands of megabytes.

A floppy disk is a single disk of flexible material coated with iron oxide, with a read-write head given access to the disk through a slot in the cardboard or plastic protective cover. They give between 360,000 and 2 million characters of storage, and you can have as many disks as you wish to deal with various sets of records.

3.4 Specialised input devices

Besides the devices mentioned above there are many specialised input devices. These include **bar codes**, a unique pattern of lines which the computer can read through a light pencil. They are used to record sales of stock for stock-taking purposes, the issue of library books etc.

MICR (magnetic ink character recognition) is achieved by printing number codes on cheques, paying in slips etc which can then be read by the computer. When a cheque is made out it already has all the account details printed on it, and the only part not printed in magnetic ink is the amount of the cheque written in by the drawer of the cheque. This is encoded in the branch, or at an operations centre by the keyboard operators, before the cheque details are read, so that the message read from the cheque by the magnetic ink character reader includes the account details and the amount to be paid. The cheque can now be cleared electronically through BACS – the Bankers Automated Clearing Service.

OMR and **OCR** inputs refer to **optical mark recognition** and **optical character recognition**. These are methods of reading examination papers and other documents electronically. For example in multiple-choice examination papers the student ticks a particular box which is believed to be the correct answer. This tick reduces the light being reflected from the paper and the box ticked can thus be detected. If it is a correct answer the computer gives the student a mark for it.

A **mouse** is an input device which can rapidly move the cursor across a screen, without the use of the keyboard, to any special area of the screen which is required to be accessed. Thus in export documentation the whole export document can be displayed on the screen. The mouse is used to pick out a particular field on the document, and request its enlargement to full visibility. Suppose the box labelled 'exporter' is featured. The keyboard operator types in the exporter's name and address and then releases the completed section. It returns to its minute place on the screen, but not only has the computer remembered the data, it will reproduce it automatically on every document relating to that consignment – bills of lading, invoices, banking documentary collection form, insurance certificate, etc.

3.5   The processing of data

The computer itself is called the **central processor unit** or **CPU**. It consists of a control unit, an arithmetic and logic unit and a main memory or main storage for immediate access. The stages of processing are as follows:

   (a)   the appropriate program is 'loaded' into the main memory from storage, either in the backing store discs or magnetic tapes associated with the computer or from a floppy disc through a disc-drive unit.
   (b)   the current data situation for the program concerned is then also loaded. Thus with a payroll it would be the situation on the last pay day; all the personal files of employees, pay to date, PAYE (Pay As You Earn) codes, etc. This would either be in the backing store or on a separate floppy disc called the 'data disc'.
   (c)   the new data to be processed would then be input. It might be keyed in individually from a keyboard, or, if this had been done earlier in batches and stored, this stored material, either on tape or disc, would be fed in.
   (d)   the control unit would now carry out the program, at speeds of between 5 and 12 'mips'. The word mips stands for 'million instructions per second'. At this enormous speed the computer reads the instructions one at a time, designates some part of the arithmetic or logic unit to carry out the instruction and stores the various results ready for output.

The detailed procedures by which an instruction is read, data values are loaded into the arithmetic unit, the calculation is performed and the results are unloaded and stored at an appropriate 'address' in the main memory is too complicated for an introductory book of this sort, but at several million instructions per second an individual item is completed almost instantaneously.

4   OUTPUT DEVICES

Once data has been processed and the results achieved the 'output data' (unless it is required immediately for display on a VDU) will be held in main storage until a sufficient volume is available to present it to an output device. The output device may be a storage device which will preserve the data in electronic form (as where the revised payroll records are sent to a data disc for storage until required on the next payday). Alternatively it may be sent to a printer or other device which will convert the binary code into characters (letters and numbers) in readable form.

4.1   VDU outputs

These are instantaneous, non-permanent screen displays which can also provide hard copies if a printer is attached. The speed of response makes them ideal for certain activities like hotel bookings, home-banking services (which enable the customer to see his/her bank account on a domestic television set), airline reservations, etc.

4.2 Printers

There are many different types of printers but their common feature is that they all produce the computer's results on paper, in legible form. The printout may be in the form of correspondence, tabulated statistics, invoices, statements of account, salary slips and many other documents. The types include line printers (which print a line at a time, usually of 132 characters and at speeds of up to 4,000 lines per minute. Another type, the matrix printer, builds up the characters by printing a series of dots. They are slower than line printers, and print about 200 characters per second. A third type is the daisywheel printer, which has characters embossed on petals like a daisy. The daisywheel rotates until the correct character is in position. It is then struck through a ribbon onto the paper. Speeds are slow, about 90 characters per second (CPS), but the quality of the print is high, like a good typewriter.

A more specialised printer is the thermal printer, which makes characters by bringing heated wires into contact with special heat-sensitive paper. There is no impact, so the printer is quiet, but the speeds are low, about 100 cps. Another type is the ink-jet printer, which sprays droplets of ink to make the characters and can now be used to print several different colours. A laser printer is another non-impact printer capable of printing a whole page at a time. It is very fast, printing 200 pages per minute on the fastest machines.

4.3 Graph plotters

These are devices which are able to reduce the data to diagrammatic form, giving graphs, bar diagrams, pie diagrams, maps and drawings. Used mainly in the scientific and engineering industries, they also have business applications. Basically they consist of pens whose movement is controlled by computer programs.

4.4 COM

Computer output to microfilm (or microfiche) is a method of storing images on rolls or sheets of film. The reduction that can be achieved is such that up to 270 A4 pages can be held on a $6'' \times 4''$ microfiche sheet of film. Some of the main uses of COM are long-term records, for example library records, the records at Companies House, banking records of customers' statements and insurance records. The reduced images can be read in special viewers, which magnify the image to full size again. The Viewers also permit copies to be taken from the full size image concerned, so that – for example – customers at banks can be given a copy of statements when required.

For our purposes in this book this outline of computer components and activities is perhaps sufficient, but a more detailed **Glossary of Computer Terms** is given at the end of this chapter. One further aspect that needs mentioning at the moment is the transmission of data over the telecommunications network.

5 TELECOMMUNICATIONS AND THE TRANSMISSION OF INFORMATION

Large mainframe computers can handle work from all areas of the country and, indeed, the world. As such they are dependent on communications services made available by British Telecom and other companies. The ordinary telephone lines are not usually satisfactory for this type of transmission and whenever possible better quality lines are provided. Eventually a fibre optics network of nationwide digital communications is to be provided. Fibre optics is a new science which transmits light impulses along thin glass fibres at very high speeds. Data can be carried in this form in a very clear way, without the loss of data that sometimes occurs in ordinary cables. In the meantime private speech circuits and private data circuits give relatively inexpensive and trouble-free connections for businesses needing direct connections. They go under the title 'Connect Direct', and take the form of either private speech circuits, or private data circuits, or both. The banks are important users of 'Connect Direct' lines, and will eventually move over to the fibre-optic lines as they become available.

At present the types of line in use are:

(a) *Speechline* These lines are designed for use within a company – for example head offices to area offices and branches. They connect directly, without dialling, and without interference from other lines.

(b) *Access lines* These lines connect up outside calls from the public telephone network to branches, through a central switchboard. Thus a connect line goes direct from a branch to an Area Office switchboard without dialling, and may then be switched to any intra-company extension. The access lines are not charged in a use-related way – there is a flat charge for the line and after that it is available for use when required.

(c) *Keyline* is a private service which sends data along ordinary telephone lines in sound code called 'analogue'. Thus it can be used for linking the head office of a retailing company to all its distribution points and to tills in the actual shops. The electronic point of sale facility records each sale made, and collects records of stock sold which will be stored in the daytime and used to up-date stock records at the end of each day. These sales, if made against credit cards or EFTPOS cards (Electronic Funds Transfer at the Point Of Sale), may be routed through to an agency which will queue the data for onward transmission each night to the bank concerned. They are not, as yet, on-line to the banks' computers, but this may be developed in the future.

A modem at each terminal links the data to be transmitted to the lines.

(d) *Kilostream and Megastream* are two systems of private digital transmission which offer high speed and very high speed data and image transmission as well as speech transmission to major companies with networks of branches. Digital transmission sends data over special lines in the form of 'bits', each bit being a part of the message. With fibre optic cables 140 million bits per second can be transmitted, and higher speeds up to 585 million bits per second are possible.

(e) *Electronic Funds Transfer – SWIFT* SWIFT is the Society for Worldwide Interbank Financial Telecommunications. It is a joint foundation which permits banks to supply computer tape for transmission to major centres abroad. In this way funds can be passed to make payments around the world. For example Barclays Cash

Management (Barcam) operates the Barclays Overseas Automated Transfer System (BOATS) over the SWIFT network to process payment tapes from customers.

6   THE USES OF COMPUTERS IN BUSINESS

While the applications of computerised techniques are numerous and almost every business can find some uses for them, it is impossible in this book to do more than mention a selection of them. Some of the most common uses are in the banking field, which has been particularly referred to here, but many of the activities mentioned could be used in almost any business. A more detailed account of computerised branch accounts is given in Chapter 19.

6.1   Real-time situations

A real-time situation is one where the actual procedures occurring at this very moment are subject to computerised control and the computer can make decisions. For example there are some rapid-transit real-time systems on railways in major cities around the world where the computer senses the position of every traction unit in the system and lets them go − or detains them − in such a way as to use the lines to a maximum efficiency. In booking holidays, hotel accommodation and airline seats a real-time system is essential, since travel agents all over the country are coming on-line at all hours of the day to find out if accommodation or seats are available, and to book them if they are. As each seat or room is booked the computer has to be up-dated to reduce the number of rooms still available, until eventually the plane or hotel is full and further enquiries are shut out.

In banking many cash dispensers or ATMs (Automated Teller Machines) are on-line in a real-time situation. The insertion of the card connects the machine to a central computer, where it enters the queue for attention. As the computer is very high powered handling several mips (million instructions per second) the machine is soon attended to; the amount required by the customer is checked with the balance available; the card is returned, the cash and a paper receipt dispensed and the records in the computer up-dated. Where real-time access is not possible the card itself will carry a daily or weekly limit. Safety devices permit the retention of cards suspected of being misused and a printed voucher is dispensed expressing regret if the customer has been inconvenienced.

6.2   Branch networking

The degree of sophistication in such areas as banking is developing all the time and the description which follows is gradually becoming reality, though some areas may not yet be fully on-line. Every branch has a terminal linked to the main computer, or computers, at Head Office. Almost all branches are directly 'on-line' to their own accounts, and can debit or credit a customer's account in the computer without any delay, although the up-dating of accounts may take place overnight. They may not yet be on-line to accounts at other branches, though eventually they will be, but many cheques, giro transfers, etc, must in any case be sent to central clearing where they can be handled more economically in bulk. Transfers to accounts at another bank are encoded and keyed in during the day as they are paid in. The stored data is then sent daily after closing hours to central clearing to go through BACS, the Bankers Automated Clearing Service, in due course.

6.3   Management information

Computers can easily produce information for managers, sometimes almost too much. For example, statistics about sales, purchases, capital expenditure, value-added tax, payrolls etc. can give excellent control of cash flow, credit allowed to customers, departmental expenditure in relation to budgets etc. The danger in some cases is that statistics on the amount of work done by, for example, check-out operators or typists using word-processors linked to a computer, may be used by managers to discipline members of staff, or decide rates of pay, without looking into the different circumstances in which the members of staff may be operating. For example a typist dealing with complex legal documents will almost certainly have a slower rate of output than a typist dealing with very straightforward letters. The moral is that computer information, like all statistics, must be treated with care and one should not make important decisions based on a single piece of information in isolation.

Bank managers have always collected information about their customers to help them control lending, obtain new business etc. With the aid of computers, the same information can be found much more quickly, sorted and selected in a chosen order, reported only when something goes wrong, and so on. In this way the manager can make the most of his/her time by avoiding the need to search manually through files full of paper for the information needed.

Computerised management information may be delivered in the form of a display on a VDU (visual display unit) for instantly required items, or may be printed out either by a printer in the branch or department, or by a central printer for despatch to reach the branch the next morning.

The types of reports which can be produced to give management information are virtually limitless. They may be designed by the Head Office or Regional Office to be standard for all branches or they may be specified by the particular manager concerned.

The simplest example perhaps is the response to a balance enquiry. Each bank will have its own particular format, but most will have a system by which a member of staff in a branch can tap in a simple enquiry over their terminal key-board and obtain a picture or print-out of the balance of a customer's account, perhaps showing whether the balance is cleared, whether any overdraft limit has been agreed, whether any debits or credits have been presented in that day's clearing which will affect the balance, and whether there are any other associated accounts held by that customer.

Other examples are:

1   Warning lists of accounts which will go overdrawn or over-limit if cheques presented in the morning clearing are paid.
2   Notices of items in the clearing which cannot be automatically applied to the relevant account (perhaps an item drawn on a closed account, or one which has been transferred to another branch).

3 Lists of accounts with limits which are due for review.

4 Accounts which have not received any credits within a certain period. (Failure to pay in cheques is a feature of businesses that are getting into difficulties and is a possible early warning sign of default, which needs investigation. The same applies to personal accounts where a customer whose salary was paid by bank giro credit has lost his/her job and has not yet found alternative employment.

5 Printouts for regional management comparing one branch's performance with another: number of accounts, volume of lending, level of bad debts, achievement of targets, and so on.

6 Analyses of the various accounts, plastic cards and other services used by a customer – this is used in marketing campaigns to help identify possible sales targets. (Such analyses can be adapted to corporate as well as personal accounts.)

7 A printout of the charges to be levied on each account can be prepared prior to the passing of the charges, to give the manager an opportunity to adjust them in the light of his personal knowledge of the account. This is an example of a situation in which what the computer has calculated may be strictly accurate, but the human touch is needed to make it also appropriate.

All the various printouts which your branch or department receives are forms of management information. The examples above relate particularly to branch banking, but if you work in a merchant bank, an investment bank or some other financial institution, I am sure you can draw up your own list of the useful computer-produced printouts you or your manager receive.

Management information is only of value if it is accurate, timely, appropriate and correctly interpreted:

● accurate, because incorrect information can lead to wrong decisions being made
● timely, because out-of-date information may be too old to be of use and may be misleading
● appropriate, because a mass of irrelevant information will just obscure that which is useful
● correctly interpreted, because unless the person receiving the information understands what it means and how to make use of it, it will be of little value.

6.4 EFTPOS

Electronic funds transfer at the point of sale is a further use of computerisation. The customer's credit card, or bank card is wiped across a terminal at the point of sale (the till). The amount to be spent is checked with the available balance and if there are funds to cover it the sale is authorised. The customer's account is debited and the stores account is credited (it has effectively deposited funds to the amount of the sale).

6.5 Account maintenance

This topic has been covered fully in Chapters 10–14. All aspects of accounts can be handled by computerised methods: sales, purchases, payments, receipts, and, in banking, giro transfers, direct debits, standing orders, loans and charges are all routinely handled. Statements of account are handled at enormous speeds – one major credit card company has 8 million accounts to send out each month, 400,000 every working day. A computerised installation can handle about 8,000 an hour.

6.6 Provision of information direct to customers

Computers can supply information to customers in many ways, either directly or by application to a keyboard operator at a terminal. Some of the best examples are in banking, travel and tourism. The customer who inserts a bank card into an automated teller machine (an autobank) can enquire what balance is available on his/her account. The printout that appears shows the balance to the previous evening, unless a real-time situation exists when it shows the balance available at the moment the application for information is made. Similarly customers with one of the home and office banking terminals can call up their accounts onto the domestic television set to view their balances. They can transfer funds from one account to the other, request statements cheque books etc. Customers checking holidays at their travel agents can see a screen display of their booking, date, destination, hotel room number, facilities requested, insurance cover provided, etc. etc.

7 A GLOSSARY OF COMPUTER TERMS

Address The location of an item in the memory.

Analogue device One in which the data is represented by physical variables (for example a wave varying with the human voice as in the ordinary telephone). The word analogue is used because it means 'parallel' and the change in the device is exactly proportional to a change in the physical variable. Thus the change in the current in a telephone circuit exactly represents the change in the voice wave as the caller speaks. (Contrast with Digital (q.v.).)

Array A series of storage locations arranged in a continuous pattern like pigeon holes in a filing system.

Arithmetic and logic unit That part of the central processor which carries out specific instructions assigned to it by the control unit (q.v.). The instructions tend to be arithmetical in nature (e.g. 'add one number to another' or 'compare one number with another number').

Backing storage A storage device to hold programs and data 'off-line' from the computer when they are not required by the CPU. For example after a pay-roll run the updated records of all employees would be put out to backing store until required in the run-up period to next pay day. The usual backing storage devices are magnetic tape and magnetic disc.

Bar codes A specialised input device which can be read with a light pencil or wand, or by passing the strip over a light-sensitive window. The computer then searches its memory to name the item, record its price and to adjust stock records. This increases the rate of stock turnover since re-orders only take place when existing stocks reach an agreed low point.

BASIC A simple computer language – the Beginners All-purpose Symbolic Instruction Code.

Batch A collection of documents or other computer work collected together prior to running. The term is also used to refer to a process being run on a computer in the background, so as to not to slow down real-time access too much.

Binary code This is the representation given by the binary system (qv) to any numeric or alphabetical character using only the digits 1 and 0. Each character is represented by a different combination of ones and zeros to give it a unique code. An input device gets information into the computer by translating the information into its binary coded form which the machine can then recognise and process.

Binary number The representation of a character in numerical form using the binary system (qv).

Binary system A number system based on two, where each place value is not 10 (as in the decimal system) but 2 (i.e. when we get more than 1 unit we move into the next place). Thus the numbers 0–7 in binary code are respectively 0; 1; 10; 11; 100; 101; 110 and 111.

Bit An abbreviation for **binary digit**. Each position (i.e. each place value) in a binary number is called a bit. Thus the number seven, 111, has three bits; 1 unit, 1 two (the second place in the binary system is a two, not a ten) and 1 four (the third place in a binary system is 2 squared (four) not 10 squared (one hundred) as in the decimal system. So 111 is a 1, a 2 and a 4 which is 7.

Blank A space; character where nothing is printed. In a computer memory the space takes just as much room as any other character.

Bug An error in coding which causes a program to fail, or perform incorrectly.

Bus A data highway; a number of transmission lines along which data is moved.

Byte A byte is 8 bits, and can be used to hold two numbers (because any number up to 15 only needs 4 bits – for example 15 is 1111) or one alphabetic or special character.

Cassette A storage medium for micro and personal computers with narrow tape only 0.15 inches wide. Data is written along the length of the tape, not across it, so the speed of reading and writing is slow.

Central processor unit The CPU, the central unit of a computer, consisting of three elements; (a) control unit (b) arithmetic and logic unit and (c) main storage (sometimes called 'main memory' or 'immediate access memory'). The function of the CPU is to process data according to a program of instructions.

Chips Small portions of a wafer of silicon on which photograph-like images have been printed and developed to give integrated circuits of great complexity; virtually a computer on a chip.

COBOL A programming language which is designed to solve business-based problems.

COM Computer output to microfilm or microfiche. These specialised outputs are used for archiving vital records – 2,000 pages on a 30 metre roll of film – 98 or 270 pages on a 6″ × 4″ microfiche. Main uses in insurance companies, banks, libraries and public record offices.

Compiler A program which translates statements made in a high-level language into machine code (qv), so that the machine can actually execute the program.

Console A typewriter keyboard used by a computer operator to interrupt the computer and feed in further instructions. It may have a VDU attached to assist the process of inputting instructions, and to receive responses from the computer. The term is also used for sophisticated telephone systems to denote the telephone operator's control unit.

Control unit That part of the central processor unit which accesses the program instructions held in main storage one at a time, and in the correct sequence, interprets the coded instructions and assigns one of the other elements in the CPU to carry out the instruction, whatever it may be. It operates at a great speed, measured in mips (millions of instructions per second).

Core Another term for memory.

CPU The central processor unit (qv).

Daisy-wheel printer A printer which works from a daisy-wheel – a circle of metal or plastic with the characters embossed on petals sticking out from the edge of the circle. The wheel rotates to bring the correct character to the ribbon, where a hammer strikes it to print the character through the ribbon. This can be done at about 90 characters per second (cps). Mainly used in word processing because of the high quality output.

Data Any item of information (qv) in machine-readable form – the stuff that computers process. Data may be numbers, letters, words or facts.

Data checking *See* data validation.

Data processing The automatic performance of operations on data, as a result of a program of instructions to the computer.

Data transfer The action of transferring data from one unit to another within the computer (for example from storage into main memory), or to the computer from an input device or from the computer to an output device. It also covers long distance transmissions.

Data transmission The communication of data from one location to another. It may be local (within the computer, or between the computer and a peripheral input or output device), or it may be from one remote terminal to another over the telephone network – usually on direct-connect lines but eventually over a full network of fibre optic lines. Data transmission by satellite is a future possibility.

Data validation A system for checking data to ensure it is within a permitted range of values – for example a percentage must usually be within the range 0–100. Works numbers for personnel may lie within certain limits. If we insert an account number the computer may be able to check that such an account does exist, or check its validity by means of an algorithm (formula).

Degrees of integration A way of expressing the number of transistor circuits on a silicon chip (e.g. SSI = small scale integration, MSI = medium scale integration, etc).

Digital device A device where the data is measured by counting, and is represented by numerical quantities. For example the wave of an ordinary telephone message is sampled 8,000 times a second to measure the amplitude of the wave and these measurements are turned into a binary code of numerical data. The original wave is reconstituted from the measurements transmitted on arrival at destination by a device called a modem (modulator-demodulator).

Dump The transfer of the contents of a memory or a file to another device, such as a printer.

EFTPOS Electronic funds transfer at the point of sale. A system which permits the computer to be accessed by wiping a banker's card through a reader machine to check that funds are available in a customer's account and sanction payment, the customer being debited (he/she has received back some of the funds on deposit) and the store is credited with the amount paid.

File A body of information on a particular topic which can be accessed at any time to accept input, answer queries, show the state of the system at any time, and keep a log of events as an audit trail. A file is usually held on a disk.

Floppy disk A single disk of plastic coated with magnetic oxide, and protected by a thin card 'envelope' or plastic case. They may be 8″, 5¼″, 3½″ or 3″ in diameter. The read-write head of the disk drive operates in a slot in the protective envelope to access the data or programs on the disk. They have a capacity between 360k bytes and 2 megabytes.

Flowchart A graphical representation of the steps involved in a procedure or program, showing the flow of information and decisions.

FORTRAN A programming language designed to deal with arithmetical problems.

Generation A term used to describe the development of computers (1st generation computers used valves; 2nd generation used transistors; 3rd generation used integrated circuits; 4th generation used VLSI (very large scale integration). The term can also be used to describe the ease of use of computer languages. Fourth generation computers can be programmed in English rather than in code, and fifth generation machines will be able to learn from the user.

Gigo Garbage in, garbage out. A maxim which reminds us that no computer can produce good output from bad input. Any results cannot be better than the input supplied.

Graph plotters Devices which produce graphs, maps, charts, etc. They consist of a pen, or several pens, driven by a computer program. There are two types, drum plotters and flat-bed plotters.

Hard copy A permanent record on paper of data or of a program. Often taken from what appears on a VDU screen, by attaching a printer.

Hardware The durable mechanical, electrical and electronic components of a computer configuration, for example the central processor, terminal, keyboard, VDU, printer, disk drive, etc.

Immediate access memory The main memory in the central processor, where data and programs are held while awaiting processing.

Information The useful output from a computer, when raw data has been processed, analysed, sorted and manipulated into an easily understandable form.

Inkjet printers A non-impact printer which sprays characters onto the paper at about 150 characters per second. They are silent, and are therefore useful in hospitals, offices, etc.

Input Data from an external source for processing by a computer.

Input device A means of passing information into a computer. The information is passed in machine-readable form and may be data, or instructions about how data is to be processed – the program. The chief input devices are punched cards, paper tape, keyboards, magnetic tape, magnetic disk, floppy disks, bar codes, magnetic ink character recognition (MICR), optical mark recognition (OMR), optical character recognition (OCR) and tags and magnetic strips of various sorts.

Integrated circuit A very small electronic circuit on a chip of semi-conducting material such as silicon.

Joystick An attachment that allows an operator to move the field of view on a screen, and draw a line or a curve, or store a position, by hand, without the use of keys.

K An abbreviation for 1000 (actually 1024) and used to denote the number of transistors on a silicon chip memory. Thus 1k = 1024 bits per chip, and we have 4k,

16k, 64k and 256k bit chips available. Also used to describe the capacity of a computer's memory, e.g. 512k, 640k, etc.

Keyboard A communicating device used to input data and commands to the computer. In many ways it is similar to a typewriter keyboard.

Key-to-disk system A system whereby large volumes of data can be keyed by VDU operators directly to a disc file. When all the data has been keyed the data on the disc can be input into the computer, or transferred to magnetic tape for submission to the central processor.

Laser printer Top quality printers, printing a page at a time and up to 200 pages a minute, i.e. 26,000 characters a second. As the machines are relatively expensive and the output is of the highest quality, the main users are companies with mainframe computers and those requiring cheaper type-setting facilities. Bank statements are printed in this way and they are increasingly being used for word processing because of the quality of output and the choice of typefaces.

Light pen Also called the sensing wand; a photosensitive detector housed in a case which can be held in the hand, and connected to the VDU controls by a cable. The computer can detect the position of the pen on the screen and display the details on record of the particular item pointed at, e.g. customer's address if a list of names is displayed.

Line printer A fast printer for the commercial field printing a line at a time at speeds of 4,000 lines per minute, on continuous stationery. Normal line width is 132 characters.

Listing The printed output from a computer. Often used to describe a printout of a computer program.

Loop The repeated execution of a program instruction, or series of instructions. An infinite loop occurs when this repeated execution carries on indefinitely. It can only be stopped by aborting the program.

Machine code The basic code on which a machine actually operates, a low-level numeric format. Early programs were written in this format. Today they are written in higher-level languages, but this language has to be converted by a compiler (q.v.) to the machine code applicable to the computer before it can be executed.

Magnetic disk A pack of disks (or platters) coated with magnetic oxide on which data can be recorded in – say – 800 tracks per disk, with about 20 recording surfaces in each pack. Access is by a read-write head, which can access about 2,500 million bytes (megabytes) on a fixed disk unit, or about 200 megabytes on an exchangeable disk drive. It takes about 50 milliseconds (thousandths of a second) to locate data on the disk, which can then be read at 2 megabytes per second.

Magnetic ink character recognition A system for reading documents such as cheques, paying in slips, etc, at speeds of 2,400 documents per minute. The vital details are printed on the cheque with magnetic ink in special type faces. The magnetic ink character reader can detect the electric field created by each magnetic pattern as the characters pass under the read-head.

Magnetic strips A specialist input device used by some major retailers to record point of sale data for stock taking and customer billing. They act rather similarly to bar codes.

Magnetic tape A tape coated with ferrous oxide, chiefly used as a backing-store medium but also as an input (and output) device. It is usually $\frac{1}{2}$ inch wide and 2,400 feet long. Characters are recorded across the width of the tape and are read in sequence along the tape. Tape can hold either 1,600 characters per inch (bytes per inch) or 6,250 bpi. A full tape at 1,600 bpi holds 46 million bytes (46 megabytes). The tape is read, or written to, at speeds of 112.5 inches per second (about 180,000 bytes per second).

Main storage The short-term storage medium, part of the central processor unit, in which programs and data are stored temporarily while they are being processed. This also includes data that has been processed and is waiting to be put out to a particular output device. It is also known as 'main memory'.

Mainframe computers Very large computers; direct descendants of the original valve computers; great power and many functions, but expensive to build, program and operate.

Matrix printer A printer that prints by building up characters from sets of dots made by firing needles at an inked ribbon which makes a dot on the print paper below it.

Memory That part of a computer capable of storing programs and data being used for manipulation (*see* main storage).

MICR See magnetic ink character recognition.

Microcomputers Small computers, at very low cost, flexible in application and adequate for most small businesses and for home use.

Microfiche See COM.

Microfilm See COM.

Microprocessor A complex set of integrated circuits on a silicon chip, which is therefore virtually a computer on a chip of silicon. Introduced in 1971 by the Intel Corporation, of California's Silicon Valley'.

Minicomputers Medium size computers – a competitor for mainframe computers at a medium size, functionality and price.

Mips Millions of instructions per second – the speed at which the central processor operates. Most mainframe computers work at speeds between 5 mips and 12 mips.

Modem A modulator-demodulator. A device which codes and decodes computer data from wave to digital form and vice versa so that it can be transmitted along telephone lines (digital device q.v.).

Mouse An input device which can direct the cursor very quickly to any part of the screen of a VDU by hand, without the use of the keyboard. It can pinpoint fields on the screen where particular data are displayed. This part of the screen can then be enlarged for the purpose of adding data or amending the data displayed. After updating, the enlarged area can be returned to its original size and position on the overall display. The mouse may also be used to select options from a menu.

Network An inter-connected pattern of communications which permits access to computers with large data bases from anywhere in the network. One such system is DIANE (Direct Information Access Network for Europe). British Telecom is developing System X as a network which will handle all communications in digital form. A LAN (Local Area Network) is a series of terminals connected to each other (e.g. within an office) which can communicate with each other. Networked computers may share resources such as printers.

OCR *See* optical character recognition.

Off-line A term used to describe any device such as a backing-store disk which is not on-line (q.v.) to the central processor but is in reserve until required.

OMR *See* optical mark recognition.

On-line Describes equipment which is connected to and controlled by the computer and available for immediate use or access.

Optical character recognition Similar to optical mark recognition (q.v.), but the computer can recognise alphabetical and numerical characters printed in one of the special type styles. The light reflected by a character creates a special pattern on the detector which is unique to the character concerned.

Optical mark recognition A specialised input device, used on pre-printed questionnaires and other documents. The respondent fills in a box, or joins a pair of dots to show his/her choice of answer. The documents are fed into a hopper, light beams are fed onto each document and reflected back to a detector. The selected answer reflects back less light and can be detected. 10,000 copies per hour, with a failure rate of 1%, can be processed. Unreadable forms are rejected into a special stacker and must be checked manually.

Output Computer results or information ready for transfer to an outside device.

Output devices Devices which will pass on the processed results of the computer's calculations to the computer user, or to a storage device for further use when required. Until sufficient data has accumulated results from the central processor are held temporarily in main memory. The chief output devices are VDUs, printers of various types, graph plotters and COM (computer output to microfilm or microfiche).

Paper tape An early method of inputting data and outputting data, by punching characters across paper tape with a pattern of holes. Ten characters per inch can be punched on the tape. They are read by a paper-tape reader at about 1,000 characters per second. The punching is a much slower operation because the punch is mechanically operated. Paper tape is rather outdated now.

Peripheral device The collective name for any device which is not part of the central processor itself, but is in the surrounding area to input data, or output data, or store it in some permanent way until required.

POS Abbreviation for 'point-of-sale'. A POS device can read bar codes, credit cards etc and call up data from the memory to give customer activity in each trading area, the price of the good etc, (*see* also EFTPOS).

Printer An output device that produces the results on paper; the most common form of computer output especially in the commercial field, where bank statements, wage slips, invoices, etc are the end products after processing. The common types of printer are line printers, matrix printers, daisy-wheel printers, laser printers and ink-jet printers (q.v.).

Printout The listing from a computer.

Processor The part of the computer actually performing the computing.

Program A set of instructions in correct order which tells the computer how to carry out the task it is being asked to perform.

Punched card An early input device, still in use, which is punched with 80 columns, with 12 punchable rows in each column. A character is punched so as to give a unique pattern in a column, and there can therefore be 80 characters per card. They are read by photo electric cells at speeds of 1,500 cards per minute, but punching the cards is a slower process. Their use is declining because of their slow speeds and bulky nature when stored.

Punched tags POS tags used in clothing stores to identify garments, sizes and prices.

The codes are punched into the tag in two places. One half is torn off and these tags are sent at the end of the day to the central computer where they give daily update of sales from all stores, and the stock position. They are a way of capturing POS data.

RAM Random access memory. The components of a memory that can be both read from and written to. A computer advertised as 64k has 64×1024 bytes of random access memory. A RAM is a volatile memory, i.e. its contents are lost when the computer is switched off. (*See* ROM)

Read The process of transferring information from an input device or a backing store into the central processor.

ROM 'Read only Memory', the components of a memory which can be read from but not written to. It is used for holding the operating system and utility programs. This is a non-volatile memory. The data is retained after the computer is switched off and can be recalled after it is switched on again.

Semi-conductor Any device which restricts electron flow to one direction only – for example a valve, transistor or silicon chip.

Silicon chips *See* Chips.

Software The operating system and application programs which organise the computer's resources and make the whole set of separate elements operate together to function as a computer.

Terminal A device made up of a keyboard and a visual display (VDU), which has become the standard means of communicating with a remote computer. Input is achieved via the keyboard, and output appears on the VDU screen. What appears on the screen can be produced as hard copy if a printer is attached. Used more generally the term can mean any device at the end of a transmission of data, i.e. a VDU, teleprinter, cash receipting machine, credit card reader, modem or mini-computer.

Thermal printer A non-impact printer, which makes characters appear on a special heat-sensitive paper by means of heated wires in the print head. They are silent and therefore useful in hospitals, but their speeds are slow (100 characters a second).

Transistor A semi-conductor device, smaller than the original device (the thermionic valve – q.v.) It restricts electron flow to one direction. Transistors are more efficient than valves, since they do not require heat to stimulate electron flow, and replaced valves in computers about 1950.

Validating The process of proving the correctness of a piece of data.

Valve The thermionic valve was the original semi-conducting device, which restricts the flow of electrons to one direction. In America it is called a vacuum tube. It can act as an amplifier of electrical signals and as an on/off switch. Valves were used in the earliest computers, but are bulky and use a lot of energy.

VDU A visual display unit, or monitor, usually part of a terminal and giving instantaneous displays of output from the computer. Hard copies may be taken if a printer is attached. The VDU with a keyboard also acts as an input device either on-line (e.g. having direct access to the central processor as in air-line bookings) or off-line (e.g. the key-to-disk system, q.v.).

Visual Display Unit *See* VDU above.

Volatility The property of a component to lose its data if switched off or if there is a power failure. We must always guard against loss of data by having back-up records, and having sound layouts which are clear so that wrong plugs will not be pulled out, wrong switches turned off, etc.

Winchester disks Hard discs for micro-computers, either single platter or multi-platter, and either integral parts of the computer or 'stand-alone' versions as separate units. More expensive than floppy discs they have faster performance and larger storage capacities (5–40 megabytes).

■ EXERCISE 18.1

1   What is a mainframe computer? What is a microcomputer?
2   Write short notes (3–5 lines) on each of the following:

(a) a VDU   **(b)** a floppy disk   **(c)** bar codes
(d) line printers   **(e)** real-time systems   **(f)** COM

3   What is meant by 'branch networking' in banking?
4   Explain MICR, OMR and OCR.
5   Why is Charles Babbage called 'the father of modern computing'?
6   What is meant by a 'user-friendly' system? Refer in your answer to the use by a customer of an ATM machine. The customer has **(a)** put the plastic card in upside down. **(b)** uses a card which the computer refuses to acknowledge **(c)** is an anti-litter enthusiast.
7   What is a graph plotter? How might a graph plotter be used to show management that out of £1,000,000 profit 35% had gone in Corporation Tax, 8% in bonus payments to staff, 20% in dividends to shareholders and the rest had been retained for use in the business as reserves. Draw the vertical bar chart as displayed on the screen.
8   Why is telecommunications essential to computerised banking? What is digital transmission and what is its importance to bank systems?
9   List the chief methods of input used in computerisation.
10 List the chief methods of output used in computerisation.

(*For the answers to this section the student should re-read the text*).

19 The use of computers in banking

OBJECTIVES

By the end of this chapter you should:
1 Appreciate some of the commonest uses of the computer in banking.
2 Have reviewed your own work and written a short report on the impact of the computer on you personally in your present working environment.
3 Have some understanding of the Data Protection Act and the implications of the Act for bankers and their staff.

1   THE USE OF COMPUTERS IN BANKS

The introduction of computers to the operation of the major banks' branches, which started around 1970, revolutionised the way the branches operated.

Tasks which had previously been carried out laboriously by hand or using cumbersome ledger posting machines could be processed much faster and in greater numbers by computer. At first, it was assumed, as in many industries, that this would result in a significant reduction in the numbers of staff required to carry out the basic clerical tasks. In fact it soon become clear that the development of computerisation was taking place at the same time as a huge rise in the numbers of people wanting to open bank accounts. As a result staff were re-deployed to tasks involving more direct customer contact, while the computer dealt with the basic bookkeeping tasks. The following areas of work are some of those with which you are likely to be concerned.

1.1   Cashiering

In the last few years, many banks have adopted a system of counter terminals, where the cashier can enter details of items cashed or paid in over the counter directly, via a keyboard, to the central computer. The procedure may update the customer's account directly, or more probably will queue the data for updating overnight. Similarly, depending on the individual bank's practice, the cashier may be able to make balance enquiries before cashing a cheque. Clearly this is a safeguard to prevent cashing a cheque where the customer does not have the funds to honour it. A third type of service is the ability of the cashier to carry out transfers between accounts, at a customer's request – for example transfer of funds to a deposit account where a current account balance is considerable, or in the reverse direction where a customer has to increase his/her current account balance to meet obligations arising in the near future.

1.2   Account maintenance

As we saw in Chapter 15 about branch accounts, almost all transactions to do with customers' accounts are now recorded by electronic means. The customer who pays in money and cheques to a cashier will find the credit recorded by the computer on his/her next statement. Similarly when a cheque is drawn by the customer and eventually presented by the person to whom it was sent, a computerised debit entry will appear (showing that the customer has received back the use of his/her money, formerly placed at the bank's disposal). Other parts of account maintenance are:

(a)   Standing orders

Before computerisation, a series of index cards had to be maintained: one for every standing order, for every customer, filed in date order. The standing order clerk had to create a Bank Giro credit or internal voucher for every payment to be made, with corresponding debit to the customer's account (often the card itself). The card then had to be re-filed carefully at the date of the next payment due. With computerisation the clerk fills out a standing order input form, on first receipt of the customer's instructions or any future amendment. This programs the computer to make the necessary payments, on the due dates, either until the final payment or until further notice, as appropriate. The BACS sheet showing the debit to the customer's account is received by the branch a few days before the debit is made, giving the manager time to return or 'bounce' the payment if the customer does not have enough money in his/her account to cover it. The credit to the beneficiary is also made through the BACS system, on the same day as the debit removes the funds from the payer's account. The chance that the bank might overlook a standing order through some event such as misfiled cards, staff illness, etc, is greatly reduced now that the computer is handling the series of payments.

(b)   Direct debits

The introduction of computers made possible the system of direct debits which is now a widespread method of settling bills, particularly annual, quarterly or monthly amounts which may vary from payment to payment. Effectively, a direct debit is a standing order initiated by the recipient rather than the customer. The customer signs a Variable Amount Direct Debit mandate authorising the beneficiary to request payment. In cases where the direct debit is in use it is the beneficiary who knows what amount has to be paid and there is no need for the customer to sign a new mandate each time the amount changes. Thus the local authority knows what community charge or business rate it has set for the citizens or ratepayers in its area and is consequently better able to request payment than the payer – who does not know the amount until advised by the authority. Similarly professional bodies know what the current subscription is, and for them to request payment of the correct amount is more sensible than to have a standing order payment which, when it arrives, proves to be for the wrong amount. The request for payment is made through the BACS system again, from the customer's account on the due date. A printout showing payments due to be requested is received by the paying bank a few days in advance, to enable payments to be stopped if the customer does not have sufficient money in his or her account, or has requested that payment of the direct debit be stopped. It is even possible now to pay telephone bills, electricity bills and gas bills by direct debit. The system is also widely used by such firms as brewery companies, to obtain payment for supplies delivered to tied houses.

(c) Cheque processing

The volume of cheques is now so enormous, about 15 milliuon a day on the BACS clearing alone to a value of about £34,000 million, that the whole system would break down were it not for the ability of the computer to read the MICR (magnetic ink character recognition) numbers and letters on the cheques. Cheque reader/sorter machines in the clearing houses read and sort cheques at speeds of about 3,000 per minute.

(d) Customer information

The most useful piece of customer information is the monthly statement. Formerly handwritten, these are now fully computerised, producing high quality statements personally addressed and automatically folded and stuffed into well-designed window envelopes. To make the machines economic the vast majority of statements are prepared on a cyclical-billing basis, with about 5% of statements being sent out each working day.

Rather similar are the statements sent out by the major credit card companies, each of which has about 8 million customers in the UK requiring detailed printouts showing every transaction, the interest added on the outstanding balance and instructions to the client about payment. These have to be individualised, to pick up such matters as customers who have failed to pay their monthly instalment, changes in credit limit etc.

Customers who require up-to-the-minute information about the balances on their bank accounts may enquire from the cashier who can check the balance on a computerised screen. A printout can be supplied but some banks are beginning to charge for this service since some customers are inclined to ask for one daily. An alternative approach adopted by other banks is to provide automated statement machines where a customer can use his or her cashcard and PIN to request a printout of recent transactions on their account while they wait. This service is free of charge at the time of writing.

(e) Management information

From the bank's point of view VDU displays and/or printouts also supply a great deal of management information, particularly featuring:

- Accounts becoming overdrawn.
- Accounts exceeding the credit limits sanctioned for an overdraft facility.
- Charges made on customers' accounts.

● Product activity – the use being made by customers of various facilities so that marketing decisions can be made and mailshots and similar campaigns accurately targeted.

There are countless potential new uses for this sort of management information. A major need in banking is to make management at all levels aware of the marketing potential available to the bank in its network of customer accounts.

2 INFORMATION TECHNOLOGY

In the UK information technology is handled by the British Telecom Special Service Sales Office. Their telephone number is available in every telephone directory. The term 'information technology' (IT) refers to the transmission of information along sophisticated telephone lines. Every company and organisation has potential uses for IT, which is widely used in banking for all the electronic systems described in this chapter. Thus the transmission of data from branches to Head Offices via a computer centre, is an overnight miracle which has been described in detail in Chapter 1 for branch and Head Office accounting. The work of ATMs is very similar. One of the earliest uses of IT was developed by the credit card services, so that, for example, American credit cards used in the UK could be checked against the complete file of stolen American credit cards, kept in the USA, in about six seconds. Less than a 10 second telephone charge to check every credit card.

The full use of information technology depends upon the conversion of traditional wiring in telephone communication to a glass fibre system. Enormous costs are involved and the only country in the world with a full glass fibre system installed is Iceland – where the task has been less demanding than in some other countries. Glass fibre networks make it possible to transmit data as a pulsed bitstream by a system known as 'pulsed code modulation' at much higher speeds than can be sent over the normal telephone lines. By clever devices it is possible to send, for example, 2,000 telephone conversations over a single cable without getting them muddled, which requires 140 million bits of information to be sent every second.

Information technology permits the knowledge in data banks all over the world to be accessed and used by those needing information. It enables management information to be compiled and distributed at a relatively trifling cost so that all are informed, however remote from Head Office, and all can similarly contribute to the conclusions management draws from the company's business activity around the world.

2.1 Home banking

Not all banks have developed a home banking service. The Bank of Scotland's HOBS (Home and Office Banking Service) works via the Prestel computer to give customers a direct link to the bank's computer (subject to certain safeguards). The link is made via a special HOBS terminal through a telephone jack socket (or a customer who has a modem can use the modem). The link throws up an image on the domestic TV set or on a dedicated VDU if preferred. The customer can:

● Monitor his/her various accounts and review them at any time.

- Transfer funds between accounts to maximise interest on balances.
- Pay bills, either at once or at any future time up to 30 days ahead, knowing that the computer will not overlook the payment. For offices this gives the maximum benefit from credit periods offered by suppliers.
- Review standing orders and direct debit authorisations.
- Order cheque books and printed statements.

The service also supplies a key card for use in cash dispensers around the country. TSB's Speedlink is a similar system and Clydesdale also has a Home Banking service.

2.2 Bank terminals (ATMs)

The automated teller machine is now so much a part of everyone's life that there is little need to describe the computerised activities it performs. The systems in use vary and at any given moment reflect the 'state of the art' at the time. For example, most ATMs are not yet directly on line to the bank's computerised accounts, but only to a bank of information which is at 'overnight' status. The actual withdrawal of cash will not be debited to a customer's account in real-time, but only queued for up-dating that evening. The machines take considerable pressure off the cashiering system, enabling many withdrawals to be made without personal attention. They can also allow customers to check their balance, print out a mini-statement, transfer money between accounts or order a cheque book depending on the bank and type of machine.

2.3 EFTPOS

Electronic funds transfer at the point of sale, although meeting some resistance from stores and other business outlets over the charges incurred, is likely to become in the future the main way of payment in most large shops, and cash-and-carry outlets in the wholesaling field. EFTPOS places the onus on the shopper to have the funds available when they make a purchase, and consequently restores to the consumer some measure of responsibility for his/her actions. The computer offers a range of invaluable services to retailers at the point of sale – not just electronic funds transfer but stock recording, re-ordering of items when a minimum stock position is reached, analysis of business activity in particular areas, etc.

2.4 Securities Department

Full details of the security held against a loan may be maintained on the computer, allowing checks to be made that security has been completed, that insurance payments on a property are up-to-date, etc. This also means central management may analyse the security held throughout the bank – the percentage cover on mortgage loans for example. The calculation of interest on mortgages, particularly with the complications of MIRAS (mortgage interest relief at source), are made much simpler by the use of a computer, which can take in its stride the numerous changes in interest rates and consequent changes in monthly repayments, which are inevitable at a time of rapidly fluctuating rates.

There is no need to run through all the departments which use the computer. This will have given you a flavour of the difference the computer has made to banking.

3   THE DATA PROTECTION ACT 1984

Certain European countries, which had already passed data protection legislation, were wary of sending data to countries where no such laws were in place, as their data might be misused there. The Council of Europe Data Protection Convention was therefore established to lay down internationally agreed data protection laws, allowing countries which have ratified the agreement to send data freely to each other. In the UK there was already pressure from consumer groups to introduce protection for individuals against misuse of personal data. In 1984 the Data Protection Act was passed, in line with the Convention, requiring all data users to register certain automatically processed files at the Data Protection Registry.

The Data Protection Act 1984 is designed to regulate the use of personal data, which is defined as information about a living individual who can be identified from that information, or from that and other information held by the data user. Data is defined as information which can be processed by equipment operating automatically which includes word processors and personal computers as well as mainframes. (So written records are not data under the Act.)

The Act imposes specific duties on data users, computer bureaux, etc and gives certain rights to individuals (including employees) on whom data is held.

The Act lays down certain 'Data Protection Principles', contravention of which may lead to the removal of the offending party from the register of those permitted to hold and transfer information held on data banks. These principles are:

(a)   Information to be contained in personal data shall be obtained fairly and lawfully, and processed fairly and lawfully.

(b)   It shall be held only for one or more specified and lawful purposes. (These are made clear when the data user registers with the Data Protection Registrar.)

(c)   The data must not be used or disclosed in any manner that is incompatible with the purpose or purposes specified on registration.

(d)   The data must be adequate, relevant, not excessive, accurate and kept up to date.

(e)   Data shall not be kept for longer than is necessary for the purposes stated.

(f)   An individual shall be entitled at reasonable intervals and without undue delay or expense to be informed whether personal data is being kept on him/her, and to have access to it.

(g)   Appropriate security measures must be taken to prevent unauthorised access to, or alteration, disclosure or destruction of data.

Exemptions

The Act does not apply to (a) payroll or pension records, (b) accounting records, (c) records of purchases and sales, (d) records aimed at financial or management forecasts, (e) matters of national security.

However payroll records may not be disclosed except to an individual seeking his/her own records, or for purposes for which the person concerned has given his/her consent.

There are a number of other exemptions, for example data may be held for the prevention or detection of crime; apprehension or prosecution of offenders; the assessment or collection of taxes, community charges, etc. Purely mailing lists are exempt, as are club membership records, provided the members agree to their details being stored on computer, and they are not disclosed to others.

Under the Data Protection (Regulation of Financial Services etc) (Subject Access Exemption) Order 1987 personal data held for the purpose of discharging designated statutory functions designed to protect members of the public from dishonesty, incompetence or malpractice by persons with banking, insurance and investment services are exempt from the rules of the Act.

Implications for banks

The Data Protection Act has two main implications for banks in the conduct of business with their customers:

(a)   The Act requires a credit provider to reveal to any customer who so requests, the name of any credit reference agency which the provider consulted before making a decision on whether to lend. In practice this is usually invoked by a customer who has been refused credit. Once the customer has been advised by the bank of the name of the credit reference agency used, the customer may approach the agency for a copy of any information held against his or her name. If this turns out to be incorrect, the Act requires the agency to correct the information held.

(b)   A customer may request the bank to disclose all personal information, held in the data banks, relating to that customer. This can be a cumbersome, laborious and expensive procedure for a bank with numerous branches, departments and computer systems but under the Act the bank has no option but to comply.

Data security

Even without the requirements of the Data Protection Act, commercial businesses have always been concerned to protect the security of their computer systems. There is a need to protect against industrial espionage and against fraud or sabotage by unscrupulous or embittered members of staff.

Unauthorised access can be prevented in three main ways:

1   **Physical means** Locks on equipment, identity card checks on access to buildings, shredders to destroy unwanted printouts and magnetic tape.

2   **Access codes** Passwords can be incorporated into systems at various levels, known only to a limited number of people. Special, often highly complex codes are used to control entry to the telecommunication network used to transfer huge sums of money daily between financial institutions. The receiving bank or branch must decode the message before allowing the payment to go through. Customers are often issued with Personal Identification Numbers (PINs) to operate automated cash machines, confirming that the card is being used by its rightful owner.

3   **Audit trails** These do not prevent unauthorised access but record all transactions passing through the system. Any changes can thus be traced back to the person who initiated them.

The importance of these precautions is clearly demonstrated by the occasional dramatic frauds, or potential frauds which hit the headlines. It is the existence of rigorous controls which ensures these are very rare.

The Banking Ombudsman receives many complaints from customers who claim that their accounts have been debited by 'phantom' cash withdrawals through ATMs. Virtually all these are subsequently shown to be the result of the customer revealing their PIN number to a friend or relative, who has misused the card; or recording the number with the card in such a way that a thief can decipher it. Used properly, PINs are a foolproof way of maintaining the security of a customer's account.

4   A PROJECT ON THE IMPACT OF THE COMPUTER ON YOUR OWN WORK

Examination questions often call for examples of the use made of computers in banking and there is much to be said for answering such a question with a clear and interesting account of the impact the computer has made on your own particular sector. For one thing, we all write well about the things we know best and a clear explanation of the way the computer serves a particular department, with which the examiner may not actually be familiar, is refreshing. You are therefore asked to prepare a brief account of the impact of the computer on your own work. The following ideas may help you analyse your own situation. If there are some parts which you are unable to answer you might like to ask around and find out (for example) exactly what the computer is doing with the inputs you make, and what exactly happens to any outputs that result.

The points you might like to review are:

(a)   What actual parts of your daily work involve the use of, or reference to, the computer?

(b)   If inputs are involved, what exactly is it that you input? Is any preparatory work necessary before you make the input? If so, what exactly do you do? What checks do you carry out?

(c)   Do you refer to any outputs from the computer? If you do, is the output in permanent form (for example a printout) or is it transitory: called up onto a VDU and cleared once you have noted the detail?

(d)   Does the computer, as far as you are concerned, produce anything directly of benefit to the customer? Do you, for example, provide customers with printouts of any sort? Is there a charge for this?

(e)   Does the computer produce any management data? Is the use of this management information beneficial to you personally? Is it irksome (does it get you into trouble, for example)?

Whether this project is one which you do for a tutor or lecturer, or only one that you do for your own satisfaction, it should finish up as a reasonable comprehensive account – say up to four A4 pages – about your own use of the computer. File it away and read it through in the week before your examination.

■ EXERCISE 19.1

1 Explain the services offered to customers by automated teller machines (ATMs). What safeguards have banks introduced to regulate their use?

2 What is meant by 'home banking'? Explain how computers and telecommunications have made this service possible.

3 Distinguish between a standing order and a direct debit. How are each of these dealt with by the computer? What triggers the computer into action and what is the final result?

4 What does MICR stand for? Explain what is already encoded on the MICR line of a cheque which is still in the cheque book. What is added to the MICR line once the cheque has been issued by the customer and paid in by the payee? How is the MICR line of use to the bank in processing the cheque?

5 How does the computer help a manager decide which cheques must be returned ('bounced')? If you are not sure, ask your manager or supervisor to explain how the system works in your bank.

6 Does the Data Protection Act 1984 cover all data? Explain your answer.

7 List as many of the requirements of the Data Protection Act 1984 as you can remember.

8 Give five examples of exemptions from the Data Protection Act 1984.

9 You are the secretary of the local drama group and keep details of your members, including names and addresses, which plays they have acted in and when they are available for rehearsals, etc on your home computer. Do you need to register under the Data Protection Act?

10 Describe the three types of measures which banks and other businesses can take to safeguard the security of their computer systems. List as many examples of each type as you can.

■ ANSWERS

1 See text for details of services. Safeguards include PINs (personal identification numbers) to ensure the card is used by the rightful owner; 'hot card' lists to enable stolen cards to be retained by the machine; daily or weekly limits incorporated in the magnetic strip on the card; and a check against the customer's balance where the machine is on-line to the central computer.

2–5 See text or ask your manager or supervisor.

6 No, only data stored in an automated way and only personalised data (so written records and information which cannot be linked to an individual are not covered). Additionally there are various types of data exempt from the requirements of the Act.

7–8 See text.

9 No, provided that your members have been made aware that their details are stored on a computer and they have indicated that they have no objections. If the names and addresses were being used solely as a mailing list then this would also be exempt from the need to register.

10 See text.

20 An introduction to statistics

OBJECTIVES

After studying this chapter you should:
1 Understand the elementary concepts of statistics as a system of collecting and analysing data so that we can be better informed about any matter we care to study;
2 Know the difference between a census and a sample, and the various types of sample that are in common use in statistics;
3 Know how to draw up arrays and tabulations of data;
4 Understand frequency distributions.

1 DEFINITIONS OF STATISTICS

Statistics may be defined as numerical facts, systematically collected and presented. The word has its origin in the Latin word for state, for from the earliest times the state has been interested in such matters as the number of its citizens, the wealth that they are creating every year, the volume of foreign trade, etc. Today managers are equally interested in the numerical facts affecting their businesses, in particular production figures, sales figures, financial projections, measurements of productivity and many other statistics. Bankers are interested in the number of accounts that might be opened in an area; the spending power that is available; the ranges of incomes in local industries; the prospects of profitability in local industries; the capital requirements of each major firm; the likely market for bank services, etc.

Viewed in this way, as numerical facts systematically collected we speak of the statistics as **data**.

Sometimes when we use the word 'statistics' we do not mean data, but the technique, or method of investigating problems by analysing statistical facts. This **statistical method** is essentially a branch of mathematics. It requires us to understand such ideas as averages, trends, distributions, probabilities, etc. Viewed in this way we may define statistics as a range of mathematical techniques for analysing problems in the real world. In fact, mathematical statistics is of increasing importance in a wide range of activities, for example, in industrial mass production, medicine, biology, economics, politics, psychology, analysis of public opinion and other social sciences, agriculture, traffic studies, meteorology, physics and engineering.

In all of these areas data is used to test hypotheses and models can be developed for planning and forecasting purposes. However this is an elementary book, and such advanced techniques need not concern us here though we may meet some of them at higher levels of our banking studies. Every bank has its financial statistics division and presents data in interesting ways in such reports as the Annual Report to shareholders. The Bank of England, in its Quarterly Bulletin, produces a huge set of statistics dealing with all aspects of banking, the money supply, etc. Students should certainly take any opportunity they get to study this sort of material.

2 CONDUCTING A STATISTICAL INQUIRY

Much data is collected as a matter of routine, as reports are fed into Head Offices. Weekly or monthly returns from branches give many businesses data which bears upon profitability, marketing success or failure, labour turnover and many other aspects of business. Other data is the result of specialist inquiries set up to discover the true facts about a particular situation or development.

The stages of a statistical inquiry may be listed as follows:

2.1 The problem must be clearly stated

An inquiry cannot be launched in general terms. We must identify the cause for concern and state explicitly what the problem is. For example, an investigation into labour turnover may not affect all parts of a firm equally. No inquiry may be necessary in many departments where labour turnover is not abnormal. The area giving trouble may be a particular department, or a particular process or product. Stating the problem carefully gives those conducting the inquiry **terms of reference** from which they can start to collect relevant data for analysis.

2.2 The best approach must be decided upon

In the light of the terms of reference provided by Section 2.1 above how shall we tackle the problem? Statistical evidence may already be available from past records. Someone may already have faced the same problem, and it will be a waste of time to repeat an investigation. Many inquiries begin with a '**literature survey**' in which we read all the published material already available on this, or related, topics. Other inquiries begin with a thorough survey of all past records available '**in house**'. For example, a 'labour turnover' investigation might begin with an examination of 'closed' personnel files. Why did people in this area leave? Did the explanations they gave fit into a pattern of behaviour that pinpoints the cause of our problem? Was it working conditions, levels of remuneration, supervisory problems or what?

2.3 Census or sample survey

If available material cannot solve our problem we must commence the collection of data. An immediate problem is the extent of the inquiry. Shall it extend to include the whole '**population**'? This word has a special meaning in statistics – it refers to the whole of the material affected by the inquiry in hand. In some cases, such as the United Kingdom Census (held every 10 years in the first year of the decade) the population is every person living in the United Kingdom, and the word, therefore, has its ordinary dictionary meaning. In other cases, for example, an inquiry into labour turnover in the machine shop, it refers to every individual working in the machine shop. Probably an inquiry of this sort should investigate the views of every person concerned, but this might be a lengthy process if the numbers were large. We could perhaps get just as good a result by asking every tenth member for his/her views. This is called a **sample survey**. Special precautions are necessary to ensure that those interviewed are a **random sample**, not a biased sample which will give a biased result. For example, suppose the most convenient group to interview were those who arrived early for work. This might well be a biased sample. People who arrive early for work are frequently enthusiastic about their work and unlikely to be disgruntled and considering a transfer. Therefore, to ask only such employees may not produce a true answer to our problem.

2.4   Is a questionnaire necessary?

One of the simplest ways to conduct an inquiry is to draw up a questionnaire. This ensures that all interviewees are asked all the questions we feel are relevant to the problem in hand. The questions should be posed in the same way to all so as to avoid biasing the answers by slightly different wording, or even an inflection of the voice. A **pilot inquiry** may be necessary (preferably in a different department) to test out the form and discover any weaknesses – ambiguous questions often produce irrelevant answers, not foreseen by those drawing up the questionnaire.

2.5   Collecting the data

Many inquiries take the form of interviewing people, and it is essential to appoint interviewers, brief them adequately and ensure that they conduct the interviews in a proper manner. Any conclusions drawn from a badly conducted series of interviews will be meaningless. Other inquiries do not involve interviewing, data is collected by **enumerators** who record facts as they become available. Thus a traffic census requires enumerators to record traffic passing a specific point, using the five-barred gate principle illustrated in Fig. 20.1.

Other data may be recorded electronically, by metering devices detecting the information required, or clocking up the number of times a particular service or facility is used.

2.6   Editing and classifying the data

The result of Section 2.5 above is a mass of raw data, in a very indigestible form. Some of it may need editing to tidy it up. For example, in Fig. 20.1 the editor will add up the total number of vehicles recorded on each part of the form and record it as shown in a circle. These should then be carried to a master sheet which will provide the total for the day under each heading.

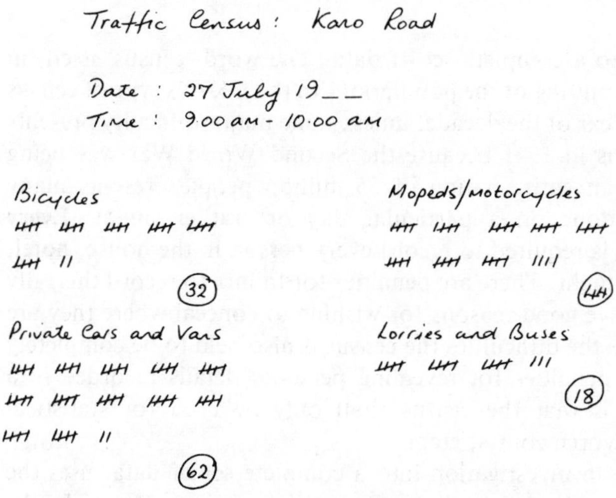

Traffic Census : Karo Road

Date : 27 July 19_ _
Time : 9·00 am - 10·00 am

Bicycles

⊬⊬⊤ ⊬⊬⊤ ⊬⊬⊤ ⊬⊬⊤ ⊬⊬⊤
⊬⊬⊤ //

(32)

Mopeds/motorcycles

⊬⊬⊤ ⊬⊬⊤ ⊬⊬⊤ ⊬⊬⊤ ⊬⊬⊤
⊬⊬⊤ ⊬⊬⊤ ⊬⊬⊤ ////

(44)

Private Cars and Vans

⊬⊬⊤ ⊬⊬⊤ ⊬⊬⊤ ⊬⊬⊤ ⊬⊬⊤
⊬⊬⊤ ⊬⊬⊤ ⊬⊬⊤ ⊬⊬⊤ ⊬⊬⊤
⊬⊬⊤ ⊬⊬⊤ //

(62)

Lorries and Buses

⊬⊬⊤ ⊬⊬⊤ ⊬⊬⊤ ///

(18)

Fig. 20.1 The five-barred gate system of enumeration

2.7 Analysing the data

We are now in a position to analyse the data. Up to this point much of the work may have been done by enumerators who were neither skilled in statistical method nor knowledgeable about the matter under investigation. It might even be preferable to use such people during the collection of the data, since an enumerator who is vitally interested in the results may introduce unconscious or – worse still – conscious bias into the data. When analysing the data it is essential to have those who are knowledgeable about the subject matter and skilled in statistical method taking part. The various parties will act as a check upon one another and ensure valid conclusions.

2.8 Presentation and report writing – including recommendations

The result of any survey is a set of proposals to remedy the problem originally faced, or to choose between alternative programmes and policies. In making these recommendations it is necessary to present the data in a simple and convincing style, as part of a report to the appropriate authority. The report will be addressed to the authority that ordered the investigation and will usually begin by quoting the terms of reference given to the team at the commencement of the inquiry. Tables, charts and diagrams will show what the survey found, suggest the causes or reasons for the original problem and make firm recommendations to resolve the difficulty.

In any statistical inquiry the object of the exercise is to solve a problem. It may be a matter of product quality, market penetration, provision of an adequate service at reasonable cost or the improvement of the environment. There is no point in collecting statistics for their own sake, or to demonstrate our erudition. Statistical surveys are expensive, and we shall generally be judged by our cost effectiveness in demonstrating the true facts and recommending the most likely cure in the circumstances.

3   TAKING A CENSUS

A census is an investigation into a complete set of data. The word 'census' itself, in everyday language, means the counting of the population. In the UK this type of census is held every decade in the first year of the decade, unless some major difficulty presents itself. Thus there was no census in 1941 because the Second World War was being fought at the time. To count an entire nation of 55 million people presents many problems, and it has to be done on a particular day or, rather, night. Every householder, hotel-keeper, etc, is required to record every person in the house, hotel, caravan site, etc, on the chosen night. There are penalties for failure to record this tally properly – some people may have good reasons for wishing to conceal where they are on a particular night. To reduce the difficulties the census is also held to be completely confidential, so that there are penalties for revealing personal details recorded in a census paper – the intention is that the census shall only be used for statistical purposes, not as evidence in divorce courts, etc.

More generally, a census, as an investigation into a complete set of data, uses the word 'population' in a special way. It means 'all those people, or things, affected by the inquiry. Thus an investigation into the incomes of students might have as its 'population' the students of a particular college class. We could not expect to conduct a census of the views of all students in the UK. We should need to use some sort of sample of the population.

4   SAMPLES

If we cannot take a census of the whole population because of the amount of work involved we have to settle for discovering data from a **sample survey**. The idea of a sample survey is that a small group of people, or objects, is taken to represent the whole population. We therefore use the term **representative sample**. By investigating the sample we discover information which is relevant to the whole population. Consider the possible samples that might be extracted from an organisation like the US Army. Suppose we decide our sample should consist of 50 persons. We might take 50 generals, 50 colonels, 50 technical corporals or 50 master-sergeant cooks. Could we regard these as a representative sample of the US Army? Clearly we could not, for there are no privates or corporals. We should feel a lot happier about our 'representative' sample if it had representatives of each rank in the army, and also represented the variety of skilled and unskilled trades in such a large organisation. Indeed, we might decide that 50 was too small a group to give adequate representation to the full range of ranks and trades – 500 might be a better sample, or even 5,000.

Having decided the general composition of our sample we now have to pick the actual individuals to be interviewed or to be sent our questionnaire. If there is to be one master-sergeant cook who shall it be? We cannot pick the one who happens to be most conveniently situated, in the camp up the road from our headquarters. The individual should ideally be selected **'at random'**. This means that all the master-sergeant cooks should have an equally good chance of being selected. This might be done, like picking a number in a raffle, by putting all the names on similar sized pieces of paper, putting them in a hat and choosing one.

The essential features of a random sample are as follows:

(a)   All members of the population are included in the selection procedure.

(b)   Every member of the population has the same chance of being selected. (In one investigation where numbers were written on cardboard discs and placed in a revolving drum, some of the discs were of shiny card and the others were on card of a rougher material. It was found that the shiny discs slipped easily to the bottom of the drum, and the majority of the discs selected were of the rougher materials. The selection was not therefore random, but biased.)

(c)   There is no way of predicting which item will be selected for inclusion in the sample.

4.1   The sample 'frame'

At a race meeting the runners and riders names appear in a frame, and those, obviously with little understanding of statistics, who propose to back a horse, may choose any name in the frame. There is no point in picking a name that is not in the frame, for those are the only horses running. In selecting a sample from a 'population' the sample 'frame' is a list of members of the 'population'. Every member of the 'population' should appear in the frame, so as to have a chance of selection. An inaccurate frame, which is out of date or contains errors, will reduce the accuracy of the results obtained from any sample chosen. Typical population frames are the register of electors, the lists of members of professional organisations (doctors, dentists, lawyers, clergymen), the list of members of clubs and societies, etc.

Theoretical considerations about the selection of a sample to represent a population often come up against practical difficulties, especially time factors and cost factors. Consequently, a variety of 'short-cut' methods of sampling have been developed, each of which inevitably reduces the perfection of the sample chosen − but samples are inherently imperfect anyway. If we have 100 motor vehicles, 5 of which are in fact faulty, any 10% sample chosen could include 5, 4, 3, 2, 1 or no faulty cars. If a sample happened to include all 5 we might conclude that 50% of the cars were faulty − much worse than the true position − whereas if the sample included no faulty cars we might conlude that all were in excellent condition. Even a satisfactory sample can therefore give an unsatisfactory result, and any conclusions drawn must bear in mind the possibility that a particular sample is unrepresentative in some way. When we start to use a sampling method that takes short cuts to save expense we may distort results again. Let us look at some of these methods of sampling.

(a)   Random samples

Ideally all samples should be random samples, defined as samples selected without any bias whatsoever, every individual in the population having an equal chance of selection. The best example of everyday use of a random sample is the game of 'Bingo'. Players are issued with cards each of which has a selection of numbers from 1 to 99 on it. Tiny pieces of card are also available to cover up the numbers on the card as they are selected. A caller selects the numbers at random and calls them out − the players covering over each number as it is called if it happens to appear on their cards. The first player to cover all the numbers on on his/her card wins a prize. To ensure random selection the numbers drawn are inscribed on identical wooden discs, or in some cases they are painted upon table tennis balls which are captured in a jet of air and trapped in turn as the selected items.

(b) Systematic, periodic or equal interval sampling

In practice random sampling can be very tedious, for every single item selected has to be chosen by random methods. An easier method is to select systematically. This can best be explained by considering an example. Suppose we wish to have a 10% selection from a population of 30 individuals. This means that 3 of the 30 are to be selected. We could systematically select every 10th one. However, this would not be random, since the 10th, 20th and 30th items would be certain of selection and the others would have no chance of selection at all. We can restore random selection by choosing the starting point by random methods. Thus if we put the first 10 numbers in the hat and select one of them (say 7) by random methods, our choice of items starts at the 7th and continues with the 17th and 27th items. This is shown in Fig. 20.2.

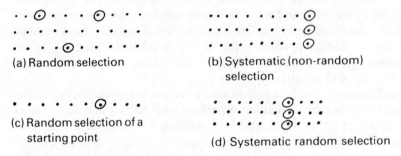

(a) Random selection

(b) Systematic (non-random) selection

(c) Random selection of a starting point

(d) Systematic random selection

Fig. 20.2 Systematic random selection

(c) Stratified (representative) sampling

It is sometimes possible to reduce the costs of random sampling by using a smaller group than the entire population, but taking steps to ensure that the various strata in the population are included in the sample used. Thus an inquiry into the opinions of car users which only questioned the owners of Rolls-Royce cars would give an unrepresentative sample. If motor vehicles can be separated into strata – the Rolls-Royce stratum, the luxury-saloon stratum, the popular-saloon stratum and the mini-car stratum – and selections are made at random for these groups we can obtain a relatively unbiased sample. If the numbers selected are proportional to the number of cars in the various strata, in the whole population we have a 'proportional stratified random sample', and come as near as possible to a representative sample of the whole population. In a purely random sample the proportion of car users in the various groups would be left to chance, but in the stratified sample it is not and the final sample consequently is more representative of the whole population than a purely random sample. The selection process is shown in Fig. 20.3.

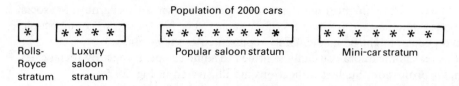

Fig. 20.3 A proportional stratified representative 1% random sample

(d) Multistage sampling (area sampling)

Rather similar to stratified sampling – which may be built into it – but a system of sampling designed to reduce the volume of work to manageable proportions, multistage sampling is a method of reducing a national survey to a number of local inquiries. The essence of the scheme is that random selection on a national basis is abandoned in favour of the random selection of a few areas (hence the alternative names 'area sampling and cluster sampling'). In the UK the most convenient basis chosen for stage 1 is the random selection of a number of rating authorities out of a total of some 400 authorities available. At this stage a certain amount of stratification might be introduced by ensuring that a fair selection of metropolitan, industrial, residential and rural authorities is included. Within the selected areas at stage 2 we now choose by random methods a further selection of subareas – possibly the electoral wards. Within the few areas now selected for our inquiry we select the actual households from the electoral roll by random methods – probably by systematic random selection as described earlier. We now have the problem of actually locating and interviewing these householders, but they are conveniently clustered together in a few areas – not necessarily very close to one another – but each area a compact base for a small team of interviewers. Multistage sampling is illustrated in Fig. 20.4.

Stage 1	400 rating authorities	
	Select 2% = 8 rating authorities	
Stage 2	8 rating authorities	= 70 electoral wards
	Select 10%	= 7 wards
Stage 3	7 wards	= 25,000 households
	Select 5%	= 1,250 households

Fig. 20.4 Multistage sampling

(e) Quota sampling

One of the problems with random sampling is the low level of responses. The individuals found in the sample may not be available, or may refuse to give their views. Repeat calls can be expensive and there is often no way of compelling replies from those who refuse to cooperate. One way of overcoming such difficulties is to allow the interviewer to substitute any other person who is available. Probably one view is as good as another. However, bias might creep in if the interviewer only has to fulfil his/her quota without any considerations of stratification. A paid interviewer might reduce the effort required by always asking the same group of people, neighbours and acquaintances. They might reflect the interviewer's own social group or social inclinations – middle-aged frequenters of the same public bar, perhaps. Young people, or retired people, might be inadequately represented in the quota.

For this reason the quota is usually stratified to some extent: by age, by social class, by trade or profession. Such stratifications are illustrated in Fig. 20.5.

Age	Sex Male (No required)	Female	Socio-ethnic group	Caucasian	Negro	Asian
Under 15	0	0	Profession/managerial	8	2	2
15–29	4	4	White-collar	10	3	2
30–44	9	9	Blue-collar	10	3	1
45–59	7	7	Senior citizen	6	2	1
60 and over	5	5				
Total	25	25	Total	34	10	6

Fig. 20.5   Quotas for sampling

(f)   Attribute sampling

This is a very simple method of sampling because it selects individuals who display a certain attribute – such as those born in April. In one long-term inquiry all children in the UK born on a particular day were followed up throughout their lives – so far. The early data were about weight, height, etc. As they passed successively through infancy, childhood and adolescence they proved to be a valuable source of data about educational attainments, intelligence, etc, and the intention is to continue the process throughout their lives. One disadvantage of such attribute sampling is that you cannot predict how many people will be caught by such a sampling method.

■ EXERCISE 20.1

(a)   Define statistics? Why are modern states interested in statistics?

(b)   Observers are to be stationed on a bridge overlooking a motorway to record (i) the number of vehicles and (ii) the types of vehicles using the motorway. Suggest how this should be done, and design a form to be used. What practical difficulties might arise and how may they be overcome? Mention in particular any decisions that might need to be made about the timing of the investigation.

(c)   A bank manager suspects that the various cashier's positions are badly used – some being too busy and others partly neglected. There is a position in the foyer from which all windows can be observed. Suggest how accurate data might be collected to provide clear evidence about the use of the various windows.

(d)   You are conducting an inquiry into business-studies teaching at your college and the contribution it has made to the careers of students who left five years previously. You propose sending out a questionnaire to the 160 students in that year, whose addresses are available. You wish to know the following points:

- The subjects studied.
- The examination successes achieved.
- Their present employment (and salary earned per annum).
- Their previous employments.
- Their opinions about the importance to them in their actual employment of (1) typewriting, (2) book-keeping and accounting, (3) economics, (4) secretarial studies, (5) business calculations, (6) banking studies and (7) English language.
- You also wish to know which subject has been the most directly beneficial in their careers.
- Finally, do they consider they benefitted greatly, only a little, or not at all from their business studies course?

Devise a questionnaire to obtain these answers.

(e) A manufacturer of a new window-cleaning product wishes to discover

- the extent of the market,
- the relative popularity of other brands and
- the likely price price customers would be willing to pay.

He proposes to conduct a survey in three areas:

- a rural area,
- a suburban area and
- an inner city area.

You are required:

    (i) To draw up a questionnaire which will discover the necessary information.

    (ii) To advise him how best to select his three areas, bearing in mind the nature of the product.

(f) Write notes on three of the following:

(i) Simple random sampling

(ii) Quota sampling

(iii) Stratified sampling

(iv) Multistage sampling (area sampling)

(g) What is a random sample? A personnel officer conducting an inquiry decides to ask the first 25 members of staff who enter the gates on the first Monday in June to complete his questionnaire. Discuss whether he has a random sample.

(h) What is a systematic sampling? Mr A proposes to select interviewees for an inquiry systematically by selecting the 50th, 100th, 150th, etc, member of the published list of the professional body concerned. Advise him about the random nature of his sample.

(i) What is quota sampling? An interviewer is asked to pose three questions about local education to 50 people, made up as follows:

- 10 boys under 18 years of age who are still at school/college
- 10 girls under 18 years of age who are still at school/college
- 10 male parents
- 10 female parents
- 10 other adults

Criticise this quota structure.

(j)   A bank is to conduct research into the leasing potential of a particular area, by finding out how much of the capital of firms and companies is tied up in fixed assets (other than premises). There are 24,000 businesses in the area. Would you recommend a census or a sample? What are the difficulties of such an investigation and how could they be overcome?

5   THE CLASSIFICATION AND TABULATION OF DATA

5.1   Discrete and continuous data

The result of any census or sample inquiry is a mass of data. This is usually called 'raw data'. The things we are seeking to measure are called **variables**. The data we collect will vary considerably, for example an inquiry about wages might reveal pay ranges from £0–£2,000 per month. Some variables are said to be **discrete variables** in other words, they can only change by a complete unit – the items being quite separate and distinct from one another. Thus a farmer keeping the breeding records of sows can only record, 8, 9, 10 or 12 piglets born per farrowing. There will be no such thing as a litter of 9.75 piglets. Other variables are said to be **continuous variables** – for example cars tested for mileage per gallon of fuel used might cover 39.75 miles or 39.89 miles, etc. There is a continuous path of increase or decrease, and vehicles may finish up with a result that appears anywhere on the scale. When classifying data these differences may be important in deciding how to present the data in classes.

5.2   Scrutinising raw data

The first task of the statistician is to reduce the mass of data to manageable proportions by classifying it and summarising it so that we can pick out the shape of the wood from the trees. The process is one where we extract from the questionnaires or interview schedules the answers to each separate question, and discover the range of replies to each.

Before doing this it is usual to scrutinise the questionnaires, as they arrive, to eliminate manifest absurdities. Some people send in 'joke' replies, others did not understand the nature of the inquiry and their replies will consequently be useless. Some forms may be incomplete, and may need to be followed up. Once the responses have been scrutinized, the valid questionnaires can now be examined in detail and the answers to individual questions recorded and collated. If this task is performed manually it can be very time consuming and tedious. Fortunately mechanical and electronic methods of analysing responses are now available.

5.3   Classification

First it is necessary to classify the data, i.e. arrange them into classes. Every inquiry will have its obvious classes into which a particular statistic naturally falls. Thus if we classify cars according to their colour we shall group all the black cars together. If we classify them by engine size we shall have all the 2 litre cars in the same class. A 1,000 cc car will not be in the 2 litre class, but naturally belongs in the 1 litre class. When we classify data we arrange them into classes, each member of which displays the same attributes as the others. Thus businesses may be classified according to turnover, and the classes used may be narrow ranges of turnover per annum, say: under £10,000; £10,000 but under £20,000; £20,000 but under £30,000, etc. In the class £20,000 but under £30,000 there will be many items – all of them businesses whose turnover falls within this narrow range. They all display this attribute, and businesses displaying a smaller turnover or a larger turnover do not appear. Any attribute that can be displayed in quantitative terms (such as turnover) is called a **variable**. Where a variable changes over time, and regular measurements of the data can be taken to bring out changes, the result is a 'series', or 'time series'. Attributes measured according to location are referred to as 'spatial distributions' – for example, sales of a firm may be collected on a geographical basis.

The rules for classifying data are as follows.

(a)   The categories must be comprehensive

We have a mass of responses to a particular inquiry. Every response must be capable of being included in one of the classes chosen. In some inquiries we deliberately have one class which is used to collect together any items which do not appear to fit in other categories. This class might be labelled 'other items', or 'other activities', according to the nature of the inquiry.

(b)   The categories should not be too numerous

Generally speaking six to ten classes is enough. Too many classes makes it difficult to draw conclusions from the data. The whole purpose of classification is to reduce the data to manageable proportions. A few large classes reduces the bulk of the data, while at the same time leaving a sufficient spread of information to bring out the range of data under consideration.

(c)   The categories should not overlap

If categories overlap there is a difficulty in deciding where to place a particular statistic. Thus if ages are classified as 0–5, 5–10, 10–15 and 15–20 we are not quite sure whether to put a 5-year-old into the first or the second group, while a 10-year-old could go in both the second and the third group. If the classes are reclassified as 0–5, 6–10, 11–15 and 16–20 the overlap is eliminated and the difficulty is resolved.

(d)   The categories should be homogeneous

In general, the members of any class will display the same characteristics, and the names given to the classes will describe the characteristic clearly. Where a class is used to collect together those items which do not fit into any other class the membership may not display the same characteristics and consequently few valid conclusions can be drawn from it. Thus in an inquiry about fish caught by vessels from a certain port we might find a number of miscellaneous varieties lumped together in a group 'other varieties'. They might include a shark, a sting ray, five lobsters, two crabs and some whitebait. Such groupings will be largely irrelevant to the main inquiry, and only included for the sake of comprehensiveness (see (a) above).

Bearing these rules for classifying data in mind, the work proceeds by rearranging the data in the form of an array, from which a frequency distribution can be developed.

5.4   Arrays and frequency distributions

Consider the responses to an inquiry about average monthly turnover shown in Table 20.1. There are 50 responses, a very confusing collection of replies at first glance. On a more detailed look we find that the smallest turnover is £7,965 and the largest £406,253. This spread, from £7,965–£406,253, is called the **range** of the data.

Table 20.1   Average monthly turnover: year 19..
(Correct to nearest £1 sterling)

£	£	£	£	£
9,160	371,162	264,238	72,295	385,492
17,184	236,324	355,426	49,425	249,265
214,319	99,297	275,326	24,276	172,624
119,385	36,179	101,164	138,254	25,426
365,626	136,326	166,157	319,186	96,265
7,965	153,325	406,253	281,166	87,171
189,172	52,331	214,246	9,160	403,318
13,296	372,264	320,321	121,632	236,724
17,295	19,333	11,626	378,188	159,621
21,185	49,721	366,262	274,246	403,184

One way of sorting out these data is to rearrange them in the form of an array. This means that we rearrange them in increasing order of size – starting with the smallest turnover. £7,965 and finishing with the largest, £406,253. The array therefore displays the full range, as shown in Table 20.2.

Table 20.2   Monthly turnover arranged as an array
(Correct to nearest £1 sterling)

£	£	£	£	£
7,965	25,426	119,385	214,319	355,426
9,160	36,179	121,632	236,324	365,626
9,160	49,425	136,326	236,724	366,262
11,626	49,721	138,254	249,265	371,162
13,296	52,331	153,325	264,238	372,264
17,184	72,295	159,621	274,246	378,188
17,295	87,171	166,157	275,326	385,492
19,333	96,265	172,624	281,166	403,184
21,185	99,297	189,172	319,186	403,318
24,276	101,164	214,246	320,321	406,253

A slightly simpler arrangement is to prepare a frequency distribution. The array is still in increasing order of size but this time the frequency with which each individual statistic occurs is indicated, instead of repeating the quantity as with 9,160 in the partial array shown above.

The frequency distribution would start:

£	
7,965	1
9,160	2
11,216	1
etc.	

It so happens that in our set of data the figure £9,610 is the only figure that occurs twice, so arranging the figures in a frequency distribution is not much help. To clarify the picture it must change to a **grouped frequency distribution**. This is shown in Table 20.3.

Table 20.3 Grouped frequency distribution of average monthly turnover: Year 19.. (Correct to nearest £1 sterling)

£	Frequency
Less than 50,000	14
50,000–99,999	5
100,000–149,999	5
150,000–199,999	5
200,000–249,999	5
250,000–299,999	4
300,000–349,999	2
350,000–399,999	7
400,000–449,999	3
Total	50

The number of groups or classes has been reduced to nine 'natural' divisions which are easily assimilated. The frequencies in each group are sufficiently large to be readily comparable with the whole – for example, statements such as '14 out of the 50 firms have turnovers below £50,000' are quite meaningful and convey a clear impression of a large section of the firms in the survey.

A grouped frequency distribution may be defined as 'a table which shows the frequency of occurrence of variables within specified classes, or bands of value'.

The full range of data is divided into a number of subgroups or classes, using subdivisions as naturally as possible. Thus to divide a range into classes of 50,000 assists comprehension while the choice of 70,000 as a subdivision for each class would not be 'natural' since we do not usually think in terms of £70,000. Overlapping of classes has been avoided, and there is no difficulty in deciding which group a business comes into.

5.5 Cumulative frequencies

The grouped frequency distribution can be extended to present the data in cumulative form. The accumulation is usually done from start to finish, but may be reversed (from finish to start). In Table 20.4 below the two cumulative columns may be used to read off such statements as the following: 34 of the firms had turnovers of less than £250,000 per annum. Twelve firms only had turnovers of £300,000 or more.

Table 20.4 Cumulative columns on a grouped frequency distribution of average monthly turnover: year 19.. (Correct to nearest £1 sterling)

£	Frequency	Cumulative frequency	Reversed cumulative frequency
Less than 50,000	14	14	50
50,000–99,999	5	19	36
100,000–149,999	5	24	31
150,000–199,999	5	29	26
200,000–249,999	5	34	21
250,000–299,999	4	38	16
300,000–349,999	2	40	12
350,000–399,999	7	47	10
400,000 and over	3	50	3
Total	50		

5.6   The essentials of tabulation

Tabulation is the most widely used and the simplest method of presenting data. A general layout is given in Fig. 20.6 and the salient points about each part of the layout are given as notes below the table. An example is given in Table 20.5.

1 A clear title (possibly including the time of the inquiry and the units used)
2 A source reference

3 Class description   4   5   6   (etc) Column headings

7 Row headings (the data will appear in columns in the rows)
8 (Not more than 10 classes if possible)
9 etc

10 Totals   (the columns will be totalled here)

11 Footnotes (but keep these as brief as possible)
12 Source notes (but keep these as brief as possible)

Fig. 20.6   A general layout for statistical tables

Notes
1   A table should have a clear and concise title, stating exactly what the table is about. Do not sacrifice clarity for brevity. Make it quite clear what units are being used. For example, dollars are used by many countries – make it clear: US\$; A\$; Hong Kong \$; etc.
2   A source reference should be given.

3   The class descriptions should appear as a heading above the various classes shown on the rows lower down. Thus the words Class of holder appear in Table 20.5 below, in the individual rows, the classes of holder are listed, with the number and value of their holdings in the columns alongside.

4   The column headings may be for actual data, or for derived data such as percentages, cumulative frequencies, etc.

10   Totals should always be checked for accuracy.

11 and 12   Sometimes footnotes and source notes are required, but these should be kept to a minimum. They are often needed in a time series collected over several years, to pinpoint a break in the table caused by a change of classification – so that earlier statistics and later statistics are not strictly comparable.

Now read these notes again, looking at Table 20.5 to see how it complies with the general layout.

Table 20.5   Investors in International Producers Plc, December 19.. (Source: company secretary's report)

Class of holder	Number of holdings	Amount of holdings (US$)	%
Banks and discount houses	4,883	1,068,750	2
Financial trusts	112	310,499	1
Insurance companies	843	8,118,631	18
Investment trusts	180	577,000	1
Pension funds	236	2,484,055	6
Trade unions	3,585	12,989,658	28
Other companies	1,235	2,234,728	5
International Producers' Trust	1	8,443,887	18
Individuals	61,831	9,539,607	21
Totals	72,906	45,766,815	100

The importance of tabulation and frequency distributions

What, it might be asked, is the point of all this? The answer depends very much on the inquiry we are conducting. Statistics is a technique for examining problems. Many tabulations are the result of the routine collection of data month after month and year after year. Because they are organised routinely does not mean they have lost their point – we are still examining the original problem, trying to detect changes which will throw our plans awry. If production starts to fall we shall not be able to fulfil the orders we are taking from customers. If people start to spend their money in different ways the Treasury's plans for the economy may be upset. If banks start to loan money on easy terms people will go ahead with expenditure which perhaps they – and perhaps the nation – cannot afford. So firms keep track of production, the Treasury keeps track of expenditure and the Central Bank monitors the banks' loan policies.

Frequency distributions are a way of sorting out data, and tables are a way of presenting data so that we can understand them almost at a glance. The manager or accountant who goes home with the latest statistics in his brief case and ponders them at home over the weekend, lifts the phone on Monday morning and starts to give orders which will correct adverse trends in the firm. Cut down output of tyres and increase the production of gear boxes. Put pressure on our debtors who are overdue and arrange for a loan from the bank until they actually pay. Statistics is not a dull activity with a mass of raw data – it is decision-making material for management.

6 SOME EXAMPLES OF TABULATION

Simple tabulation

Many tables are made up of relatively simple data, presented to display the data in a straightforward manner, bringing out totals wherever possible and possibly such derived statistics as percentages. Thus the following data might be presented as shown in Table 20.6.

Example 1

Weekly production of two different models of an appliance in a certain factory taken from weekly reports were as follows during the month of March: Standard model: week 1: 37,285; week 2: 42, 656; week 3: 40,758; week 4: 39,500. Deluxe model: week 1: 7,853; week 2: 8,594; week 3: 9,251; week 4: 12,285. Arrange these in a table to bring out weekly and monthly totals.

Note: The best layout for such a table shows the weekly production figures side by side in rows, and added to give the weekly total, while the monthly totals are in columns, to give a grand total. Now see Table 20.6.

Table 20.6 Production of appliances: March 19.. (Source: weekly reports)

Week	Standard model	De luxe model	Weekly total
1	37,285	7,853	45,138
2	42,656	8,594	51,250
3	40,758	9,251	50,009
4	39,500	12,285	51,785
Monthly total	160,199	37,983	198,182

6.2 Simple tabulation, with rounding

Frequently, sets of data contain more figures than can be readily comprehended by most people, and it is better to round the figures to simplify them. Thus to say that the UK has 55,295,321 people may be 'true' at a particular moment, but is it meaningful? It is difficult to visualise 55 million people, but quite impossible to visualise 55,295,321. We could round the figure to thousands (55,295 thousands), or better still, to millions (55 million).

Example 2

The populations of the 12 states in the EC are found to be as follows in the year 19..: UK 55,930,000; France 52,605,802; Germany 61,645,000; Belgium 9,650,944; Holland 2,215,876; Luxembourg 338,500; Italy 56,024,000; Eire 2,978,248; Denmark 4,921,156; Greece 8,736,367; Spain 38,832,000 and Portugal 10,212,000. Round these populations to the nearest tenth of a million and present them in tabulated form to show the total population of the EC. Using these rounded statistics calculate the percentage of the total EC population in each country. Include these statistics in your table.

The result is shown in Table 20.7.

Table 20.7 Population of the European Community, 19..

Country	Population (millions)	%
United Kingdom	55.9	18.4
France	52.6	17.3
Germany	61.6	20.3
Belgium	9.7	3.2
Holland	2.2	0.7
Luxembourg	0.3	0.1
Italy	56.0	18.4
Eire	3.0	1.0
Denmark	4.9	1.6
Greece	8.7	2.9
Spain	38.8	12.8
Portugal	10.2	3.4
Total	303.9	100.0

Note: The % column does not total to exactly 100 because of rounding errors.

■ EXERCISE 20.2

(a) Sales of strawberries at a 'pick-your-own' farm were as follows in the third week of June, according to the weekly sales records: Sunday, 387.5 kg; Monday, 145 kg; Tuesday, 195.5 kg; Wednesday, 394.5 kg; Thursday, 203.5 kg; Friday, 295 kg; Saturday, 624.5 kg. Arrange them in tabular form bringing out the sales by weight and by value each day, and the total for the week. The charge to pickers is 50 pence per kilogramme.

(b) Output from two mills owned by a firm in the cotton industry is as follows according to the production reports for the 4-week period 4–31 July inclusive: week 1: mill A 24,702 m; mill B 13,975 m; week 2: mill A 31,560 m; mill B 15,295 m; week 3: mill A 28,850 m; mill B 16,170 m; week 4: mill A 34,252 m; mill B 15,850 m. Present these figures in tabular form to show the weekly production, the total weekly production the monthly production of each mill and the total production of the firm for the month.

(c) Employment figures in the year 19.. are given in a Department of Employment Report as follows: agriculture 432,754; mining and quarrying 363,175; manufacturing industries 7,830,495; construction 1,379,500; gas, electricity and water 344,395; transport and communication 1,523,850; distributive trades 2,743,975; insurance, banking and finance 1,058,490; professional services 3,250,499; catering and hotels 793,895; miscellaneous services 1,388,733; national government service 607,845; local government service 977,490. Round these figures to the nearest thousand, and present them in tabular form, showing the total in employment.

(d) Capital expenditure in the New York distributive and service industries for the year 19.. is investigated by a research organisation. The results are as follows: wholesale distribution $394,273,816; retail distribution $738,246,712; shipping $386,959,090; leasing $572,498,389; other finance $1,251,826,374; other industries $1,656,738,240. Round these figures to the nearest million dollars and present them in tabular form, to show the total capital expenditure, and also the percentage of capital expenditure (to the nearest 0.1%) invested in each industry.

7 FREQUENCY DISTRIBUTIONS

The full procedure for drawing up frequency distributions has already been discussed earlier in this chapter. It consists of the following stages:

(a) Arrange the data in an array, in ascending order of magnitude;

(b) Draw up a frequency distribution showing the number of times each item appears.

(c) If there are too many items decide how to group them together (i.e. decide the class intervals to be used in the classification). From these groups we can now draw up a grouped frequency distribution.

(d) Add cumulative frequency columns, or other derived statistics if these are helpful in understanding the table.

(e) Use the rules for tabulation to draw up the table in proper form.

A short-cut procedure may be used as follows:

(a) Examine the data to discover the range, i.e. find the smallest item and the largest item.

(b) Having found the range decide upon the number of classes or groups to be used, and the class interval for the body of the table. There may be classes at the beginning or the end of the table which are different – collect together scattered items towards the limits of the range.

(c) Prepare a draft table with class intervals on the left-hand side and a space for frequencies on the right-hand side. Using the original data and the five-barred gate system of recording record the actual items in the various groups at once. This eliminates the 'array' and 'ungrouped frequency' stages and enables us to prepare the final table more quickly.

Example 3

Examination marks scored by 50 candidates in an examination in Business Calculations were as follows:

25	72	96	54	92	67
42	35	72	56	63	46
36	81	100	72	57	38
84	49	14	64	55	49
72	75	34	73	48	56
95	36	84	62	43	55
63	25	25	48	44	93
66	88	56	53	72	45
46	52				

The lowest score is 14, the highest is 100.

It is decided to have an open class 'under 30' to begin with and then build in tens, 30 and under 40, 40 and under 50, etc. The final group will be 90 and over, and will thus include 100. The sorting out process is then done as shown in Fig. 20.7. The table might then be laid out as in Table 20.8 on page 262.

Examination Scores

Class intervals	Frequency	
Under 30	IIII	4
30 and under 40	IHT	5
40 and under 50	IHT IHT	10
50 and under 60	IHT IIII	9
60 and under 70	IHT I	6
70 and under 80	IHT II	7
80 and under 90	IIII	4
90 and over	IHT	5

Fig. 20.7 Raw data recorded as a frequency distribution

Table 20.8   Examination scores: Business Calculations

Scores	Frequency	Reverse cumulative frequency
Under 30	4	50
30 and under 40	5	46
40 and under 50	10	41
50 and under 60	9	31
60 and under 70	6	22
70 and under 80	7	16
80 and under 90	4	9
90 and over	5	5

Note

The reverse cumulative frequency is chosen because we can tell from this how many people will pass the examination if a particular cut-off point is chosen. Thus if the pass mark is 50 the number passing the examination will be 31, for 31 people altogether scored 50 or more marks.

■ EXERCISE 20.3

(a)   The lives of 60 electric light bulbs subjected to a quality control investigation were as follows:

Hours	Hours	Hours	Hours	Hours	Hours
72	5 minutes	424	724	97	712
594	242	127	636	537	615
624	363	363	719	479	495
836	1,846	725	824	629	12
137	5,042	616	243	516	139
449	395	494	240	724	725
347	696	727	371	638	623
626	727	1,046	268	456	304
594	816	952	1,724	395	180
1,726	96	121	23	327	175

Arrange these 'lifetimes' in an array. What is the range of the data?

(b)   Earnings of office juniors per month are found by questioning 30 young people about their gross monthly pay (pay before deductions). The results are as follows:

£	£	£	£	£
340	380	820	348	440
420	440	520	380	500
480	340	446	575	580
520	420	342	780	342
800	480	540	480	380
420	550	550	575	340

Arrange these earnings in a frequency distribution and add a cumulative frequency distribution column to bring out the total number earning a given amouint, or less.

(c) Houses in a certain town are on offer at the following prices. Draw up a grouped frequency table in bands of £10,000, the first group being £1–30,000, the second £30,001–£40,000, etc

£	£	£	£	£
88,000	72,500	42,500	51,250	74,250
75,500	46,750	85,000	33,550	43,500
50,000	48,500	49,050	58,750	21,500
67,250	73,250	75,000	47,500	50,500
18,000	55,000	67,750	72,500	61,500
44,000	21,250	88,750	57,500	83,850
38,000	38,250	33,750	35,000	42,500
15,000	99,000	85,000	92,750	28,500
59,500	65,000	79,850	87,950	66,250
78,250	58,000	56,000	97,250	88,000

(d) Output by operatives in a newly industrialised country are listed below. The figures show the number of garments made. Prepare a grouped frequency distribution in bands of 100 garments. Present it as a table, with a cumulative frequency column.

72	320	720	240	320
165	460	186	460	800
850	54	142	320	780
560	186	59	760	630
490	290	180	480	320
360	580	480	360	240
120	660	650	429	560
800	420	720	512	780

(e) Weekly turnovers for 50 shops in a pedestrian precinct in Newtown are found to
be as follows:

Turnover (£)

£	£	£	£	£
3,350	980	2,500	15,000	14,250
2,350	380	2,000	775	740
10,000	4,200	1,980	400	11,750
12,500	3,780	380	5,850	625
790	1,470	5,950	630	12,500
1,230	695	3,680	8,650	6,950
670	4,800	13,600	3,890	8,750
800	1,820	6,880	2,460	6,400
500	480	1,020	9,500	2,750
9,750	1,600	9,500	980	14,500

(i) From these figures prepare a grouped frequency distribution, in bands of £2,500,
the first group being £1–£2,500.

(ii) Add a column showing the percentage of shops in each group, and another
column showing the cumulative percentage of shops from the lowest turnover to
the highest turnover.

■ **ANSWERS**

Exercise 20.1   Refer to text.

Exercise 20.2   **(a)** 2,245.5 kg; £1,122.75   **(b)** monthly totals 119,364 m; 61,290 m,
grand total 180,654 m   **(c)** 22,694(000)   **(d)** $5,000m; percentages 7.9%, 14.8%,
7.7%, 11.4%, 25.0%, 33.1%.

Exercise 20.3   **(a)** Range 5 minutes – 5,042 hours   **(b)** no numerical answer required
(c) groups contain 5, 5, 9, 8, 5, 8, 7 and 3 respectively   **(d)** groups contain 3, 6, 3, 6,
7, 4, 3, 7 and 1 items respectively   **(e)** groups contain 25, 7, 5, 6, 3 and 4 items
respectively.

21 The presentation of statisics

OBJECTIVES

At the end of this chapter you should:
1 Be able to present data in graphical form;
2 Be able to draw pictograms, bar charts and pie charts;
3 Understand histograms as a method of displaying frequency distributions;
4 Be able to draw scatter diagrams and draw from them the degree of correlation between variables.

1 GRAPHICAL COMMUNICATION

In the last quarter of a century a new art – graphical communication – has appeared. It is an extension of old skills, such as surveying and engineering drawing, into much wider fields. We now see in a single day more illustrations than our ancestors saw in a lifetime; our children build up 'graphics' on their home computers, the advertising world invades every waking moment with attempts to convey, in pictorial form, the essence of its customers' products and no statistical presentation is complete without its diagram or chart.

The chief feature of graphical communication is the display, in a simple pictorial form, of the essential facts of any situation. Tabular presentation is one way of presenting statistical facts in a table of figures, rounded to reduce complexity and promote understanding, but there are many people who are not particularly 'numerate'; people for whom some pictorial representation would be more appropriate. This chapter is about the use of such pictorial methods of displaying data, to promote wider statistical understanding.

The chief types of pictorial representation may be listed as follows:

(a) graphs
(b) pictograms
(c) bar charts
(d) pie charts
(e) histograms
(f) scatter diagrams.

2 GRAPHS

Graphs are pictorial representations of data which show the relationship between two variables. Two lines called axes are drawn at right angles to one another on special graph paper which is ruled up in squares. The squares assist the 'plotting' of the data, because the eye can follow the rulings easily to locate any point on the chart. In any pair of variables there is usually one variable which is dependent on the other – the **independent variable**. Thus if we are plotting the temperature of a patient in intensive care, taking the readings every two hours, the time is the independent variable and the temperature is the **dependent variable** – what the patient's temperature will be depends upon the time you take it, as the disease progresses. Figure 21.1 below and the notes below it explain the basic features of a graph.

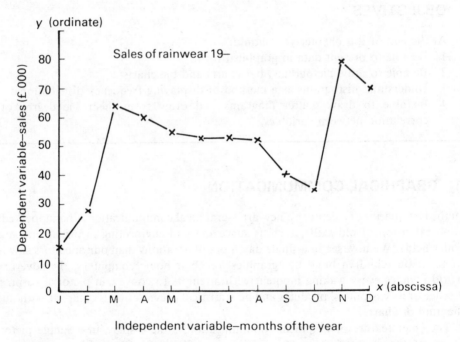

Fig. 21.1 Constructing a graph

Notes
1   The two axes are called the coordinates of the graph. The horizontal axis is called the abscissa, or *x* axis. It is used to plot the independent variable – in the case shown the months of the year, January, February, etc.
2   The vertical axis is called the ordinate, or *y* axis. It is used to plot the dependent variable – in the case shown sales for the month.
3   A scale is chosen which enables the data to be shown on the graph. In the case shown the largest monthly sale was £79,000 so that the scale used enabled this to be shown easily. Had the largest monthly sale been £179,000 the scale used would have been inappropriate, since £179,000 could not have been shown on the graph. We could only show it by changing the scale to, say 20, 40, 60, 80, 100, 120, 140, 160, 180 on the *y* axis. The point where the two axes meet, and from which the scales start, is called the origin, and is labelled 0.

4   Points are plotted by making a tiny dot, or perhaps a tiny cross, on the space available between the two axes – for example, if sales in August were £52,000 this gives a unique point on the graph, marked with a tiny cross as shown.

5   The points can then be joined by a curve (even if the lines are straight it is convenient to refer to them as a curve). The curve may be continuous, or discontinuous as in this example. Discontinuous lines show up the actual plotting points more easily.

3   SIMPLE GRAPHS

For simple graphs the intention is to display the data and there is no attempt to use the graph to make predictions. The use of graphs in this way is explained below (*see* Section 21.4). For comparison purposes it is possible to put two or more lines on the same graph, differentiating between them by using different patterns for the lines. Thus we could use a dotted line, a line of interrupted dashes, a mixture of dots and dashes, etc. Such a graph is shown in Fig. 21.2 below.

Where the data to be displayed are large, and yet the variations are only small, it is best to use a graph with an interrupted vertical scale as shown in Fig. 21.3 on page 268. The data compare the circulation of two national daily papers, each of which sells over three million copies. It would waste much of the paper to show the full scale, but the origin must still be shown, with the interruption slightly above it.

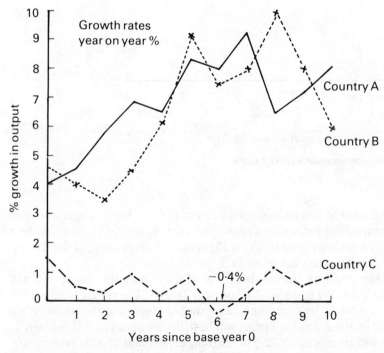

Fig. 21.2   Several sets of data plotted to show comparative achievements (*source:* Finance and Development)

Notes
1 Every graph should carry a caption showing what it is about.
2 The source of the data should be given wherever possible.
3 The axes should be labelled with the name of the variable, and the scales used.
4 The vertical scale should start at zero. If the data are remote from zero the axis should still start at zero, but be broken above the zero mark (see Fig. 21.3 for an example) continuing with the scale at the upper levels.
5 Three-dimensional effects are not desirable in examinations, though they may be used in house magazines, etc, where the aim is communication rather than statistical clarity.
6 If more than one line is shown they should be varied by dots, dashes, etc.

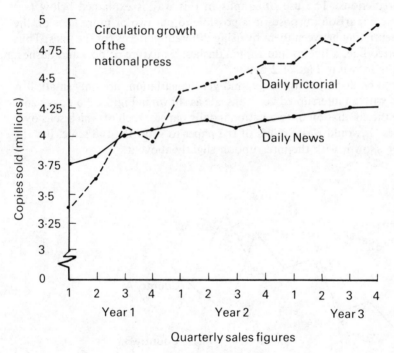

Fig. 21.3   Graph with interrupted vertical scale

Some sets of data consist of component parts of a grand total. For example, the sales of a firm are made up of the individual department sales figures, which add up in a series of layers to give a multilayer total. In Fig. 21.4 the official reserves of the UK are shown in a layer graph. The data are given in Table 21.1.

To plot such a layer graph we start with one set of data. As gold is heavy we will show it as the bottom layer. We first plot this layer and label it. The second layer – IMF special drawing rights – has to be superimposed on the gold layer and should therefore be plotted at the total of these, i.e. the figures will be 4,504 for year 1, 7,547 for year 2, etc. The third layer will be plotted at 22,538, 26,168, 21,834 and 15,429, respectively (adding up the three sets of figures), while the fourth layer will be the total reserves. Note that in year 1 there was no fourth layer.

Table 21.1   United Kingdom official reserves, year 19..

Reserve	Year 1 ($m)	Year 2 ($m)	Year 3 ($m)	Year 4 ($m)
Reserves deposited with the IMF	—	1,308	1,513	1,568
Convertible currencies at Bank of England, etc	18,034	18,621	13,457	9,634
IMF special drawing rights	1,245	560	1,043	1,233
Gold	3,259	6,987	7,334	4,562
Total	22,538	27,476	23,347	16,997

(Source: *The Pink Book*)

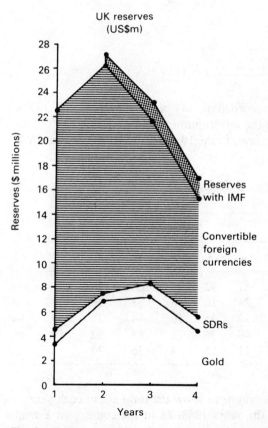

Fig. 21.4   A layer graph (Source: The Pink Book)

■ EXERCISE 21.1

(a) A finance house has monthly activities in three fields as shown in the table below. Plot these figures on a single graph, using distinctive lines to differentiate the three classes. Note that the bank collates its statistics in 13 equal four-weekly months.

Activity (£ millions)

Month	Hire	Leasing	Block discounting
1	62	48	43
2	67	49	47
3	75	66	49
4	76	72	51
5	81	91	50
6	84	95	48
7	85	85	62
8	89	83	63
9	91	76	65
10	94	79	68
11	87	85	72
12	86	91	66
13	84	76	60

Note: Since the lowest figure to be recorded is £43 million you should use an interrupted vertical scale starting above the interruption at £40 million.

(b) Foreign aid to Latin American countries in the 10 years shown below is made up as follows:

Foreign aid (US$m)

Type of aid	

Type of aid	1	2	3	4	5	6	7	8	9	10
USA official	33	42	47	51	82	94	106	120	111	128
USA private	84	72	36	24	16	86	88	94	120	108
World Bank, etc	17	24	27	32	35	56	74	29	59	84
Comecon (estimated)	14	32	38	46	36	22	88	92	60	66
Other	7	3	8	11	15	4	36	24	3	12

Plot these figures in the form of a layer graph, to show the total aid in each year.

(c) National expenditure figures over the years 1968–88 in the country of Europa were made up as follows:

Form of expenditure	1968 (%)	1973 (%)	1978 (%)	1983 (%)	1988 (%)
Private expenditure	68	66	60	56	54
Public expenditure (goods and services)	16	16	17	19	20
Public expenditure (welfare)	8	9	10	12	13
Public expenditure (debt interest)	4	5	9	10	11
Public expenditure (investment)	4	4	4	3	2

Draw the figures as a layer graph, showing the way national expenditure varied over the course of the 20-year-period.

4 PICTOGRAMS

As its name implies, a pictogram conveys statistical facts in picture form. The usual method is to choose some appropriate symbol to represent the data concerned. Thus wine production might be represented by a vat of wine, or wine consumption by a bottle, or perhaps a glass, of wine. Sometimes the symbol is obvious and springs naturally to mind. Others may not be so obvious, and it is up to the ingenuity of the designer to choose an appropriate symbol. For the purposes of this discussion we will use a bottle of wine as an appropriate symbol.

Imagine that wine consumption in country A in year 19.0 is 1 million litres per year, but that due to a change of taste or fashion it doubles to 2 million litres per year in year 19.1. There are two different ways of showing the increase – we can double the number of symbols or we can increase the size of the symbol. This is illustrated in Figs. 21.5a and 21.5b.

a *Doubling the number of symbols*   b *Increasing the size of the symbol*

Fig. 21.5 Alternative ways of sharing an increase in consumption

Notes

1   The difficulty with method **b** is that the increase in size has to be related to the area of space enclosed by the symbol. If the dimensions are doubled the area is quadrupled. This method is therefore unsatisfactory for it is difficult to calculate the dimensions for a symbol of twice the area, nor can the average eye detect the size of the change.

2   By contrast, doubling the number of symbols is easy to follow, so method **a** is acceptable.

It helps if the symbol can be divided into at least four parts, to represent fractions of a unit. Thus a drawing of a television set is still comprehensible as half a television set or one-quarter of a television set. By contrast half a glass of wine may be meaningful in a pictogram, but one-quarter of a glass of wine is rather less satisfactory. Some appropriate scale must be chosen to enable the full data to be displayed on the page where it is to appear. Thus if wine consumption in various countries ranges from 5 million bottles per year in the least convivial country to 14 million bottles per year in the country with the largest consumption, we might need to use 1 bottle to represent a million bottles.

Wine consumption in Europe is shown in Fig. 21.6 below. The notes on page 273 deal with certain difficulties encountered with pictograms.

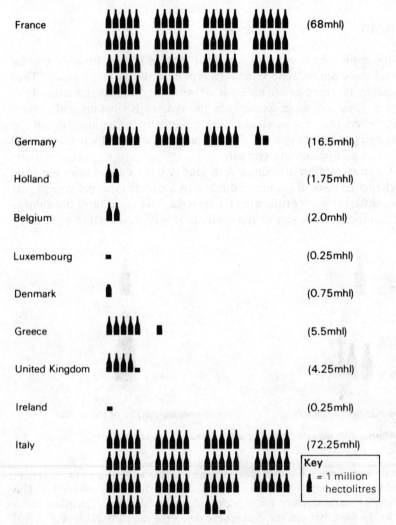

Fig. 21.6 Wine consumption in the European Common Market (year 19—) (Source: Annual Reports: European Community)

Notes

1   The symbol chosen must be appropriate to the data being presented.

2   The symbol should, if possible, be divisible into four parts, so that halves and quarters of a unit can be portrayed. In this illustration three-quarters of a bottle and half a bottle are comprehensible but a quarter of a bottle is less satisfactory. If we wish to represent smaller fractions than one-quarter (and in a decimal world tenths are often represented) it is usual to break up the height of a symbol, rather than the width as in Fig. 21.6.

3   The scale is chosen to represent the data on the size of page available – in this example 1 bottle represented 1,000,000 hl. The figures are given to the nearest $\frac{1}{4}$ million hl. To have chosen 1 bottle to represent 1,000 hl would have made it quite impossible to draw the diagram in the space available.

4   Frequently, comprehension is improved by giving at the end of each row the total figure represented by the pictogram.

5   The source of the data must be given – though in this illustration, to save endlessly revising the illustration, we have taken the liberty of not revealing the actual year to which the data relates.

■ EXERCISE 21.2

(a)   New housing construction in the country of Domestica for the last five years has been as follows:

Year 1	25,000 new houses
Year 2	38,000 new houses
Year 3	45,000 new houses
Year 4	62,000 new houses
Year 5	94,000 new houses

Draw a pictogram to illustrate these data. The source is the Domestica Annual Abstract of Statistics.

(b)   A manufacturer of baby carriages is considering the expansion of his factory. He asks you to sanction a loan for the project and includes in his proposal a pictogram showing that the number of live births has been as follows in the last six years, according to a report of the Population Bureau:

Year 1	750,000
Year 2	728,000
Year 3	685,000
Year 4	675,000
Year 5	650,000
Year 6	598,000

Draw this pictogram and suggest in a few sentences what the implications of the data are for the proposed extension of the factory.

(c)   You are asked by your manager to draw up a report about leasing (the provision of finance for the purpose of buying capital assets such as motor vehicles and machinery for lease to business customers). Your research reveals that the Finance

Houses which usually handle such purchases have provided, for cars alone, the following sums in recent years.

Year	Finance provided (£ million)
19.2	100
19.3	225
19.4	275
19.5	350
19.6	425
19.7	650
19.8	800
19.9	1,000

Draw a pictogram to illustrate this data for inclusion in your report.

(d) Holidays financed by the use of credit cards are shown by the major travel agents to have risen in the following way.

Year	Credit card transactions (£ million)
19.1	400
19.2	450
19.3	575
19.4	625
19.5	850
19.6	1,000
19.7	1,125
19.8	1,225
19.9	1,275
19.0	1,500

Draw a pictogram to illustrate this data.

5   BAR CHARTS

Although pictograms are useful in presenting data in an attractive way with symbols relevant to the data, they can be tedious to draw and require some artistic ability. A bar chart is almost as useful for comparing sets of data, and is more easily drawn. Information is related to the horizontal or vertical length of a bar or thick line. Bar charts should not be confused with histograms (see pp 283–5) which are used to display frequency distributions. Bar charts are used to display sets of data from different times, or from different places. Thus they might be used to compare one year with another, or one place with another. The length of the bar is the basis of the comparison, not the area or volume of the bar, even though, for artistic purposes, a three-dimensional view may be given.

Not everyone has the artistic ability to draw three-dimensional figures correctly and they are not recommended for examinations. They waste time and may even distort the comparisons that the student is trying to convey. A plain, two-dimensional, bar is preferable.

In Fig. 21.7 the group profits of Helpful Bank Plc are shown over a decade, as a horizontal bar chart. The profits are large, and have had to be shown in £100 million gradations. Although drawn originally on graph paper the graticule has not been allowed to appear on the finished chart, and to assist appreciation of the actual figures symbolised by the length of the bar they have been inserted on the bar itself. In the examination you will not be provided with graph paper, but should make a neat drawing on the lined paper of the answer book.

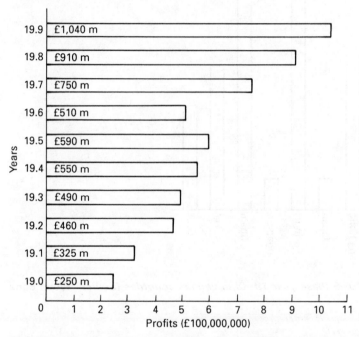

Fig. 21.7   Group profits over a ten-year period (Source: Helpful Bank Plc annual report)

In designing such a bar chart we have to decide on the following points:

(a)   *Scale*   The scale must be chosen so that all the data can appear easily in the space available. The largest piece of data should use up almost the whole scale. Where one figure is much larger than the others and would make the others appear totally unimportant if a scale was chosen to accomodate it, it is usual to break the bar – as shown in Fig. 21.8. Students may find it helpful to remember that squared paper can be turned through 90° (landscaped) to give more room when required.

(b)   *Bars*   The bars should all be of the same width, since only the length of the bar is used to compare the data. The length of each bar is a matter of simple calculation. If the scale chosen in Fig. 21.7 was 1 cm = £100m then 19.8 profit requires

$$\frac{£910m}{£100m} = 9.1 \text{ cm}$$

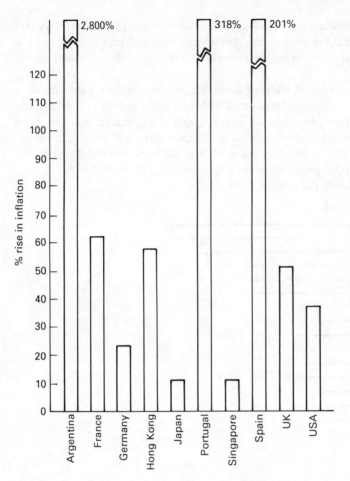

Fig. 21.8   Inflation by 19–6 (base year 19–0) in various countries (Source: World Bank World Tables*)*

(c)   *Horizontal or vertical* Bar charts may be drawn either horizontally or vertically and a choice must be made as to which is more appropriate. In Fig. 21.9 inflation rises and falls over the years, and vertical presentation was adopted.

(d)   *Shading or colouring* Colour, or cross hatching, can be helpful in differentiating between the bars.

5.1   Positive and negative bar charts

Bar charts can also be used to illustrate a positive or negative effect where this is required by indicating a scale above and below zero. In Fig. 21.9 the earnings per share of the Helpful Bank Plc are shown. In one year when enormous provisions were made against Third World debts the earnings became negative (i.e. losses were actually made). The scale of the chart starts at zero, and moves both positively and negatively

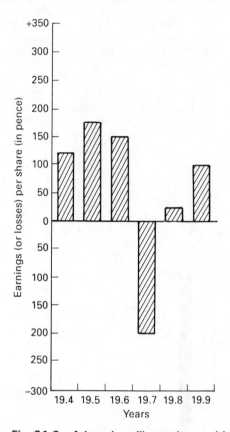

Fig. 21.9   A bar chart illustrating positive and negative data

from zero. The earnings per share are shown in pence, for instance 120 pence per share in year 19.4 and − 200 pence in year 19.7.

Students should appreciate that these are earnings per share, not distributions per share. Successful and prosperous companies heep huge sums back in reserves (partly for distribution in bad years when profits would not otherwise be available). It is not shown on the chart, but in fact distributions per year were at the rate of 30 pence per share every year, being paid out of reserves in the bad year, 19X7.

5.2   Multiple or grouped bar charts

If we wish to compare a number of items over a number of years we can draw a multiple bar chart, showing how each item varied over the period. In Fig. 21.10 we see the contributions made by visible exports and imports (goods) and invisible exports and imports (services) to the Balance of Payments and their net effects (i.e. the current balance). The bar chart is worked out from the figures published each year in the United Kingdom Balance of Payments (*The Pink Book*) which were according to the 1989 edition as shown below. The Pink Book may be purchased each year in August from Her Majesty's Stationery Office.

	'84	'85	'86	'87	'88
Visibles	− 5,169	− 3,132	− 9,364	− 10,929	− 20,826
Invisibles	7,054	6,335	9,430	7,258	6,209
Current Balance	1,885	3,203	66	− 3,671	− 14,617

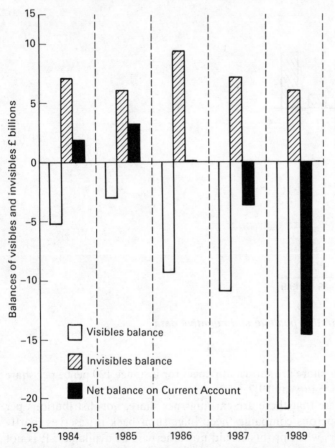

Fig. 21.10   Multiple (or grouped) bar chart. UK Balance of Payments on Current Account (*Source:* **The Pink Book** *1989 Edn*)

5.3   Component (or stacked) bar charts

Where a set of data combines to form a total of some sort it is possible to draw a component bar chart which shows the total as the length of the bar, each component being shown as a shaded section of the bar. If the bar is vertical, as in Fig. 21.11, the term 'stacked' bar chart is sometimes used to describe the chart.

■ EXERCISE 21.3   BAR CHARTS

(a)   Sales in a department store during a year are as follows: furniture, £7.48 million; fashions, £11.89 million; domestic and garden appliances, £5.88 million; soft furnish-

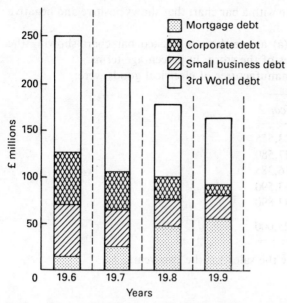

Fig. 21.11   A 'stacked' bar chart. Provisions for bad debt in banking (Source: Helpful Bank Plc Annual Report)

ings, £3.23 million; restaurant, £1.78 million; menswear, £7.33 million; electronics, £12.44 million. Correct these figures to the nearest tenth of a million and draw a bar chart presenting the data.

(b) A multinational company sells its products in the following regions in two successive years as shown. All figures are given in US$, to the nearest million. Draw a multiple bar chart to present this data.

Region	Year 1 $m	Year 2 $m
Europe	8,258	9,149
Asia	11,246	15,168
Africa	2,785	3,258
North America	16,356	18,252
South and Central America	5,495	3,958
Australasia and Oceania	4,725	3,584

(c) Growth rates (changes in the national output) of a certain country were as follows in a 10 year cycle:

Year 1	1.5%	Year 6	− 1.5%
Year 2	2.0%	Year 7	− 2.3%
Year 3	3.7%	Year 8	− 0.5%
Year 4	4.2%	Year 9	1.1%
Year 5	8.3%	Year 10	3.2%

Illustrate these changes in growth rate with a bar chart that shows positive and negative changes.

(d) Using the figures in Exercise (a) above draw a stacked bar chart showing the departmental shares in the total sales of the store, in percentage terms.

(e) Sales in successive years by a manufacturer of electrical goods were:

Product	Year 1	Year 2
Vacuum cleaners	20,850	23,555
Hair dryers	18,560	27,580
Toasters	14,250	16,385
Blow-heaters	11,380	13,590
Electric fires	34,960	43,890
Total	100,000	125,000

Draw component bar charts to show the sales for the two years.

6 PIE CHARTS

One of the commonest concepts in economics is the concept of the 'national cake'. The output of the nation is conceived as a large cake, which can be sliced up and allocated to the various groups within the community. The same idea is used in statistics, though the name applied to the diagram is a pie chart. Any total may be conceived as a round pie, which is divided into slices according to the size of the component parts which make up the total.

Table 21.2 United Kingdom visible imports and exports, 19.. (£m)

Item	Imports	Exports
Food, beverages and tobacco	6,606	3,924
Basic materials	3,311	1,355
Minerals, fuels and lubricants	7,091	11,193
Semi-manufactured goods	12,967	14,112
Finished manufactures	21,905	23,221
Unclassified items	1,547	1,741
Total	53,427	55,546

(Source: *The Pink Book*)

Consider the data supplied in table 21.2. When drawn as a pie chart both parts of the table can be presented as a circular pie, with the component parts shown as slices of the pie. The $360°$ in a circle must be shared in the same proportion as the parts of the table bear to the total. This is simple enough, especially if an electronic calculator is used. Thus the slice of the pie to be allocated to basic materials in the case of imports is:

$$\frac{3,311}{53,427} \times 360° = 22.3°$$

When drawn the pie charts appear as shown in Fig. 21.12.

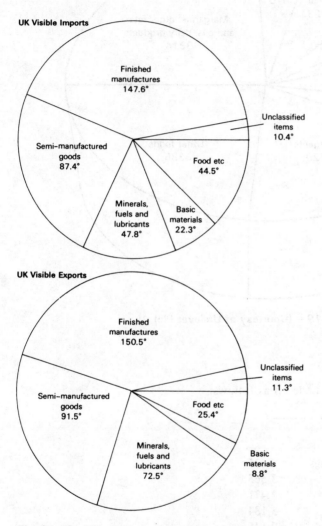

Fig. 21.12   UK visible imports and exports, as pie charts (*Source:* The Pink Book)

Notes
1   The pies are divided into slices in proportion as the class of imports or exports bears to the total figure.
2   The number of degrees in each slice need not be shown on the final diagram, they are put in here to assist the reader.
3   A three-dimensional view should not be attempted in an examination, but Fig. 21.13 on page 282 shows such a presentation from a business publication.

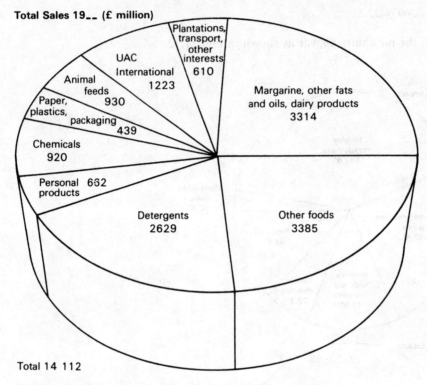

Total Sales 19__ (£ million)

Plantations, transport, other interests 610

UAC International 1223

Animal feeds 930

Paper, plastics, packaging 439

Chemicals 920

Personal products 662

Margarine, other fats and oils, dairy products 3314

Detergents 2629

Other foods 3385

Total 14 112

Fig. 21.13   Sales for year 19— (Courtesy of Unilever Plc)

■ EXERCISE 21.4

(a)   Invisible exports are made up as follows:

Item	£m
General government earnings	435
Sea transport	3,565
Civil aviation	2,471
Travel and tourism	3,184
Financial services (net)	2,145
Other services	5,782

(Source: *The Pink Book*)

The word (net) on financial services implies that this is the earnings left after imported financial services had been set off against earnings. Ignore this for the purposes of the present exercise. Draw a pie diagram to illustrate these statistics.

(b)   A multinational company has sales totalling £800 million in the year. The details are:

Product	£m
Dairy products	160
Other foods	240
Detergents	180
Hygiene products	80
Chemicals	72
Paper, plastics	12
Animal feedstuffs	56

Draw a pie diagram to illustrate the data.

(c) According to its Central Bank, the country of Garibaldia has total debts of $11,200 million. This is made up as follows:

Debtor	£m
Civil Service borrowing	6,981
Central Bank borrowing	696
Banking sector debt	426
Commercial firms' indebtedness	1,433
Private borrowing	1,664

Draw a pie chart to illustrate this data.

7 HISTOGRAMS

A histogram is a diagram which displays a frequency distribution as a series of contiguous rectangles each of which represents one class interval. It is sometimes called a block frequency diagram. Because the blocks stand alongside one another they show the pattern of the distribution. It might, for example, be symmetrical, rising to a peak and then falling away. It may be more erratic, with a number of peaks separated by ranges where the frequency is much smaller.

The basic principle is that the *area* of each block is proportional to the data. The class intervals are measured along the horizontal axis, and if these intervals are all equal, the height of the blocks is proportional to the frequency but this does not change the basic principle that the areas are proportional to the frequencies displayed.

If the data are arranged in equal class intervals the width chosen for the blocks is immaterial and may be selected to suit the space available. A simple illustration referring to Table 20.3 on page 255 is shown in Fig. 21.14.

Where the class intervals are not equal it is necessary to adjust the height of the blocks to take account of the frequency density. This is defined as the frequency per standard unit of class interval. The frequency given in the data has to be reduced to take account of the extra width of those class intervals which are larger than the rest. It

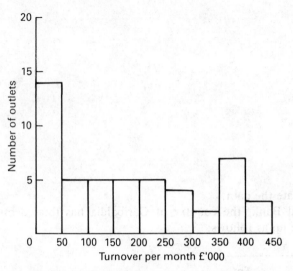

Fig. 21.14   A histogram showing monthly turnover

Notes

1   The data (see Table 20.3 on page 255) are in equal class intervals of £50,000 turnover.

2   The class intervals are marked along the horizontal axis, using a scale appropriate to the space available.

3   The frequencies are marked up the vertical axis. In this case, since the widths used for each block are the same, the height of the blocks varies with the frequency.

4   Using the midpoint of the class interval, mark in a height above the horizontal axis which is proportional to the frequency. Draw a horizontal line at this point equal to the width of the class interval. Now join up the sides of the rectangle. The result is as shown. Note that the pattern of turnover is clearly shown with a large number of relatively small businesses in the first group and then a fairly even distribution over the next few groups with the very largest businesses slightly more variable in frequency.

is found by the formula:

$$\text{Frequency density} = \frac{\text{frequency (area)}}{\text{number of standard units in the class interval}}$$

This is shown in Fig. 21.15 on page 285.

■ EXERCISE 21.5

(a)   Houses are on offer in Suburbia as follows:

Price range (£)	Number on offer
Under 20,000	18
20,000 and under 40,000	38
40,000 and under 60,000	196
60,000 and under 80,000	270
80,000 and under 100,000	86

Draw a histogram to present this data diagrammatically.

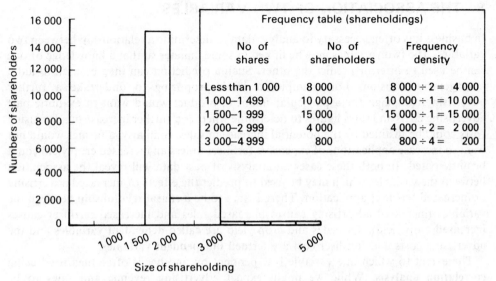

Frequency table (shareholdings)		
No of shares	No of shareholders	Frequency density
Less than 1 000	8 000	8 000 ÷ 2 = 4 000
1 000–1 499	10 000	10 000 ÷ 1 = 10 000
1 500–1 999	15 000	15 000 ÷ 1 = 15 000
2 000–2 999	4 000	4 000 ÷ 2 = 2 000
3 000–4 999	800	800 ÷ 4 = 200

Fig. 21.15   Histogram with unequal class intervals (referred to on page 284)

(b)   Commercial property in a city is available as follows:

Rentals (£ per annum)	Number on offer
Under 2,000	12
2,000 and under 4,000	16
4,000 and under 6,000	24
6,000 and under 8,000	20
8,000 and under 10,000	8
10,000 and under 12,000	2
12,000 and under 20,000	8

Draw a histogram to present this data diagrammatically.
(c)   A survey of wages in an industrial town shows the following results for the first week in the financial year.

Class range (£)	Number in class
50 and under 100	438
100 and under 150	850
150 and under 200	1,350
200 and under 250	820
250 and under 300	460
300 and under 350	320
350 and under 400	240

Draw a histogram to present this data diagrammatically.

8   THE ASSOCIATION OF TWO VARIABLES

In business it is often necessary to analyse data to determine a relationship between two variables. The two variables may be linked in some manner so that a knowledge of one can be used to infer or predict the other. Such a prediction can then be used to aid a management decision. For example, a bank proposing to undertake a further advertising campaign for a particular financial product would want to examine past advertising costs and sales figures to determine whether a further increase in advertising costs could be justified by the potential increase in sales. Similarly, a farmer would not want to increase applications of expensive fertiliser unless an increased crop yield could be anticipated. In both these cases an analysis of past data will reveal the association between the variables which may be used to predict the effects of increased advertising or increased fertiliser application. There is said to be a **causal relationship** between the variables (increased advertising causes increased sales and increased fertiliser causes increased crop yield). The sales and crop yield are called **dependent variables** and the advertising costs and fertiliser cost are termed **independent variables**.

The extent to which one variable is dependent on another is often measured using **correlation analysis**. While we might expect advertising revenue and sales to be **positively correlated** we would be surprised to see any correlation between variables such as the sales of paint brushes and chairs, unless people stand on new chairs to paint their houses, which is rather unlikely. It is possible, however, to come across **spurious correlations** and an example of this is the relationship between interest rates and house prices. When interest rates are falling people can afford larger mortgages and house prices tend to rise. A **negative correlation** is obtained between interest rates and house prices. If this correlation applied for all time then when interest rates rise we would expect house prices to fall. However, this does not happen because people are more reluctant to move and cannot afford the higher mortgage rates with the result that prices stagnate or rise more slowly, rather than fall. Thus the correlation is spurious when applied over the longer time scale. Quite often business decisions are made on the basis of spurious correlations, with disastrous results for the company involved. It is important therefore, to understand correlation analysis and to be able to use it effectively as an aid to business management. Unfortunately in this text it is not possible to go into the subject too deeply – students will meet more detailed discussion of correlation in later courses.

7.1   Scatter diagrams

The simplest method of investigating the relationship between two variables is to plot a scatter diagram. In Fig. 21.16 the rewards earned by bank branches when making a loan have been plotted against the envisaged risk of non-payment. The resulting scatter shows a wide variety of rewards and risks. If we now calculate the average reward over-all and the average risk we can plot these averages against one another. By drawing a line through this point parallel to the x axis and another line parallel to the y axis we divide the scatter diagram into four quadrants. These quadrants show a high reward – low risk quadrant, a high reward – high risk quadrant, a low reward – high risk quadrant and a low reward – low risk quadrant. Future loan sanctioning can then be varied to eliminate high risk loans and favour high reward loans.

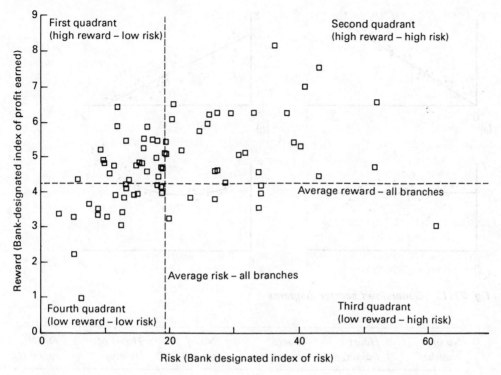

Fig. 21.16 *A scatter diagram plotting rewards against risks as a guide to credit risk management*

7.2 Generalised scatter diagrams

In general, the vertical axis is used for the dependent variable and the horizontal axis for the independent variable. A scatter of points is obtained by plotting one set of values against the other set of values and making a series of dots on the graph. The pattern of these points often indicates immediately whether the two variables are associated in any way and whether the relationship is linear or not. The relationship is linear if the points tend to cluster about a straight line as indicated in Fig. 21.17 (a) and (b). In the first diagram the variables may be said to have a strong positive linear correlation since y is increasing with increasing x. In the second diagram, y is decreasing with increasing x and the relationship has a strong negative linear correlation. In Fig. 21.17(c) there is no obvious relationship and zero-correlation is assumed. However, in Fig. 21.17(d) there does seem to be a relationship since a curved line can be drawn through the points. In this case a non-linear or curvilinear relationship exists between the variables.

Consider the following data about 20 branches of the Helpful Bank Plc. They show the hours of training undergone by members of the branch in marketing techniques for bank products and the funds collected by the branch for investment in various investment schemes.

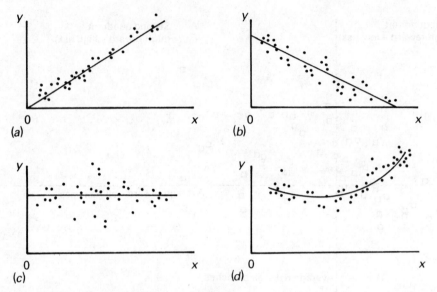

Fig. 21.17 Generalised scatter diagrams

No of branches	Hours training	Funds raised (£)	No of branch	Hours of training	Funds raised (£)
1	4	32,000	11	4	6,000
2	12	36,000	12	16	54,000
3	10	26,000	13	6	10,000
4	8	12,000	14	24	100,000
5	18	64,000	15	12	35,000
6	14	31,000	16	6	12,000
7	6	16,000	17	18	84,000
8	20	80,000	18	16	60,000
9	24	56,000	19	10	30,000
10	4	8,000	20	8	28,000

We wish to discover whether there is any correlation between the training given and the effectiveness of the branch as a fund raiser. We proceed as follows:

(a)   Draw a scatter diagram plotting 'hours of training' aginst 'funds raised'.

(b)   Make a rough guess as to whether there is any correlation at all in the scatter points.

(c)   If so, it is helpful to draw in a line central to the scatter of points (i.e. with an equal balance of points and distances from the line on either side of it). This is called the **'line of best fit'**. Before trying to do this, one helpful point is that as we are seeking an average line of best fit, this line will always pass through the average of the two sets of data. It therefore gives us a good starting point if we plot the average number of hours instruction against the average funds raised.

These averages are 12 hours and £39,000. If we plot these against one another our line of best fit will pass through that point. A good way to find the line of best fit is to use a piece of cotton stretched taut between your two hands and find the most central line, passing over the mean point mentioned above. Remember, we do not have to have an equal number of points on either side of the line – it is the combination of points and distances which have to be equal. Thus one point 4 cm from the line balances out two points each two cm from the line.

(d) Fig. 21.18 shows such a line arrived at by inspection only (i.e. the piece of cotton method). There are more accurate ways of finding the line of best fit, but they are too difficult for our purposes in this text. What we can say from Fig. 21.18 is that there is a strong positive correlation between training hours received and funds collected. We may therefore assume that further training for the least effective branches will improve their fund-raising performances. If the line had sloped downwards from left to right we would have said there was a negative correlation; in other words more training led to less funds being raised. If the dots had been randomly scattered with no obvious line of best fit, we would have said there was no obvious correlation between training and funds raised.

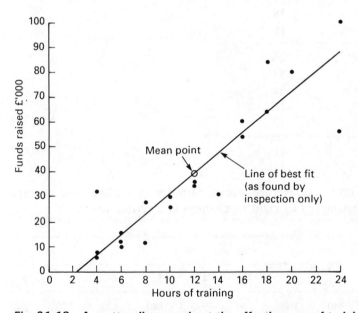

Fig. 21.18   A scatter diagram about the effectiveness of training

■ EXERCISE 21.6

(a) The following data show (i) the number of GCSE passes achieved by 10 entrants to banking at age 16, and (ii) the salaries being earned five years later.

Draw a scatter diagram from these data and find by inspection a line of best fit. From your line of best fit comment on the usefulness of GCSE results as a predictor for success in the banking field.

	A	B	C	D	E	F	G	H	I	J
Passes	5	6	8	9	10	7	2	5	3	8
Salary (£'000)	6	8	10	6	11	9	5	9	6	12

(b)   The following data shows the funds loaned by a bank to 12 new businesses, and the average profits made by these businesses per year for the first five years.

Draw a scatter diagram and a line of best fit to decide whether there is any correlation between bank help and business profitability.

Business	Loans made £'000	Average Profits per annum £'000
Z	10	20
Y	8	8
X	5	9
W	2	18
V	8	16
U	26	40
T	30	34
S	12	24
R	4	12
Q	16	10
P	5	11
N	10	14

(c)   The figures below show the average weekly turnover (£ sterling) and average weekly profit (£ sterling) achieved by eight retail shops in a certain town:

	Shop							
	1	2	3	4	5	6	7	8
Average profit	340	360	280	590	840	420	370	540
Average turnover	1,250	1,200	1,400	2,400	2,400	1,800	1,350	2,200

(i)   Draw a scatter diagram to represent this data.
(ii) Draw in a line of best fit, by inspection.
(iii) State the degree of correlation to your mind between turnover and profitability.

■ ANSWERS

Exercise 21.6   (a) Mean figures: 6.3 passes earning £8,200. There is a reasonably strong correlation and the GCSE is therefore a fairly good predictor of banking ability.

(b) Mean figures: loans of £11,300; profits of £18,000. The scatter is fairly wide. There is some correlation but other factors seem to be important too.

(c) Mean figures: turnover £1,750 and profits £467.50. There is a fairly close correlation between turnover and profitability; the more we turn over, the more profit we make.

22 Averages

OBJECTIVES

At the end of this chapter you should:
1 Understand the importance of averages in statistics;
2 Be able to calculate the arithmetic mean;
3 Understand the median as the central item in an array, and the uses and limitations of this average;
4 Understand the concept of the mode as an average which tells us which value occurs most frequently in a distribution.

1 AVERAGES IN STATISTICS

It is frequently difficult to describe a set of data. Any mass of statistics consists of a huge range of information from which we have to draw conclusions, yet a reference to any one statistic may be quite inappropriate because it may be unrepresentative. We have to see if there is any pattern in the data, and one of the best ways to start is to find an average. An average is a point within a group of data which is central to the group, and around which the other values are distributed. It is therefore a **measure of central tendency** – a measure which starts to summarise the data by fixing one point, the centre. The position of the central item fixes the location of the distribution and averages are therefore sometimes called measures of location.

Unfortunately, there are several possible 'centres' or 'averages', which we must list and look at in turn. Before we do so let us notice the common feature to them all; that they stress the middle items in the set and reduce the significance of the extreme values. If we take the simple average of production in a factory which turns out 27, 25, 3 and 46 units of product in a 4 week period – the third week's production having been affected by a strike, compensated by overtime working in the fourth week – we find that the average is $101 \div 4 = 25.25$ units per week. This average figure replaces the extreme values 3 and 46 by an average figure much closer to the two 'normal' weeks. This average figure does not coincide with any of the actual figures in the series, nor is it in fact an actual number of whole units, but it does describe a week's typical production more clearly than any of the four actual figures, and much more accurately than either of the extremes.

The types of average most commonly used in banking may be listed as follows:

(a)   the arithmetic average – often called the arithmetic mean
(b)   the median – or central item
(c)   the mode – or most fashionable item

2   THE ARITHMETIC MEAN

The arithmetic mean is the most commonly used average, and is often referred to simply as 'the mean'. It is found by adding together the individual values and dividing by the number of items. Thus consider a batsman in cricket who scores as follows in a five match series: 168, 27, 52, 1, 17, 0, 256, 88, 19, 22 – there being two innings in each match. The total runs scored are 650. Dividing by 10, the average score is 65. Note that none of the original scores was 65, so that every original score was really unrepresentative of the batsman's ability. The most extreme scores, 0 and 256, were very unrepresentative, but they have contributed to the calculation of 65 as the average score. Note also that the centrality of 65 as an average can be proved by showing how much the other numbers varied from 65. We can set this out as:

Scores below average	Variation from mean	Arithmetic mean	Variation from mean	Scores above average
27	– 38	65	+ 103	168
52	– 13	65	+ 191	256
1	– 64	65	+ 23	88
17	– 48	65		
0	– 65	65		
19	– 46	65		
22	– 43	65		
Total	– 317		+ 317	

The variations above and below the average are equal, and 65 is therefore central to the distribution.

Such simple average calculations are very elementary. Variations on them are as follows.

2.1   Weighted average calculations

Where a particular item occurs a number of times it is said to weight the statistics in its favour. Thus consider the average wage of the employees in the factor of the X Co Ltd shown below. There are five rates of pay:

Weekly wages (£)	Number of employees	Total pay (£)
85	30	2,550
90	62	5,580
95	25	2,375
100	40	4,000
120	30	3,600
Total	187	18,105

To find the arithmetic mean we must multiply each rate of pay by the number of employees receiving that rate (this is the weighting) to give a total pay at each rate. Then we must divide the grand total not by 5, but by the sum of the frequencies (i.e. the number of employees). The result is:

$$\frac{£18,105}{187} = £96.82 \text{ (correct to the nearest penny)}$$

2.2 The average of large numbers

With very large numbers it is sometimes convenient to work from an **assumed mean**. We know that the mean will lie somewhere above the lowest figure on the list of large numbers, so this could be our assumed mean. Consider the average of the following numbers:

     23,874   23,525   23,004   24,156   23,126

The smallest of these is 23,004 so this could be our assumed mean, but in fact the calculations are made rather simpler if we take a round figure – in this case 23,000 – as our assumed mean. Obviously the true mean will be a little above this. To find it we find the average of the residue of the numbers when 23,000 has been deducted from them. They are then 874, 525, 4, 1156 and 126. The sum of these is 2,685. Dividing by 5 the average of these residues is 537. Therefore the true mean is 537 above 23,000. which is 23,537.

2.3 The arithmetic mean of a grouped frequency distribution: method I

Many statistics are given in the form of grouped frequency distributions, such as the one given in Table 22.1. Note that in this type of grouped distribution we have no idea what the individual outputs of the operatives were. Seven operatives produced between 21 and 30 units in the 4-week period but whether they produced 22, 23, 27 or 29 is not known. We can only find an average if we make some sensible assumption about the actual outputs. The assumption is that they are evenly distributed throughout the band of 21–30, which is the same as saying that the average within that particular band is the midpoint of the band. Since there are an even number of items in the band (21–30 inclusive is ten items) we assume that the midpoint is half-way between 25 and 26, i.e. 25.5 (a quick method of fixing the midpoints is to add up the extreme items 21 and 30 and divide by 2 = 25.5). The midpoints of all the classes are found in the same way, as shown in the table. We now multiply this midpoint figure for each class by the frequency (the number of operatives whose output came within that band). The resulting products are entered in the end column and totalled. We now divide this total by the number of operatives (i.e. the sum of the frequencies = 45):

$$\text{Average output per operative} = \frac{1,977.5}{45}$$

$$= 43.9 \text{ (correct to one decimal place)}$$

Table 22.1 Output of operatives: weeks 1–4 inclusive

Output in units	Midpoints	Number of operatives	Products
21–30	25.5	7	178.5
31–40	35.5	11	390.5
41–50	45.5	14	637.0
51–60	55.5	8	444.0
61–70	65.5	5	327.5
Total		45	1,977.5

■ EXERCISE 22.1

(a) Students attending a certain evening course are aged as follows:

17, 17, 17, 18, 19, 19, 19, 19, 21, 22, 23, 23, 35, 37, 38, 44

What is the mean age?

(b) In a certain factory gas consumption per month is as follows:

Month	Therms consumed	Month	Therms consumed
January	17,318	July	10,725
February	14,924	August	11,846
March	15,618	September	14,925
April	14,212	October	18,203
May	13,168	November	19,214
June	12,849	December	21,174

What is the mean consumption per month?

(c) Theatre tickets are sold as follows: 386 front stalls at £8.50; 436 rear stalls at £6.50; 86 dress circle at £7.50; 240 upper circle at £5; 296 gallery at £3.50. What is the mean price of a ticket? (Answer correct to nearest penny.)

(d) Mass-produced cylinder blocks have internal diameters as follows: 8 blocks are 9.456 cm, 7 are 9.457 cm, 3 are 9.458 cm, 12 are 9.459 cm. What is the mean diameter? (Answer correct to 3 decimal places.)

(e) What is the average of (i) 48,016, (ii) 48,156 and (iii) 48,176?

(f) What is the average of (i) 28,385, (ii) 29,268, (iii) 28,721 and (iv) 28,522?

(g) Sales by representatives employed by a toy wholesaler are as follows:

Sales (£'000)	No. of representatives
Under 10	3
10 and under 20	8
20 and under 30	16
30 and under 40	15
40 and under 50	8
50 and under 60	4

Calculate the mean sales. (Answer correct to the nearest £100.)

3   THE MEDIAN

The median is a very simple average to find. All we do is arrange the data as an array (i.e. in increasing order of size) and take the middle item. Thus if the average output of 11 operatives is given as follows in units per week:

27   29   13   14   12   48   37   25   32   19   23

Rearranged as an array we have:

12   13   14   19   23   25   27   29   32   37   48

The median item is the middle item of the array, which is 25. The median separates the array into halves – in this case with the weaker performers on the left and the better performers on the right:

(12, 13, 14, 19, 23)   25   (27, 29, 32, 37, 48)

3.1   The formulae for the median

To find the median item we use the formula:

$$\text{Median} = \frac{n+1}{2}$$

Thus with 11 items the median item is $(11 + 1)/2 = $ 6th item. In the example given above the median item is 25, which has 5 items below it (making it the 6th item) and 5 items above it, to give 11 items in all. Where the number of items is even we find that the formula results in a figure ending in $\frac{1}{2}$. Looking back to Table 20.2 (see page 254) we find there were 50 items in the array. The median item in the array is $(50 + 1)/2 = 25\frac{1}{2}$ item. We cannot have a $25\frac{1}{2}$th item so the median must be the average of the two items at the centre of the array – which means the average of the 25th and 26th items. We find that the 25th item was £153,325 and the 26th item was £159,621. The average of these items is:

$$\frac{£153,325 + £159,621}{2}$$

$$= \frac{£312,946}{2}$$

$$= £156,473$$

The median figure for monthly turnover is £156,473. This illustrates a very common student error which is to confuse the median with the median item. Thus many students would state in examination answers that the median in the above examples is $25\frac{1}{2}$, whereas of course it is £156,473. *The median is defined as the* **value** *of the central item in an array.*

3.2   The median of grouped data

Where data are grouped, as in Table 22.1 on page 295, we cannot find an exact median, because the individual values within the groups are not available. As with the arithmetic mean we must make an assumption – that the items are spread evenly within the group. We cannot of course know this – they might all be bunched at the top of the group, or towards the bottom of the group – we can only assume they are evenly spread.

Table 22.2   Output of operatives: weeks 1–4 inclusive

Output in units	Number of operatives	Cumulative frequency
21–30	7	7
31–40	11	18
41–50	14	32
51–60	8	40
61–70	5	45

We have to decide where the median item is, and to do this we arrange the table, with a cumulative frequency column added. This is done in Table 22.2. There are 45 items so what is the median item? Here we must learn a rather tricky point. The median item in a group distribution is found by the formula $n/2$ not $(n + 1)/2$. The reason for this is that in assuming that the items are evenly spread throughout the group we imagine a number of subdivisions, each with 1 in it. The formula $(n + 1)/2$ finds the upper end of a subdivision, not the middle of it, and we must drop back $\frac{1}{2}$ division to $n/2$. This formula gives $45/2 = 22\frac{1}{2}$. We therefore need to find the $22\frac{1}{2}$th item in the distribution. This is clearly in the 41–50 group and is the $4\frac{1}{2}$th item out of the 14 in the group. The value of the median output is therefore:

$$40 + \left(\frac{4\frac{1}{2}}{14} \times 10\right) \text{units} = 40 + \frac{90}{28}$$

$$= 40 + 3.21$$

$$= 43.21 \text{ units}$$

To the nearest whole unit this is 43 units. Remember that as the median is the central item of a distribution it will be an actual item, and it is most sensible to give the answer as a round number.

4   FEATURES OF THE MEDIAN

The median lies at the centre of the distribution, with half the data on one side of it and half on the other side. Where the position of the centre is important the median can therefore be a useful average.

Where the data contain extreme items which distort the picture the median pays no attention to them and gives a more correct picture. Thus if 20 students in a class are aged 18 but two mature students are, respectively, 60 and 64 years of age, the median declares the average age to be 18, and ignores the extreme values. The arithmetic mean, by contrast gives an average age of 22 which really distorts the picture.

The disadvantage of the median is that it is unsuitable for mathematical calculation. It is the value of a central item in an array. This does not mean that it can be put to mathematical use – for example, the arithmetic mean × frequency gives the aggregate value of all the items in a set of data, but the median × frequency does not give any such result.

■ EXERCISE 22.2

(a)   Children using a die to play a board game throw successively as follows:

1, 6, 3, 4, 1, 2, 5, 6, 4, 3, 2, 5, 3, 1, 4

What was the score of the median throw?

(b)   A soccer team in successive matches scores as follows:

1, 3, 7, 2, 1, 0, 5, 1, 2, 3, 0, 0, 2, 0, 4, 4, 3, 0

What is the median score?

(c)   In an examination the marks obtained by 140 pupils (rounded to the nearest whole number) are as follows. What is the median score? (*To the nearest whole number.*)

Marks	Frequencies
0– 9	3
10–19	7
20–29	11
30–39	14
40–49	29
50–59	31
60–69	17
70–79	11
80–89	9
90 and over	8
Total	140

(d) The following monthly take-home pay of employees in a company was recorded for January 19... Find the median take-home pay.

Earnings (£)	Number of employees
450 and under 500	31
500 and under 550	47
550 and under 600	83
600 and under 650	185
650 and under 700	106
700 and over	48

(e) Construction costs and selling prices of new houses in the city of Developia were as follows in the year 19...

Cost per house (£)	Number of houses built	Selling price per house (£)	Number of houses sold
Less than £30,000	181	Less than £45,000	142
30,000–39,999	326	45,000–59,999	276
40,000–49,999	284	60,000–79,999	324
50,000–59,999	135	80,000–99,999	186
60,000–69,999	74	100,000–119,999	72

Find (i) the median cost of houses and (ii) the median selling price of houses in Developia. (Answers correct to the nearest £1.)

(f) A stock-exchange broker drew up a table to illustrate the profitability of his dealings in the year 19.. as follows:

Profit (£'000)	Number of deals
Less than 1	18
1 and less than 2	27
2 and less than 3	5
3 and less than 4	3
4 and less than 5	7

Calculate the median value of profit per deal from this table (answer correct to the nearest £1).

5 THE MODE

Sometimes neither the mean nor the median give the best description of a set of data. The mean takes account of all the values in a set of data but does not draw any attention to extreme items which may be of great significance. The median is the value of the central item and divides the set of data into halves, but in many cases this item may be quite unrepresentative. For example, there are about $1\frac{1}{2}$ million business in the UK, of which $1\frac{1}{4}$ million are very small, while the 500 largest are of such importance that they employ more capital and more people than all the rest put together. The median item in this array of $1\frac{1}{2}$ million businesses is quite insignificant.

Statements are frequently made which use the word 'average' in a different sense from either the mean or the median. For example, a statement 'The average family with young children enjoys a visit to the circus' means that the vast majority of families with young children find a visit to the circus an enjoyable and memorable occasion. This type of 'average' draws attention to the value which is most frequent within a distribution. It is called the 'mode' – a word which has some link with the world of fashion – and the concept of the 'modal' item as the most popular, or fashionable may help the reader to remember this average. The mode is defined as that value which occurs most frequently in a distribution.

The mode is most helpful and its value may be very obvious where the set of data consists of discrete items. Thus the modal number of legs for human beings is two, although one occasionally sees people who have lost a leg, or even both legs. The number of bedrooms in houses is a common feature of advertisements, and the numbers are discrete. We can have 1, 2, 3, 4 or 5 bedrooms, etc, but we cannot have a house with 1.87 bedrooms, or 3.45 bedrooms. Suppose the accommodation available in a town consists of 2,000 houses made up as follows:

Accomodation in Suburbia

Number of bedrooms	1	2	3	4	5
Frequencies	32	484	963	434	87

Clearly the modal type of house is a 3-bedroomed house, for its frequency is greatest. The 3-bedroomed house best describes the average accommodation available in Suburbia.

5.1 Bimodal and multimodal series

Sometimes, especially where there is a large variety of items in the distribution, we may have two or more which are equally popular. Thus if a team of 11 cricketers score as follows:

> 69, 36, 27, 14, 9, 36, 4, 14, 3, 1, 0

we have a bimodal series – two batsmen scored 36 and two scored 14. If the scores had been:

> 69, 36, 27, 14, 9, 36, 9, 14, 3, 1, 0

we should have had a multimodal series with 36, 14 and 9 runs being scored by two batsmen each.

It is of course possible to have a series with no modal frequency as where all the scores are different and each value only occurs once.

5.2   The mode of a grouped distribution

If data are in the form of a grouped distribution it is not possible to state the modal value accurately. Consider the data in Table 22.3. We cannot know where the mode is – for example, if all 6 of the representatives in the final group had sold £32,000 of goods in the month, and no other group had a similar concentration of results, the mode would be £32,000. We have no way of knowing this unless the full data are available elsewhere.

Table 22.3   Sales by representatives, October 19..

Sales (£'000)	Number of representatives
10 and under 15	10
15 and under 20	36
20 and under 25	28
25 and under 30	10
30 and under 35	6
Total	90

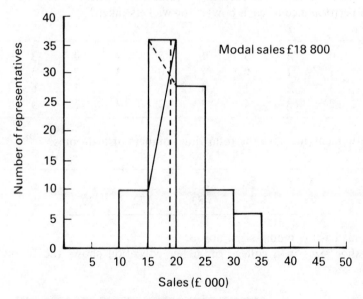

Fig. 22.1   Finding the mode by interpolation

Notes

1   The histogram is drawn in the usual way.
2   A line is then drawn from the top left-hand corner of the modal class (the tallest rectangle) to the top left-hand corner of the next group, as shown.
3   Similarly a line is drawn from the top right-hand corner of the modal class to the top right-hand corner of the group below.
4   Where these lines intersect, a vertical line is dropped to the *x* axis to find the modal sales figures – £19,000.

When asked to give the mode of a grouped distribution we therefore have to make some assumptions. These are:

(a) that the mode lies in the group with the highest frequency – in Table 22.3 this is the second group
(b) that the frequencies in all the groups are evenly spread within the group

This does not mean that we would place the modal item at the midpoint of the second group in Table 22.3 because the pattern of the whole distribution influences our idea of where the mode should be. Since there are more representatives achieving sales in group 3 than in group 1 we would expect that the mode came above the midpoint of group 2. Had the position been reversed – with more representatives achieving sales in the group below the modal group than in the one above it – we should have expected the mode to be below the midpoint of its group.

We can find out where the mode is by interpolation on a histogram. (*See* Fig 22.1)

To conclude, the mode is most useful when discussing discrete variables, where it is an actual item, and therefore more meaningful.

■ EXERCISE 22.3

(a) Four bowlers have the following records of success in a series of ten matches. What is the modal performance of each bowler for wickets taken?

Bowler A	2	4	4	3	1	0	4	4	3	4
Bowler B	3	1	1	0	1	0	3	2	5	1
Bowler C	7	3	2	1	4	5	2	1	6	8
Bowler D	3	2	3	4	3	2	4	3	4	4

(b) Houses in Retirementville have the following numbers of bedrooms:

Number of rooms	1	2	3	4	5	6	7
Frequency	387	542	483	172	39	28	4

How many bedrooms has the modal-sized house?

(c) A survey of shoe sizes in a college of higher education shows the following frequencies of shoe sizes:

Size of shoes (male)	5	6	7	8	9	10	11	12		
Frequency	3	23	284	301	139	60	22	8		
Size of shoes (female)	3	$3\frac{1}{2}$	4	$4\frac{1}{2}$	5	$5\frac{1}{2}$	6	$6\frac{1}{2}$	7	$7\frac{1}{2}$	8
Frequency	47	88	195	163	195	142	83	47	27	8	5

What is the modal size of shoes for *a* males and *b* females?
(d) The following data relates to the salaries of civil servants in certain categories. Draw a histogram of the data and hence estimate the modal earnings before tax.

Earnings before tax (£)	Number
7,500 but under 8,000	200
8,000 but under 8,500	450
8,500 but under 9,000	800
9,000 but under 9,500	650
9,500 but under 10,000	320
10,000 but under 10,500	180

(e)   Draw a histogram to represent the following data. Then use the histogram to find the modal output.

Output of operatives in units	Number of operatives
500–509	46
510–519	84
520–529	284
530–539	362
540–549	72
550–559	38
560–569	14

■ **ANSWERS**

Exercise 22.1   (a) 24.25 years   (b) 15,348 therms   (c) £6.23   (d) 9.458 cm
(e) 48,116   (f) 28,724   (g) £30,400

Exercise 22.2   (a) 3   (b) 2   (c) 52   (d) £624.05   (e) (i) £39,875 (ii) £65,679
(f) £1,444

Exercise 22.3   (a) A = 4,   B = 1,   C = 1   and   2,   D = 3   and   4   (b) 2 bedrooms
(c) males – sizes 8, females – sizes 4 and 5   (d) £8,855 (but this is an approximate answer and readers with a result within £25 may consider they have the correct answer
(e) 532 units (but again, this is an approximate answer).

Index